Designing Trustworthy Immersive Systems at the Convergence of Metaverse, AI, and Cybersecurity

Omar Almomani
https://orcid.org/0000-0003-3160-6542
Al-Ahliyya Amman University, Jordan

Ammar Almomani
https://orcid.org/0000-0002-8808-6114
Higher Colleges of Technology, UAE

Mohammad Alauthman
https://orcid.org/0000-0003-0319-1968
University of Petra, Jordan

IGI Global
Scientific Publishing
Publishing Tomorrow's Research Today

Vice President of Editorial	Melissa Wagner
Director of Acquisitions	Mikaela Felty
Director of Book Development	Jocelynn Hessler
Production Manager	Mike Brehm
Cover Design	Jose Rosado

Published in the United States of America by
IGI Global Scientific Publishing
701 East Chocolate Avenue
Hershey, PA, 17033, USA
Tel: 717-533-8845 | Fax: 717-533-7115
Website: https://www.igi-global.com E-mail: cust@igi-global.com

Library of Congress Cataloging-in-Publication Data

LCCN: 2026009788 (CIP Data Pending)
ISBN13: 979-8-3373-7882-4
Isbn13Softcover: 979-8-3373-7883-1
EISBN13: 979-8-3373-7884-8
British Cataloguing in Publication Data
A Cataloguing in Publication record for this book is available from the British Library.

Table of Contents

Detailed Table of Contents

The rise of immersive technologies like virtual reality (VR) and augmented reality (AR) have enabled means of gathering biometric data regarding behaviour, including gaze patterns, gait signatures, voice characteristics and neurophysiological signals. These technologies produce continuous streams of personal data for which existing privacy frameworks were never intended. This chapter presents the Immersive Biometric Privacy Threat Taxonomy (IBPT), a framework for analysing privacy threats unique to immersive environments. The IBPT model of threat categorisation is three-dimensional and proposes four novel privacy threats: Immersive Identity Disclosure; Environmental Attribute Inference; Cross-Reality Correlation; and Temporal Behavioural Reconstruction. The chapter examines the regulatory landscape across jurisdictions, validates the framework through case studies, and offers practitioners a threat prioritisation matrix. By bridging the gap between biometric security research and immersive technology privacy requirements, this work contributes to trustworthy immersive system design.

Immersive technologies, including Virtual Reality (VR), Augmented Reality (AR), Mixed Reality (MR), and Extended Reality (XR), are transforming the way people learn, cooperate, and are entertained. To provide a responsive and realistic experience, the user's location, gaze, and gestures, as well as sometimes physiological information, need to be constantly sensed. To this end, a range of processing needs to be carried out on the device, as well as edge servers and cloud platforms. However, it also expands the attack surface: motion data can uniquely identify users, digital twins linking physical and virtual systems introduce vulnerabilities across multiple layers,

Immersive multi-user metaverses combine persistent identity, real-time interaction, virtual assets, and digital-physical linkages, which creates a cybersecurity problem that extends beyond isolated authentication or perimeter controls. This chapter examines how swarm intelligence can support resilient cybersecurity in these environments through distributed sensing, cooperative risk analysis, graded containment, recovery orchestration, and policy-aware federation. To this end, it introduces the Swarm-Intelligence for Resilient Metaverse Cybersecurity (SIRMC) framework as a layered reference architecture spanning avatars, spaces, services, assets, and cybersecurity digital twins under zero-trust principles. In addition, the chapter synthesizes current literature, defines a metaverse-specific threat model, outlines resilience requirements, and provides figures, tables, scenarios, and an implementation blueprint. Overall, the chapter positions resilient metaverse defense as a coordinated capability grounded in local intelligence, twin-assisted foresight, and privacy-aware governance.

Metaverse ecosystems pose new challenges that have never been seen before in ensuring that digital identities are consistent across heterogeneous platforms. The chapter suggests a new twin architecture based on the digital twin principles of managing identity that introduces a federated model that includes credential, behavioral, context, and authorization sub-twins. In our methodology, we use privacy-preserving protocols of synchronization using zero-knowledge proofs. On benchmark datasets (LFW, VGGFace2, KeyRecs) the system has been shown to achieve 99.1% authentication accuracy, 0.7% EER (22% better than current systems) and 127ms average latency and 99.8% cross-platform synchronization reliability. These results provide a roadmap to the next-generation authentication systems that would enable the smooth experiences across the physical-virtual metaverse boundaries.

AI-driven metaverse platforms are evolving into core infrastructure for work, learning, commerce, and services, but their blend of identity data, behavioral telemetry, sensing, virtual assets, and automated decisions creates complex security and privacy risks. This chapter proposes a trustworthy architecture using zero-trust, privacy-preserving analytics, confidential computing, explainable AI, and continuous risk monitoring to secure scalable, interoperable immersive systems across sectors now.

The interaction between human beings and computers is changing in the fields of healthcare, education, and entertainment with the help of Extended Reality technologies. Nevertheless, there are serious issues of accessibility, safety and user sovereignty that pose a threat to equitable adoption. The chapter offers an inclusive Trustworthy XR Framework to such interrelated issues by means of empirical analysis of publicly accessible datasets such as BOXRR-23 motion capture data, cybersickness physiological records, and XR accessibility test protocols. The suggested approach combines the multimodal accessibility characteristics, real-time cybersickness detection with the F1-score of 91.1% with the Bi-LSTM networks and data augmentation, as well as privacy-preserving strategies in accordance with GDPR and future XR regulations. Experimental validation shows that there are important improvements in user safety measures such as 23% decrease in the severity of cyber sickness, and 34% increase in accessibility compliance scores.

The rapid expansion of immersive systems and spatial computing within the metaverse introduces unprecedented security challenges that traditional perimeter-based models fail to address. This chapter presents a zero-trust architecture (ZTA) tailored for extended reality (XR) environments, ensuring secure, continuous, and context-aware authentication and authorization across dynamic virtual spaces. By integrating principles of least privilege, micro-segmentation, and real-time behavioral analytics, the proposed framework safeguards against threats such as unauthorized avatar access, data interception, and session hijacking. Emphasis is placed on securing biometric telemetry streams—including gaze, gesture, and voice data—while maintaining low-latency performance essential for immersive experiences. The chapter also explores implementation considerations for edge computing, 5G/6G networks, and cross-platform interoperability, providing a blueprint for deploying zero-trust models in enterprise, healthcare, and educational metaverse applications.

Preface

INTRODUCTION

The rapid evolution of immersive technologies—encompassing Virtual Reality (VR), Augmented Reality (AR), Mixed Reality (MR), and Extended Reality (XR)—is reshaping how individuals interact with digital environments. Collectively forming what is increasingly described as the metaverse, these immersive ecosystems enable persistent digital worlds where users socialize, learn, work, and conduct economic activities. While these innovations promise transformative societal benefits, they also introduce complex challenges related to privacy, security, governance, and trust. As immersive systems become deeply intertwined with artificial intelligence and distributed computing infrastructures, designing trustworthy platforms has become a critical interdisciplinary priority.

Trust in immersive environments is not merely a technical problem but a multidimensional challenge that spans cybersecurity, ethical governance, privacy protection, system architecture, and human–computer interaction. The convergence of AI and immersive technologies has dramatically expanded the attack surface of digital systems. Behavioral biometric data, persistent avatars, digital assets, and cross-platform identities generate continuous streams of sensitive information. At the same time, edge–cloud infrastructures, decentralized identity frameworks, and autonomous security mechanisms are being developed to address these emerging vulnerabilities. The intersection of these technological trends demands new research frameworks capable of balancing innovation with robust safeguards.

This edited volume was conceived to address these pressing issues by bringing together scholars and practitioners from cybersecurity, artificial intelligence, immersive computing, and digital governance. The chapters in this book explore theoretical foundations, architectural frameworks, security models, and practical applications that collectively advance the design of trustworthy immersive systems. Through interdisciplinary perspectives and cutting-edge research, the book aims to provide readers with a comprehensive understanding of how trust can be embedded into the design, deployment, and governance of metaverse technologies.

CHAPTER OVERVIEWS

The chapters in this volume collectively examine the technological, ethical, and governance dimensions required to establish trustworthy immersive systems.

Chapter 1, "Behavioral Biometric Privacy Threats in Immersive Systems," by Deepti A. R., Farzeen Basith, and Manimekala B., introduces the Immersive Biometric Privacy Threat Taxonomy (IBPT). The chapter examines how immersive technologies capture sensitive behavioral biometric signals—including gaze, movement, voice, and neurophysiological responses—and proposes a multidimensional framework for identifying privacy risks unique to immersive environments. Through regulatory analysis and case studies, the authors provide a structured approach to threat prioritization and privacy-aware system design.

Chapter 2, "Edge–Cloud Continuum Security for Immersive Systems: Latency, Scalability, and Attack Resilience," by Salam Al-E'mari, Yousef Sanjalawe, and Fadi Fataftah, explores the architectural challenges of securing immersive systems that rely on distributed computing across devices, edge nodes, and cloud platforms. The chapter analyzes how immersive data flows introduce vulnerabilities across computational layers while emphasizing strategies to balance performance requirements with robust security controls.

Chapter 3, "Redefining Safety in Digital Realms: Advanced AI and Cybersecurity Strategies for Trustworthy Immersive Systems," by Barkha Dange and colleagues, examines advanced defense strategies for immersive platforms. The authors present a layered safety-by-design framework that integrates AI-driven threat detection, federated learning, blockchain-based identity systems, zero-trust architectures, and quantum-resistant cryptography to mitigate emerging threats in VR and XR ecosystems.

Chapter 4, "Reinforcement Learning for Autonomous Threat Mitigation in AI-Driven Metaverse Environments," by Mohammad Alauthman and collaborators, proposes an ontology-guided reinforcement learning framework designed to support autonomous cybersecurity responses within metaverse ecosystems. The chapter emphasizes context-aware decision-making, explainability, and governance-aware AI agents capable of adapting to evolving threats in dynamic virtual environments.

Chapter 5, "Reshaping Global Education with the Help of Extended Reality and Artificial Intelligence," by Thair Al-Fararjeh, Ammar Almomani, Omar Almomani, and Mohammad Alauthman, explores the transformative potential of XR technologies in education. The chapter introduces the International XR Driving License (IXRDL) framework as a standardized model for developing competencies, curricula, and certification pathways that support immersive learning across global educational systems.

Chapter 6, "Swarm Intelligence for Resilient Cybersecurity in Immersive Multi-User Metaverses," by Mohammad Alauthman and co-authors, examines how distributed swarm intelligence techniques can enhance resilience in complex immersive ecosystems. The chapter proposes the Swarm-Intelligence for Resilient Metaverse Cybersecurity (SIRMC) framework, which integrates cooperative detection, distributed response mechanisms, and digital twin technologies to strengthen cybersecurity coordination across metaverse platforms.

Chapter 7, "Synchronized Digital Identities: Twin-Based Architectures for Consistent Authentication Across Physical-Virtual Metaverse Boundaries," by Khalil Omar and colleagues, presents a digital twin–based identity architecture designed to synchronize authentication across heterogeneous metaverse environments. Using privacy-preserving synchronization techniques and federated identity components, the chapter demonstrates how reliable cross-platform authentication can be achieved while maintaining strong privacy guarantees.

Chapter 8, "Trustworthy Security Architectures for AI-Driven Metaverse Experiences," by Abdelraouf Ishtaiwi and Ahmad Hajyasien, proposes a comprehensive security architecture grounded in zero-trust principles and privacy-preserving analytics. The chapter integrates confidential computing, explainable AI mechanisms, and continuous risk monitoring to secure scalable immersive systems across multiple sectors.

Chapter 9, "Trustworthy XR: Accessibility, Safety, and Sovereignty in Immersive Environments," by Khalil Omar and colleagues, addresses the critical challenges of accessibility, cybersickness mitigation, and user sovereignty in XR systems. Through empirical analysis and machine learning techniques, the authors present a framework designed to improve user safety and inclusivity in immersive platforms.

Chapter 10, "Zero-Trust for Immersive Systems and Spatial Computing," by Rachna Rana and Pankaj Bhambri, explores the application of zero-trust architectures within XR ecosystems. The chapter demonstrates how principles such as continuous authentication, least-privilege access, and behavioral analytics can secure immersive environments while maintaining the low-latency performance required for spatial computing.

CONCLUSION

Collectively, the contributions in this volume highlight that trustworthy immersive systems require more than isolated technical solutions. Trust must be embedded across every layer of immersive ecosystems—from biometric data protection and identity management to network architecture, governance frameworks, and ethical AI deployment. The chapters demonstrate that cybersecurity, artificial intelligence, and immersive computing must evolve together in order to support the safe and responsible growth of the metaverse.

Another key insight emerging from this work is the importance of interdisciplinary collaboration. Addressing the challenges of immersive technologies demands cooperation among computer scientists, cybersecurity experts, policymakers, educators, and industry practitioners. By integrating perspectives from these diverse domains, this book offers a holistic view of how trustworthy immersive infrastructures can be designed, implemented, and governed.

We hope this volume will serve as a valuable resource for researchers, developers, policymakers, and graduate students interested in the future of immersive systems. As the metaverse continues to evolve, the principles, frameworks, and research presented in this book aim to guide the development of secure, ethical, and human-centered immersive technologies that enhance digital experiences while safeguarding the trust of their users.

Omar Almomani
Al-Ahliyya Amman University, Jordan

Ammar Almomani
Higher Colleges of Technology, UAE

Mohammad Alauthman
University of Petra, Jordan

Chapter 1
Behavioral Biometric Privacy Threats in Immersive Systems

A. R. Deepti
http://orcid.org/0009-0003-4320-517X
Acharya Institute of Graduate Studies, India

Farzeen Basith
http://orcid.org/0009-0003-5475-684X
Acharya Institute of Graduate Studies, India

B. Manimekala
http://orcid.org/0000-0002-4776-867X
Christ University, India

ABSTRACT

The rise of immersive technologies like virtual reality (VR) and augmented reality (AR) have enabled means of gathering biometric data regarding behaviour, including gaze patterns, gait signatures, voice characteristics and neurophysiological signals. These technologies produce continuous streams of personal data for which existing privacy frameworks were never intended. This chapter presents the Immersive Biometric Privacy Threat Taxonomy (IBPT), a framework for analysing privacy threats unique to immersive environments. The IBPT model of threat categorisation is three-dimensional and proposes four novel privacy threats: Immersive Identity Disclosure; Environmental Attribute Inference; Cross-Reality Correlation; and Temporal Behavioural Reconstruction. The chapter examines the regulatory landscape across jurisdictions, validates the framework through case studies, and

DOI: 10.4018/979-8-3373-7882-4.ch001

offers practitioners a threat prioritisation matrix. By bridging the gap between biometric security research and immersive technology privacy requirements, this work contributes to trustworthy immersive system design.

1. INTRODUCTION

Biometric monitoring involves the systematic collection and analysis of unique physiological and behavioural characteristics of individuals in digital environments. Physiological biometrics refers to those characteristics confined within the body and usually remains constant over time, which cannot be voluntarily transferred from one person to another (e.g., fingerprint ridge patterns, facial bone structure, iris texture, DNA sequences). These modes involve physical contact with the scanning device which accounts for their high precision being due to the underlying physical properties that are hard to change or produce (Jain et al., 2004). Behavioural biometrics, on the other hand, is defined as statistical recognition based on measurable patterns in learned human conduct and activities, such as keystroke dynamics, speaker verification (voice), signature identification and gait analysis. Such systems allow for continuous authentication alongside normal human behaviour, without needing extra hardware or disrupting the workflow (Piugie, (2023); Yampolskiy & Govindaraju, (2008).

Immersive environments have introduced fundamentally new classes of behavioural biometric data that simply do not exist in traditional computing systems. VR and AR devices records 3D movement patterns, spatial navigation behavior, gesture recognition data, head tracking motions, or eye tracking patterns. Behavioural signals are continuously recorded by these systems as users interact with them, allowing detailed representations of both conscious and unconscious movement behaviour to be built within long interaction sessions (Bailenson, 2018); Hanisch et al., 2021).

The phenomenon of behavioural normalization is a defining feature of immersive biometric data collection: when users are immersed in virtual environments, they tend to act more naturally and distinctively than they would have under traditional computing contexts, thus producing a detailed and also more personally distinctive behavioural dataset. In contrast to static biometric modalities like fingerprints or facial recognition, immersive behavioural metrics encompass dynamic patterns that characterise individual differences in performance within three-dimensional interactive environments.

VR systems are clearly designed to collect massive quantities of non-verbal data such as user's movement, biometrics and interaction patterns. Modern VR headsets have many sensors that gather explicit user input as well as implicit non-verbal information, which is used to model the virtual world by the engine generating it.

As (Bailenson 2018) showed, this information is highly revealing and can be used for anything from personalised advertising to performance assessment. The current and expected future exponential growth of the metaverse and immersive technologies has transformed platforms into never-before-available means for sensitive data collection, where used behavioural characteristics are individually specific entities linked to highly sensitive personal traits (e.g., emotional state, health condition) (Hanisch et al., 2021).

1.1 Scope and Significance of Behavioural Biometrics

Behavioural biometrics research began in the 1990s when researchers noticed that human behaviour is made of noticeable patterns unique to each person. Behavioural habits, as opposed to genetically coded physical attributes, arise through learning experiences from external and internal sources through mechanisms of disposition and preference, and they become learned behaviours that are highly automatic. These can occur inadvertently by individuals, and even in the case that an individual knows he/she is being watched, it is hard to consciously change a behavioural pattern (Yampolskiy & Govindaraju, 2008).

Behavioural biometric authentication is based on three established principles of theoretical foundation. Underlying this is the principle of behavioural reliability that individuals perform actions in a similar way in similar situations over time. The very basic premise of the behavioural feature principle is that behaviour, meaning combinations of learnt behaviours, physiology-based abilities, and individual preferences create unique patterns exclusive to individuals. The principle of multiple complexes acknowledges that human behavior has multiple interdependent scopes, effectively making it impossible for one individual to completely recreate the behavioral signature of another.

Behavioural biometric systems operate through three distinct phases, each with unique privacy concerns. The first phase of enrolment captures initial behavioural samples over several occasions to obtain baseline measurements, including natural variation in average behaviour. In this phase, the template is created by applying various machine learning algorithms to the gathered data and extracting features, which are then converted into a profile that is stored and used for future comparison. The verification stage captures real-time behaviour and compares it with the enrolled template to authenticate identity (Jain et al., 2004; Piugie, 2023). Standardised metrics are used to evaluate the system performance. The False Acceptance Rate (FAR) is the rate at which an unauthorised user is incorrectly granted access. The False Rejection Rate (FRR) represents the percentage of legitimate users whose access attempts are incorrectly denied. Other ratio-based metrics include the Failure to Enrol Rate (FTE), which refers to users for whom the system cannot derive a reliable behavioural profile, and the Failure to Acquire Rate (FTA), which denotes failed attempts where sufficient behavioural data could not be captured.

Recent advances have established eye movement behaviour as a distinctive biometric signature, owing to its high degree of individual change. That is, gaze patterns from individuals are shaped by their own visual experiences in an acquisition process that leads to unique examples of personal imprint D'Amelio et al., (2023). In such a way, the connection between individual uniqueness and gaze behaviour creates a basis for biometric recognition that could be used in immersive and metaverse environments. Electroencephalogram (EEG) signals have also gained significant research attention as a potential secure modality for authentication, primarily due to their inherent complexity which resists imitation; however, they also allow for emotional-state inference, raising additional privacy concerns Becerra et al., (2025). Therefore, the involvement of user biometric identification and emotion recognition within immersive systems can provide novel opportunities for enriched usage but conversely also introduces increasing privacy concerns.

1.2 Market Growth and Industry Context

The behavioural biometrics market shows considerable growth potential, with estimates of a $5.5 billion market size by 2033 at an 18.2% compound annual growth rate the driving force behind cybersecurity needs and digital transformation in banking, healthcare and government, Data Insights Market, (2025). As of 2025, there are more than 171 million VR technology users worldwide and about 77 million in the United States (Statista, 2025). After two years of declines, global AR/VR headset shipments increased 10% in 2024 to approximately 9.6 million units (IDC, 2025). Meta leads the VR headset market, with a (74.6%), Apple ranks in second (5.2%) and Sony third (4.3%) (IDC 2025)) The global VR market valued at USD 36.13 billion in 2024 is expected to grow further and reach a value of USD 284.04 billion by 2034, with a compound annual growth rate (CAGR) of22.9% (Precedence Research, 2015). Key hardware milestones include Meta Quest 3 (October 2023) and Apple Vision Pro (February 2024), a platform with the rare distinction of being major new entrant in immersive headsets to hit the scene in a decade.

Commercial usage spans across various sectors like retail, real estate, healthcare, and manufacturing as well as tourism with industry estimates indicating ongoing growth in immersive technology adoption across enterprise applications TechCrunch (2019). Enterprise adoption continues to be driven by commercial applications, which will make up around 56% of VR market revenue (Precedence Research, 2025). Market surveys found that commercial headset shipments were up by 14.9% in 2024 compared to the previous year, and deployments in education alone grew by a whopping 69.4% (IDC, 2025). Guidelines to protect biometric data privacy have been provided or are being developed by industry bodies like the Biometrics Institute (2019) and governments including the Office of the Victorian Information Commissioner (2023), which may be used to support designing privacy-preserving systems.

1.3 Research Methodology

The theoretical basis of this chapter derives from two independent published systematic reviews. Rahartomo et al. (2025) detailed a systematic review of 114 metaverse-specific security and privacy publications from 2013 till 2024, concluding that the most widely prioritised security property across immersive spaces was authentication. Hanisch et al. (2021) conducted a review of 142 academic works on anonymisation techniques for behavioural biometric data from 2007 to 2024, emphasising the need to protect behavioural data against identity disclosure and attribute disclosure attacks, while preserving utility.

This chapter synthesises findings from both reviews and adds to them new primary sourcing. The synthesis is performed according to systematic review guidelines given by Kitchenham (2004), employing searches across IEEE Xplore, ACM Digital Library, Scopus, Web of Science, Google Scholar and arXiv. The search terms included various combinations of behavioural biometrics, privacy, security, immersive virtual reality [VR], augmented reality [AR] and the metaverse. Peer-reviewed publication or preprint status from recognised sources, explicit treatment of privacy or security considerations regarding behavioural biometric data and relevance to immersive or extended reality systems were required for inclusion.

Table 1 present the combined findings from both systematic reviews, structured by time period to show how research has developed over time, from early experimental studies to current privacy-by-design frameworks.

Table 1. Systematic review summary statistics

Modality	Accuracy	Privacy Risk	Complexity	VR Fit	Key Features	Source(s)
Gaze Tracking	94–98%	High	Medium	Excellent	Fixations, saccades, pupil dilation	D'Amelio et al. (2023); Griffith et al. (2021)
Gait Analysis	88–95%	Medium	High	Good	Step patterns, balance, movement	Bouchiba et al. (2019); Pfeuffer et al. (2019)
Voice	92–97%	Medium	Low	Excellent	Vocal patterns, rhythm, prosody	Reynolds et al. (2000); Piugie (2023)
EEG Signals	96–99%	Very High	Very High	Limited	Brainwave patterns, cognitive states	Becerra et al. (2025); Bidgoly et al. (2022)
EMG Signals	89–94%	High	High	Good	Muscle activity, gestures	Pereira et al. (2023)
Haptic/Controller	85–93%	Medium	Low	Excellent	Grip force, button press dynamics, manipulation signatures	Syed et al. (2020); Kulesza et al. (2025)

The overall evidence base includes 142 publications from four time periods. The 18 papers from 2007 to 2012 are from Hanisch et al. s (2021) systematic review of prior research on gaze and physiological signal analysis. The 124 publications from 2013 to 2024 are the deduplicated union of both reviews, and growth was most notable during the 2018 to 2020 period.

1.4 Chapter Structure

The structure of this chapter is as follows. The background section describes the main concepts of biometric recognition, privacy theory, behavioural biometric modalities and existing approaches to privacy protection. In the regulatory landscape section, GDPR Article 9 requirements, BIPA, and CCPA/CPRA apply in cases involving immersive biometric systems have been analysed. Threat landscape section documented case studies demonstrating known (i.e., theoretical) privacy threats. The section of IBPT framework introduces the three-dimensional threat categorisation model along with four new threat classifications. Future research directions and a summary of contributions are provided at the end of this chapter.

The IBPT framework introduced in Section (5) suggests four new classes of privacy threats which are specific to immersive environments: Immersive Identity Disclosure (IID), that concerns the disclosure of physical identities through behaviouristic pattern clustering; Environmental Attribute Inference (EAI), a class privy to detecting sensitive personal attributes from spatial activity traces; Cross-Reality Correlation (CRC), linking user's activity across virtual and real domains; and Temporal Behavioural Reconstruction TBR, reconstructing psychological embeddedness from longitudinal behavioural data. These categories are used throughout the case study analysis in Section 4 and formally defined in Section 5.3.

2. BACKGROUND AND RELATED WORK

2.1 Foundational Biometric Recognition and Security

Biometric authentication is a basic shift from conventional user validation based on knowledge factors or possession factors. Unlike what you know or have, biometric modalities recognize users by degrees of individual variation that make each person unique and have several benefits in terms of security and usability. But while this transition is promising, it also raises fundamental privacy issues: whereas passwords or tokens can be revoked and replaced (Ratha et al., 2001; Prabhakar et al., 2003), there are classes of biometric data that cannot be easily done away with once lost.

This data is normally processed through a structured framework regardless of the modality, which generally consists of acquiring data using modality-specific devices; processing this data to reduce noise and normalising it; extracting unique features that are used to produce a mathematical template; matching this live sample to the database templates stored in memory, and finally authenticating them by means of statistical thresholds (Jain et al., 2004). Pioneering work identified key properties of systems, such as distinctiveness, stability, collectability and circumvention resistance. Ratha et al. (2001), classified eight attack surfaces in biometric systems, illustrating that security issues exist in biometric systems not present in the traditional cryptographic schemes. Prabhakar et al. (2003), including scope expansion, surveillance, cross application data linkage, and secret recognition.

These foundational difficulties are intensified in immersive systems. This non-reversibility problem is exacerbated by the continuous as opposed to discrete nature of biometric capture. The risk of function expansion is also increased, as behavioural data collected for the purpose to render VR are used to identify. The usability-security trade-off is further complicated by the need for privacy mechanisms to be executed modestly within immersive usage contexts. The unique compounding challenges of immersive biometric privacy versus traditional biometric security are what drives the motivation to develop the IBPT framework.

In immersive systems, biometric data is collected in real-time on an ongoing basis that fundamentally differs from traditional applications that use data only at authentication checkpoints. Immersive Systems track user behaviour within entire sessions lasting hours with hundreds of thousands of data points. Moreover, immersive systems capture many behavioural dimensions (e.g., gaze tracking, hand gestures, body orientation, spatial navigation and response timing) at the same time which can yield highly detailed behavioural fingerprints via multimodal data fusion. Behavioural traits possess more private information than traditional biometric modalities (Yampolskiy & Govindaraju, 2008), correlating with cognitive, neurological and social factors. It is important to recognize that VR/AR headsets function as networked IoT devices, transferring biometric data over wireless channels subject to interception, Talukder et al., (2024); Alsaaidah et al., (2024), lending itself to the necessity of network-level information security. This scale of identifiability risk has been confirmed at population level: Nair et al. (2023) revealed that 55,541 actual VR user behaviours could be uniquely identified with 94.33% accuracy from only 100 seconds of head and hand motion data demonstrating that the biometric of VR behavior serves as a unique identifier on par with facial or fingerprint recognition

2.2 Theoretical Foundations of Privacy

Informational privacy emerged in the legal and ethical tradition as a value meant to protect human dignity and personal autonomy against unnecessary collection and use of information about individual persons. Privacy covers physical, decisional, informational and communicational dimensions that map onto different components of individual autonomy. Modern privacy theory acknowledges that our conception of what it means to be private extends beyond how secret something is and also involves some idea of control, where privacy expectations are constructed at the individual level; influences include cultural and generational factors.

Constitutes the derived fundamental principles from classical privacy theory that can be applied to biometric immersive systems. (Westin, 1967) in Privacy and Freedom laid out key principles such as privacy being control over personal information, the trade-off between privacy and social benefit, and the need for legal frameworks. These principles may be revisited in the context of immersive systems that capture sensitive physiological and behavioural data.

One particularly pertinent framework is that of contextual integrity (Nissenbaum, 2004). Because of its core proposition: that privacy violations take place when pieces of information move across contexts inappropriately, it applies literally to immersive environments where the borders between private and public, physical and virtual or personal and professional are often blurry. The monitoring infrastructure of immersive environments condenses multiple layers of informatic context into a single modality of data collection: someone engaging in immersive social interaction is producing biometrics that, in non-immersive contexts, would be spread across discrete domains. This collapse of context allows for violations of the information norms governing each of these unique variables, as they are aggregated through the various data streams collected by a single platform, creating new privacy threats that would not have surfaced if these contexts had remained separate.

In building towards Nissenbaum's model, (Solove, 2006) also created a comprehensive taxonomy of privacy, categorising privacy harms into four broad classes: Information collection (surveillance and interrogation), information processing (aggregation, identification, insecurity, secondary use and exclusion), information dissemination (breach of confidentiality; disclosure; exposure) and invasion (intrusion and decisional interference). This taxonomy applies directly to the privacy threats of immersive biometrics: both the Immersive Identity Disclosure threat and category Solove identifies as identification; Environmental Attribute Inference correlates with aggregation and secondary use; Cross-Reality Correlation maps onto increased accessibility across contexts; and Temporal Behavioural Reconstruction represents surveillance in combination with temporal aggregation. Consequently, Solove's framework serves as a granular theoretical approach to the understanding of the specific categories of privacy harms that each IBPT threat category embodies.

These theoretical perspectives are further contextualised by empirical research into privacy behaviour. Acquisti et al. (2015) synthesised three important trends: individuals are noticeably uncertain about the implications of privacy-related behaviours; privacy considerations are extremely reliant; and privacy preferences are variable and susceptible to influences by commercial interests. These findings have a direct bearing on immersive systems such as VR, in which the phenomenon of behavioural normalisation (users acting more like themselves while present in VR) might lead to reduced vigilance around privacy, and continual data collection leads to conditions under which meaningful informed consent is especially challenging to uphold.

2.3 Behavioural Biometric Modalities in Immersive Systems

Eye tracking is one of the most advanced behavioural biometric modalities, documenting fixation, gaze shift, and pupil dilation profiles that create stable, uniquely identifiable. D'Amelio et al. (2023) revealed that different oculomotor patterns are reproducible across contexts and time. Earlier foundational work showed that gazing behaviour was correlated with individual personality traits, so that eye movements revealed psychological characteristics of a person beyond simple identification (Rauthmann et al., 2012). Previous theory suggests that decision of personality using gazing behaviour is possible and also indicates the potential of eye movement data to reveal, beyond identification: typical psychological features, (Rauthmann et al., 2012), with supporting findings indicating specific variations in individual personalities can influence eye movements for viewing natural scenes (Risko et al.,

2012). Individual variation for biometric identification in DOVES (Van Der Linde et al., 2009) while segmented linear regression advances (Pekkanen & Lappi, 2017) improved reliable feature extraction.

Gait analysis quantifies movement patterns of individual including step length, timing, posture and overall motion. A combination of biomechanical factors (e.g., leg length, muscle strength, neurological condition) and learned habits cause each individual to have their own unique gait that is quite challenging to modify at a conscious level (Bouchiba et al., 2019). Voice and speech analysis studies acoustic features and verbal patterns to establish vocal fingerprints that remain fairly consistent across settings. Neurophysiological biometrics, which involves electrical recordings of brain and nervous system activity such as electromyography (EMG) and electroencephalography (EEG), represents a way to authenticate a user with very high security, but raises the privacy concern of creating an internal profile around mental or even emotional states (Becerra et al., 2025; Vadher et al., 2023; Khan Khalil et al., 2024).

Five major modalities of behavioural biometric are investigated in this section as shown in Table 2, and compared for the deployment towards immersive systems.

Table 2. Behavioural biometric modalities comparison

Compliance Aspect	GDPR Article 9	BIPA	CCPA/CPRA	EU AI Act
Consent Standard	Explicit consent	Prior written consent	Opt-in for sensitive data	Prohibited for real-time biometric ID in public spaces; conformity assessment for high-risk
Enforcement Model	Regulatory (DPA enforcement)	Private right of action	Regulatory + limited private	Regulatory (national authorities + EU AI Office)
Financial Penalties	Up to €20M or 4% global revenue	$1,000–$5,000 per violation	$2,500–$7,500 per violation	Up to €35M or 7% global revenue (prohibited); €15M or 3% (high-risk)
Jurisdictional Scope	EU residents/processing	Illinois residents	California residents	EU market (providers and deployers)
Profit Restriction	Purpose limitation	Absolute prohibition on sale	Opt-out right	Risk-based: prohibited, high-risk, limited-risk, minimal-risk
Data Subject Rights	Access, rectification, erasure, portability	Limited; enforcement-focused	Know, delete, correct, limit, opt-out	Transparency, human oversight, right to explanation
Retention Requirements	Data minimisation principle	Published schedule; mandatory deletion	Limited retention periods	Logging and documentation obligations for high-risk
Class Action Capability	No (complaints to DPA)	Yes (private lawsuits)	Limited (attorney general)	Complaints to national authorities; no private right of action
Biometric Definition	Broad (physiological, behavioural)	Limited (traditional identifiers)	Comprehensive (includes behavioural)	Biometric identification and categorisation (risk-classified)

There is a positive correlation between authentication accuracy and privacy risk: modalities achieving higher identification accuracy also capture greater revelation of sensitive personal data. Because implementation is more complex than deploying any one of the single modality approaches, this multi-modal fusion framework has low global readiness to be brought to current VR deployment (George & Routray, 2016) but it approaches accuracy higher than any single modality can achieve while introducing a privacy risk since intermodality correlations will show up details not obtainable from any single one.

2.4 Traditional Privacy Protection Approaches

Biometric data has led to the development of four main classes of privacy-preserving techniques. The enablement of differential privacy, which provides a well-founded mathematical framework for quantifying the loss of privacy incurred from releasing data summary, has recently been demonstrated to apply to VR eye-tracking data through the DPGazeSynth framework (Ren et al., 2024) Anonymisation and pseudonymisation seek to eliminate identity-linking information, but both encounter limits on biometric data that ultimately possesses identifying features (Hanisch et al., 2021). Cryptographic measures that secure stored biometric data are used in template protection schemes. Katoikos et al. (2025) combines EEG classifiers with authentication systems. Federated learning facilitates the improvement of models across multiple devices without having to centralise sensitive data, allowing for biometric information to remain with the local device while simply model updates are shared.

The relative strengths and limitations of these approaches are complementary: differential privacy provides strong formal guarantees, but with accuracy trade-offs; anonymisation maintains utility, though re-identification protection can be weaker; template protection secures stored data against local compromise, but does not address capture-time risks; and federated learning mitigates centralisation risk, but offers no protections in the case of an individual's compromised device. Each domain, however, fails to encompass the extensive set of immersive privacy issues associated with continuous capture, multimodal fusion and temporal accumulation. The newest methods provided by explainable AI, e.g., SHAP-based feature attribution (Shambour et al., 2025), and studies devoted to transform data representation (AL-Essa et al., 2025) are also new pillars to be used towards transparent and interpretable biometric processing decisions.

In opposition to these defensive techniques are the adversarial machine learning methods, the offensive side of cybersecurity within ML. Model inversion attacks can derive biometric inputs from trained classification models, membership inference attacks can ascertain whether the data for a specific individual was among that which was used to train a biometric model, and property inference attacks can obtain aggregate information about training populations. These techniques are directly applicable to the privacy risks that identified with immersive systems: a biometric authentication model trained on VR movement data could, in theory, be subject to either model inversion to reconstruct individual movement signatures or membership inference to determine whether they were used in the training set even when there is no direct access of the raw biometric data.

2.5 Limitations of Existing Frameworks on Privacy

Standard privacy-preserving paradigms are limited by their nature in immersive situations, where the biometric is acquired continuously and multimodal. Existing methods are usually discrete interaction models, where biometric data is collected during the authentication process at specific points, in contrast to continuous monitoring used by immersive systems. Rahartomo et al. (2025) notes that authentication is still the most scrutinized security property with no framework capturing the dynamics of continuous biometric surveillance in virtual spaces. The IBPT framework introduced in this chapter is motivated by the aforementioned gap.

3. REGULATORY LANDSCAPE ANALYSIS

3.1 GDPR Article 9: Special Category Data

The European Union's General Data Protection Regulation (GDPR), widely considered to be one of the strongest data protection frameworks in the world, treats biometric data processed for identification purposes as special category under Article 9 (Xynogalas & Leiser, 2024). According to article 4(14), biometric data is personal data resulting from specific technical processing concerning the physical, physiological or behavioural characteristics of a natural person which allow or confirm the unique identification of that natural person. In immersive environments, this refers to eye-tracking data, walking gait, voice signatures, facial gestures and neurophysiological signals.

Studies show that VR behavioural biometrics exhibit a high chance of re-identification. Pfeuffer et al. (2019) demonstrated that means of machine learning models can distinguish between individual VR users with 94.33% accuracy based only on 100 seconds of head and hand movement data, largely bringing all immersive behavioural data within the scope of Article 9. Data subjects in immersive spaces are particularly vulnerable to behaviour pattern re-identification (Sorrentino & López-Guzmán, 2025). From the provider standpoint, robust compliance augments Data Protection Impact Assessments, privacy by design, enhanced security and opt-in protocols (Xynogalas & Leiser, 2024).

3.2 BIPA Requirements for VR/AR Environments

The Illinois Biometric Information Privacy Act (BIPA) creates one of the most protective biometric privacy regimes in the United States, even providing a private right of action. BIPA defines biometric identifiers and biometric information separately, creating uncertainty for immersive technologies as full-body movement data (the position of limbs, glances) could be classified under a definition of biometric information if it was used for identification purposes. BIPA has five main requirements: (a) notice requirements requiring disclosure of the purpose for which data will be collected and how it will be handled; (b) prior written consent is required prior to collection of biometric data; (c) defendant must have schedules for storing and disposing of the captured information, with deletion triggered when its purposes have been satisfied or three years after the last interaction with a person; (d) security measures must be at least as protective as those used by that person with respect to any other confidential information not subject to coverage under BIPA with particular care given in determining these factors; and (e) Opt-out provisions preventing sale, lease or trading of biometrically-collected data. These enforcement provisions allow for penalties ranging from USD1,000–5,000 per infraction and class action authorisation (Sorrentino & López-Guzmán 2025).

3.3 CCPA/CPRA Biometric Data Provisions

The California Consumer Privacy Act, strengthened by the California Privacy Rights Act, classifies biometric data as sensitive personal information with enhanced requirements. The broad definition covers all immersive biometric data categories including gaze patterns, voice characteristics, gait signatures, facial geometry from avatars, and neurophysiological signals. Consumer rights include the right to know, delete, correct, limit use, and opt out of biometric data sale. Enforcement penalties range from \$2,500 to \$7,500 per violation. As regulatory authorities increasingly recognise XR-specific challenges, the absence of XR-specific guidance exposes developers to legal risk (Allen & Barrett, 2025; Future of Privacy Forum, 2025).

3.4 Cross-Jurisdictional Comparison

A comparative matrix of the three main regulatory approaches is provided in Table 3.

Table 3. Regulatory compliance matrix

Threat	Evidence	Impact	Priority	Key Evidence
IID	Strong	High	Critical	94.33% re-identification at N=55,541 (Nair et al., 2023); 95% at N=511 (Miller et al., 2020); N=22 (Pfeuffer et al., 2019); gaze signatures (D'Amelio et al., 2023)
TBR	Moderate	High	High	GazeBase, EyeT4Empathy datasets; personality prediction (Hoppe et al., 2018)
CRC	Moderate	Medium–High	High	Cross-dataset identification (Al Zaidawi et al., 2022); uncoordinated protections (Aziz & Komogortsev, 2024)
EAI	Preliminary	Medium	Medium	Attribute inference from VR telemetry (Nair et al., 2023); platform capabilities (Meta Quest sensors); avatar features (Sorrentino & López-Guzmán, 2025)

The previously compared three frameworks are complemented by the EU Artificial Intelligence Act (Regulation 2024/1689), entered into force in August 2024, which creates an additional regulatory layer of specific relevance for immersive biometric systems. Under Article 5, real-time biometric identification systems in publicly accessible spaces are prohibited practices under the AI Act; and other forms of biometric identification and categorisation systems are considered high-risk according to Annex III. This risk-based taxonomy directly impacts immersive systems that utilize behavioural biometric identification, because the nature of continuous motion- based or gaze-based user-identification in collaborative-VEs is likely to fall under high-risk or even prohibited categories depending on its use-context and deployment purpose. Notable examples of converging trends involve the tightening measures regarding consent, fixed retention periods and stronger security obligations alongside special status for biometric data (Xynogalas & Leiser, 2024). In fact, existing law is ill-suited to immersive technologies: traditional definitions of biometrics may not include data derived from the brain or inferred from behaviour; most laws revolve around discrete capture versus continuous monitoring; and there is little guidance on multimodal data fusion in machine learning architectures or fusing biometric input into said architectures.

4. THREAT LANDSCAPE ANALYSIS AND CASE STUDIES

This subsection provides a collection of documented privacy threats identified in deployed immersive systems against evidence from practice, both serving to validate threat models with concrete examples and mapping their occurrences to the corresponding IBPT threat categories.

4.1 Platform-Level Privacy Incidents

Case Study 1: Meta Quest Data Collection Practices

Meta's Quest headsets collect biometric data via their sensors, microphones, cameras, room mapping and tracking ability from millions of users. To offer contextual awareness, studies show that more than 94.33% of VR movement data is able to be accurately re-identified (Bailenson, 2018; Aziz & Komogortsev, 2024). This threat maps to the Environmental Attribute Inference and Temporal Behavioural Reconstruction threat categories via home-layout mapping and continuous motion-profile logging

Case Study 2: VR Behavioural Identification Research

Pfeuffer et al. (2019) used 100 seconds of data from head and hand motion (22 subjects) to differentiate individuals in a virtual reality environment with an accuracy of 94.33% using a random forest classifier. This validates the Immersive Identity Disclosure attack: nominalisation of VR interactions allows user identities to be reconstructed via behavioural analysis.

At considerably larger scales, this result has been replicated. Miller et al. (2020) reported a 95% identification accuracy rate among 511 participants during realistic viewing of 360-degree VR videos with no uniquely tailored identifying task, drawing data from Bailenson's Virtual Human Interaction Lab. Most critically, Nair et al. (2023) validated 94.33% re-identification accuracy in a pool of 55,541 real VR users using exclusively head and hand motion data, demonstrating that behavioural biometric identification in VR generalises to population-level datasets rather than being an artefact of small samples.

4.2 Gaze-Based Privacy Threats

Case Study 3: Eye Movement Biometric Signatures

D'Amelio et al. (2023) showed that gaze behaviour represents unique biometric signatures. Hoppe et al. (2018) showed that people's everyday eye-movement patterns predict wounds and traits, expanding the threat from identification to psychological profiling. Temporal persistence in gaze patterns is evidenced by the GazeBase dataset (Griffith et al., 2021). Abdrabou et al. (2025) documented emerging risks when gaze data enters machine-learning systems.

Case Study 4: Cross-Dataset Identification

Al Zaidawi et al. (2022) showed that user identification based on eye movements is stable across datasets and experimental conditions, establishing an empirical basis for user tracking across immersive platforms, thus corroborating the Cross-Reality Correlation threat.

Case Study 5: Avatar-Based Biometric Inference

According to Sorrentino and López-Guzmán (2025), avatars often represent physical traits of creators, and that unified avatar creation technologies allow for linking avatar between platforms. In their review, they found that metaverse platforms did not obtain consent for biometric data collection despite having the potential to infer facial geometry.

4.3 Neurophysiological and Multimodal Threats

Case Study 6: EEG-Based Authentication and Inference

Becerra et al. (2025) proved comprehensive EEG biometric identification and emotion recognition capabilities. The ability and relative ease of using EEG signals for adherence-preserving authentication and emotional state inference (Bidgoly et al., 2022) not only has military dual use concerns (Vadher et al., 2023), but also opens up applications for authentication that carry the same issues presented by these systems in identifying an individual based on their brainwaves or emotional states.

Case Study 7: Multimodal Fusion

George and Routray (2016) proposed score-level fusion for eye-movement biometrics and Bouchiba et al. (2019) demonstrated gait-ECG fusion. These confirm that the combination of individually harmless modalities forms rich behavioural profiles with serious privacy implications.

Case Study 8: Temporal Pattern Analysis

The EyeT4Empathy dataset (Lencastre et al., 2022) shows that longitudinal gaze data collection allows for the assessment of empathy and emotional state. Individual data points might seem benign, but collected over time it allows for a complete psychological judgement.

Case Study 9: Educational VR Monitoring

The use of VR in education also raises implications for student privacy, as eye movement during VR (and patterns of interaction) can identify learning and cognitive difficulties (Lim et al., 2020), which may lead to risks under protections intended for students.

4.4 Threat Prioritisation

The prioritisation assigns three levels: Critical, High, and Medium based on two factors: the strength of peer-reviewed empirical evidence demonstrating the threat, and the potential impact on user privacy as assessed through the documented case studies in Sections 4.1– 4.3. Table 4 presents a threat prioritisation matrix based on empirical evidence strength and potential impact.

The prioritization assigns three levels: Critical, High, and Medium based on two factors: The strength of peer-reviewed empirical evidence indicating the threat, and the potential impact on user privacy as evaluated through the standard case studies in Sections 4.1– 4.3. Table 4 present a threat listing matrix based on empirical evidence strength and potential impact.

Table 4. IBPT Threat Prioritization Matrix

Year Range	Papers	Primary Focus	Methodology	Key Contributions
2007–2012	18	Foundational gaze and physiological signal analysis	Experimental laboratory studies	Baseline behavioural biometric recognition
2013–2017	34	VR/AR emergence and privacy concerns	Human experimentation	Early immersive biometric systems
2018–2020	42	Authentication and security applications	Benchmarking studies	Multimodal fusion techniques
2021–2024	48	Metaverse privacy and trustworthy AI	Qualitative and user-centred approaches	Privacy-preserving frameworks and GDPR compliance
Total	**142**	18 papers (2007–2012) from Hanisch et al. (2021); 124 papers (2013–2024) from combined reviews		

Immersive Identity Disclosure is the most instant and threatening of these three use cases backed by strong empirical evidence indicating high-accuracy re-identification. Temporal Behavioural Reconstruction and Cross-Reality Correlation are high-priority threats with growing evidence bases. Environmental Attribute Inference has the wakest empirical ground and additional research is needed to quantify specific attribute disclosure accuracy.

Most empirical evidence underpinning these threat analyses comes from controlled laboratory or platform-specific data However, need to investigate how reported accuracy generalises to real-world deployments involving diverse user populations, disparate hardware configurations and naturalistic usage patterns. Nonetheless, the consistency of results across various sample sizes from Pfeuffer et al. 22 participants (2019), to Miller et al. to Nair et al. 's 511 participants (2020). It provides good reason to believe that behavioural biometric re-identification is a stable effect that increases in strength with increasing population size.

5. IMMERSIVE BIOMETRIC PRIVACY THREAT TAXONOMY (IBPT) FRAMEWORK

5.1 Framework Development Methodology

The IBPT framework was derived from a structured process that combines threat modelling principles, best practices of privacy engineering, and empirical validation using documented case studies (Hanisch et al., 2021; Rahartomo et al., 2025). The methodology involved a four-phase process: scoping (to determine the parameters of the analysis); mapping data flow (the flow of personal information), systematic threat identification for each stage in each data flow, and risk assessment (of likelihood and consequences based on technical vulnerabilities through contextual factors).

Existing biometric privacy models assume one-time capture of traits at segment points of interaction (Yampolskiy & Govindaraju, 2008), while immersive systems continuously monitor user inputs to create adaptive profiles through an extended exchange session. By integrating principles of time stability, multimodal fusion, and environmental context as critical threat dimensions, the IBPT framework captures this paradigm shift.

The classification method is based on existing taxonomies of cybersecurity threats. Classifications of threats for the security of data bases (which distinguish in separate analytical categories threats, vulnerabilities and countermeasures) provide a structural model which is transferable to the aspects related to biometric privacy. In addition, the work on robust malware detection through machine and deep learning classifiers (Almomani et al., 2025) shows how hybrid classification approaches can and is informing the multi-layered threat categorisation methodology employed in IBPT framework. Network-level attack detection in IoT environments has been documented by multiple studies (Alsaaidah et al., 2024) and the results are key to how the IBPT framework factors data-in-transit threats, as immersive biometric systems run like networked devices.

5.2 Three-Dimensional Threat Categorisation

The IBPT framework offer a three-dimensional threat categorisation from the finding that privacy threats in immersive environments cannot be fully understood through single-dimension examination.

Modality Integration Hierarchy adds further complexity when mix with multiple biometric modalities. The varied threat posed by individual modalities; no single modality may be critical, but a combination yields complete behavioural profiles (D'Amelio et al., 2023). Specific modalities are added, that outline threat increase structures with a hierarchical level.

Patterns of Temporal Evolution, are derived from long term monitoring to identify emerging dangers. In contrast to classical systems which work with discrete samples, immersive systems produce continuously flowing behavioural time series and are therefore available for psychological profiling (Hoppe et al., 2018). As more observations gather, inferential power grows, which changes the privacy calculus.

Context-Aware Threat Assessment deals with threat variation varies based on context. VR in healthcare creates unique privacy challenges compared to entertainment or education, requiring a purpose-fit assessment (Becerra et al., 2025). This dimension allows a structured exploration of how deployment context, user population and regulation environment influence variance in threat severity.

This approach is further encouraged by regulatory gaps. Interviews with developers suggest that the existing UK frameworks approach immersive technology through a web-first, two-dimensional frame, which insufficiently accounts for spatial and corporeal technologies (Allen & Barrett, 2025). The structure of the overall IBPT framework is as shown in Figure 1.

Figure 1. IBPT Framework Overview

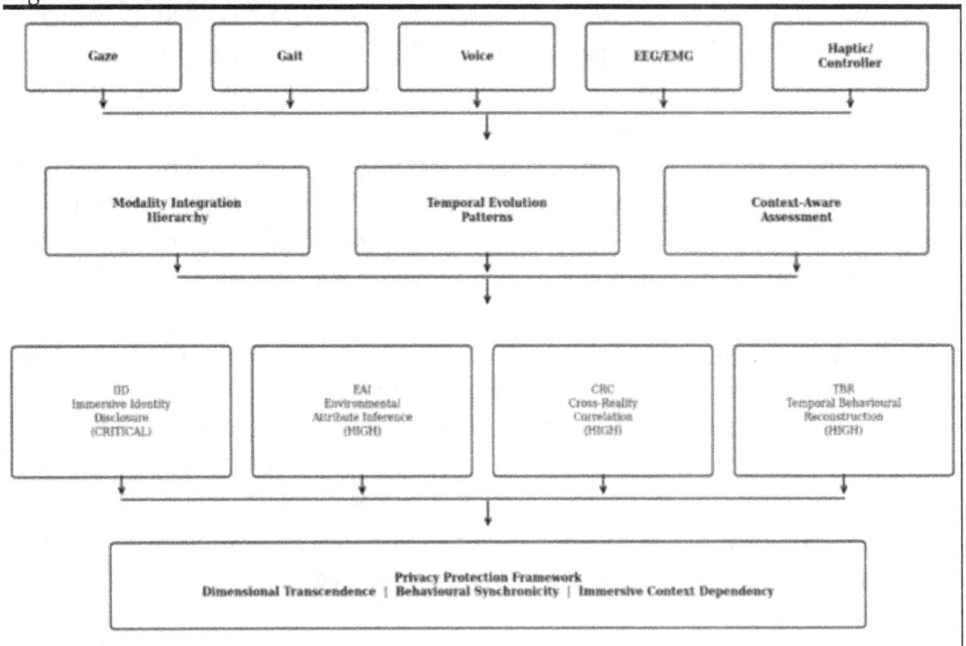

The complete framework structure is depicted in figure 1, wherein data from four biometric inputs (gaze, gait, voice, EEG/EMG) can propagate through three intersecting analytical dimensions (Modality Integration Hierarchy, Temporal Evolution Patterns and Context-Aware Assessment), towards the formulation of four threat classifications (IID–Critical; EAI–Medium; CRC–High; TBR–High), culminating in a Privacy Protection Framework output supported by the underlying theoretical principles: Dimensional Transcendence, Behavioural Synchronicity and Immersive Context Dependency.

5.3 Four Novel Privacy Threat Classifications

The IBPT framework identifies four classes of threat in immersive environment, shown in Figure 2.

Immersive Identity Disclosure (IID) refers to an attack type that takes advantage of virtual social interactions to disclose real world identities, despite the fact that they are anonymised. Pfeuffer et al. (2019) found a random forest classifier yielded with an extremely low number of 22 participants and with only 100 seconds worth of VR movement data for each participant- the date re-identification accuracy reached far into the 90s with at least to 94.33%.

This observation was validated at population scale by Nair et al. (2023), with a 94.33% re-identification accuracy across real VR users (55,541) and by Miller et al. (2020), showed 511 participants achieved 95% accuracy with naturalistic VR viewing, there appears to be a scalable threat of immersive identity disclosure that extends beyond lab-based paradigms.

Environmental Attribute Inference (EAI) refers to the problem of discovering sensitive personal attributes from spatial interaction data. Meta Quest's room-mapping sensors capture physical environment layouts and avatar characteristics derived from a creators' own physical features and Sorrentino and López-Guzmán (2025) showed that avatar characteristics mirror creator physical features. No peer-reviewed quantification of attribute inference accuracy for specific attributes is yet available, constituting a top priority area for future research.

Cross-Reality Correlation (CRC) deals with the mapping of activities between virtual and physical environments. Al Zaidawi et al. (2022) revealed that eye movement identifiers were robust across datasets, and Aziz and Komogortsev (2024) leaked evidence of possible exploitation from uncoordinated privacy protections implemented on eye tracking data as well as VR motion data to enable unauthorized re-identification.

Temporal Behavioural Reconstruction (TBR) refers to reconstruction user histories and psychological profiles based on longitudinal data. Acknowledging the persistence of gaze patterns over time in the GazeBase dataset (Griffith et al., 2021, Hoppe et al., 2018) predicted personality from eye movements, while the EyeT4Empathy dataset captured emotional state from summarize of gaze data (Lencastre et al., 2022).

The IBPT framework therefore offers four threat classifications, tailored specifically for use in the immersive environments the case studies analysed in Section 4 relate to, and which have been identified as having empirical basis within them. These classifications consider privacy threats that result specifically from thoroughly continuous, multimodal, and context-rich biometric data collection in VR/AR systems as opposed to threats tackled by well-established conventional privacy models aimed at discrete computing environments. These four classifications with supporting evidence and assigned priority levels (as per the threat prioritisation methodology in Section 4.4) are illustrated within Figure 2.

Figure 2. Four Novel Threat Classifications From IBPT Framework

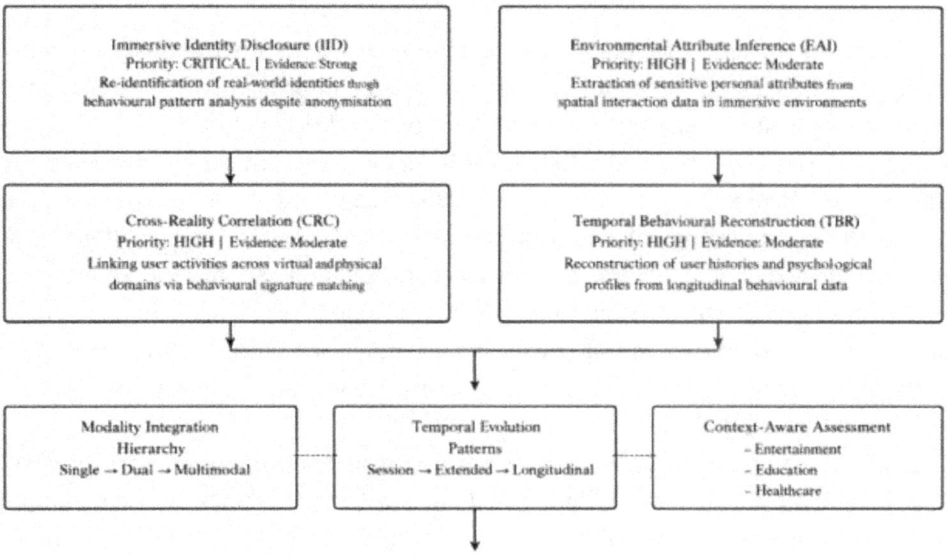

5.4 Theoretical Principles

Principle of Dimensional Transcendence: Privacy risks manifest differently in two-dimensional or immersive environments, due to the spatial–temporal and contextual dimensions of data propagation. Conventional privacy models are founded on the assumption of distinct user-system interfere (Yang et al., 2016) while immersive systems give users with multi-dimensional embodied spaces in which threat characteristics change dynamically as context changes.

Behavioural Synchronicity Theory acknowledges that immersive systems induce synchronised data collection across numerous biometrics, leading to consequential risk profiles in excess of the modal sum. The ability to record gaze, movement, vocalisation and autonomic responses simultaneously allows for highly detailed profiling that would not be achievable through serial or standalone collection (Vadher et al., 2023).

Immersive Context Dependency Principle states the contextual aspect of privacy is such that the user must take into consideration industry domain, audience demographics (or social graph), interaction pattern and surroundings. A privacy threat that is acceptable in entertainment may not be one in healthcare or education (Khan Khalil et al., 2024), requiring context-dependent privacy engineering.

6. FUTURE RESEARCH DIRECTIONS

The rapid evolution of immersive technologies yields continuously evolving privacy challenges. By combining brain-computer interfaces with VR/AR systems, neurophysiological privacy considerations additional to current biometric modalities arise (Becerra et al., 2025). With enhanced eye-tracking, including iris scanning, medical privacy becomes a concern since pupillary responses can serve as indicators of neurological conditions (Lim et al. 2020). Artificial intelligence at the confluence of semi-immersive biometric data, and more sophisticated inference from everyday patterns of behaviour (AI-derived impact evidence), (Hoppe et al., 2018). Age verification technologies raise privacy risks but also aim to mitigate safety concerns at the intersection of children's privacy and online safety (Future of Privacy Forum, 2025).

Legislative frameworks must be dealt with to consider both continuous monitoring, in this context biometric surveillance, and cross-referential matches of data points via the integration of multiple forms of behavioural datasets over time (Xynogalas & Leiser, 2024). Cross-border enforcement on global immersive platforms (Tu & De Castro e Silva, 2025) will also take international cooperation frameworks. Immersive specific considerations such as continuous consent mechanisms, multimodal data minimization, and context-aware controls must be integrated into privacy engineering frameworks (Ren et al., 2024). The new data collection properties of spatial computing environments necessitate privacy-first design principles for practitioners creating immersive experiences (Kalsha, 2025). Collaboration across the industry, through common standards, threat intelligence sharing, and certification programmes, would greatly accelerate the adoption of privacy technologies (Rahartomo et al., 2025). The follow up studies and novel privacy metrics that consider temporal accumulation (a.k.a., long-tail effects) and multimodal integration are also essential (Hanisch et al., 2021; Pfeuffer et al., 2019).

7. CONCLUSION

This chapter, have introduced the Immersive Biometric Privacy Threat Taxonomy (IBPT), a novel theoretical structure for analysing and framing privacy threats resulting from behavioural biometric data harvesting in immersive settings. Based on two extensive independent systematic reviews, the framework bridges the gap between traditional privacy models and the reality of data collection in constant operation with a high degree of multimodality, across multiple contexts enabled by virtual and augmented reality systems. Three-dimensional threat model and four novel taxonomy classifications are analytical tool sets that can potentially guide human agent privacy risk assessment in a variety of immersive deployment settings. The analysis regarding regulation finds both common trends toward greater biometric protection and ongoing deficiencies in adapting these measures to immersive-specific concerns. The threat prioritisation matrix provides actionable guidance for allocation of privacy engineering efforts. These are essential contributions in the effort to get researchers, developers, policy makers and industry practitioners working towards the design of immersive systems that balance technological ability with meaningful privacy protection. As immersive technologies develop further, constant scrutiny of these matters will be necessary because privacy frameworks may keep up with the nature and scale of these new threats.

REFERENCES

Abdrabou, Y., Ozdel, S., Maquiling, V., & Kasneci, E. (2025). From gaze to data: Privacy and societal challenges of using eye-tracking data to inform GenAI models. In *ETRA '25: 2025 Symposium on Eye Tracking Research and Applications*. ACM. https://doi.org/DOI: 10.1145/3715669.3726788

Acquisti, A., Brandimarte, L., & Loewenstein, G. (2015). Privacy and human behavior in the age of information. *Science*, *347*(6221), 509–514. DOI: 10.1126/science.aaa1465 PMID: 25635091

AL-Essa, M., Alsharo, M., Alnsour, Y., Ali, W. A., & Almomani, O.AL-Essa. (2025, December 31). M., Alsharo, M., Alnsour, Y., Ali, W. A., & Almomani, O. (2025). Transforming data representation: A comparative analysis of tabular and image-based approaches with XAI. *Journal of Computational and Cognitive Engineering*. Advance online publication. DOI: 10.47852/bonviewJCCE52026581

Al Zaidawi, S. M. K., Prinzler, M. H., Lührs, J., & Maneth, S. (2022). An extensive study of user identification via eye movements across multiple datasets. *Signal Processing Image Communication*, *108*, 116804. DOI: 10.1016/j.image.2022.116804

Allen, C., & Barrett, E. (2025, October 3). Why XR developers in the UK need accessible and authoritative guidance: The role of regulators in mapping existing laws on to the risks of immersive technologies. *The Log*.

Almomani, O., Arabiat, A., Al Tayeb, M., Amin Almaiah, M., Obeidat, M., Aldhyani, T. H. H., Shehab, R., & Rowad, M. (2025). A robust model for Android malware detection via ML and DL classifiers. *Mesopotamian Journal of Big Data*, *2025*, 261–277. DOI: 10.58496/MJBD/2025/017

Alsaaidah, A., Almomani, O., Abu-Shareha, A. A., Abualhaj, M. M., & Achuthan, A. (2024). ARP spoofing attack detection model in IoT network using machine learning: Complexity vs. accuracy. *Journal of Applied Data Sciences*, *5*(4), 1850–1860. DOI: 10.47738/jads.v5i4.374

Aziz, S., & Komogortsev, O. (2024). Exploiting the uncoordinated privacy protections of eye tracking and VR motion data for unauthorized user identification. *arXiv*. https://arxiv.org/abs/2411.12766v1

Bailenson, J. (2018). Protecting nonverbal data tracked in virtual reality. *Journal of the American Medical Association*, *320*(2), 716–717. DOI: 10.1001/jama.2018.0764 PMID: 30083770

Becerra, M. A., Duque-Mejia, C., Castro-Ospina, A., Serna-Guarín, L., Mejía, C., & Duque-Grisales, E. (2025). EEG-based biometric identification and emotion recognition: An overview. *Computers*, *14*(8), 299. DOI: 10.3390/computers14080299

Bidgoly, A. J., Bidgoly, H. J., & Arezoumand, Z. (2022). Towards a universal and privacy preserving EEG-based authentication system. *Scientific Reports*, *12*(1), 2531. DOI: 10.1038/s41598-022-06527-7 PMID: 35169248

Biometrics Institute. (2019). *Biometrics privacy guidelines*. https://www.biometricsinstitute.org/

Bouchiba, G., Tlemsani, R., Chouraqui, S., & Benouis, M. (2019). An improved behavioral biometric system based on gait and ECG signals. *International Journal of Intelligent Engineering and Systems*, *12*(6), 147–156. DOI: 10.22266/ijies2019.1231.14

D'Amelio, A., Patania, S., Bursic, S., Cuculo, V., & Boccignone, G. (2023). Using gaze for behavioural biometrics. *Sensors (Basel)*, *23*(3), 1262. DOI: 10.3390/s23031262 PMID: 36772302

Data Insights Market. (2025, April 14). *Behavioral biometrics competitive strategies: Trends and forecasts 2025–2033*. https://www.datainsightsmarket.com/reports/behavioral-biometrics-1950776

Future of Privacy Forum. (2025). *What to expect in global privacy in 2025*. https://fpf.org/blog/what-to-expect-in-global-privacy-in-2025/

George, A., & Routray, A. (2016). A score level fusion method for eye movement biometrics. *Pattern Recognition Letters*, *82*, 207–215. DOI: 10.1016/j.patrec.2015.11.020

Griffith, H., Lohr, D., Abdulin, E., & Komogortsev, O. (2021). GazeBase, a large-scale, multi-stimulus, longitudinal eye movement dataset. *Scientific Data*, *8*(1), 184. DOI: 10.1038/s41597-021-00959-y PMID: 34272404

Hanisch, S., Arias-Cabarcos, P., Parra-Arnau, J., & Strufe, T. (2021). Privacy-protecting techniques for behavioral biometric data: A survey. *arXiv*. https://doi.org//arXiv.2109.04120DOI: 10.48550

Hoppe, S., Loetscher, T., Morey, S. A., & Bulling, A. (2018). Eye movements during everyday behavior predict personality traits. *Frontiers in Human Neuroscience*, *12*, 105. DOI: 10.3389/fnhum.2018.00105 PMID: 29713270

IDC. (2025, March 25). Growth expected to pause for AR/VR headsets. International Data Corporation. https://my.idc.com/getdoc.jsp?containerId=prUS53278025

Jain, A. K., Ross, A., & Prabhakar, S. (2004). An introduction to biometric recognition. *IEEE Transactions on Circuits and Systems for Video Technology, 14*(1), 4–20. DOI: 10.1109/TCSVT.2003.818349

Kalsha, S. (2025, August 1). Privacy first: Critical considerations in immersive experiences. *Qodequay*.https://www.qodequay.com/privacy-first-critical-considerations-in-immersive-experiences

Katoikos, I., Fidas, C. A., & Koukopoulos, D. (2025). Strengthening graphical password security through EEG-driven classifiers based on image content familiarity. *International Journal of Human-Computer Interaction*. Advance online publication. DOI: 10.1080/10447318.2025.2504195

Khan Khalil, A. E., Perez-Diaz, J. A., Cantoral-Ceballos, J. A., & Antelis, J. M. (2024). Unlocking security for comprehensive electroencephalogram-based user authentication systems. *Sensors (Basel), 24*(24), 7919. DOI: 10.3390/s24247919 PMID: 39771656

Kitchenham, B. (2004). *Procedures for performing systematic reviews* (Technical Report TR/SE-0401). Software Engineering Group, Department of Computer Science, Keele University.

Lencastre, P., Bhurtel, S., Yazidi, A., Denysov, S., & Lind, P. G. (2022). EyeT4Empathy: Dataset of foraging for visual information, gaze typing and empathy assessment. *Scientific Data, 9*(1), 752. DOI: 10.1038/s41597-022-01862-w PMID: 36463232

Lim, J. Z., Mountstephens, J., & Teo, J. (2020). Emotion recognition using eye-tracking: Taxonomy, review and current challenges. *Sensors (Basel), 20*(8), 2384. DOI: 10.3390/s20082384 PMID: 32331327

Miller, M. R., Herrera, F., Jun, H., Landay, J. A., & Bailenson, J. N. (2020). Personal identifiability of user tracking data during observation of 360-degree VR video. *Scientific Reports, 10*(1), 17404. DOI: 10.1038/s41598-020-74486-y PMID: 33060713

Nair, V., Guo, W., Mattern, J., Wang, R., O'Brien, J. F., Rosenberg, L., & Song, D. (2023). Unique identification of 50,000+ virtual reality users from head & hand motion data. In *32nd USENIX Security Symposium* (pp. 895–910). USENIX Association. DOI: 10.48550/arXiv.2302.08927

Nissenbaum, H. (2004). Privacy as contextual integrity. *Washington Law Review (Seattle, Wash.), 79*(1), 119–158.

Office of the Victorian Information Commissioner. (2023). *Biometrics and privacy: A resource for Victorian public sector organisations*. State Government of Victoria.

Pekkanen, J., & Lappi, O. (2017). A new and general approach to signal denoising and eye movement classification based on segmented linear regression. *Scientific Reports*, *7*(1), 17726. DOI: 10.1038/s41598-017-17983-x PMID: 29255207

Pfeuffer, K., Geiger, M. J., Prange, S., Mecke, L., Buschek, D., & Alt, F. (2019). Behavioural biometrics in VR: Identifying people from body motion and relations in virtual reality. In *Proceedings of the 2019 CHI Conference on Human Factors in Computing Systems* (pp. 1–12). ACM. DOI: 10.1145/3290605.3300340

Piugie, Y. B. W. (2023). *Performance and security evaluation of behavioral biometric systems* [Doctoral dissertation, Normandy University]. GREYC Laboratory.

Prabhakar, S., Pankanti, S., & Jain, A. K. (2003). Biometric recognition: Security and privacy concerns. *IEEE Security and Privacy*, *1*(2), 33–42. DOI: 10.1109/MSECP.2003.1193209

Precedence Research. (2025). Virtual reality market size, share, and trends 2025 to 2034. https://www.precedenceresearch.com/virtual-reality-market

Rahartomo, A., Merino, L., & Ghafari, M. (2025). Metaverse security and privacy research: A systematic review. *arXiv*. https://arxiv.org/abs/2507.14985

Ratha, N. K., Connell, J. H., & Bolle, R. M. (2001). Enhancing security and privacy in biometrics-based authentication systems. *IBM Systems Journal*, *40*(3), 614–634. DOI: 10.1147/sj.403.0614

Rauthmann, J. F., Seubert, C. T., Sachse, P., & Furtner, M. R. (2012). Eyes as windows to the soul: Gazing behavior is related to personality. *Journal of Research in Personality*, *46*(2), 147–156. DOI: 10.1016/j.jrp.2011.12.010

Ren, X., Fan, J., Xu, N., Wen, Z., Chen, J., Zhao, S., Zhang, Y., & Gao, W. (2024). DPGazeSynth: Enhancing eye-tracking virtual reality privacy with differentially private data synthesis. *Information Sciences*, *675*(2), 120720. DOI: 10.1016/j.ins.2024.120720

Risko, E. F., Anderson, N. C., Lanthier, S., & Kingstone, A. (2012). Curious eyes: Individual differences in personality predict eye movement behavior in scene-viewing. *Cognition*, *122*(1), 86–90. DOI: 10.1016/j.cognition.2011.08.014 PMID: 21983424

Shambour, Q., Al-Zyoud, M., & Almomani, O. (2025). Quantum-inspired hybrid metaheuristic feature selection with SHAP for optimized and explainable spam detection. *Symmetry*, *17*(10), 1716. DOI: 10.3390/sym17101716

Solove, D. J. (2006). A taxonomy of privacy. *University of Pennsylvania Law Review*, *154*(3), 477–564. DOI: 10.2307/40041279

Sorrentino, G., & López-Guzmán, J. (2025). Rethinking privacy for avatars: Biometric and inferred data in the metaverse. *Frontiers in Virtual Reality*, *6*, 1520655. DOI: 10.3389/frvir.2025.1520655

Statista. (2025). Virtual reality (VR) – statistics & facts. https://www.statista.com/topics/2532/virtual-reality-vr/

Talukder, M. A., Sharmin, S., Uddin, M. A., Islam, M. M., & Aryal, S. (2024). MLSTL-WSN: Machine learning-based intrusion detection using SMOTETomek in WSNs. *International Journal of Information Security*, *23*(3), 2139–2158. DOI: 10.1007/s10207-024-00833-z

TechCrunch. (2019). *Immersive technology industry projections.*

Tu, X., & de Castro e Silva, B. (2025). Are we ready for the metaverse? Implications, legal landscape, and recommendations for responsible development. *Digital Society : Ethics, Socio-Legal and Governance of Digital Technology*, *4*(9), 9. Advance online publication. DOI: 10.1007/s44206-025-00163-0

Vadher, H., Patel, P., Nair, A., Vyas, T., Desai, S., Gohil, L., Tanwar, S., Garg, D., & Singh, A. (2023). EEG-based biometric authentication system using convolutional neural network for military applications. *Security and Privacy*. Advance online publication. DOI: 10.1002/spy2.345

Van Der Linde, I., Rajashekar, U., Bovik, A. C., & Cormack, L. K. (2009). DOVES: A database of visual eye movements. *Spatial Vision*, *22*(2), 161–177. DOI: 10.1163/156856809787465636 PMID: 19228456

Westin, A. F. (1967). *Privacy and freedom*. Atheneum Publishers.

Xynogalas, V., & Leiser, M. R. (2024). The metaverse: Searching for compliance with the General Data Protection Regulation. *International Data Privacy Law*, *14*(2), 89–105. DOI: 10.1093/idpl/ipae004

Yampolskiy, R. V., & Govindaraju, V. (2008). Behavioural biometrics: A survey and classification. *International Journal of Biometrics*, *1*(1), 81–113. DOI: 10.1504/IJBM.2008.018665

Yang, S. C. H., Wolpert, D. M., & Lengyel, M. (2016). Theoretical perspectives on active sensing. *Current Opinion in Behavioral Sciences*, *11*, 100–108. DOI: 10.1016/j.cobeha.2016.06.009 PMID: 30175197

KEY TERMS AND DEFINITIONS

Behavioural Biometrics: Measurable patterns in learned human actions and activities that can be used to distinguish individuals, including gaze patterns, gait characteristics, voice features, and neurophysiological signals.

Biometric Telemetry: The remote, continuous, and often passive transmission of biometric data from sensors embedded in immersive devices to processing systems.

Contextual Integrity: A privacy framework positing that privacy violations occur when information flows across contexts without appropriate authorisation, particularly relevant to immersive environments that collapse multiple informational contexts.

Cross-Reality Correlation (CRC): A privacy threat involving the linking of user activities across virtual and physical domains through multi-sensor data fusion and behavioural signature matching.

Environmental Attribute Inference (EAI): A privacy threat involving the extraction of sensitive personal attributes from spatial interaction data collected in immersive environments.

Immersive Identity Disclosure (IID): A privacy threat in which virtual interactions reveal real-world user identities through behavioural pattern analysis despite anonymisation attempts.

Multimodal Fusion: The combination of data from multiple biometric modalities to create integrated behavioural profiles, which may achieve higher identification accuracy but correspondingly amplify privacy risks.

Psychographic Inference: The derivation of sensitive personal attributes such as emotional states, personality traits, or health conditions from behavioural biometric data through computational analysis.

Temporal Behavioural Reconstruction (TBR): A privacy threat involving the reconstruction of user histories and psychological profiles from longitudinal behavioural data collected over extended immersive sessions.

Chapter 2

Edge-Cloud Continuum Security for Immersive Systems Latency, Scalability, and Attack Resilience

Salam Al E'mari
http://orcid.org/0000-0002-2134-4158
University of Petra, Jordan

Yousef Sanjalawe
http://orcid.org/0000-0002-4442-1865
University of Jordan, Jordan

Fadi Fataftah
http://orcid.org/0000-0002-3299-0972
University Canada West, Canada

ABSTRACT

Immersive technologies, including Virtual Reality (VR), Augmented Reality (AR), Mixed Reality (MR), and Extended Reality (XR), are transforming the way people learn, cooperate, and are entertained. To provide a responsive and realistic experience, the user's location, gaze, and gestures, as well as sometimes physiological information, need to be constantly sensed. To this end, a range of processing needs to be carried out on the device, as well as edge servers and cloud platforms. However, it also expands the attack surface: motion data can uniquely identify users, digital twins linking physical and virtual systems introduce vulnerabilities across multiple

DOI: 10.4018/979-8-3373-7882-4.ch002

layers, and 6G networks will connect billions of devices requiring sub-millisecond security decisions. This chapter examines how latency, scalability and attack resilience can be balanced in immersive systems.

1. INTRODUCTION

Immersive technologies have shifted from their role as entertainment media to their use in the interaction of human societies, education, industrial control, and medical care. The latest VR, AR, MR, and XR devices can display photorealistic scenes, provide realistic haptics, and offer spatialized sound. These technologies can also facilitate remote work through the display of avatars in a common virtual space. These technologies rely on a loop of sensing, computation, and display. Sensing technologies detect user input and environmental information, computation modules interpret the sensor data, and display technologies render images in real-time, within tens of milliseconds. The computational requirements of real-time physics, stereoscopy, scene reconstruction, and AI are beyond those of portable devices. As a result, immersive applications utilize the distributed computing architecture referred to as the edge-cloud continuum. Local computing handles latency-sensitive activities such as head tracking and haptic feedback, near-edge servers are utilized for computationally intensive activities such as heavy graphics rendering and initial AI inference, whereas deep analytics, extensive model training, and storage are done in the cloud data centers. This collaborative architecture ensures the user has a seamless and realistic experience, while the system scales appropriately in different regions and use cases (Nair et al., 2023).

The growth of 5G connectivity has further fueled the growth of immersive technologies. According to the Boston Consulting Group (BCG), the growth of 5G connectivity has led to the generation of over $1 trillion in economic impact and is likely to rise to over $6 trillion by the end of 2030. Data consumption in the United States alone reached 132 trillion megabytes in 2024. The growth of 5G connectivity has enabled the services to reach nearly three billion people. The growth of these technologies indicates the impact of high-speed connectivity on the development of the Internet of Things and AI services. AI agents are shifting from cloud-based tools to permanent and multimodal agents in phones, cars, wearables, and XR devices. Agents produce continuous flows of uplink heavy, latency-critical, and context-dependent traffic. The connectivity of devices also plays an essential role in the performance of AI systems, as devices can offload tasks effortlessly when connected reliably and with low latency. To cater to the requirements of AI-native services, 6G networks are expected to deliver predictable low latency, uplink capacity, and sensing as well as multilayer coverage. The 6G network is expected to include non-terrestrial networks, context-aware agentic intelligence, and continuous edge collection of real-world data. The marriage of AI and connectivity is expected to open doors to novel business opportunities such as remote robotics, autonomous vehicles, and immersive telemedicine.

However, these opportunities bring new challenges. The spread of computation across devices, edge nodes, and the cloud creates new issues with respect to the optimal allocation of computation tasks and the quality of service. The problem of security in the new landscape of devices and the spread of computation also needs to be addressed. The question of the balance between latency, scalability, and security in immersive technologies is the subject of this chapter. The latest literature and technologies will be analyzed in order to identify the best practices and gaps in the research.

Immersive mediums, which include VR, AR, and MR, have revolutionized education, entertainment, remote collaborations, and training in industrial environments. These mediums allow users to be immersed in a digital world or allow digital information to be mapped onto the physical world, which enables surgeons to practice on virtual organs, engineers to view their prototypes in situ, or remote colleagues to collaborate with co-presence. To ensure that there is believability in the experience and prevent simulator sickness, immersive mediums have extreme performance requirements that include latencies of less than 20 ms in motion-to-photon time and minimizing frame loss. As the fidelity of experiences increases, so too does the volume of sensor and render data that must be processed and delivered. Traditional centralised clouds cannot meet these stringent requirements because network delays accumulate over wide-area links and throughput is constrained by shared backhaul. Consequently, distributed computing paradigms that bring computation and storage closer to the user have become critical for next-generation immersive applications.

This paradigm shift is underscored by the rapid relocation of enterprise data from central data centres to the edge. OTAVA's 2025 report on edge computing security notes that data processing is moving away from centralised data centres, predicting that by 2025 about 75% of enterprise data will be handled at the edge compared with only 10% in 2018. At the same time, the proliferation of connected devices is driving up the volume and diversity of data produced at the network periphery; with approximately 75 billion connected devices expected by 2025, organisations must adopt distributed architectures to collect, process and interpret this information. These trends emphasise the necessity of edge–cloud integration so that latency-sensitive workloads can be handled locally while heavy compute tasks are off-loaded to the cloud. Immersive systems sit at the forefront of this trend because headsets and haptic devices continuously generate motion, gaze and environmental data that must be processed in real time.

New mobile network generations further catalyse the deployment of immersive applications. The same OTAVA report highlights how fifth-generation (5G) networks accelerate the adoption of edge computing by lowering latency and increasing connectivity, enabling use cases such as remote healthcare, smart factories and autonomous vehicles. However, the benefits of 5G are accompanied by new attack vectors because multi-access edge computing introduces additional entry points and endpoint vulnerabilities. Beyond 5G, sixth-generation (6G) research envisions AI-native, spatially aware networks that provide high uplink capacity, predictable low latency and integrated sensing across terrestrial and aerial layers. In this context, the edge–cloud continuum will be the default computing substrate for immersive systems, making security and resilience fundamental design criteria.

2. THE EDGE–CLOUD CONTINUUM

The edge–cloud continuum describes a dynamic distribution of computing and storage resources spanning devices, local edge servers, fog nodes and central cloud data centres. Instead of treating computation as a binary choice between device and cloud, the continuum allows tasks to migrate among tiers based on latency requirements, available resources, energy constraints, privacy policies and network conditions. This section outlines the architectural principles that enable immersive systems to exploit this continuum. Figure 1 illustrates the layered architecture of the edge–cloud continuum in immersive systems, highlighting the distribution of computation, data flow, and latency-sensitive operations across device, edge, network, and cloud layers.

Figure 1. Edge–Cloud Continuum Architecture for Immersive Systems.

2.1 Micro-Services, Virtualization and Containerization

Modern applications are decomposed into micro-services—small, loosely coupled components that each provide a specific function (e.g., user authentication, scene reconstruction, physics simulation). Micro-services are typically packaged in containers (e.g., Docker) that include the code and its dependencies, enabling them to run on heterogeneous hardware and migrate seamlessly across the continuum. Sofia et al., 2024 note that next-generation IoT applications are increasingly adopting containerised micro-services and that approximately 40% of IoT data is already captured and processed at the edge. They argue that flexible cross-layer orchestration is necessary to support decentralisation, mobility and multi-tenant environments. Projects such as CODECO integrate reinforcement learning and graph neural networks to predict resource exhaustion, automate placement decisions and provide context-aware scheduling (Subramanian et al., 2026).

Virtualization technologies, including Virtual Machines (VMs), containers and unikernels, allow multiple services to share hardware resources while isolating faults. Hypervisors enable VMs to run unmodified operating systems; containers share the host kernel for lightweight deployment; and unikernels compile applications and minimal OS components into a single binary for fast boot times. Virtualisation is complemented by hardware accelerators (GPUs, TPUs, NPUs) that support parallel processing for graphics and AI inference.

2.2 Offloading and Resource Management

Deciding where to execute each component of an immersive application, on-device, at an edge node or in the cloud, is crucial. The offloading strategies include assessing the sensitivity of latency, data volume, computational requirements, energy budget, and privacy. In split rendering, there is still latency-sensitive tracking and fusion of sensors on the device, but the rendering is offloaded to edge servers. The edge servers then render frames and send them back using high-bandwidth wireless communication. This enables headsets to be both lightweight and energy-efficient with high-quality graphics. Research on Integrated Communication and Computing (ICC) frameworks extends this concept by placing compute modules directly within radio access network nodes and coordinating bandwidth and computer resource management. Queueing-theoretic analysis shows that ICC increases service capacity, defined as the maximum arrival rate that meets a specified latency budget, by 98% compared with traditional 5G multi-access edge computing. System-level simulations using transformer-based generative AI workloads demonstrate a 60% improvement in service capacity. These findings illustrate that co-designing communication and computation stacks is essential for future immersive systems (Volico, 2024).

Offloading decisions may be static (e.g., pre-defined in application code) or dynamic. Dynamic offloading algorithms use real-time monitoring of network conditions, user context and device status to decide where to execute tasks. Machine-learning-based schedulers, including reinforcement learning, multi-armed bandits and deep Q-networks, can learn policies for optimal offloading under uncertainty. In addition to computation offloading, data offloading (where raw data is preprocessed at the edge before being sent to the cloud) reduces bandwidth and protects privacy. Edge catching stores popular content, such as 3D models, at edge servers to reduce retrieval latency during collaborative sessions.

2.3 Heterogeneity, Mobility and Interoperability

Immersive systems involve diverse hardware—from lightweight headsets, smart glasses and gloves to powerful game consoles, smartphones, IoT sensors and autonomous robots. Each of them has various computational capacities, energy limitations, operating systems, and communication interfaces. Network heterogeneity refers to the diversity of wired and wireless links, such as Wi-Fi, 5G, mmWave, sub-Terahertz, satellite, etc., with various levels of bandwidth, latency, and reliability. Mobility is another challenge, which, in the context of physical space, causes users to move from one base station to another, as well as devices joining or terminating sessions, and network conditions changing. Orchestration frameworks should be able to concurrently monitor all levels of computing, networks, and data in order to adjust accordingly. Interoperability requires standards for data formats, APIs and protocols so that applications can seamlessly exchange geometry, physics information and user state across platforms. Initiatives like Gaia-X and the International Data Spaces Association promote secure and interoperable data spaces.

2.4 Network Function Virtualization and Software-Defined Networking

Network Function Virtualization (NFV) decouples network functions (firewalls, load balancers, intrusion detection systems) from dedicated hardware appliances and implements them as software that can run on general-purpose servers. Software-Defined Networking (SDN) centralizes control over network devices, allowing dynamic configuration of routing, quality-of-service policies and security rules. NFV and SDN enable network slicing: multiple virtual networks can run on a shared physical infrastructure with isolated performance and security properties. For immersive applications, slices may reserve bandwidth and compute resources to guarantee motion-to-photon latency. NFV also allows deployment of security functions at the edge; for example, a distributed firewall or deep packet inspection engine can be spun up near users to detect anomalies. Combining SDN with AI analytics can enable self-healing networks that reroute traffic around congestion or compromised nodes.

2.5 Edge AI and Distributed Intelligence

The development of edge computing is accompanied by the development of edge AI. Edge AI is the application of AI models on resource-constrained devices or edge servers. In immersive systems, edge AI can be used for various functions such as pose estimation, gaze prediction, hand gesture detection, audio noise reduction, and natural language processing. Reinforcement learning agents can be used to manage the network resources. Federated learning enables devices to learn the same model without the need to share raw data. The updates are aggregated centrally. Differential privacy and secure aggregation are used to preserve the privacy of the raw data. Distributed intelligence can be used in context-aware services. Edge nodes can be used to analyze environmental data and adjust lighting effects in an immersive scene (Industrial Cyber, 2025, Shambour, Al-Zyoud & Almomani, 2025).

At the architectural level, modern immersive platforms make extensive use of virtualization technology to virtualize applications and efficiently utilize hardware. VMs virtualize hardware and have their own operating system. This gives good isolation at the cost of resource overhead and slower instantiation. The alternative to VMs is containerization, which virtualizes the operating system rather than hardware.

This allows many micro services to be run concurrently with minimal overhead. Containers require fewer resources and thus make it easier to scale applications finely and speed up deployment due to their ability to start in milliseconds. However, the absence of a full hypervisor means that containers share the kernel, which can lead to kernel-level exploits if misconfigured. To mitigate such risks, container orchestration platforms such as Kubernetes implement role-based access control, network policies and admission controllers to restrict privileges and enforce best practices.

Building on containerisation, the serverless paradigm abstracts away infrastructure management by decomposing applications into discrete functions that are executed on demand. Escaleira et al. (2025) describe serverless computing as a pivotal paradigm that offers unprecedented scalability and operational agility because the cloud service provider abstracts the hardware and software stack up to the application layer. In this model, applications are deconstructed into micro-services called functions, and even the execution environment and data are managed by the provider. Developers only implement business logic and rely on the platform to scale and patch underlying components. The architecture appears more secure at first glance because the provider controls most computation layers and performs software updates, which reduces the risk of outdated dependencies. However, Escaleira et al. point out that serverless systems remain susceptible to misconfiguration and closed-source infrastructure; a vulnerability in the underlying platform can affect all tenants. Moreover, application-level vulnerabilities persist because functions are still software, and the distributed nature of serverless increases the attack surface for access control and event-driven dataflows. An emergent threat specific to serverless is the denial-of-wallet attack, where adversaries trigger a large number of function executions to exhaust a tenant's budget. Such attacks illustrate how cloud economics intersect with security in the edge–cloud continuum.

These deployment models co-exist with emerging orchestration frameworks that optimise resource placement across edge and cloud resources. In addition to container orchestrators, researchers have proposed decentralised solutions like CODECO that integrate reinforcement learning and graph neural networks to predict resource exhaustion and optimise placement decisions. This framework not only schedules containers across heterogeneous devices but also adapts to context in real time, improving the execution of interactive tasks. Similarly, integrated communication and computing frameworks in 6G networks embed computing capabilities within radio access network nodes, coordinating bandwidth and compute resources to support AI-enabled workloads with ultralow latency. While containerization, serverless functions, and cross-layer orchestration provide the building blocks for scalable and flexible immersive services, the complexity of these solutions increases the attack surface and the need for effective security solutions.

3. SECURITY CHALLENGES IN THE EDGE–CLOUD CONTINUUM

The immersive experience provided by immersive systems also expands the threat landscape. The threats can be in the form of hardware attacks, software attacks, protocol attacks, authentication attacks, and even insider attacks. The distributed nature of the edge-cloud continuum provides the ability for attacks to spread across devices and edge-cloud continuum. The security issues were previously discussed in the above section. Figure 2 presents a structured taxonomy of security threats in the edge–cloud continuum, categorizing risks across device, network, infrastructure, application, and human layers while relating them to core security objectives of confidentiality, integrity, and availability.

Figure 2. Threat Taxonomy in the Edge–Cloud Continuum.

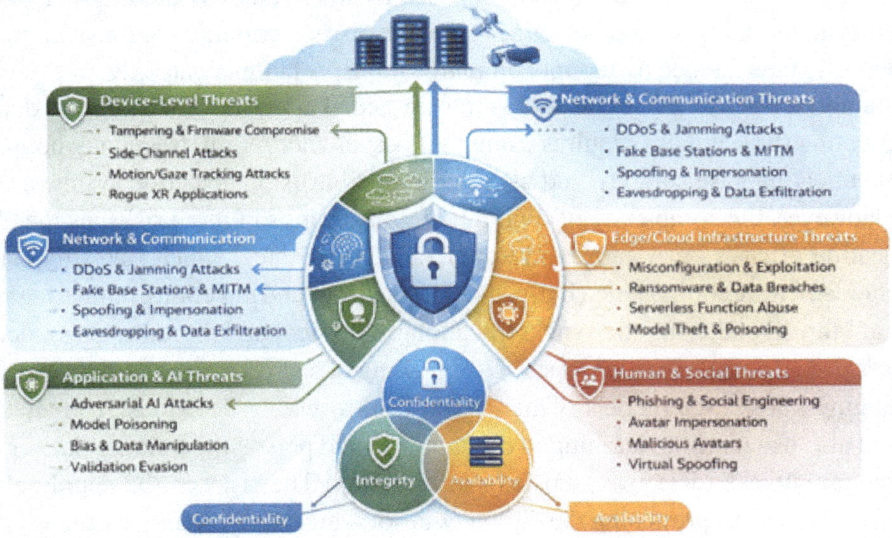

Besides the privacy issues associated with biometric and behavioral data that were discussed in the previous sections, devices may also be tampered with. This means that devices like controllers may have keyloggers installed in them, and wearables like headsets may have malicious chips installed in them. The devices may be used in areas like operating rooms, industrial areas, and military training areas, and as such, the consequences of compromised devices will be severe. There is also the possibility that machine learning algorithms running on devices may be vulnerable to attacks like adversarial attacks. This means that if an attacker wants to deceive a gesture recognition model running on a device, he or she may be able to do that by feeding it adversarial examples. Supply chain attacks are also possible, and as such, devices may be tampered with before they reach users.

3.1 Communication and Network Attacks

Immersive technologies are also subject to sophisticated network attacks, malicious actors can exploit weaknesses in session initiation protocol used for voice and video communications. They can also inject fake avatars. Ransomware-as-a-Service groups can attack edge servers, causing them to encrypt rendering services. Quantum key distribution is expected to provide security for long-distance communications in the future. However, presently, classical cryptography is used. In addition, quantum computing poses a threat to breaking classical cryptography. Malicious actors can also use 5G stingrays to attack communications. They can also analyze communications to obtain sensitive information, such as when a user is talking to a virtual therapist. Jamming is another attack used to disrupt communications. Jamming uses radio interference to disrupt communications. A jammer can only react during certain times of the day when data is transmitted. This makes it difficult to detect. Mitigating these attacks requires using multi-layer encryption, frequency hopping, authenticating base stations, and using AI-based intrusion detection systems.

However, the complexity of digital twins also brings in more risks, as the classification of risks by Alcaraz and Lopez (2022) indicates, which states that risks include software components (buffer overflows, command injection), tampering with digital threads (altering the synchronization of physical and digital spaces), denial of service (flooding simulation servers), stealing of secrets (industrial secrets), and changing knowledge models, which could lead to wrong decisions. The attacker could also use machine learning in digital twins and poison the training data or use inversion attacks to recover sensitive information. The risks in the supply chain could include compromising the digital twin software and spreading wrong logic in different plants. The security of digital twins requires different security measures, which include secure communication protocols, anomaly detection in physics models, redundancy, and access control.

The IoT devices used in immersive systems vary from smart lights and speakers in a VR room to industrial sensors used in digital twin applications. These devices are resource-constrained devices with outdated software and are rarely updated. Botnets such as Mirai and Mozi exploit weak authentication mechanisms to recruit millions of IoT devices to launch coordinated DDoS attacks. Edge servers are also used in DDoS attacks to disrupt VR applications. In DDoS attacks, attackers often use reflection and amplification attacks, in which attackers send small queries to weak servers such as DNS and NTP, which in turn send large responses to flood the target. In order to defend against DDoS attacks, rate limiting, filtering, anomaly detection, and load balancing are used. Edge computing can be used to absorb or redirect malicious traffic closer to its source. Machine-learning-based DDoS detection models also need to be robust against adversarial examples.

Side-channel attacks can also be performed against immersive devices. For example, the electromagnetic radiation given off by the processor of a headset could potentially be used to deduce encryption keys. Similarly, sound could be used to detect keys pressed or voice commands given to a device. Another example is the use of heat sensors to track the pattern of movement of the head or hand of the user of the immersive device. Proximity attacks could include bumping into the user of an immersive device in order to cause them to make gestures, or the use of haptic devices to feed false information to the user in order to affect their decision-making processes.

The attackers use human psychology, rather than any particular vulnerability in the system. The immersive experience dissolves the line between physical and virtual presence, making the user more prone to such attacks. Social engineering can include phishing emails sent through chat in VR, avatars of trusted co-workers or authorities, or even the use of deepfake voices in a simulation for training purposes. Harassment, stalking, and unwanted touch, in the form of avatars, can have serious effects on the user's psychology. The attackers can force the user to download malware in the form of mods or software updates. Trust in an immersive environment relies on strong user verification, moderation, reporting, and education of users about phishing and privacy. The interface should also offer safety indicators, such as personal space bubbles (Almomani et al., 2025).

3.2 Regulatory and Compliance Issues

The data collected by the immersive technologies might include biometric data such as iris scans and voice patterns. The data might also include health-related data such as heart rate and breathing patterns. The data might also be location-based. The regulations such as the GDPR require that data be collected with the informed consent of the data subject. The regulations also require data minimization and the right to access, correct, and erase the data. The data flows across borders might raise issues of jurisdiction and the law that applies. For instance, the user might be in Europe and connect to an edge server in North America. Which privacy law applies? The platform operators need to be transparent about the data processing and sharing. The data retention policy needs to take into consideration the fact that the data collected might be uniquely identifying and cannot be revoked like the password. The IEEE and ISO are developing guidelines for the responsible design of XR technologies.

Securing the edge–cloud continuum also requires attention to the socio-technical systems that support immersive applications. One often overlooked vector is the supply chain. OTAVA reports that approximately 40% of cyber security breaches originate from weak links in the supply chain. Edge devices are frequently deployed in remote facilities, warehouses and retail environments where they run outdated firmware and lack physical protection. Attackers exploit these conditions to plant malware or backdoors that later propagate through the network. A resilient security strategy therefore includes rigorous vendor assessments, encryption of data at rest and in transit, and automated patch management to close vulnerabilities before they are exploited. Hyper-converged edge solutions that integrate compute, storage and security can help organisations segment networks, isolate compromised devices and perform rapid restoration after an incident.

The massive scale of connected devices projected for the near future further magnifies the attack surface. With an estimated 75 billion connected devices by 2025, zero-trust architectures that eliminate implicit trust are essential. In a zero-trust model, every user, device and application must authenticate and authorize each request and network micro-segments limit lateral movement. OTAVA's S.E.C.U.R.E.™ framework emphasises shrinking the attack surface through strict authentication, data encryption and real-time monitoring. In addition, AI-powered threat detection systems that examine network activity and automatically respond to anomalies are becoming indispensable as attack speeds outpace human response times. Global spending on edge AI is projected to grow from US$1.92 billion in 2024 to US$7.19 billion by 2030, underscoring the rapid adoption of automation. Nevertheless, reliance on AI also introduces new risks such as adversarial attacks and model poisoning, necessitating robust validation and monitoring protocols (Alnaim & Alwakeel, 2025).

Emerging technologies also intersect with security in less obvious ways. Quantum computing threatens to render many current encryption schemes obsolete; OTAVA stresses that quantum computers may be capable of breaking traditional encryption methods, so organisations need to adopt post-quantum cryptography to protect financial transactions, healthcare records and IoT communications. The development of quantum-resistant encryption is therefore a priority for long-term secure edge deployments. At the same time, sustainability considerations are becoming intertwined with security. Energy-efficient hardware such as analog edge chips can perform certain computations with one-tenth the power consumption of their digital counterparts. Deploying such chips not only reduces carbon footprints but also enables secure processing in power-constrained environments. Moreover, data localization laws are driving the need for regional edge data centres that comply with local privacy regulations. These legal requirements shape the architecture of immersive systems, necessitating secure and energy-efficient infrastructures that respect local sovereignty. Table 1 summarizes the key security threats across different layers of the edge–cloud continuum along with their corresponding impacts and mitigation strategies, providing a consolidated view of the threat landscape and defense approaches.

Table 1. Threats vs. Mitigation Strategies in Immersive Edge–Cloud Systems

Layer	Threat Type	Example Attack	Impact	Mitigation
Device	Physical tampering	Malicious chip in headset	Data leakage	Secure boot, hardware attestation
Network	DDoS / jamming	Reflection attacks	Service disruption	Rate limiting, edge filtering
Edge	Ransomware	Encrypted rendering servers	Downtime	Backup, segmentation
AI	Adversarial input	Gesture spoofing	Wrong decisions	Robust training
Human	Social engineering	Fake avatars	Credential theft	User awareness, verification

4. ATTACK RESILIENCE AND EMERGING DEFENSE MECHANISMS

As immersive systems advance, it is expected that defenders will need to be prepared for an adaptive and stealthy opponent. The notion of attack resilience also means that, in addition to preventing attacks, it is important to be able to detect attacks in a timely manner and contain and recover from attacks. This section further discusses existing defence strategies and additional defence strategies.

Implementing ZTA requires more than MFA and continuous monitoring. The access control policies need to be contextual, i.e., they need to consider device posture, user behavior, network conditions, and location. Adaptive authentication may need to involve stronger factors if anomalies are detected. The trust scores may be updated based on machine learning models that analyze patterns of interactions within the network. In 6G, ZTA will need to operate effectively within a highly distributed edge, fog, and cloud nodes environment. Automating the management of ZTA policies will be required, as policy misconfigurations may create security risks or deny legitimate access. The integration of ZTA and SDN allows for the dynamic deployment of security policies within slices. Figure 3 illustrates the attack resilience framework in the edge–cloud continuum, highlighting a defense-in-depth strategy across device, edge, network, and cloud layers through integrated prevention, detection, response, and recovery mechanisms.

Figure 3. Attack Resilience Framework

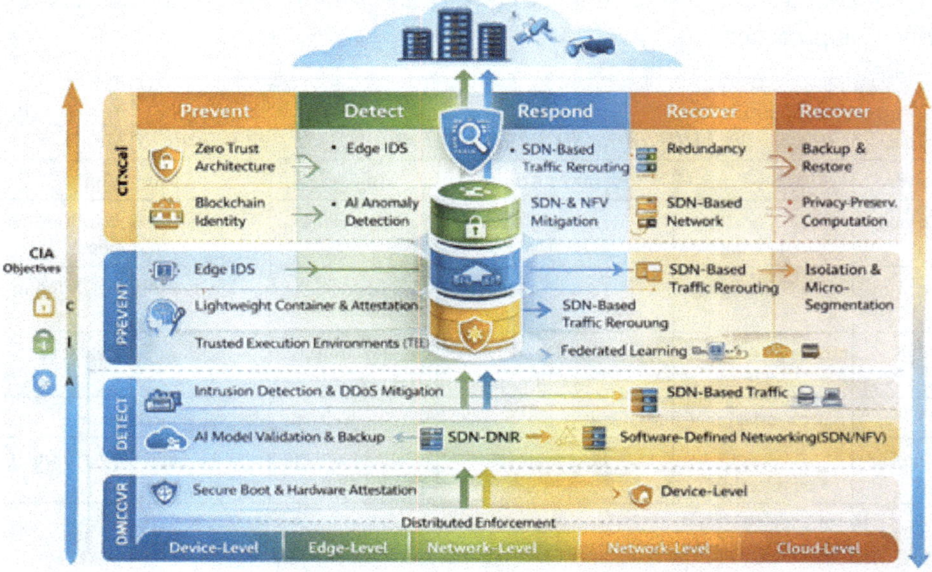

Furthermore, the Blockchains facilitate the implementation of tamper-proof audit trails. However, they also have scalability issues. For instance, public blockchains such as Ethereum have low throughput and high energy consumption. However, private and consortium blockchains can be optimized for speed by implementing proof-of-authority and PBFT consensus algorithms. The identity data can be stored off the blockchain with only references stored on the blockchain. Self-sovereign identity solutions enable users to manage their own identity and share verifiable information without revealing underlying data. Decentralized identifiers and verifiable credentials can be used to represent users, devices, and services. Zero-knowledge proofs can be used with blockchains to verify user attributes such as age and profession without revealing the data.

The communication overhead and statistical heterogeneity are the main problems faced in federated learning. To reduce the communication overhead, the updates are compressed or quantized. Split learning is another technique where the neural network is divided into two models, and the intermediate results are shared. However, there is some leakage of information. Secure methods include the use of homomorphic encryption and secure multi-party computation. Currently, the focus is on personalizing the federated learning, where each device has its own personal model derived from the global model. Immersive applications use federated learning to improve hand-tracking or gesture recognition using headsets, while maintaining user privacy.

The previously discussed micro-layer intrusion detection system architecture is a good example of how the proximity of the system to the source of the data improves the system's response time. Other techniques include collaborative anomaly detection, where edge nodes are utilized to share the detected intrusion and pool the detected anomalies to improve the detection of distributed attacks. Light machine learning models, such as one-class SVM, isolation forests, and autoencoders, are utilized in edge nodes. However, the attacker may employ techniques to manipulate the learning process; therefore, the system must be designed to provide updates and effective learning algorithms. Signature-based and anomaly-based intrusion detection provide defense against attacks; the former is effective in detecting well-known attacks, whereas the latter is effective in detecting unknown attacks.

Digital twin security requires that both data flows, which update models, and logic, which defines behavior, be secured. This is achieved through formal verification of control algorithms to validate safety, monitoring behavior against expected models, and through redundancy, whereby multiple digital twins operate in parallel. Digital twins are also required to adhere to the principle of least privilege, whereby only specific sensors and actuators are available to specific sub-modules. For instance, AI-driven digital twins may be trained to respond to simulated cyber-attacks. The integration of digital twins and blockchain technology ensures that updates and logs are tamper-proof.

Besides the technical aspect, there is the socio-behavioral aspect. This includes the moderation of the immersive platforms. This could be community-based, AI-based, or a combination of both. There is also the need to rethink the concept of consent in the context of continuous sensing. This would involve giving the user more granular control over the data they are willing to share. There is also the need to create privacy dashboards that provide real-time data. Ethical considerations would involve more than just privacy; they would include fairness, accessibility, and sustainability. There is the need to think about the concept of avatars and identity, personal space in the context of VR, and how to deal with cultural sensitivities. There is also the need to involve psychologists and sociologists in the development of immersive environments.

A Software-Defined Perimeter (SDP) is a technique that involves designing a network architecture where services are not discoverable for unauthenticated users. A software-defined perimeter utilizes a control plane that authenticates and authorizes a user before a data plane connection is made. Micro-segmentation involves dividing a network into small segments, and this helps in reducing the blast radius in the event of a network compromise. In immersive networks, micro-segmentation can be used to segment rendering services, sensor networks, and administrative services. The policies can be implemented through SDN controllers, and access can be dynamically managed based on risk indicators.

Homomorphic encryption enables computation on encrypted data, allowing the server to perform rendering or analysis without decrypting the data. Although fully homomorphic encryption is still computationally expensive, partially homomorphic encryption and secure enclaves (e.g., Intel SGX, ARM TrustZone) can be used to protect critical computations. Another technique is Secure Multiparty Computation (SMPC), which involves dividing data between different parties and allowing them to compute the output together without disclosing their data. Another technique is trusted execution environments, which protect code and data from an untrusted OS. These techniques could be used in immersive systems to allow the edge node to process biometric data for authentication or calibrate the digital twin without exposing the data to the network.

The attackers and the defenders are in a dynamic game. Game theory models can be used to predict the attackers' behavior and the defender's strategy. For instance, the defender can allocate resources for monitoring and patching the system based on the payoff of the attackers. Dynamic defence strategies respond to changes in the system in real-time according to the threat levels and the system's behavior. Machine learning algorithms can be used to make predictions about the attackers' behavior. This will allow the defender to take proactive steps in patching the system and making configurations. However, the problem is that it might cause oscillations.

To get an idea of the implications of edge security, one only needs to remember the Mirai botnet. In 2016, this malware caused worldwide concern after it recruited hundreds of thousands of vulnerable IoT devices such as routers, cameras, DVRs, and other embedded devices into a botnet that carried out distributed denial-of-service attacks that exceeded 600 Gbps. Antonakakis et al. (2017) offer a retrospective analysis that indicates that the ease of the Mirai code was the key to the recruitment of low-end devices on such an unprecedented scale. In the first 20 hours of the botnet's operations, it recruited nearly 65,000 devices. The devices were concentrated in several geographical areas. In particular, Brazil, Colombia, and Vietnam accounted for 41.5 percent of the infections. The Mirai variants were continuously evolving and competed with each other in the recruitment of vulnerable devices. The Mirai botnet attack against the domain name service provider Dyn caused disruptions to several popular websites such as Twitter and Netflix. Mirai demonstrates the necessity of defense-in-depth strategies that extend to device firmware, network protocols, and cloud orchestration (Almomani et al., 2026).

The Mirai attack also led to further studies on new defensive mechanisms. Intrusion detection using micro-layers involves deploying anomaly detection logic in between devices and gateways. For example, in the Edge AI Bridge architecture, there is a micro-computing layer that performs local anomaly detection and signature matching.

This reduces detection time from 500 ms in traditional gateway-based architectures to 50 ms, with CPU utilization at around 20%. Such architectures reflect a zero-trust approach in that all incoming packets are assumed not trustworthy and inspected at entry. When federated learning and blockchain-based identity management are used in conjunction with micro-layer-based detection, there is promise of scalable and privacy-preserving security for IoT environments. Apart from anomaly detection, there have been significant changes in supply chain security in response to Mirai. For example, there is greater emphasis on removing default passwords, ensuring that there is compliance with secure boot mechanisms, and that there is automated patching. Such lessons reflect that edge security is not just about solutions but also involves legislative action.

5. LATENCY AND SCALABILITY CONSIDERATIONS

Latency and scalability are considered the two pillars of performance for immersive systems. Latency relates to the total time taken from user input, such as head movements, and system responses, such as visual feedback. Scalability, on the other hand, relates to the number of users and devices that can be supported without compromising performance. This section presents additional information on network and computational latencies, as well as new topics such as next generation communication technologies and Quality of Experience (QoE).

5.1 Networking Latency, Scalability and Load Balancing

In immersive apps, there is a stringent delay constraint that should be met. The delay constraint is that motion photon delay should not exceed 20 ms. This is because if it is exceeded, there is likely to be motion sickness. The total delay is made up of propagation delay, transmission delay, processing delay, and queuing delay. 5G reduces round-trip delay time to 5-10 ms. However, there is jitter in wireless channels that is caused by handovers. 6G is targeting user plane delay that is less than 1 ms. This is achievable by using new spectrum bands that include mmWave at 30-300 GHz and THz at 0.1-10 THz. Furthermore, massive MIMO is used in 6G. IAB uses the same frequency band for user access and backhaul communication. This makes it cost-effective. Non-terrestrial networks include low Earth orbit satellites. This is in addition to high-altitude platforms (Gherari et al., 2026).

For photorealistic rendering, heavy matrix operations and shading calculations are required. Cloud gaming services make use of powerful GPUs in data centers to perform rendering and transmit compressed video to clients. However, in immersive VR applications, where even slight delays cause discomfort, rendering should be done closer to the user. The load can be reduced using foveated rendering, where rendering of high-resolution images is done only in the foveal area of the gaze of the user. However, this method requires eye-tracking devices. Another method is predicting head movements to pre-render potential frames of the video. AI inference operations such as natural language understanding and gesture recognition can be performed more efficiently by pruning, quantizing, and knowledge distillation of the models. Edge AI accelerators can be used to run optimized models with low power consumption. The frameworks should also take into account the energy consumption of devices in the case of computing and offloading frameworks, as repeatedly sending data to the cloud can cause battery drain of devices in the future, and other areas of research could include neuromorphic computing and analog AI processors.

The radio spectrum for wireless communication affects aspects such as latency, throughput, and reliability. The sub-6 GHz spectrum supports reliable coverage but lacks sufficient bandwidth. The mmWave spectrum supports gigabit-level throughput but requires line of sight. The sub-THz and THz bands have even higher throughput, supporting features such as streaming of uncompressed video and holographic communication. The Visible Light Communication (LiFi) network utilizes the optical spectrum, supporting high bandwidth within indoor environments. The combination of these networks, referred to as a hybrid network, allows devices to utilize different networks for communication. A device may utilize the mmWave network for the downlink, sub-6 GHz for the uplink, and LiFi for indoor locationing. The multi-connectivity feature allows devices to maintain simultaneous connectivity to different access points. In the context of the 6G network, devices will utilize the Integrated Sensing and Communication (ISAC) technique, where a single waveform supports both communication and environmental sensing. The device will be able to sense the environment and communicate simultaneously. The integration of edge computing supports features such as mixed reality.

Scalability includes horizontal scaling, which adds more servers, and vertical scaling, which adds resources to existing servers. For micro-service architecture, auto scalers monitor metrics like CPU load, memory, and request latency. However, for immersive applications, it is not easy to move the state of a VR session to another server. The state migration involves moving positions, states, and parameters without disrupting the session. Techniques for state migration include state replication, in which multiple servers replicate states and then promote one server for scaling. Another technique is consistent hashing, which allows for uniform distribution of sessions over servers and minimizes changes in server additions and removals. Queueing theory is also applicable for load balancing. Table 2 presents a comparative analysis of key techniques in immersive systems, highlighting the trade-offs between latency, scalability, and security to support informed design decisions within the edge–cloud continuum.

Table 2. Latency vs. Security vs. Scalability Trade-offs.

Technique	Latency Impact	Scalability Impact	Security Impact	Notes
Edge computing	Low latency	Medium	Improves (local control)	More attack surface
Cloud computing	High latency	High	Centralized security	Not real-time friendly
Split rendering	Low latency	Medium	Moderate risk	Needs secure channels
Federated learning	Medium	High	Strong privacy	Communication overhead
Zero Trust Architecture	Slight overhead	Scalable	Strong security	Policy complexity
Blockchain identity	High latency	Low–Medium	Strong integrity	Not real-time suitable

5.2 Quality of Experience and Human Perception

While the metrics of latency and throughput are not sufficient to guarantee user satisfaction, the QoE includes the user's subjective experience of smoothness, visual clarity, and comfort. Other factors affecting the QoE include the frame rate, resolution, field of view, audio-visual synchronization, and haptic feedback. Network jitters are more critical than increased average latency. Packet loss may lead to visual artefacts. Studies in perceptual psychology show that users may be willing to accept longer latencies for some types of interaction (e.g., asynchronous collaboration) but demand ultra-low latency for others (e.g., controlling a robot). Adaptive streaming techniques are used to manage the streaming of the video according to the network conditions to provide the best QoE. Using the human perception of the video would provide more efficient system performance, e.g., sacrificing the video fidelity instead of allowing the motion-to-photon latency to exceed the threshold (Laghari et al., 2024).

Immersive systems require not only strong security but also low-latency and scalable performance in a heterogeneous network environment. Fifth-generation mobile networks are already offering low-latency connectivity, although their capacity and reliability are restricted by the accessible spectrum and network topology. In addition, sixth-generation network visions are proposed to address these limitations through the integration of terahertz communications, satellite and aerial networks, and multi-layer network coverages combining terrestrial cells with high-altitude platforms and low-earth-orbit satellites. These networks are expected to provide devices with integrated sensing and communication capabilities, which enable devices to localize themselves and sense their environment concurrently with communicating with other devices. In addition, in immersive systems, it is expected that devices will be able to sense their environment, such as user location and gesture, in order to allocate network resources appropriately. In addition, low-latency and high-uplink-capacity sixth-generation networks are expected to support complex interactions such as multi-user holographic meetings and tactile internet applications, in which users are expected to manipulate remote objects in real time.

For the realization of these visions, there is research into Integrated Communication and Computing (ICC) frameworks that manage both bandwidth and computing resources in radio access networks. Compared to the multi-access edge computing solutions enabled in fifth-generation networks, ICC integrates computing components into base stations and manages them using machine learning techniques to jointly manage both spectrum and computing resources. Xu et al. (2025) demonstrate the potential benefits of ICC solutions, which include increases in service capacity of up to 98% compared to disjoint solutions, together with potential reductions in latency of up to 60% for transformer-based AI applications. As future networks are developed in the context of the 6G vision, the interplay between the potential of advanced radio solutions, network slicing, and edge computing solutions will be critical in determining the potential quality of experience enabled in immersive systems.

At the software level, load balancing and adaptive scheduling again remain key factors in enabling scalability. Hybrid models of render engines are currently used, which enable the offloading of heavy graphics processing to edge servers, with latency-sensitive tracking and prediction remaining on the user's device. Adaptive streaming protocols are used to dynamically adjust the resolution of the video, as well as the frame rate, in accordance with the available network conditions, thus minimizing stalls in the video playback. Additionally, cross-layer optimization, which takes into account information from the physical, network, and application layers, enables the network to anticipate spikes in the volume of data to be transmitted, thus enabling the pre-provisioning of resources. These optimizations, however, have to be carried out in such a manner that they do not compromise security, such as in the case of dynamic scaling, where decisions have to be validated to prevent resource exhaustion attacks, as well as in the case of slicing configurations, which have to be monitored for unauthorized flows.

6. FUTURE DIRECTIONS FOR IMMERSIVE SYSTEMS SECURITY

The edge–cloud continuum and immersive technologies are evolving rapidly. While current research provides a foundation for secure and scalable systems, numerous open questions remain. This section outlines additional future directions.

6G is seen as an AI-native network where AI is integrated into each layer, ranging from the physical layer's optimization and beamforming to the application layer's personalization. Sensing and multi-layer coverage will enable the network to be aware of its surroundings, adapting to environmental changes and user mobility. Therefore, policy interventions are required to ensure coordination among nations in the allocation of the spectrum and investment in research and training. Further, the open standardization bodies (3GPP, IEEE, etc.) must include AI explainability, fairness, and security considerations. Additionally, cross-domain collaboration between the telecom, cloud, AI, and immersive tech sectors is critical (Zawish et al., 2024).

Techniques such as federated analytics, homomorphic encryption, and secure multi-party computation are expected to enable the immersive platforms to gain insights without the need to access the underlying data. Research is also being undertaken to develop privacy-enhancing technologies for sequential data, e.g., RNN-friendly encryption schemes. Personalized privacy settings are expected to enable users to make compromises between accuracy and privacy. For instance, coarse-grained hand tracking may be sufficient in some cases. New policies, e.g., the European Union's AI Act, are expected to regulate the use of biometric data. Interdisciplinary collaboration is essential to develop frameworks that ensure both individual privacy and public safety are addressed.

Current trust models mainly concentrate on authentication and access control in one layer only. Future models should be able to combine information from different layers, including device attestation information, network behavior, application usage patterns, and user feedback, to generate comprehensive trust values. Graph-based trust propagation methods can be used to establish relationships between devices and users, and update trust values based on interactions between them. Machine learning methods can be used to identify abnormal patterns in trust evolution, such as sudden decreases in trust values of devices. Standardization of trust metrics and developing interoperable frameworks will also be helpful in wider acceptance of technology. Research is also needed to address the representation and exchange of trust information in a secure way and prevent manipulation of trust values.

Aside from security, there are also ethics to consider with immersive technologies. For instance, how can we avoid harassment and discrimination in an immersive environment, considering that people interact with each other through avatars? How can we promote fair representation of identities in an immersive environment, considering that there are differences in cultures, genders, and abilities? Some people may prefer to be anonymous in an immersive environment, whereas some may prefer to be identified in an immersive environment. How can we balance freedom of expression with protection from abuse in an immersive environment? How can we avoid exploitation in an immersive environment, considering that there can be exploitation in a virtual environment? How can we promote access to education in an immersive environment, considering that there can be inequality in the availability of infrastructure in an immersive environment? It is essential to include social scientists, psychologists, and ethicists in the development of immersive technologies.

The carbon footprint of immersive technologies can be attributed to the production of devices, the operational energy, and the data center operations. Cloud gaming and streaming of VR content can consume substantial amounts of energy, with the rendering of high-definition images and the use of AI for inference at high frames per second increasing the energy footprint. Some of the sustainable design strategies include energy-aware scheduling, energy-efficient hardware design, using renewable energy sources for edge devices, and sustainable design principles such as circular economies, which include modular design for upgradability rather than disposability. It is recommended that the researchers measure the environmental footprint of immersive technologies and propose metrics for sustainable design. It is recommended that government policies offer incentives for sustainable design, as well as corporate social responsibility for sustainable design.

Quantum computers have the potential to compromise existing public key cryptography (e.g., RSA, ECC), which is used for much of today's internet. Lattice-based, code-based, and hash-based cryptographic schemes are being standardized by NIST. The immersive platforms need to adopt post-quantum cryptographic schemes. Hybrid cryptographic schemes have also been proposed that could be used in conjunction with classical schemes. Research is also needed on optimizing post-quantum cryptographic schemes for resource-constrained edge devices. The impact of post-quantum cryptographic schemes on latency is also an open issue.

This means that, as AI assistants in immersive environments become more powerful, users will interact with them to get things done, solve problems, and access content. For effective interaction, there is a need for transparency (where the AI explains what it is doing to the user), controllability (where the user can control the AI, including turning it off if needed), and trust. There is also a need for digital literacy, which should include educating users on security concerns, privacy, and how to use immersive environments safely. Human-in-the-loop approaches can be used to take advantage of the speed of AI systems, such as in moderation or in developing security models.

Standards enable interoperability, safety, and reliability. Immersive technologies overlap with telecommunications, computing, gaming, healthcare, and transportation.

Integrating into these areas is challenging but vital. A framework for regulation must cover platform liability, intellectual property rights, interoperability, accessibility, environmental concerns, and international data flows. Creating certification schemes for immersive technologies, such as those used in cybersecurity for IoT devices, can give consumers confidence in products meeting certain security and privacy criteria.

However, there are concerns regarding space, dissipation of heat, and environmental issues. The solutions to these issues include utilizing the waste heat generated by edge servers for heating buildings, embedding edge servers in street furniture, and using renewable resources (solar panels fixed on lampposts). The edge servers may also be located near renewable sources like wind farms or hydroelectric stations. The cost-benefit trade-off for edge server deployments will be modeled to ensure sustainability.

Looking into the future, immersive technology, edge computing, and AI will be influenced by technological, regulatory, and social factors. Energy-efficient computing is becoming increasingly important. For achieving immersive experiences without contributing to climate change, researchers are developing analog computing chips that can perform computations with only one-tenth the power consumption of digital computing chips. This technology will increase the life of headset batteries, reduce cooling requirements for micro-data centers, and reduce carbon footprint for immersive technology. Moreover, software architects are also developing energy-efficient scheduling algorithms that take into account not only performance and latency but also energy consumption for task allocation between edge computing and cloud computing.

Another feature that is likely to be part of immersive technologies is post-quantum security. Quantum computers have been known to have the potential to crack certain types of cryptographic algorithms, including asymmetric key algorithms that include RSA and elliptical curve cryptography. If these cryptographic algorithms are cracked, malicious actors could manipulate software updates, impersonate devices, or even decrypt data. However, in order to avoid all these potential threats, researchers have been working on creating quantum-resistant cryptographic algorithms. According to OTAVA, using post-quantum cryptography is crucial in protecting sensitive data. Therefore, in order to ensure business continuity, it is crucial that organizations make the transition to new cryptographic algorithms. However, in order to do that, there is a need to plan appropriately, including hybrid approaches that allow both classical and quantum-resistant cryptographic algorithms. For edge devices, lattice-based or hash-based signatures will be crucial.

Ethical and social factors will be equally relevant. For instance, the process of behavioral identity detection in the context of VR enables the recognition of people between sessions with more than 80% accuracy, even if they attempt to disguise their actions. This has implications for surveillance and manipulation. It is essential that legislators and standardization bodies develop guidelines around the collection, storage, and sharing of biometric data, while engineers need to ensure the integration of privacy-preserving analytics. Another aspect is the need to ensure equal access to immersive technology, which would involve addressing the digital divide and avoiding the disproportionate burdening of security measures on the less privileged. Finally, there is the need to ensure collaboration between technologists, ethicists, sociologists, and legislators to develop regulations that strike the right balance between safety and human rights.

Another area is the creation of unified trust management models that include devices, network slices, and cloud services. With billions of devices interacting independently, static trust management models are no longer manageable. Dynamic trust scoring models, as envisioned in the zero-trust architecture of 6G, assess the behavior and reputation of devices to allocate access rights. These models also include AI-driven anomaly detection and blockchain-driven identity management, which can dynamically allocate access rights in real time and provide traceable audit trails. However, to deploy these models, future research should address challenges related to scalability, privacy, and interoperability in implementing these models in real-world scenarios. Future research should also include the creation of unified protocols for trust negotiation, efficient protocols for edge devices, and data sharing protocols that preserve privacy (IJCSPUB, 2025).

7. CONCLUSION

While providing unprecedented opportunities in the realms of communication, creativity, and productivity, their realization is contingent upon the establishment of a secure, scalable, and low-latency continuum of computing. This chapter has reviewed the architectural principles underlying the edge-cloud continuum, where the intelligent distribution of workload is achieved through the deployment of microservices, virtualization, containerization, offloading techniques, NFV, SDN, and edge AI. Security challenges were identified at the device, network, virtualization, and application levels, which include biometric privacy, digital twin risks, side-channel attacks, DDoS attacks, social engineering, and regulatory complexities. Zero trust architecture, blockchain-based identity management, federated and split learning, micro-layer intrusion detection, digital twin security, socio-behavioral safety, SdP, privacy-preserving computation, and adaptive defence are the emerging defence techniques against the aforementioned attacks. Latency and scalability considerations were reviewed, which include networking (sub-6 GHz, mmWave, THz, NTN), computing (split rendering, rendering, model optimization), balancing techniques, and quality of experience. Proposals were put forward for future research directions, which are AI-Native Networks, privacy-preserving analytics, cross-layer trust management, ethical and societal considerations, sustainability, post-quantum security, human-AI collaboration, standardization, and sustainable edge infrastructures. Real-life examples highlight the need to address the above research directions, which include the ability of motion data to uniquely identify users, the ability of ZTF-6G to provide significant gains in latency and throughput, the ability of edge AI bridges to reduce intrusion detection latency to 50 ms, and the ability of ICC frameworks to increase service capacity by 98%. Advances in the above research directions would ensure that immersive systems empower users, are privacy-preserving, and are safe at scale globally.

REFERENCES

Alcaraz, C., & Lopez, J. (2022). Digital twin: A comprehensive survey of security threats. *IEEE Communications Surveys and Tutorials, 24*(3), 1475–1503. DOI: 10.1109/COMST.2022.3171465

Almomani, O., Arabiat, A., Al Tayeb, M., Almaiah, M. A., Obeidat, M., Aldhyani, T. H., & Rowad, M. (2025). A robust model for android malware detection via ML and DL classifiers. *Mesopotamian Journal of Big Data, 2025*, 261–277. DOI: 10.58496/MJBD/2025/017

Almomani, O., Arabiat, A. M., Hind, A. A., & Alsariera, E. (2026). Hybridization of Deep Learning Models for Multiclass Attack Detection in Wireless Sensor Networks. *Journal of Communication, 21*(1). Advance online publication. DOI: 10.12720/jcm.21.1.20-34

Alnaim, A. K., & Alwakeel, A. M. (2025). Zero-trust mechanisms for securing distributed edge and fog computing in 6G networks. *Mathematics, 13*(8), 1239. DOI: 10.3390/math13081239

Antonakakis, M., April, T., Bailey, M., Bernhard, M., Bursztein, E., Cochran, J., Durumeric, Z., Halderman, J. A., Invernizzi, L., Kallitsis, M., Kumar, D., Lever, C., Ma, Z., Mason, J., Menscher, D., Seaman, C., Sullivan, N., Thomas, K., & Zhou, Y. (2017). Understanding the Mirai botnet. In *Proceedings of the 26th USENIX Security Symposium* (pp. 1093–1110). USENIX Association., https://www.usenix.org/system/files/conference/usenixsecurity17/sec17-antonakakis.pdf

Boston Consulting Group (BCG). (2026). 6G: The network for the future of AI and immersive connectivity. BCG and Qualcomm. https://web-assets.bcg.com/9c/73/4ac7634848a0b0bb31cf8dae40cb/6g-the-network-for-the-future-of-ai-and-immersive-connectivity-report-feb-2026-edit-03-web.pdf

Escaleira, P., Cunha, V. A., Barraca, J. P., Gomes, D., & Aguiar, R. L. (2025). A systematic review on security mechanisms for serverless computing. *Cluster Computing, 28*(465), 1–31. DOI: 10.1007/s10586-025-05371-4

Gherari, M., Maia, A., Dieye, M., Elbiaze, H., Ghamri-Doudane, Y., & Glitho, R. H. (2026). Optimizing Immersive Services with Parallel In-Network Rendering and Deep RL. *IEEE Transactions on Machine Learning in Communications and Networking, 4*, 491–513. Advance online publication. DOI: 10.1109/TMLCN.2026.3666742

IJCSPUB. (2025). Zero trust and 6G: Enhancing security in next generation networks. *International Journal of Current Science, 15*(2), 175–179. https://www.rjpn.org/ijcspub/papers/IJCSP25B1021.pdf

Industrial Cyber. (2025). Edge AI emerges as cyber force multiplier, enhancing operations and safeguarding critical installations from evolving threats. Industrial Cyber. https://industrialcyber.co/threat-landscape/edge-ai-emerges-as-cyber-force-multiplier-enhancing-operations-and-safeguarding-critical-installations-from-evolving-threats/

Laghari, A. A., Zhang, X., Shaikh, Z. A., Khan, A., Estrela, V. V., & Izadi, S. (2024). A review on quality of experience (QoE) in cloud computing. *Journal of Reliable Intelligent Environments*, *10*(2), 107–121. DOI: 10.1007/s40860-023-00210-y

Nair, V., Guo, W., Mattern, J., Wang, R., O'Brien, J. F., Rosenberg, L., & Song, D. "Unique identification of 50,000+ virtual reality users from head & hand motion data." In *32nd USENIX Security Symposium (USENIX Security 23)*, pp. 895-910. 2023. https://www.usenix.org/system/files/usenixsecurity23-nair-identification.pdf

OTAVA. (2025). 2025 trends in edge computing security. OTAVA. https://www.otava.com/blog/2025-trends-in-edge-computing-security/

Shambour, Q., Al-Zyoud, M., & Almomani, O. (2025). Quantum-inspired hybrid metaheuristic feature selection with SHAP for optimized and explainable spam detection. *Symmetry*, *17*(10), 1716. DOI: 10.3390/sym17101716

Sofia, R. C., Salomon, J., Ferlin-Reiter, S., Garcés-Erice, L., Urbanetz, P., & Touma, R.. (2024). A framework for cognitive, decentralised container orchestration. *IEEE Access : Practical Innovations, Open Solutions*, *12*, 79979–80002. DOI: 10.1109/ACCESS.2024.3406861

Subramanian, S., Prabu, P., Jain, K., & Krishnan, P. (2026). Edge AI bridge: A micro-layer intrusion detection architecture for smart-city IoT networks. *Preprints*, 202602.0606. DOI: 10.20944/preprints202602.0606.v1

Volico. (2024). Edge computing security: Challenges and best practices. Retrieved from https://www.volico.com/edge-computing-security-challenges-and-best-practices/

Yang, C.-S., Ku, Y.-J., Lou, Y.-Y., Tenny, N., & Hsu, A. C.-C. (2025). 6G EdgeAI: Performance evaluation and analysis. arXiv preprint arXiv:2504.16529. /arXiv.2504.16529DOI: 10.48550

Zawish, M., Dharejo, F. A., Khowaja, S. A., Raza, S., Davy, S., Dev, K., & Bellavista, P. (2024). AI and 6G into the metaverse: Fundamentals, challenges and future research trends. DOI: 10.1109/OJCOMS.2024.3349465

Chapter 3
Redefining Safety in Digital Realms:
Advanced AI and Cybersecurity Strategies for Trustworthy Immersive Systems

Barkha S. Dange
http://orcid.org/0009-0009-3804-2090
Ramdeobaba University, Nagpur, India

Sagar P. Tete
http://orcid.org/0009-0000-6787-7489
Ramdeobaba University, Nagpur, India

Paritosh P. Nagarnaik
Priyadarshini Bhagwati College of Engineering, Nagpur, India

Tintu Erlin Philip
http://orcid.org/0009-0008-7770-0466
Ramdeobaba University, Nagpur, India

ABSTRACT

The convergence of metaverse, AI, and cybersecurity demands a redefinition of safety in immersive systems to ensure trustworthiness amid escalating threats like avatar hijacking, data exfiltration, and adversarial manipulations. This chapter synthesizes advanced strategies—including AI-driven anomaly detection, federated learning for privacy-preserving models, blockchain-based decentralized identities, zero-trust architectures, and quantum-resistant cryptography—to fortify VR/AR/XR environments against real-time risks. Through architectural overviews, threat

DOI: 10.4018/979-8-3373-7882-4.ch003

taxonomies, case studies from 2025-2026 incidents, and future directions like edge AI hybrids, we propose a layered "safety-by-design" framework. Empirical insights reveal 60-90% risk reductions via proactive defenses, addressing scalability, ethical biases, and regulatory gaps. Ultimately, this work provides researchers, developers, and policymakers with actionable blueprints for persistent digital realms where immersion enhances human potential without compromising security or privacy.

INTRODUCTION

The rapid evolution of immersive systems—encompassing virtual reality (VR), augmented reality (AR), extended reality (XR), and broader metaverse ecosystems—has led to a significant convergence with advanced artificial intelligence (AI) and cybersecurity infrastructures. This convergence creates substantial opportunities for persistent, interactive, and context-aware digital experiences, while simultaneously introducing complex and evolving risk vectors (Awadallah et al., 2024; Farid et al., 2024). These risks include, but are not limited to, avatar impersonation and hijacking, unauthorized extraction of biometric and behavioural data, adversarial manipulation of sensory inputs, and poisoning of AI models that underpin system intelligence (Chow et al., 2022). In response to these emerging challenges, this chapter, titled *"Redefining Safety in Digital Realms,"* proposes a comprehensive and layered framework aimed at enhancing trustworthiness and resilience. The framework draws conceptually on recent developments in federated learning, decentralized identity management using blockchain, zero-trust security architectures, and ongoing standardization efforts in post-quantum cryptography (Kairouz & McMahan, 2021; Zyskind & Nathan, 2015; National Institute of Standards and Technology [NIST], 2024). Where forward-looking technologies are discussed, they are framed as emerging or anticipated directions rather than fully standardized deployments.

The chapter begins with an architectural overview of immersive system stacks, outlining key layers such as perception (e.g., sensors, cameras, inertial measurement units), edge and cloud-based processing pipelines, and distributed storage or persistence layers that may incorporate blockchain technologies (Awadallah et al., 2024). Enabling infrastructures, including next-generation communication networks and advances in generative AI, are discussed as facilitators of scalability and realism, while also contributing to increased system complexity. Building on this foundation, a structured threat taxonomy is introduced to systematically categorize risks (Farid et al., 2024). These include identity spoofing through synthetic media, environmental manipulation that may result in cognitive or physical harm, economic exploitation within tokenized or asset-driven virtual economies, and large-scale service disruption attacks such as distributed denial-of-service (DDoS) targeting immersive platforms (Chow et al., 2022). Rather than presenting these threats as isolated phenomena, the chapter emphasizes their interconnected nature within highly dynamic and persistent environments.

To address these challenges, the discussion advances toward AI-driven security strategies that move beyond reactive detection toward proactive and adaptive defence mechanisms. Techniques such as variational autoencoders are examined in the context of anomaly detection within multimodal interaction streams (e.g., gestures, gaze, and movement patterns), while sequential models, including recurrent neural networks, are considered for predictive threat modelling based on temporal behavioural data (Almomani et al., 2025). Reinforcement learning is explored as a potential approach for automated response and mitigation in complex environments, although its practical deployment remains an area of ongoing research. Additionally, adversarial training is highlighted as a method for improving model robustness against manipulated inputs (Achuthan et al., 2025). Importantly, performance-related statements are treated cautiously, and where metrics are referenced, they are framed as illustrative of reported findings in controlled or experimental settings rather than universally generalizable outcomes.

Privacy-preserving mechanisms are examined as a core component of trust in immersive ecosystems. Approaches such as federated learning are discussed in conjunction with differential privacy to enable distributed model training without centralized exposure of sensitive data (Kairouz & McMahan, 2021; Dwork & Roth, 2014), while decentralized identity frameworks (e.g., self-sovereign identities supported by cryptographic proofs) are considered for enhancing user control and authentication integrity (W3C, 2022; Buterin, 2022). Behavioural biometrics, including gaze dynamics and locomotion patterns, are presented as continuous authentication mechanisms; however, the discussion also acknowledges the ethical and regulatory implications of collecting and processing such sensitive data. Rather than asserting fixed parameter thresholds or guarantees, these techniques are described in terms of their design principles, trade-offs, and implementation challenges.

The chapter further considers the role of emerging technologies in addressing constraints related to scalability, computational overhead, and future cryptographic risks (NIST, 2024). Case-based illustrations are incorporated to provide contextual grounding; however, these examples are framed cautiously, with an emphasis on their illustrative value rather than as definitive empirical benchmarks. For instance, references to reported improvements in breach reduction or risk mitigation are presented as outcomes observed in specific pilot studies or industry reports, with the expectation that such claims require detailed methodological validation. Similarly, widely reported incidents involving virtual asset exploitation are used to highlight systemic vulnerabilities, while avoiding duplication and ensuring consistency in presentation.

Several cross-cutting challenges are identified, including performance overheads associated with advanced security mechanisms, potential biases embedded in AI-driven decision systems, and the evolving nature of regulatory and governance frameworks (Achuthan et al., 2025). In response, the chapter outlines future research directions such as tighter integration between AI and distributed ledger technologies, the exploration of hybrid reasoning models that combine statistical and symbolic approaches, and the development of internationally recognized standards for trustworthy AI systems (ISO/IEC, 2023; ENISA, 2023). References to emerging standards are positioned as part of an evolving governance landscape rather than finalized global mandates.

Overall, this chapter aims to provide a structured and critically grounded synthesis that supports the design of "safety-by-design" immersive environments. Rather than presenting prescriptive or absolute solutions, it offers a conceptual and technical foundation intended for developers, researchers, and policymakers seeking to balance innovation with user protection. By integrating architectural insights, threat analysis, and evolving defence strategies, the discussion contributes to a more nuanced understanding of how secure and human-centric immersive systems can be developed in an increasingly complex digital ecosystem.

Immersive systems have fundamentally transformed digital interaction paradigms by integrating virtual reality (VR), augmented reality (AR), and mixed reality (MR) into persistent and highly interactive environments often described collectively as the metaverse (Abdeljaber et al., 2025; Al-Adwan et al., 2025). These environments enable users to participate in shared virtual spaces that support economic exchange, social interaction, and collaborative work, often mediated through avatars and enhanced by AI-driven agents and digital representations of physical entities. This chapter critically examines how advanced AI methodologies and cybersecurity strategies can be combined to redefine safety frameworks, with particular attention to maintaining user trust and long-term system viability.

The integration of AI-driven personalization—such as adaptive content generation—and real-time security monitoring introduces new possibilities across domains including education, healthcare simulation, and digital commerce (Al-Adwan et al., 2025). While projections regarding the economic scale of these ecosystems are frequently cited in industry discourse, such estimates are treated here as indicative of potential growth trajectories rather than definitive forecasts. At the same time, the expanded functionality of immersive platforms introduces novel and complex risks. Persistent digital identities may increase exposure to long-term social engineering attacks, while sensory feedback systems could be exploited to manipulate user perception (Farid et al., 2024). Decentralized economic infrastructures, including tokenized assets and smart contracts, introduce additional layers of vulnerability that may be exploited through sophisticated financial or technical attacks (Zyskind & Nathan, 2015).

Traditional security models, particularly those based on static perimeters and periodic assessment, are increasingly insufficient in these environments. Immersive systems operate through continuous data exchange involving biometric signals, behavioural patterns, and high-value digital assets, thereby creating a fluid and expansive attack surface (Awadallah et al., 2024). This necessitates a shift toward adaptive, continuous, and context-aware security models. By synthesizing architectural, technological, and risk-oriented perspectives, this introduction establishes the foundation for a layered defence framework that emphasizes proactive resilience, responsible AI integration, and user-centric governance as essential components of future immersive ecosystems.

Defining Key Concepts

Immersive systems encompass a broad spectrum of technologies, including virtual reality (VR), augmented reality (AR), and extended reality (XR), each contributing distinct capabilities to the creation of interactive and persistent digital environments (Chow et al., 2022; Awadallah et al., 2024). VR systems typically generate fully synthetic environments using head-mounted displays and spatial audio to create a sense of presence, while AR overlays digital information onto the physical world to enhance contextual awareness. XR serves as an umbrella construct that integrates these modalities, enabling fluid transitions between physical and virtual contexts. Collectively, these systems underpin the evolution of large-scale, persistent environments often described as the metaverse, where users engage in social interaction, economic exchange, and collaborative activities through digital representations such as avatars (Abdeljaber et al., 2025; Al-Adwan et al., 2025).

The metaverse extends beyond isolated immersive experiences by incorporating persistent infrastructures, often supported by distributed technologies such as blockchain, to enable continuity of identity, ownership, and interaction (Zyskind & Nathan, 2015). Platforms such as Decentral and The Sandbox illustrate this model, where users participate in virtual economies involving digital assets, events, and user-generated content. While projections regarding the economic scale of such ecosystems are frequently cited in industry discourse, these estimates should be interpreted as indicative rather than definitive, reflecting evolving market dynamics and adoption uncertainties (Balhareth et al., 2024). Importantly, interoperability and decentralization remain aspirational goals, with many implementations still operating within partially centralized frameworks.

Artificial intelligence (AI) plays a foundational role in enabling immersive functionality. Techniques such as procedural content generation allow for the dynamic creation of environments and objects, while machine learning models support non-player character (NPC) behaviour, adaptive interfaces, and personalized user experiences (Awadallah et al., 2024). Generative models, including diffusion-based approaches, have been explored for real-time content synthesis, although their deployment in production-scale immersive systems remains an area of active research (Achuthan et al., 2025). At the same time, the integration of AI introduces new security and privacy considerations, particularly as systems increasingly rely on continuous streams of multimodal data, including visual, spatial, and behavioural inputs (Farid et al., 2024). Rather than emphasizing specific performance thresholds, this chapter focuses on the architectural and functional implications of these technologies within immersive ecosystems.

Trustworthiness within immersive systems can be conceptualized through three interrelated dimensions: robustness, explainability, and ethical integrity (Achuthan et al., 2025). Robustness refers to the system's capacity to withstand adversarial manipulation, including attacks targeting sensor inputs, machine learning models, or communication channels. Explainability addresses the need for transparency in AI-driven decision-making processes, particularly in security-critical contexts where users and administrators must understand the rationale behind system actions. Techniques such as feature attribution and model interpretability frameworks are increasingly explored to support this goal (Shambour et al., 2025). Ethical integrity encompasses privacy preservation, fairness, and responsible data usage, especially given the sensitive nature of biometric and behavioural information processed within immersive environments. Mechanisms such as differential privacy and decentralized identity management are often proposed as potential solutions (Dwork & Roth, 2014; W3C, 2022), though their practical implementation involves trade-offs related to performance and usability.

Without adequate consideration of these dimensions, immersive systems may give rise to significant risks. These include psychological impacts resulting from manipulated or misleading virtual experiences, financial losses associated with insecure digital asset ecosystems, and broader societal concerns such as harassment or identity misuse within anonymized environments (Farid et al., 2024). Accordingly, the integration of AI and cybersecurity must be approached as a unified design challenge, emphasizing user protection alongside technological innovation.

Historical Context and Evolution

The development of immersive technologies can be traced back to early virtual reality experiments in the late twentieth century, where systems focused primarily on achieving perceptual immersion through stereoscopic displays and basic motion tracking (Chow et al., 2022). Early platforms, including arcade-based VR systems and research prototypes developed by pioneers such as Jaron Lanier, emphasized the concept of "presence" as a core design objective. However, these early implementations operated largely as standalone systems, with limited consideration of security, privacy, or large-scale networked interaction.

Contemporary immersive platforms inherit both the capabilities and limitations of earlier web-based ecosystems. In particular, many current implementations reflect architectural patterns associated with centralized data control, as seen in platforms such as Horizon Worlds, where user data and interaction logs are managed within proprietary infrastructures (Farid et al., 2024). At the same time, immersive environments introduce new categories of vulnerability that extend beyond traditional web applications. For example, continuous spatial tracking data may expose users to location inference risks, while advanced rendering techniques could potentially introduce side-channel vulnerabilities under certain conditions (Chow et al., 2022). Similarly, the integration of haptic feedback and other sensory interfaces raises questions about the integrity and safety of user experiences.

Recent advances in AI, particularly in multimodal learning, have further accelerated the development of immersive systems. Modern models are increasingly capable of processing and integrating diverse data types, including visual, auditory, and contextual inputs, thereby enabling more natural and responsive interactions (Awadallah et al., 2024). While references to specific model generations are often used in industry narratives, this chapter adopts a generalized perspective, focusing on the broader class of multimodal AI systems rather than specific proprietary implementations. This approach ensures conceptual clarity and avoids reliance on unverifiable or rapidly evolving benchmarks.

The expansion of immersive platforms has also been accompanied by a growing awareness of security and social risks. Reports of synthetic media misuse, including avatar impersonation and identity spoofing, highlight the potential for adversarial exploitation in these environments (Farid et al., 2024). While quantitative estimates of such incidents vary across sources, the trend underscores the need for robust identity verification and content authentication mechanisms. Rather than relying on isolated statistics, this chapter emphasizes structural vulnerabilities and systemic risk patterns that can inform more resilient design strategies.

To address these challenges, the chapter adopts a structured approach that progresses from foundational analysis to applied frameworks:

- Cataloguing immersive architectures and associated risks: The discussion examines the layered structure of immersive systems, from sensor-based perception components to distributed processing and persistence mechanisms, identifying potential vulnerabilities at each stage (Awadallah et al., 2024). Examples include session-level identity compromise, data leakage through unintended channels, and scalability-related disruptions affecting system availability.

- Exploring AI-driven defence mechanisms: The chapter investigates adaptive security techniques, including anomaly detection and distributed learning approaches, with an emphasis on their conceptual advantages and implementation challenges rather than fixed performance claims (Almomani et al., 2025). Particular attention is given to privacy-preserving methods that enable collaborative threat detection without centralized data exposure (Kairouz & McMahan, 2021).
- Proposing integrative security frameworks: Hybrid approaches combining decentralized identity systems, continuous authentication mechanisms, and zero-trust principles are examined as potential pathways toward more resilient architectures (Zyskind & Nathan, 2015; W3C, 2022). These frameworks are discussed in terms of design principles and trade-offs, acknowledging that many remain under active development.
- Assessing case-based insights and future directions: Illustrative examples are used to highlight both vulnerabilities and mitigation strategies, while emerging areas such as post-quantum cryptography are considered in the context of long-term system security (National Institute of Standards and Technology [NIST], 2024). These discussions are framed cautiously, distinguishing between established practices and forward-looking research trajectories.

Through this progression, the chapter aims to translate conceptual risks into actionable design considerations, providing a foundation for the development of secure and trustworthy

IMMERSIVE SYSTEMS OVERVIEW

Modern immersive systems rely on a complex integration of hardware, software, and networked infrastructures that collectively support persistent and interactive digital environments (Awadallah et al., 2024; Farid et al., 2024). These systems are characterized by continuous operation, cross-device interoperability, and real-time synchronization, enabling users to maintain consistent identities and experiences across sessions. Technologies such as spatial anchoring facilitate shared reference points within virtual or augmented environments, while advances in haptic feedback contribute to more embodied and tactile interactions (Chow et al., 2022).

From an architectural perspective, immersive systems can be understood as comprising multiple interdependent layers, each with distinct functional roles and associated security considerations:

- Perception Layer: This layer includes sensors and input devices responsible for capturing user and environmental data, such as depth information, motion tracking, and physiological signals (Chow et al., 2022). While these technologies enable high levels of interactivity, they also introduce risks related to data integrity and spoofing, particularly if input streams are not adequately validated (Farid et al., 2024).
- Processing Layer: Data captured at the perception layer is processed through a combination of edge and cloud-based systems, often leveraging AI models for tasks such as rendering, object recognition, and behavioural analysis (Awadallah et al., 2024). The distributed nature of this layer introduces potential vulnerabilities related to data transmission, model updates, and system synchronization (Almomani et al., 2025).
- Interaction Layer: User engagement is facilitated through multimodal interfaces, including voice, gesture, and, in emerging cases, neural input mechanisms. This layer is particularly sensitive to manipulation, as adversarial inputs could disrupt system behaviour or compromise user intent (Achuthan et al., 2025).
- Persistence Layer: Long-term data storage and asset management are handled within this layer, which may incorporate distributed ledger technologies to support ownership and interoperability (Zyskind & Nathan, 2015). While such approaches offer benefits in terms of transparency and decentralization, they also introduce challenges related to scalability, governance, and consensus security.

At scale, immersive platforms often employ distributed architectures, including sharding and content delivery networks, to support large user populations (Awadallah et al., 2024). However, centralized components such as authentication services may still represent critical points of vulnerability (Farid et al., 2024). AI technologies further enhance these systems by enabling dynamic content generation and context-aware interactions, but also expand the potential attack surface, particularly when models interact with unverified user-generated content (Achuthan et al., 2025).

Overall, the layered architecture of immersive systems underscores the necessity of integrating security considerations at every level. Rather than treating cybersecurity as an external addition, it must be embedded within the design and operation of each component to prevent cascading failures that could compromise both technical infrastructure and user trust (Farid et al., 2024).

AI Pipelines

Artificial intelligence pipelines play a central role in enabling adaptive, responsive, and scalable immersive experiences (Awadallah et al., 2024; Achuthan et al., 2025). Reinforcement learning techniques are increasingly explored to model user behaviour and support dynamic interaction within virtual environments, allowing systems to adapt to changing contexts such as crowd density or user intent. Similarly, generative models are being investigated for their ability to produce virtual assets, environments, and interactions on demand, thereby reducing reliance on manual content creation and enabling more personalized experiences (Achuthan et al., 2025).

Despite these advantages, AI pipelines introduce distinct vulnerabilities. For instance, generative systems may be susceptible to adversarial inputs that manipulate output in unintended ways, while learning-based models trained on user-generated data may inherit biases or become targets of data poisoning attacks (Farid et al., 2024; Almomani et al., 2025). Rather than assuming fixed efficiency gains or performance improvements, it is more appropriate to view these technologies as evolving tools whose benefits must be balanced against risks related to robustness, validation, and governance. Ensuring secure model training, validation, and deployment processes is therefore essential for maintaining system integrity (Achuthan et al., 2025).

Digital Twins

Digital twins represent virtual replicas of physical objects, environments, or entities, continuously updated through real-time data streams (Awadallah et al., 2024). Within immersive systems, they enable applications such as industrial monitoring, simulation-based training, and interactive commerce, where users can visualize and interact with digital representations of real-world assets. In consumer contexts, digital twins may also extend to personalized avatars that reflect user behaviour or preferences (Abdeljaber et al., 2025).

While digital twins enhance realism and utility, they also raise concerns regarding data ownership, intellectual property, and replication risks. For example, high-fidelity models derived from publicly accessible data may be vulnerable to reverse engineering or unauthorized duplication, particularly in the absence of strong provenance mechanisms (Zyskind & Nathan, 2015). Additionally, the coupling of physical and virtual states introduces new dependencies, where inaccuracies or manipulations in one domain may propagate to the other. Addressing these challenges requires not only technical safeguards, such as secure data pipelines and cryptographic verification, but also governance frameworks that define ownership and usage rights.

A further challenge across these enabling technologies is the volume and velocity of data generated within immersive environments. Multimodal inputs—including visual streams, spatial mapping data, and interaction telemetry—can create substantial processing demands, necessitating the use of edge computing and on-device intelligence to filter, compress, and analyze data prior to transmission (Awadallah et al., 2024). Techniques such as lightweight machine learning models are increasingly explored for this purpose, enabling preliminary anomaly detection and reducing exposure during data transfer (Almomani et al., 2025). Rather than focusing on absolute data volume figures, the emphasis here is on the architectural implication: immersive systems operate under conditions of continuous, high-frequency data exchange that require efficient and secure handling.

Standardization efforts remain an important, yet still evolving, component of this ecosystem. Frameworks such as OpenXR aim to provide interoperability across hardware and software platforms, facilitating consistent development practices. However, security and privacy considerations are not always comprehensively addressed within such standards, often leaving implementation-specific decisions to platform providers (ENISA, 2023). This fragmentation can lead to inconsistencies in authentication, encryption, and data protection mechanisms, highlighting the need for more integrated and security-focused standardization initiatives.

Cybersecurity Threats

Immersive environments introduce a distinct cybersecurity landscape shaped by continuous interaction, multisensory engagement, and persistent digital identities (Farid et al., 2024; Chow et al., 2022). Unlike traditional digital systems, immersive platforms integrate visual, auditory, spatial, and sometimes tactile feedback, thereby increasing both the complexity of user interaction and the potential impact of malicious activity. At the same time, these environments often support long-term user engagement and economic activity, further elevating the consequences of security breaches (Awadallah et al., 2024).

A defining characteristic of immersive threats is their ability to combine technical exploitation with psychological influence. For example, realistic avatar representations and spatial interaction models may increase user susceptibility to deception, particularly in scenarios involving impersonation or social engineering (Farid et al., 2024). Similarly, the integration of spatial and behavioural data creates opportunities for more targeted and context-aware attacks. Rather than emphasizing speculative or extreme scenarios, it is important to recognize that these risks emerge from the convergence of technological capability and human factors.

Threats within immersive systems can propagate across multiple architectural layers, creating interdependent failure modes:

- Perception-Level Manipulation: Attacks targeting sensor inputs or environmental data may distort system perception, potentially affecting user navigation or interaction (Chow et al., 2022). Such manipulation could arise from interference, corrupted input streams, or adversarial modifications to the environment.
- Identity Exploitation: The use of synthetic media and behavioural modeling techniques may enable impersonation or unauthorized access, particularly if identity verification mechanisms are insufficient or static (Farid et al., 2024). Persistent avatars further increase the potential impact of such compromises.
- Economic Exploits: Virtual economies built on digital assets and smart contracts introduce financial risk, particularly in the presence of software vulnerabilities or flawed governance mechanisms (Zyskind & Nathan, 2015). These risks are analogous to those observed in broader decentralized finance ecosystems but may be amplified by the immersive context.
- Psychological and Social Manipulation: Immersive interaction can intensify the effects of harassment, coercion, or misinformation, as users experience these interactions in a more embodied and immediate manner (Achuthan et al., 2025). This highlights the need for safeguards that address both technical and social dimensions of security.

These dynamics illustrate that immersive security challenges are not confined to isolated technical flaws but emerge from the interaction between system design, user behaviour, and evolving threat capabilities (Farid et al., 2024). As adoption increases, the scale and diversity of potential attacks are also likely to expand, reinforcing the importance of proactive and adaptive defence strategies.

Primary Threat Categories

To provide a structured understanding, key threat categories within immersive systems can be summarized as follows (Farid et al., 2024; Chow et al., 2022):

- Identity-Based Attacks: These include impersonation, credential compromise, and unauthorized avatar control. Such attacks may exploit weaknesses in authentication mechanisms or leverage synthetic media to mimic legitimate users (Farid et al., 2024).
- Data Exfiltration: Sensitive information, including voice data, behavioural patterns, or environmental context, may be inferred or extracted through direct or indirect channels. This highlights the importance of securing both explicit data transmission and potential side channels (Chow et al., 2022).

- Environmental Manipulation: Alterations to virtual or augmented environments may disrupt user perception or interaction, potentially affecting usability, safety, or trust in the system (Awadallah et al., 2024).
- Economic Exploits: Vulnerabilities in digital asset management systems, including smart contracts or transaction mechanisms, may result in financial loss or market disruption within virtual economies (Zyskind & Nathan, 2015).
- AI-Targeted Attacks: Machine learning components may be subject to adversarial manipulation, including input perturbation, prompt injection, or data poisoning, which can degrade system performance or alter behaviour (Achuthan et al., 2025; Almomani et al., 2025).

While some reports suggest a rise in security incidents within immersive and XR ecosystems, the variability in reporting methodologies and definitions makes it difficult to establish precise quantitative trends. Therefore, the emphasis should remain on identifying systemic vulnerabilities and strengthening resilience mechanisms rather than relying on isolated statistics (Farid et al., 2024).

Overall, this section highlights that enabling technologies and associated threats are deeply interconnected. The same innovations that drive immersion—advanced networking, AI integration, and real-time data processing—also introduce new vulnerabilities that must be addressed through integrated, multi-layered security approaches (Awadallah et al., 2024). By framing these challenges in a balanced and evidence-aware manner, the discussion supports the development of immersive systems that are both innovative and trustworthy.

ADVANCED AI STRATEGIES

Artificial intelligence (AI) is increasingly reshaping cybersecurity approaches within immersive systems by enabling a transition from static, rule-based defences toward adaptive, data-driven paradigms (Awadallah et al., 2024; Achuthan et al., 2025). In contrast to traditional security mechanisms that rely on predefined signatures or periodic updates, AI-based strategies leverage machine learning techniques to identify patterns, detect anomalies, and respond to threats in near real time. This shift is particularly significant in immersive environments, where interactions occur continuously across spatial, temporal, and social dimensions, generating complex streams of multimodal data that require dynamic analysis (Farid et al., 2024).

Within these contexts, AI systems are designed to process diverse data inputs, including sensor outputs, behavioural signals, network activity, and user interactions. Rather than emphasizing absolute data scale, it is more appropriate to recognize that immersive environments produce high-frequency, heterogeneous data streams that can support advanced pattern recognition (Awadallah et al., 2024). These capabilities enable AI systems to identify subtle deviations from expected behaviour, thereby enhancing the detection of sophisticated or previously unseen attack vectors. At the same time, the effectiveness of such systems depends heavily on data quality, model design, and continuous validation, highlighting the importance of cautious and context-aware deployment (Achuthan et al., 2025).

Core AI applications in immersive cybersecurity include behavioural analytics, generative threat modelling, and automated response orchestration. Behavioural analytics focuses on interpreting continuous interaction patterns—such as gestures, navigation, and communication—to establish baselines of normal activity (Almomani et al., 2025). Generative models may be used in controlled settings to simulate potential attack scenarios, thereby supporting proactive defence strategies and system testing (Achuthan et al., 2025). Autonomous or semi-autonomous agents can then coordinate responses based on detected anomalies, contributing to a more resilient and adaptive security posture. Rather than asserting instantaneous or universal performance improvements, these approaches are best understood as augmenting existing security mechanisms with adaptive capabilities.

AI-Driven Threat Detection

Anomaly Detection

Anomaly detection represents one of the most prominent applications of AI in immersive cybersecurity, particularly in environments characterized by continuous and high-dimensional data streams (Awadallah et al., 2024). Unsupervised and semi-supervised learning approaches are commonly explored, as they allow systems to model normal behaviour without requiring exhaustive labelled datasets. Variational autoencoders (VAEs), for example, are often applied to learn latent representations of behavioural or sensor data, enabling the identification of deviations through reconstruction error analysis (Almomani et al., 2025). In the context of immersive systems, such models may be used to monitor patterns in movement, interaction, or environmental input.

Complementary techniques, such as tree-based anomaly detection methods, can be applied to multidimensional datasets to isolate irregular patterns that may indicate manipulation or intrusion (Achuthan et al., 2025). Similarly, graph-based approaches, including graph neural networks (GNNs), provide a framework for modelling relationships between users, interactions, and spatial proximity. By representing immersive environments as dynamic graphs, these models can support the identification of coordinated or anomalous behaviour patterns that may not be evident through isolated analysis (Awadallah et al., 2024). Importantly, while experimental studies often report promising detection capabilities, performance metrics vary significantly depending on dataset quality, system configuration, and evaluation methodology, and should therefore be interpreted with caution.

Predictive Analytics

Predictive analytics extends detection capabilities by attempting to anticipate potential threats based on historical and contextual data (Achuthan et al., 2025). Sequential models, such as recurrent neural networks and attention-based architectures, are frequently explored for analysing temporal patterns in security-related data, including network activity and user interactions (Almomani et al., 2025). These models can identify trends or precursors associated with specific types of attacks, thereby supporting earlier intervention.

In immersive environments, predictive systems may also incorporate multimodal inputs, combining textual, auditory, and behavioural signals to assess risk in a more holistic manner (Awadallah et al., 2024). For example, communication patterns within virtual spaces could be analysed alongside contextual metadata to identify indicators of social engineering or coordinated malicious activity. However, such applications remain dependent on robust training data and careful calibration to avoid false positives or biased outcomes (Farid et al., 2024). Rather than relying on specific numerical performance claims, it is more appropriate to emphasize the conceptual value of predictive analytics in enhancing situational awareness and enabling proactive defence.

Together, anomaly detection and predictive analytics contribute to a layered detection framework that enhances the ability of immersive systems to identify both known and emerging threats. These approaches transform the extensive data generated within immersive environments from a potential liability into a resource for improving system resilience (Awadallah et al., 2024).

Automated Response and Resilience

Beyond detection, AI also supports automated and semi-automated response mechanisms that can mitigate threats with minimal delay (Awadallah et al., 2024; Achuthan et al., 2025). Intelligent agents may be designed to isolate compromised entities, restrict suspicious activity, or trigger recovery processes based on predefined policies and learned behaviours. For instance, access controls can be dynamically adjusted, or affected system components can be temporarily segmented to prevent further propagation of an attack (Farid et al., 2024). In distributed environments, such responses may be coordinated across multiple layers, including network, application, and identity management systems (Almomani et al., 2025).

Reinforcement learning (RL) has been explored as a framework for optimizing response strategies in complex and evolving threat landscapes (Achuthan et al., 2025). By training agents in simulated environments, it is possible to evaluate different defence policies under varying attack scenarios. While this approach shows promise, its practical deployment requires careful consideration of safety constraints, interpretability, and robustness to adversarial manipulation.

Adversarial training represents another important strategy for enhancing system resilience. By exposing models to intentionally perturbed inputs during training, it is possible to improve their ability to withstand malicious manipulation in real-world conditions (Awadallah et al., 2024). Similarly, distributed learning approaches, such as federated learning, enable collaborative model improvement without requiring centralized data aggregation, thereby supporting privacy preservation while enhancing collective defence capabilities (Kairouz & McMahan, 2021).

Rather than presenting these techniques as fully mature or universally effective solutions, it is important to recognize that they represent evolving approaches within a broader security ecosystem. Their effectiveness depends on integration with complementary mechanisms, including governance frameworks, user awareness, and system-level safeguards (ENISA, 2023).

Overall, advanced AI strategies provide a critical foundation for enhancing cybersecurity in immersive systems by enabling adaptive detection, predictive insight, and coordinated response (Achuthan et al., 2025). However, their deployment must be guided by rigorous evaluation, transparency, and ethical considerations to ensure that the benefits of AI-driven security are realized without introducing new vulnerabilities or unintended consequences (Farid et al., 2024).

IMPLEMENTATION FRAMEWORKS

The deployment of advanced AI-driven cybersecurity strategies within immersive systems requires robust and scalable implementation frameworks capable of operating across distributed, heterogeneous environments (Almomani et al., 2025; Farid et al., 2024). Contemporary approaches increasingly rely on microservices-based architectures, where modular components—such as anomaly detection models, behavioural analytics engines, and response agents—are containerized and orchestrated across edge and cloud infrastructures. Technologies such as container orchestration platforms enable horizontal scaling and fault-tolerant deployment, ensuring that security services can adapt dynamically to fluctuating workloads and user densities (Achuthan et al., 2025).

Within immersive ecosystems, these frameworks are often extended to edge computing environments, where processing is distributed closer to end-user devices. This architectural shift reduces latency and enhances responsiveness, which is critical in real-time XR interactions (Farid et al., 2024). At the same time, it introduces additional considerations related to synchronization, trust management, and secure communication between nodes. To address data confidentiality concerns, advanced cryptographic techniques such as homomorphic encryption have been explored for enabling computation on encrypted data (Kairouz & McMahan, 2021). While still computationally intensive in many practical scenarios, such approaches illustrate a broader trend toward privacy-preserving analytics in distributed systems.

Privacy-enhancing technologies also play a central role in implementation frameworks. Differential privacy mechanisms, for instance, are often integrated into machine learning pipelines to limit the risk of re-identification when aggregating user data (Kairouz & McMahan, 2021). Rather than relying on fixed parameter thresholds, these mechanisms are typically calibrated based on system requirements and acceptable privacy-utility trade-offs. Integration with monitoring and analytics platforms further supports operational visibility, enabling security teams to interpret model outputs through explainability techniques such as feature attribution (Awadallah et al., 2024). These capabilities are particularly important in immersive systems, where transparency and accountability are necessary to maintain user trust.

Despite these advancements, implementation frameworks must also account for the inherent vulnerabilities of AI systems themselves. Risks such as model backdoors, data poisoning, and adversarial manipulation necessitate continuous validation and integrity checking (Awadallah et al., 2024). Techniques including model watermarking, secure aggregation protocols, and anomaly detection within training pipelines are increasingly proposed as safeguards against such threats. In practice, organizations deploying immersive training or simulation environments have begun to incorporate continuous auditing mechanisms, where system behaviour is evaluated under simulated adversarial conditions (ENISA, 2023). While reported outcomes from such deployments suggest improvements in detection and response capabilities, these results are often context-specific and should be interpreted within the scope of controlled environments.

Scaling and Future Enhancements

As immersive systems evolve toward large-scale adoption, scalability becomes a central design challenge (Almomani et al., 2025). Supporting extensive user populations and continuous interaction requires not only computational efficiency but also interdisciplinary integration. In particular, the intersection of computer science, human-computer interaction, and behavioural science offers valuable insights into how users perceive and respond to immersive environments. Understanding cognitive and spatial behaviours can inform the design of more effective security mechanisms, especially in scenarios involving social engineering or perceptual manipulation (Achuthan et al., 2025).

Future developments are likely to emphasize multimodal data fusion, where inputs from visual, auditory, and behavioural channels are integrated to provide a more comprehensive view of system activity (Farid et al., 2024). Advanced machine learning architectures, including transformer-based models, are being explored for this purpose, although their deployment in real-time immersive settings remains an area of ongoing research. Rather than focusing on specific performance metrics, it is more appropriate to view these approaches as part of a broader effort to improve situational awareness and contextual understanding within complex environments.

The integration of AI capabilities directly into hardware platforms, such as on-device processing units within XR headsets, represents another emerging direction (Awadallah et al., 2024). This approach supports continuous monitoring and localized decision-making, reducing reliance on centralized infrastructure. However, it also raises questions related to energy efficiency, model optimization, and device-level security. Overall, scaling immersive cybersecurity solutions will require a balance between performance, privacy, and adaptability, supported by advances in both software and hardware design (ENISA, 2023).

Privacy and Trust Mechanisms

Privacy and trust constitute foundational elements of secure immersive systems, particularly in environments characterized by continuous data generation and persistent user identities (Kairouz & McMahan, 2021; ENISA, 2023). Unlike traditional applications, immersive platforms often process sensitive information such as biometric signals, behavioural patterns, and contextual interaction data. As a result, centralized data management approaches may introduce significant risks related to data breaches, misuse, or unauthorized access.

To address these concerns, there is a growing emphasis on decentralized and cryptographically verifiable mechanisms that enable users to retain greater control over their digital identities and data (ENISA, 2023). Rather than relying on implicit trust in platform providers, these approaches aim to establish verifiable assurances through technical means, thereby fostering more transparent and accountable ecosystems. Privacy-preserving techniques, including zero-knowledge proofs, allow users to demonstrate specific attributes or credentials without disclosing underlying data, supporting selective disclosure in identity verification processes (Kairouz & McMahan, 2021).

This section focuses on three complementary paradigms that are particularly relevant to immersive environments: federated learning, decentralized identity systems, and zero-trust architectures. Together, these approaches provide a framework for balancing data utility with privacy protection, while addressing both technical and human-centric aspects of trust.

Federated Learning for Privacy-Preserving AI

Federated learning enables collaborative model training across distributed devices without requiring centralized data collection (Kairouz & McMahan, 2021). In immersive systems, this approach is particularly valuable, as it allows user devices—such as VR headsets or AR glasses—to contribute to model development using locally generated data while retaining control over sensitive information. Instead of transmitting raw data, devices share model updates, which are aggregated to improve global performance.

Enhancements to federated learning frameworks include the integration of privacy-preserving techniques such as differential privacy and secure multi-party computation (Kairouz & McMahan, 2021). These mechanisms aim to protect individual contributions during the aggregation process, although their implementation involves trade-offs related to computational overhead and model accuracy. Additionally, emerging approaches explore the use of distributed ledgers to validate contributions and enhance trust in collaborative training processes (ENISA, 2023).

Challenges associated with federated learning include data heterogeneity, communication overhead, and system scalability. Variations in user behaviour and device capabilities can affect model convergence, while coordinating large numbers of participants introduces logistical complexity. Ongoing research addresses these issues through adaptive algorithms, hierarchical aggregation strategies, and model compression techniques.

Decentralized Identities and Blockchain

Decentralized identity frameworks provide mechanisms for managing user identities without reliance on centralized authorities (ENISA, 2023). In immersive systems, these approaches support the concept of self-sovereign identity, where users control their credentials and determine how they are shared across platforms.

Technologies such as decentralized identifiers (DIDs) and verifiable credentials enable selective disclosure, enhancing privacy while maintaining trust.

Blockchain infrastructures are often proposed as a supporting layer for these systems, providing transparency and immutability for identity-related transactions (Farid et al., 2024). In immersive environments, this can facilitate cross-platform interoperability, allowing users to maintain consistent identities and reputations across multiple virtual spaces. However, challenges related to scalability, governance, and interoperability remain, particularly as different platforms adopt varying standards and protocols.

Zero-Trust Architecture in Immersive Contexts

Zero-trust architectures are based on the principle that no component within a system should be inherently trusted (Almomani et al., 2025). Instead, continuous verification is required for all interactions, regardless of their origin. In immersive systems, this approach is particularly relevant due to the dynamic and distributed nature of user interactions.

Implementation strategies may include continuous authentication based on behavioural patterns, dynamic access control policies, and segmentation of system components to limit the spread of potential breaches (Achuthan et al., 2025). While these mechanisms enhance security, they must be carefully designed to avoid disrupting user experience, particularly in highly interactive environments. Ethical considerations, including transparency and user consent, are also critical in ensuring that continuous monitoring does not compromise user autonomy (ENISA, 2023).

Emerging Technologies

Emerging technologies are expected to play a critical role in addressing the evolving security challenges of immersive systems (ENISA, 2023). Among these, post-quantum cryptography and edge-based AI processing are particularly significant, as they address both long-term cryptographic resilience and real-time operational requirements.

Quantum-Resistant Cryptography

Advances in quantum computing have raised concerns about the long-term security of classical cryptographic systems. In response, new cryptographic approaches are being developed to resist quantum-based attacks. Standardization efforts led by organizations such as the National Institute of Standards and Technology have identified candidate algorithms for secure communication in a post-quantum context (ENISA, 2023). These include lattice-based cryptographic schemes designed to provide resilience against emerging computational threats.

While integration into existing communication protocols is ongoing, these technologies are generally considered part of a transitional phase. Hybrid approaches that combine classical and post-quantum methods are often proposed to balance current performance requirements with future security needs (Farid et al., 2024). In immersive systems, such mechanisms may be applied to secure communication channels, identity verification processes, and digital asset transactions.

Edge AI and Distributed Security

Edge computing enables data processing to occur closer to the source, reducing latency and enhancing responsiveness (Achuthan et al., 2025). In immersive systems, this approach supports real-time analysis of sensor data and user interactions, enabling faster detection of anomalies or security events. Lightweight machine learning models are often deployed at the edge to perform preliminary analysis, with more complex processing handled by centralized systems.

Distributed security models leverage this architecture to enhance resilience, as data and processing are not confined to a single point of failure (Almomani et al., 2025). However, ensuring consistency and integrity across distributed nodes remains a key challenge, requiring robust synchronization and validation mechanisms.

Case Studies & Challenges

Case-based analysis provides valuable insights into the practical application of AI-driven cybersecurity strategies in immersive systems (ENISA, 2023). These examples illustrate both the potential benefits and limitations of current approaches, highlighting the importance of integrated and context-aware security design.

In enterprise training environments, immersive platforms incorporating AI-based monitoring and adaptive response mechanisms have demonstrated improvements in threat detection and user engagement (Achuthan et al., 2025). These systems often combine behavioural analytics with simulation-based testing, enabling continuous evaluation under controlled conditions. While reported outcomes suggest enhanced detection capabilities and reduced response times, such findings are typically derived from specific deployment contexts and may not generalize across all environments.

Conversely, widely reported incidents involving virtual asset exploitation highlight the risks associated with insufficient integration of security mechanisms (Farid et al., 2024). In particular, vulnerabilities in identity management, smart contracts, or system architecture can lead to significant financial and reputational impacts. These cases underscore the importance of proactive security design and continuous monitoring.

Mixed outcomes are also observed in large-scale social platforms, where partial implementation of advanced security measures has improved resilience but not fully eliminated vulnerabilities (ENISA, 2023). These examples demonstrate that while incremental improvements are valuable, comprehensive and integrated approaches are necessary to achieve robust protection.

Challenges and Future Directions

Immersive systems face a range of technical, ethical, and regulatory challenges that must be addressed to ensure long-term viability (ENISA, 2023). Technical challenges include scalability constraints, computational overhead, and the need for robust defence mechanisms against evolving adversarial techniques (Awadallah et al., 2024). Interoperability across platforms remains limited, complicating the implementation of unified security frameworks.

Ethical considerations are equally significant, particularly in relation to privacy, fairness, and user autonomy. The use of AI in monitoring and decision-making introduces risks of bias and lack of transparency, which must be mitigated through explainability and accountability mechanisms (Kairouz & McMahan, 2021). Regulatory frameworks are still evolving and often lag behind technological developments, creating uncertainty for both developers and users.

Future research directions emphasize the integration of AI and distributed technologies, the development of privacy-preserving learning frameworks, and the establishment of standardized protocols for immersive security (Achuthan et al., 2025). Interdisciplinary collaboration will be essential in addressing these challenges, ensuring that technological innovation is aligned with societal values and user expectations.

CONCLUSION

The convergence of AI and cybersecurity strategies provides a foundation for redefining safety in immersive systems (Achuthan et al., 2025; Farid et al., 2024). By integrating adaptive detection mechanisms, privacy-preserving architectures, and emerging cryptographic techniques, it is possible to enhance resilience and trust within complex digital environments (Kairouz & McMahan, 2021; ENISA, 2023). Rather than presenting definitive solutions, this chapter has outlined a conceptual and practical framework for addressing the multifaceted challenges associated with immersive technologies.

Key insights emphasize the importance of layered and proactive security approaches, where multiple mechanisms operate in coordination to address diverse threat vectors (Almomani et al., 2025). The integration of decentralized identity systems, federated learning, and zero-trust principles supports a shift toward user-centric and verifiable trust models (Kairouz & McMahan, 2021; ENISA, 2023). At the same time, emerging technologies such as post-quantum cryptography and edge-based AI processing offer pathways for future-proofing these systems (Farid et al., 2024).

Moving forward, stakeholders—including researchers, developers, and policymakers—must collaborate to establish standards, develop robust evaluation frameworks, and ensure responsible deployment (ENISA, 2023). The concept of "safety by design" should be embedded throughout the development lifecycle, enabling immersive systems to scale while maintaining user trust and system integrity (Awadallah et al., 2024). In this way, immersive technologies can realize their transformative potential without compromising security or ethical principles.

REFERENCES

Abdeljaber, O., Al-Adwan, A. S., Yaseen, H., Falahat, M., Abdullah, A., & Fauzi, M. A. (2025). Shopping in the Metaverse: Decoding Consumer Intentions. *The International Information & Library Review*, •••, 1–31.

Achuthan, K., Ramanathan, S., & Raman, R. (2025). Securing the metaverse: Machine learning–based perspectives on risk, trust, and governance. *International Journal of Information Management Data Insights*, *5*(2), 100356. DOI: 10.1016/j.jjimei.2025.100356

Al-Adwan, A. S., Al-Adwan, A., Li, N., Fauzi, M. A., Jafar, R. M. S., Habibi, A., & Falahat, M. (2025). Immersive Learning Meets Theory: Modeling Eduverse Adoption in Higher Education. Journal of Information Technology Education: Research, 24, 042.

Almomani, O., Arabiat, A., Al Tayeb, M., Almaiah, M. A., Obeidat, M., Aldhyani, T. H., & Rowad, M. (2025). A robust model for android malware detection via ML and DL classifiers. *Mesopotamian Journal of Big Data*, *2025*, 261–277. DOI: 10.58496/MJBD/2025/017

Awadallah, A., Eledlebi, K., Zemerly, M. J., Puthal, D., Damiani, E., Taha, K., Kim, T.-Y., Yoo, P. D., Raymond Choo, K.-K., Yim, M.-S., & Yeun, C. Y. (2024). Artificial intelligence-based cybersecurity for the metaverse: Research challenges and opportunities. *IEEE Communications Surveys and Tutorials*, *27*(2), 1008–1052. DOI: 10.1109/COMST.2024.3442475

Balhareth, H., Al-Adwan, A. S., Alsoud, A. R., Abd-Aljaber, O., Al-Rahmi, W. M., & Urbaníková, M. (2024). Journey into meta-commerce: Driving forces of consumer adoption. *Global Knowledge, Memory and Communication*. Advance online publication. DOI: 10.1108/GKMC-05-2024-0307

Buterin, V. (2022). Soulbound tokens: A vision for Web3 identity.

Chow, Y. W.. (2022). Visualization and cybersecurity in the metaverse: A survey. *Future Generation Computer Systems*. Advance online publication. DOI: 10.1016/j.future.2022.10.012 PMID: 36662109

Dwork, C., & Roth, A. (2014). The algorithmic foundations of differential privacy. *Foundations and Trends in Machine Learning*.

European Union Agency for Cybersecurity (ENISA). (2023). *Cybersecurity guidelines for emerging technologies.*

Farid, F.. (2024). Cyber security management in metaverse: A review and analysis. *Journal of Information Security and Applications.*

Kairouz, P., & McMahan, H. B. (2021). Advances and open problems in federated learning. *Foundations and Trends in Machine Learning, 14*(1-2), 1–210. DOI: 10.1561/2200000083

National Institute of Standards and Technology (NIST). (2024). *Post-quantum cryptography standardization (ML-KEM, ML-DSA).*

Shambour, Q., Al-Zyoud, M., & Almomani, O. (2025). Quantum-inspired hybrid metaheuristic feature selection with SHAP for optimized and explainable spam detection. *Symmetry, 17*(10), 1716. DOI: 10.3390/sym17101716

W3C. (2022). *Decentralized identifiers (DIDs) v1.0.*

Zyskind, G., & Nathan, O. (2015). Decentralizing privacy: Using blockchain to protect personal data. In *IEEE Security and Privacy Workshops.*

Chapter 4
Reinforcement Learning for Autonomous Threat Mitigation in AI-Driven Metaverse Environments

Mohammad Alauthman
http://orcid.org/0000-0003-0319-1968
University of Petra, Jordan

Ala Hamarsheh
http://orcid.org/0000-0002-4736-7331
Computer Science, Faculty of Information Technology, Arab American University, Jenin, Palestine

Amjad Aldweesh
http://orcid.org/0000-0001-9358-1323
Shaqra University, Saudi Arabia

Ahmad Al-Qerem
http://orcid.org/0000-0003-2187-6194
Computer Science Department, Faculty of Information Technology, Zarqa University, Zarqa, Jordan

Thair Al Fararjeh
http://orcid.org/0009-0001-8963-9761
Beyond & Universe LLC, USA

Omar Almomani
http://orcid.org/0000-0003-3160-6542
Al-Ahliyya Amman University, Jordan

ABSTRACT

Metaverse environments now blend embodied interaction, synthetic media, virtual asset trading, and platform governance in persistent multi-user worlds. But conventional cybersecurity? It's necessary yet insufficient--treating threats as isolated technical incidents ignores their social impact. This chapter proposes an ontology-guided reinforcement learning framework for autonomous threat mitigation. It models actors, assets, interactions, threats, governance constraints, and control options as a linked semantic system that shapes state construction, action boundaries, reward design, explainability, and cross-platform learning. We identify eight knowledge mechanisms that boost context awareness, ensure proportional responses, and

DOI: 10.4018/979-8-3373-7882-4.ch004

enable auditability. Privacy, fairness, scalability, accountability, and adversarial adaptation remain key challenges. Ultimately, trustworthy metaverse defense demands semantically grounded, governance-aware adaptive agents.

1. INTRODUCTION

Immersive multi-user virtual worlds extend distributed computing into persistent social, economic, and embodied environments. In these settings, users appear through avatars, interact through speech and gesture, exchange virtual assets, and increasingly rely on AI systems for content generation, assistance, and platform management. As a result, the security problem is not limited to infrastructure protection. It also includes identity integrity, economic trust, content safety, privacy, and the legitimacy of platform intervention (Chen et al., 2022; Di Pietro & Cresci, 2021; Wang et al., 2023).

This combination makes threat mitigation particularly challenging. A malicious campaign may involve cloned voices, synthetic faces, scripted avatar movement, coordinated reports, fraudulent asset transfers, or covert behavioral surveillance. The relevant signals are therefore multimodal, temporally extended, and socially meaningful. Conventional detection pipelines and rule-based moderation remain essential but insufficient on their own. While they can identify anomalies, they often fail to determine the contextual meaning, severity, or proportionate intervention required.

The choice of reinforcement learning in this context is due to the sequential nature of mitigation as a decision problem. The defender has to operate in the realm of uncertainty, balance between short term friction and long term security and adjust to the evolving tactics of the attackers. Nevertheless, the majority of RL-based cybersecurity models consider infrastructure-based states and abstractive actions like isolate host, block flow, or reconfigure service (Adawadkar and Kulkarni, 2022; Nguyen and Reddi, 2023; Uprety and Rawat, 2021). Security in the metaverse requires more: states which capture the meaning of actors, assets, interactions, and governance requirements, and actions which are mindful of proportionality, rights to appeal, and privacy constraints.

The scale of these environments also creates a coordination problem. Threats can move across spaces, services, sessions, and even platforms. Defense therefore benefits from distributed local agents and shared situational awareness. Yet unlike simple swarm-style coordination, effective metaverse defense requires a common semantic language about identity, ownership, consent, delegation, and acceptable intervention. Coordination is useful only if agents agree on what they are observing and why a response is justified.

Figure 1. Layered architecture of autonomous threat mitigation in AI-driven metaverse environments.

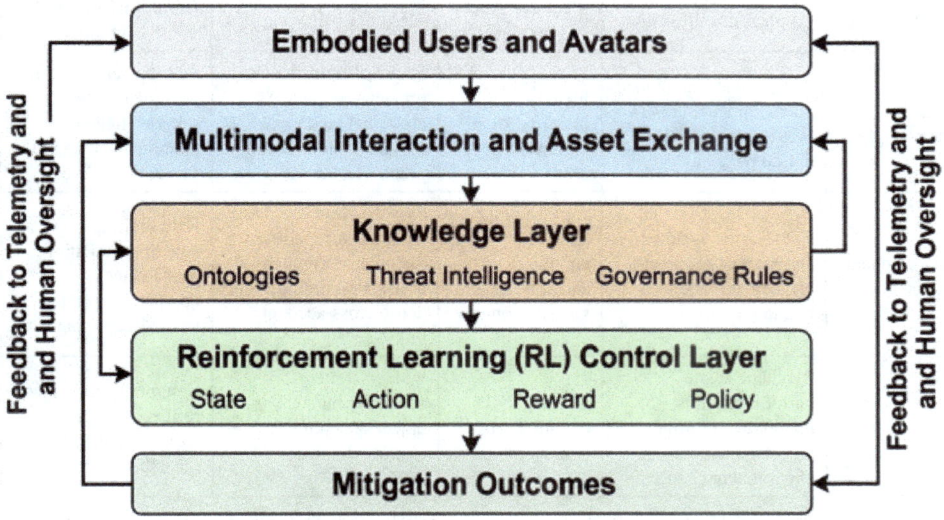

This chapter is a conceptual analysis rather than an experimental study. Its purpose is to show how autonomous threat mitigation in AI-driven metaverse environments can be reframed as a problem of semantic control: adaptive decision-making grounded in ontologies, knowledge graphs, and governance-aware constraints. Figure 1 summarizes the layered architecture used throughout the chapter, and Table 1 highlights why the metaverse threat surface differs from conventional intrusion response.

Table 1. Core threat classes in AI-driven metaverse environments and RL-relevant observables

Threat class	Typical manifestation	Primary assets at risk	RL-observable signals	Candidate mitigation actions
Identity deception	Deepfake avatar, cloned voice, impersonated moderator, copied digital persona	Identity integrity, trust, reputation	Face-voice mismatch, provenance gaps, abnormal credential use, anomalous social graph overlap	Step-up verification, provenance check, session challenge, temporary interaction freeze
Coordinated automation	Bot swarms, scripted harassment, report brigading, market manipulation	Service continuity, social order, virtual economy	Synchronized movement, repetitive dialogue, correlated transaction timing, dense cross-account links	Rate limiting, swarm partitioning, coordinated quarantine, graph-level alert propagation
Content abuse	Synthetic scams, harmful prompts, manipulated virtual objects, malicious environment changes	User safety, cognitive trust, content integrity	Sudden content similarity bursts, unsafe object spawning, multimodal toxicity markers	Content gating, object rollback, visibility reduction, supervised escalation
Asset fraud	Theft of virtual goods, wallet redirection, fake storefronts, unauthorized transfers	Ownership, economic value, transactional confidence	High-risk transfer chains, provenance discontinuity, price anomalies, unauthorized access patterns	Transfer hold, asset freeze, escrow activation, transaction verification
Privacy extraction	Covert gaze tracking, biometric inference, movement profiling, intimate space surveillance	Personal data, autonomy, dignity	Excessive sensor access, repeated proximity probes, cross-session linkage behavior	Sensor permission downgrade, data minimization, path obfuscation, access revocation
Infrastructure abuse	World instance overload, rendering abuse, bandwidth exhaustion, model abuse	Availability, latency, platform stability	Resource spikes, adversarial load patterns, repeated object generation, abnormal session churn	Load shedding, instance isolation, resource cap, adaptive routing

The remainder of the chapter proceeds as follows. Section 2 reviews the literature on metaverse security, RL for cyber defense, multi-agent coordination, ontologies, and explainable and safe RL. Section 3 presents the conceptual framework. Section 4 explains the knowledge mechanisms that connect semantics to autonomous mitigation and introduces an illustrative end-to-end scenario. Section 5 discusses the main implications and challenges. Section 6 outlines future research directions, and Section 7 concludes the chapter.

2. LITERATURE REVIEW

Research on metaverse security has grown rapidly, focusing on virtual reality safety, platform governance, cybersecurity, and artificial intelligence systems. Broad surveys of the metaverse defined it as an integration of immersive interfaces, social platforms, digital economies, AI services and networked infrastructure, all of which increase the attack surface (Chen et al., 2022; Huang et al., 2023; Wang et al., 2023). These studies are valuable for identifying the breadth of the problem but are usually more descriptive than operational. They delineate what can go wrong much better than how an autonomous defender should reason about what to do next.

A related body of work seeks to focus upon immersive safety, avatar privacy, and the risks created by embodied sensing. Users in virtual worlds create gaze traces, movement data, voice streams, proximity patterns and social graph signals that are much richer than the logs available in traditional systems. These data streams facilitate useful services but they also open the possibility of surveillance, biometric inference, harassment and exclusion (Hine et al., 2024; Giaretta, 2025; Eltanbouly et al., 2025; Laiz-Ibanez et al., 2025). This literature is especially important because it demonstrates that mitigation actions must be evaluated not only by technical success but also by their impact on autonomy, dignity, and due process.

Synthetic media makes the problem worse. Identity in metaverse spaces is often gathered through inferences from multimodal cues, including face, voice, style, and continuity of behavior. Deepfakes, voice cloning, and AI-generated personas could therefore be used not only to trick a classifier, but to manipulate trust relationships, moderation authority and economic behavior (Tolosana et al., 2020; Mustak et al., 2023). This is one of the reasons why binary detection is not satisfactory: the defender needs to reason about uncertainty, provenance, and the consequences of intervening in a live social environment.

There are tools to do sequential adaptation under uncertainty in the RL literature. Foundational work on Q-learning and deep RL determined how agents can obtain policies from interaction, while subsequent work in cyber defense determined how RL can be used in adaptive blocking, moving target defense, and response optimization (Watkins & Dayan, 1992; Mnih et al., 2015; van Hasselt et al., 2016; Wang et al., 2022; Nguyen & Reddi, 2023). Yet most cyber-defense formulations represent the environment in terms of traffic statistics, alerts, configurations, or host states. Actions are typically network controls or device controls. These abstractions are appropriate for many enterprise environments, but exclude social semantics, identity structures, and platform rules that are at the center of the metaverse experience.

The multi-agent RL literature offers a valuable contribution - defence tends to be decentralized. Research on stochastic games, decentralized response, and multi-agent cyber defense demonstrates how various agents can cooperate in the presence of uncertainty and partial observability (Hu & Wellman, 2003; Finistrella et al., 2025; Ren et al., 2024). However, these models seldom discuss durable social worlds when actions can have an effect on speech, participation, access to virtual assets, and user reputation. Semantically grounded coordination means not being able to differentiate socially different cases which could be superficially similar in terms of raw signal patterns.

Knowledge representation and cyber knowledge graphs provide the missing semantic structure. Ontologies are used to make concepts in the domain explicit, to aid interoperability, to allow reasoning over relations such as identity, ownership, delegation, policy scope and attack pattern similarity (Gruber, 1993, 1995; Iannacone et al., 2015; Sikos, 2023; Akbar et al., 2023; Bratsas et al., 2024; Wang et al., 2024). In cyber threat intelligence, knowledge graphs have already been used for, among other things, normalising events and connecting evidence in heterogeneous sources. What is still underdeveloped is the combination of these semantic assets with live policy optimization in a way that influences RL states, actions, rewards, and explanations.

Explainable and safe RL research is moving in the same direction. Explainability techniques aim to reveal the real reason for the agent's choice of action while safe RL imposes limitations on behavior that would be unacceptable (Heuillet et al., 2021; Madumal et al., 2020; Bekkemoen, 2024; Wachi et al., 2024). For metaverse defense, these ideas are not the optional add-ons. They are prerequisites for legitimacy due to the influence of autonomous interventions on expression, access, identity claims and property-like interests in digital assets.

Table 2. Literature strands relevant to autonomous mitigation in metaverse environments

Literature strand	Representative sources	Main contribution	Limitation for metaverse threat mitigation
Metaverse security and privacy	Chen et al. (2022); Di Pietro and Cresci (2021); Huang et al. (2023); Wang et al. (2023)	Defines key threats in immersive and economically active virtual systems	Usually descriptive; limited linkage to adaptive control logic
Immersive safety and avatar privacy	Hine et al. (2024); Giaretta (2025); Eltanbouly et al. (2025); Laiz-Ibanez et al. (2025)	Shows how embodied sensing and representation create new harms	Emphasizes governance concerns more than autonomous response mechanisms
Synthetic media and deepfake detection	Tolosana et al. (2020); Mustak et al. (2023)	Explains multimodal identity deception and media authenticity risks	Often stops at detection and offers limited guidance on sequential mitigation

continued on following page

Table 2. Continued

Literature strand	Representative sources	Main contribution	Limitation for metaverse threat mitigation
RL for cybersecurity	Adawadkar and Kulkarni (2022); Nguyen and Reddi (2023); Wang et al. (2022); Uprety and Rawat (2021); Hu et al. (2019)	Demonstrates adaptive defense under uncertainty	States and actions are usually infrastructure-centric and semantically limited
Multi-agent RL for defense	Hu and Wellman (2003); Finistrella et al. (2025); Ren et al. (2024)	Models coordination, competition, and decentralized response	Rarely captures persistent social environments and platform governance
Ontologies and cyber knowledge graphs	Gruber (1993, 1995); Iannacone et al. (2015); Sikos (2023); Bratsas et al. (2024); Akbar et al. (2023); Wang et al. (2024)	Supports semantic interoperability, reasoning, and structured threat intelligence	Often detached from live policy optimization and sequential control
Explainable and safe RL	Heuillet et al. (2021); Madumal et al. (2020); Bekkemoen (2024); Wachi et al. (2024)	Makes adaptive control interpretable and constraint-aware	Needs domain grounding for moderation, identity, and asset protection decisions

Taken together, the literature provides the necessary building blocks but not an integrated theory of autonomous threat mitigation in AI-driven metaverse environments. Existing work identifies the threat surface, demonstrates adaptive control, models distributed decision-making, and formalizes cyber semantics. What it does not yet provide is a unified account of how semantic knowledge and RL can be combined to produce context-aware, proportionate, and auditable mitigation. Table 2 summarizes the main literature strands and their limitations for this chapter's problem setting.

This review leads to three key takeaways. First, security in the metaverse goes beyond traditional cybersecurity. It has to account for how people interact socially, how they perform their identities, and how virtual economies function. Second, reinforcement learning shows real promise for adaptive defenses, but only if we move past abstractions focused purely on infrastructure. Third, semantic modeling, the ability to explain decisions, and built-in safety constraints aren't nice-to-have additions. They're fundamental to making autonomous systems trustworthy in immersive spaces.

3. CONCEPTUAL FRAMEWORK

The framework proposed here treats autonomous mitigation as a joint problem of semantic modeling and adaptive control. In conventional cyber defense, states are often defined over machines, alerts, or policies. In the metaverse, the defender must instead reason over hybrid environments in which users, avatars, autonomous agents, digital assets, rules, and social interactions all shape the meaning of an event. The task is not merely to classify a threat; it is to select a context-sensitive intervention over time.

The framework is organized around six interconnected layers: actor, asset, interaction, threat, governance, and control. Figure 2 illustrates these layers and their relationships. The actor layer identifies who or what is participating. The asset layer defines what is at stake. The interaction layer captures what happened. The threat layer interprets patterns of interaction as possible abuse, fraud, deception, or infrastructure attack. The governance layer specifies which obligations and limits apply. The control layer then converts this semantic structure into RL primitives-state, action, reward, policy, value, and belief.

Figure 2. Ontology-guided control framework for metaverse threat mitigation.

The actor layer is foundational because identity in immersive environments is rarely one-to-one. For example, one individual may control multiple avatars, delegate tasks to assistants, or communicate through AI-generated surrogates. Likewise, a visible avatar could represent a human, a bot, a service process or an arrangement of a combination. An autonomous defender therefore requires explicit representations of role, authority, delegation and continuity of identity between sessions. Without these sorts of distinctions, therefore, an intervention targeting impersonation or coordinated automation can easily prove ineffective or unjust.

The asset layer needs to be broader as well as in regular cyber security. In metaverse systems assets aren't only tokens and virtual goods, but also identity credentials, storefronts, objects in the world, access rights, sensor streams, creative works, and persons with a reputation. The security meaning of an event is dependent upon the way these assets are classified. Freezing a high value transfer, rolling back a manipulated object, or revoking access from the sensors each have different interests and implications. Asset semantics then influence the design of risk assessment and mitigation.

The interaction layer is the source of the temporal fabric of the state space. Raw telemetry could be movement, speech, gestures, content creation, payments, co-attendance, reports and moderation history. These signals, in their uncooked form, are of no use for control by humans until they get organized into semantically meaningful events and relationships. That translation is done by the threat layer. It maps patterns for interactions and asset states into metaverse-specific threat primitives which include impersonation, collusion, asset fraud, harmful content propagation, privacy extraction and infrastructure abuse. This transition from raw signal to threat primitive is what permits the agent to reason about general classes of behavior rather than individual observations.

Governance cannot be thought of as a layer that has been added on after the systems are rolled out. Security actions in immersive platforms directly influence user engagement by restricting the expression that can be permitted, controlling any visible content, controlling who can access a personal or restricted space, and determining the degree of control over virtual assets. Defensive mechanisms, therefore, should not be considered simply as technically effective, but rather with regard to proportionality, limited disclosure of sensitive data, protection of secured areas, age-specific policy implementation, the existence of appeal procedures, and the difference between temporary and permanent sanctions. Accordingly, governance functions as the normative framework through which appropriate actions are determined, evidentiary thresholds are specified, and the need for human explanation or review is established.

The control layer is a transformation of semantic structure to RL primitives. The state transforms into a hybrid entity, which incorporates numerical characteristics, symbolic statements, relations on graphs, and estimations of uncertainties. Actions are as type of interventions, rather than as generic controls: verify identity, slow down a transaction, reduce reach, isolate a session, freeze an asset, escalate to a human moderator, share an evidence packet with another domain. Reward is multi-objective, i.e., threat reduction vs. false positive vs. privacy intrusion vs. service disruption vs. burden of appeals. Belief is the state of uncertainty of some concealed conditions like intent, identity, collusion or source credibility. A summary of this mapping is provided in table 3.

Table 3. Mapping RL primitives to metaverse-specific security semantics

RL primitive	Metaverse representation	Example formal attributes	Security meaning
State	Hybrid semantic state over actors, assets, interactions, and beliefs	Actor role, provenance status, graph neighborhood, anomaly score, confidence level	What the defense agent currently knows or infers about the environment
Action	Typed intervention linked to governance conditions	Verification, rate limit, mute, freeze, isolate, escalate, explain	What the agent can do, subject to proportionality and feasibility
Reward	Multi-objective feedback combining protection and rights preservation	Threat reduction, false-positive cost, latency cost, privacy cost, continuity gain	What counts as successful mitigation in a shared virtual environment
Policy	Context-sensitive decision rule over hybrid states	Local policy, hierarchical policy, federated policy, uncertainty-aware policy	How the agent selects actions over time
Value	Estimated long-term utility of a state or action path	Expected safety gain, expected disruption cost, expected appeal burden	Why one mitigation path is preferable to another
Belief	Probability or confidence distribution over hidden conditions	Identity confidence, report reliability, collusion likelihood, intent uncertainty	How the agent reasons under partial observability

A further implication is architectural. The most credible implementation is not a single monolithic controller but a hierarchical and distributed one. Local agents can monitor sessions, neighborhoods, or services where latency matters, while higher-level agents reason about cross-zone patterns, portfolio risk, and policy consistency. User-behavior graphs provide a natural substrate for this design because they connect actors, assets, interactions, and historical cases in a form that supports both learning and explanation.

The central design principle is therefore straightforward: autonomous metaverse defense should operate on semantically meaningful states and governance-aware actions. RL remains valuable because it helps optimize over time, but it becomes trustworthy only when it is embedded in an explicit model of what the environment, the threat, and the intervention mean.

4. KNOWLEDGE MECHANISMS FOR AUTONOMOUS MITIGATION

A conceptual framework can only become operational when it alters the decision-making process of mitigation decisions. In this section, the knowledge mechanisms that draw the relationship between semantic modeling and RL-based control are identified. This is not to substitute learning with rules, but to ensure that learning is guided by the structured meanings that constitute the security problem.

The first is semantic state abstraction. Raw metaverse telemetry is too detailed and too volatile to be the only source of learning. A defense agent that directly reasons over all positional updates, voice packets, or object events will struggle to generalize and will be overly sensitive to noise. With ontologies and event schema in place, the system is able to convert low-level telemetry into semantically stable descriptors like suspected identity conflict, high-risk asset transfer, repeated proximity probing, or coordinated account cluster. The descriptors facilitate generalization across worlds and interfaces since the descriptors describe what is important and not just how it was measured.

The second is semantic regularization of value estimation. In ordinary value-based RL, two states may appear unrelated if their raw features differ, even when they correspond to the same underlying threat logic. Concept hierarchies, graph similarity, and threat relations make it possible to regularize value or policy estimation so that semantically similar cases are treated consistently. This is especially important in metaverse settings because the same attack may present differently across languages, avatars, worlds, or interaction modalities. Figure 3 shows how telemetry, semantic parsing, knowledge alignment, and policy evaluation co-evolve in a knowledge-enhanced RL loop.

Figure 3. Knowledge-enhanced RL cycle for autonomous mitigation.

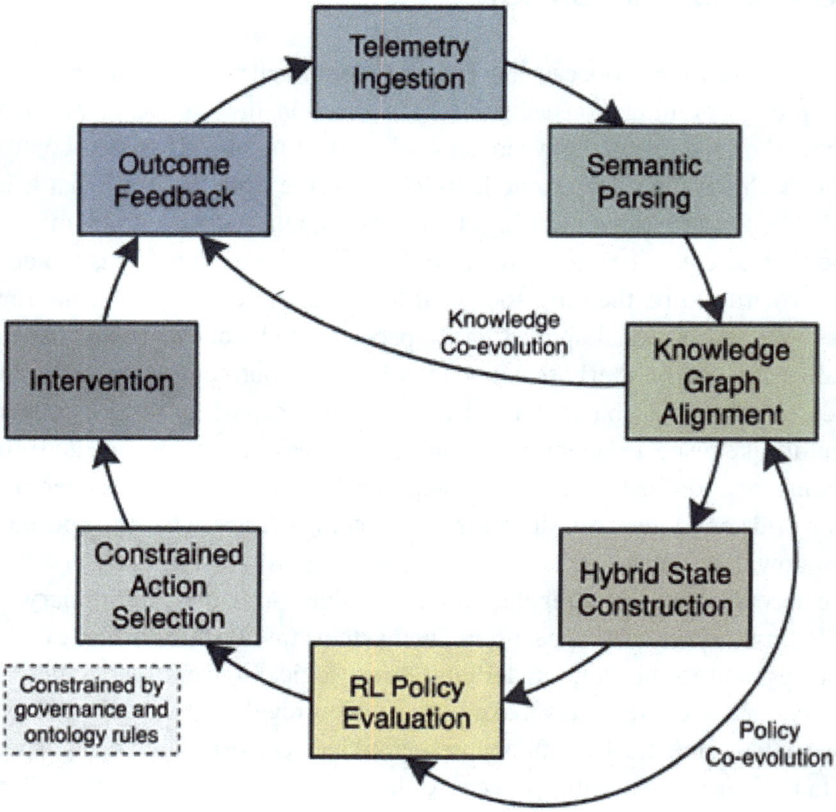

The third is knowledge-guided action selection. There are usually significant prior knowledge on platforms prior to any form of learning: secure areas, age gates, trading policies, identity verification routes, and limits to when human scrutiny is required. One can apply this knowledge to conceal unsafe actions, put reversible actions in front of the irreversible ones, and break broad interventions into small steps. The fourth is governance-based reward design. Reward design must not reward only the immediate suppression of harmful behavior. It also should impose penalties on disproportionate interventions, redundant data collection, unnecessary latency, and unwarranted appeal burden. By doing so, the governance can be included in the maximization of the agent but not as a post hoc restraint.

Table 4. Knowledge mechanisms that connect semantic modeling to RL-based mitigation

Knowledge mechanism	Primary knowledge source	RL touchpoint	Expected mitigation benefit	Governance effect
Semantic state abstraction	Ontologies, event schemas, behavior graphs	State representation	Better generalization across worlds and threat variants	Improves interpretability of state descriptions
Semantic value regularization	Concept hierarchies, threat relations, graph similarity	Value or policy estimation	Faster transfer to related attack patterns	Supports consistent treatment of similar cases
Knowledge-guided action selection	Policy rules, asset semantics, risk thresholds	Action masking and action decomposition	Reduces unsafe or disproportionate interventions	Aligns actions with formal obligations
Governance-shaped reward design	Governance rules, privacy norms, service objectives	Reward modeling	Balances security gains against user harm and operational cost	Makes trade-offs explicit and reviewable
Epistemic feedback loops	Provenance metadata, confidence models, source trust histories	Belief update and policy revision	Handles uncertainty, deception, and sparse evidence	Preserves due process under ambiguity
Explanation through semantic traces	Concept mappings, evidence lineage, decision logs	Policy justification and human review	Improves auditability and appeal handling	Makes interventions intelligible and contestable
Federated threat memory	Shared ontologies, external threat intelligence, cross-platform alerts	Transfer learning and policy priors	Accelerates response to recurring attack patterns	Supports interoperability and collective defense
Multi-agent semantic coordination	Common action vocabularies, trust schemas, case abstractions	Hierarchical and distributed control	Reduces duplication and conflicting interventions	Maintains consistency across agents and scopes

The fifth is the epistemic feedback loop. In metaverse defense, the difference between observation and knowledge is unusually consequential. A system may observe that two avatars look alike, that reports arrive in a burst, or that a transfer chain is abnormal without knowing whether the case is malicious, coordinated, delegated, or accidental. Epistemic feedback loops preserve this distinction by combining semantic interpretation with confidence estimation, evidence validation, source credibility assessment, and belief revision. When confidence is low, the policy should prefer reversible or information-gathering actions. When confidence rises, stronger interventions can become available.

Figure 4. Epistemic feedback loop for confidence-aware intervention under uncertainty.

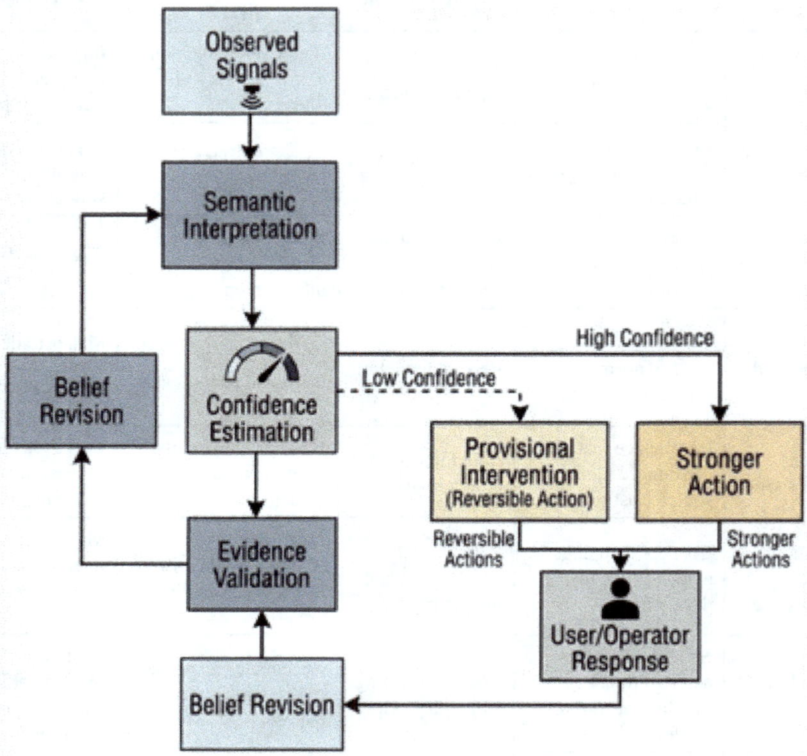

Illustrative Scenario

An illustrative scenario shows how these mechanisms fit together. Suppose a platform detects a suspected moderator impersonation incident during a high-value asset transfer. Signals that are observed are a face-voice mismatch, unusual use of credentials, high speed asset movement, and a newly thickened overlap with accounts flagged before. Semantic state abstraction transforms such observations into the actor, asset, interaction and threat descriptors. The belief model still reflects uncertainty: the transfer may have been delegated to an assistant, and the voice mismatch may reflect benign rendering conditions. Since the level of confidence is moderate, instead of immediate seizure of the assets, the policy chooses step-up verification, temporary transfer friction and augmented provenance checking. This case is described to the user using semantic language, checked by a moderator in case the threshold is exceeded, and finally to update beliefs and reward signals when the result is known. The system therefore acts adaptively without pretending to know more than it does.

The sixth is explanation through semantic traces. RL systems tend to suffer from criticism of opacity, and this criticism is more serious when interventions affect access, reputation or property-like interests. Semantic traces allow the agent to explain not only which action was chosen but also the concepts and evidence that justified it, e.g. repeated inconsistency of identity, high risk transfer topology, rule-triggered need for human review, and availability of a lower intrusion alternative. Explanations also help improve learning since appeals and moderator overrides, where concepts, thresholds, or reward weights were misaligned.

The seventh is federated threat memory. Attackers routinely test one environment, adjust, and move to another. Defenders therefore benefit from sharing semantically structured evidence about attack patterns, without necessarily sharing raw personal data. Portable evidence packets, shared ontologies, and trust vocabularies allow one platform's experience with a bot cluster, asset scam, or impersonation script to inform another platform's priors and action thresholds. Federation should not erase local governance differences; instead, it should provide a controlled basis for transfer learning and collective defense.

The eighth is multi-agent semantic coordination. In practical implementations, agents are deployed at various levels: agents can be close to session edge, market layer, or platform or cross platform level. Shared semantics enable such agents to evade conflicts, redundancy and incoherent escalation. As an example, a local guardian may tag a case as an uncertain identity conflict, a market agent may slack the corresponding transaction and a supervisory agent may determine whether the pattern is similar to a familiar campaign. The reason why coordination is important is because semantically compatible agents are able to share responsibility without losing policy.

Collectively, these mechanisms justify the idea that trustworthy autonomous mitigation is beyond being constructed by merely overlaying a policy network over alert streams. Adaptive control is still needed, and it should be complemented by semantic abstraction, uncertainty modeling, explanation, and controlled knowledge exchange. Table 4 provides the overview of the key knowledge mechanisms and the contribution of each of them in RL-based mitigation.

5. IMPLICATIONS AND CHALLENGES

The framework presented above has implications that extend beyond technical architecture. An RL agent that is capable of autonomous mitigation in the metaverse is part of the governance structure of the platform because its actions determine participation, visibility, economic access, and perceived legitimacy. The challenge is hence institutional as much as algorithmic: the platform has to determine which interventions can be automated, which ones will need to stay reviewable, and what the burdens of error will be.

The most immediate concern is privacy. Effective mitigation may require gaze, voice, gesture, movement, transaction and interaction history analysis, though these signals are very telling even in the absence of overt abuse. A poorly designed agent can over-collect data, draw unwarranted inferences, or retain evidence longer than necessary. The design response is not to not want to learn, but to make privacy limits hard constraints, to minimize the length of retention times, and to view intrusive sensing as a cost and not as free information.

Fairness is also important. Semantic abstractions have the potential of consistency, but can reproduce bias as well if concepts, priors or training data is skewed. Voice verification may work differently for different languages and accents; gesture-based models may misinterpret disability-based movement; community norms may vary between cultures & spaces. The practical implication is that explainability, appeals, concept review and continuous evaluation for disparate error rates are central governance requirements and are not an optional ethics add-on.

Scalability brings with it its own set of pressures. Metaverse environments create modality-rich data streams and massive user behavior graphs. A semantically rich but slow mitigation policy will be ineffective against coordinated attacks with fast moving viral code. On the other hand an aggressively compressed policy might lose the context to distinguish between good novelty and bad adaptation. Hierarchical control, semantic abstraction, local-global decomposition and selective retention of evidence are thus engineering necessities.

Table 5. Key challenges for RL-based autonomous mitigation in shared virtual worlds

Challenge domain	Why it is acute in the metaverse	Consequence for autonomous mitigation	Design response suggested by this chapter
Privacy and surveillance	Immersive systems collect rich biometric and behavioral traces	Learning agents may over-collect or over-infer	Encode privacy limits as formal constraints and reward penalties
Fairness and bias	Representation, speech, and behavior differ across users and cultures	False positives may disproportionately affect certain communities	Use explainable policies, ontology review, and appeal-informed updates
Scalability and latency	Continuous multimodal interaction produces massive state spaces	Slow or unstable policies may miss fast-moving coordinated attacks	Use semantic abstraction, hierarchical control, and local-global decomposition

continued on following page

Table 5. Continued

Challenge domain	Why it is acute in the metaverse	Consequence for autonomous mitigation	Design response suggested by this chapter
Interoperability	Worlds and platforms use heterogeneous semantics and evidence models	Shared defense knowledge becomes fragmented	Adopt portable evidence schemas, shared trust vocabularies, and common action descriptions
Accountability and oversight	Security actions affect participation, expression, and asset rights	Users may face opaque or unjustified intervention	Generate semantic explanations and preserve audit trails for review
Adversarial adaptation	Attackers can probe and manipulate platform responses over time	Learned policies may be gamed, poisoned, or reverse-engineered	Maintain epistemic feedback loops, uncertainty-aware actions, and periodic policy revision

There is a complicated reason why interoperability is challenging. Interoperability remains challenging for a more fundamental reason. The same event may be modeled using schemas that are incompatible, or when the same label of action suggests different legal or social consequences. It is not a mere issue of data exchange, but of semantic alignment. To address such a practice, it is proposed that the scheme of portable evidence be standardized and the vocabularies of trust and description of action be standardized whilst still permitting local rules of governance to vary.

Accountability requires not only technical justification but also that users experience the intervention as fair and intelligible. During immersive experiences, being silenced, alone, degraded visually, or experiencing transfer friction, may be stigmatized even in cases where the act is temporary and reversible. The users must have justifications that are intelligible, contestable, and clearly linked to the platform regulations. The use of human oversight is also required but not because all the cases are to be justified manually, but because of institutional learning, there should be cases of appeals, exception handling and revision of the concept.

Lastly, defenders should anticipate strategic change. Opponents are able to scan the reactions of a platform, pollute its evidence trails, create artificial obedience, or understand what activities are activated by which signals. This implies that autonomous mitigation should be uncertainty aware and periodically rewritable. This is not a very definitive policy, but a robust governance cycle where the knowledge models, thresholds and rewards can be updated over time as the environment evolves. The key challenge areas and the design responses proposed by this chapter are highlighted in Table 5.

All of these implications support the general argument of the chapter: autonomous mitigation within the metaverse must be seen as the architecture of credible institutional control, and not as the automation of incident response..

6. FUTURE RESEARCH DIRECTIONS

Several research directions follow from the framework proposed in this chapter. The first is neurosymbolic integration for metaverse defense. Current RL systems excel at extracting patterns from large-scale data, while ontologies and rules provide explicit conceptual structure. The central research question is how to combine these strengths without collapsing either into rigid rule execution or opaque end-to-end optimization. Progress here would make mitigation more adaptable while preserving interpretability.

A second direction concerns cross-platform knowledge federation. Attackers benefit from fragmentation, so defenders need ways to share threat meaning across worlds, services, and jurisdictions. The core challenge is not simple data pooling but the development of portable security ontologies, evidence packets, and trust vocabularies that allow transfer without erasing local governance differences. Figure 5 summarizes this broader research agenda.

Figure 5. Research agenda for trustworthy autonomous mitigation in the metaverse.

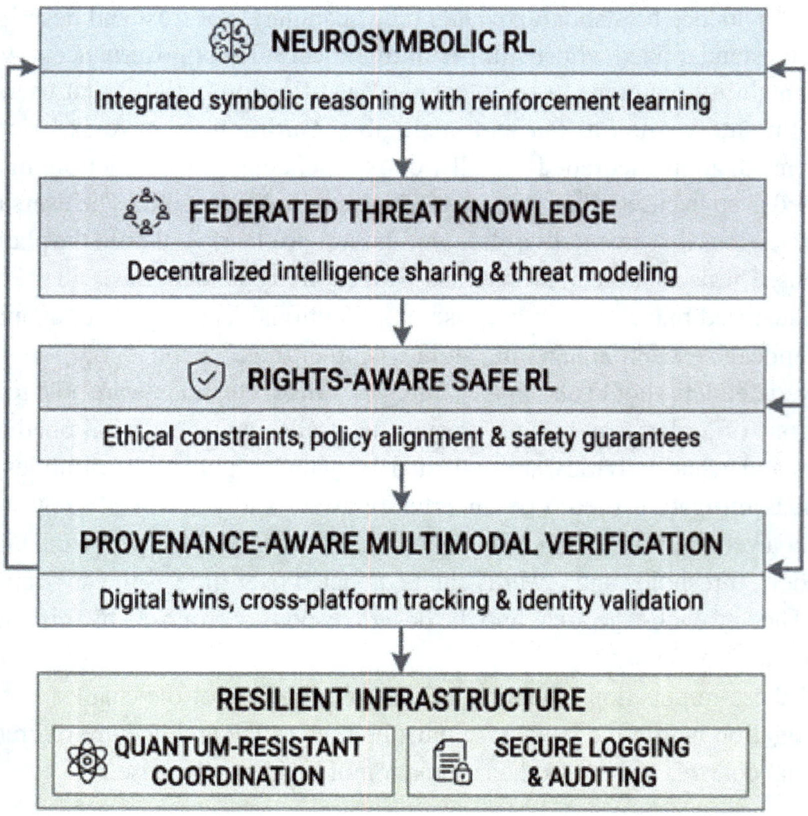

A third direction is constituted by continual and transfer learning. The environment of the metaverse evolves rapidly with the emergence of new AI tools, types of assets, and conventions of interaction, as well as conventions of moderation. An autonomous defender may not have to re-learn every time a world evolves but it cannot allow itself to drift semantically where learned policies are not connected to the original concepts on which they were originally based. This identifies the necessity of ontology versioning, concept-conscious external memory and the means of stable transfer in partially aligned settings.

A fourth way is multimodal verification that is provenance aware. Face, voice, behavior, provenance of transactions and delegation records are becoming more and more important in providing identity assurance in immersive environments. The way these streams of evidence can be combined into belief models that can be robust and explainable under deception should be explored in future work. It is not just the intention to achieve greater detection accuracy, but to choose actions with uncertainty that are to be calibrated.

The fifth direction deals with rights-conscience safe RL. The use of constraint formulations in safe RL is advancing fast, and immersive governance presents demands that are not yet well explored: safeguarded individual spaces, accessibility accommodations, reversible-first intervention rules, age-specific regulations, and auditable appeal processes. Study is required on the encoding of such obligations as hard constraints, soft costs or hierarchical control limits without turning the system into a usability nightmare.

A sixth orientation is the strong support infrastructure. It is not an assertion that cryptographic or post-quantum methods are substitutes of RL; they are not. Instead, long-term autonomous alleviation will rely on the provenance records that are secure, on the policy exchange signature, on the tamper-evident logging, and on the trust with regard to cross-platform coordination. Since evidence histories and identity attestations will be maintained over long horizons, platforms will require trust anchors which are resistant even to future cryptographic threats. The problem of post-quantum signatures, secure logging, and policy integrity mechanisms will then be better thought of as the infrastructure that renders semantic coordination long-lasting.

Table 6. Future research directions for ontology-guided RL in immersive security

Research direction	Core question	Knowledge dependency	Expected contribution
Neurosymbolic RL	How can symbolic rules and learned policies cooperate without reducing adaptability?	Ontologies, rule bases, explanation models	More context-aware and interpretable mitigation
Cross-platform knowledge federation	How can platforms share threat meaning while preserving local governance differences?	Federated ontologies, portable evidence schemas, trust vocabularies	Stronger collective defense across worlds
Continual and transfer learning	How can policies adapt to new worlds and attack forms without semantic drift?	Stable concept hierarchies, ontology versioning, external memory	Faster adaptation with lower relearning cost
Provenance-aware multimodal verification	How should evidence from voice, face, motion, delegation, and transaction provenance be combined?	Provenance graphs, belief models, authenticity taxonomies	Better identity assurance under deception
Rights-aware safe RL	Which platform obligations should be encoded as hard constraints instead of soft rewards?	Governance ontologies, policy logic, audit schemas	Security policies that remain proportionate and reviewable
Resilient support infrastructure	How can signed provenance, policy exchange, and audit logs remain trustworthy over long horizons, including against post-quantum threats?	Secure provenance, tamper-evident logs, post-quantum signatures	Durable coordination and policy integrity
Benchmark design and evaluation	How should metaverse defense systems be compared beyond raw detection or reward?	Canonical threat primitives, governance scenarios, explanation templates	More meaningful evaluation of proportionality, transfer, and auditability

A final direction concerns benchmark design. The field needs more than isolated performance leaderboards. It needs common benchmark scenarios that encode canonical metaverse threat primitives, governance constraints, uncertainty patterns, and explanation requirements. Such benchmarks would make it possible to compare architectures not only on detection or reward, but also on proportionality, auditability, transfer, and user rights preservation. Table 6 summarizes the main research directions and the knowledge assets on which they depend.

7. CONCLUSION

AI-driven metaverse environments require security models that can treat embodied interaction, synthetic media, virtual assets, and platform governance as interconnected parts of a single security challenge. Traditional controls remain important, but they are no longer sufficient when threats must be detected and mitigated inside persistent, social, and economically active virtual worlds.

This chapter has argued that autonomous mitigation should be understood as a form of semantic control. The literature review shows that existing research already provides many of the necessary building blocks, including metaverse threat analysis, reinforcement learning for cyber defense, multi-agent coordination, ontologies, knowledge graphs, explainability, and safe reinforcement learning. However, these strands have not yet been brought together into a unified framework. The proposed six-layer model, along with its supporting knowledge mechanisms, demonstrates how semantic state construction, governed action spaces, epistemic feedback, explanation, and federated memory can make adaptive threat mitigation more context-aware, accountable, and legitimate.

REFERENCES

Adawadkar, A. M. K., & Kulkarni, N. (2022). Cyber-security and reinforcement learning-A brief survey. *Engineering Applications of Artificial Intelligence*, *114*, 105116. DOI: 10.1016/j.engappai.2022.105116

Akbar, A., Rahman, F., Singhal, A., Khan, L., & Thuriasingham, B. (2023). The design and application of a unified ontology for cyber security. In. Lecture Notes in Computer Science: Vol. 14424. *Information Systems Security* (pp. 23–41). Springer., DOI: 10.1007/978-3-031-49099-6_2

Bekkemoen, Y. (2024). Explainable reinforcement learning (XRL): A systematic literature review and taxonomy. *Machine Learning*, *113*(1), 355–441. DOI: 10.1007/s10994-023-06479-7

Bratsas, C., Anastasiadis, E. K., Angelidis, A. K., Ioannidis, L., Kotsakis, R., & Ougiaroglou, S. (2024). Knowledge graphs and semantic web tools in cyber threat intelligence: A systematic literature review. *Journal of Cybersecurity and Privacy*, *4*(3), 518–545. DOI: 10.3390/jcp4030025

Chen, Z., Wu, J., Gan, W., & Qi, Z. (2022). Metaverse security and privacy: An overview. In 2022 IEEE International Conference on Big Data (Big Data) (pp. 2950-2959). Piscataway, NJ: IEEE. DOI: 10.1109/BigData55660.2022.10021112

Di Pietro, R., & Cresci, S. (2021). Metaverse: Security and privacy issues. In *2021 IEEE International Conference on Trust, Privacy and Security in Intelligent Systems and Applications (TPS-ISA)* (pp. 281-288). Piscataway, NJ: IEEE. DOI: 10.1109/TPSISA52974.2021.00032

Eltanbouly, S., Halabi, O., & Qadir, J. (2025). Avatar privacy challenges in the metaverse: A comprehensive review and future directions. *International Journal of Human-Computer Interaction*, *41*(4), 1967–1984. DOI: 10.1080/10447318.2024.2374091

Finistrella, S., Mariani, S., & Zambonelli, F. (2025). Multi-agent reinforcement learning for cybersecurity: Classification and survey. *Intelligent Systems with Applications*, *26*, 200495. DOI: 10.1016/j.iswa.2025.200495

Giaretta, A. (2025). Security and privacy in virtual reality: A literature survey. *Virtual Reality (Waltham Cross)*, *29*(1), 10. Advance online publication. DOI: 10.1007/s10055-024-01079-9

Gruber, T. R. (1993). A translation approach to portable ontology specifications. *Knowledge Acquisition*, *5*(2), 199–220. DOI: 10.1006/knac.1993.1008

Gruber, T. R. (1995). Toward principles for the design of ontologies used for knowledge sharing. *International Journal of Human-Computer Studies, 43*(5-6), 907–928. DOI: 10.1006/ijhc.1995.1081

Heuillet, A., Couthouis, F., & Díaz-Rodríguez, N. (2021). Explainability in deep reinforcement learning. *Knowledge-Based Systems, 214*, 106685. DOI: 10.1016/j.knosys.2020.106685

Hine, E., Rezende, I. N., Roberts, H., Wong, D., Taddeo, M., & Floridi, L. (2024). Safety and privacy in immersive extended reality: An analysis and policy recommendations. *Digital Society : Ethics, Socio-Legal and Governance of Digital Technology, 3*(2), 33. Advance online publication. DOI: 10.1007/s44206-024-00114-1

Hu, J., & Wellman, M. P. (2003). Nash Q-learning for general-sum stochastic games. *Journal of Machine Learning Research, 4*, 1039–1069. DOI: 10.1162/1532443041827880

Hu, Z., Chen, P., Zhu, M., & Liu, P. (2019). Reinforcement learning for adaptive cyber defense against zero-day attacks. In. Lecture Notes in Computer Science: Vol. 11830. *Adversarial and Uncertain Reasoning for Adaptive Cyber Defense* (pp. 54–93). Springer., DOI: 10.1007/978-3-030-30719-6_4

Huang, Y., Li, Y., & Cai, Z. (2023). Security and privacy in metaverse: A comprehensive survey. *Big Data Mining and Analytics, 6*(2), 234–247. DOI: 10.26599/BDMA.2022.9020047

Iannacone, M., Bohn, S., Nakamura, G., Gerth, J., Huffer, K., Bridges, R., & Goodall, J. (2015). Developing an ontology for cyber security knowledge graphs. In *Proceedings of the 10th Annual Cyber and Information Security Research Conference* (pp. 1-4). New York, NY: ACM. DOI: 10.1145/2746266.2746278

Laiz-Ibanez, H., Mendaña-Cuervo, C., & Carus Candas, J. L. (2025). The metaverse: Privacy and information security risks. *International Journal of Information Management Data Insights, 5*(2), 100373. DOI: 10.1016/j.jjimei.2025.100373

Madumal, P., Miller, T., Sonenberg, L., & Vetere, F. (2020). Explainable reinforcement learning through a causal lens. *Proceedings of the AAAI Conference on Artificial Intelligence, 34*(03), 2493–2500. DOI: 10.1609/aaai.v34i03.5631

Mnih, V., Kavukcuoglu, K., Silver, D., Rusu, A. A., Veness, J., Bellemare, M. G., Graves, A., Riedmiller, M., Fidjeland, A. K., Ostrovski, G., Petersen, S., Beattie, C., Sadik, A., Antonoglou, I., King, H., Kumaran, D., Wierstra, D., Legg, S., & Hassabis, D. (2015). Human-level control through deep reinforcement learning. *Nature, 518*(7540), 529–533. DOI: 10.1038/nature14236 PMID: 25719670

Mustak, M., Salminen, J., Mäntymäki, M., Rahman, A., & Dwivedi, Y. K. (2023). Deepfakes: Deceptions, mitigations, and opportunities. *Journal of Business Research*, *154*, 113368. DOI: 10.1016/j.jbusres.2022.113368

Nguyen, T. T., & Reddi, V. J. (2023). Deep reinforcement learning for cyber security. *IEEE Transactions on Neural Networks and Learning Systems*, *34*(8), 3779–3795. DOI: 10.1109/TNNLS.2021.3121870 PMID: 34723814

Ren, B., Tang, Y., Wang, H., Wang, Y., Liu, J., Gao, G., & Wei, W. (2024). A multiagent deep reinforcement learning autonomous security management approach for Internet of Things. *IEEE Internet of Things Journal*, *11*(15), 25600–25612. DOI: 10.1109/JIOT.2024.3368072

Sikos, L. F. (2023). Cybersecurity knowledge graphs. *Knowledge and Information Systems*, *65*(9), 3511–3531. DOI: 10.1007/s10115-023-01860-3

Tolosana, R., Vera-Rodriguez, R., Fierrez, J., Morales, A., & Ortega-Garcia, J. (2020). Deepfakes and beyond: A survey of face manipulation and fake detection. *Information Fusion*, *64*, 131–148. DOI: 10.1016/j.inffus.2020.06.014

Uprety, A., & Rawat, D. B. (2021). Reinforcement learning for IoT security: A comprehensive survey. *IEEE Internet of Things Journal*, *8*(11), 8693–8706. DOI: 10.1109/JIOT.2020.3040957

van Hasselt, H., Guez, A., & Silver, D. (2016). Deep reinforcement learning with double Q-learning. *Proceedings of the AAAI Conference on Artificial Intelligence*, *30*(1), 2094–2100. DOI: 10.1609/aaai.v30i1.10295

Wachi, A., Shen, X., & Sui, Y. (2024). A survey of constraint formulations in safe reinforcement learning. In *Proceedings of the Thirty-Third International Joint Conference on Artificial Intelligence* (pp. 8262-8271). International Joint Conferences on Artificial Intelligence Organization. DOI: 10.24963/ijcai.2024/913

Wang, G., Liu, P., Huang, J., Bin, H., Wang, X., & Zhu, H. (2024). KnowCTI: Knowledge-based cyber threat intelligence entity and relation extraction. *Computers & Security*, *141*, 103824. DOI: 10.1016/j.cose.2024.103824

Wang, H., Ning, H., Lin, Y., Wang, W., Dhelim, S., Farha, F., Ding, J., & Daneshmand, M. (2023). A survey on the metaverse: The state-of-the-art, technologies, applications, and challenges. *IEEE Internet of Things Journal*, *10*(16), 14671–14688. DOI: 10.1109/JIOT.2023.3278329

Wang, W., Sun, D., Jiang, F., Chen, X., & Zhu, C. (2022). Research and challenges of reinforcement learning in cyber defense decision-making for intranet security. *Algorithms*, *15*(4), 134. DOI: 10.3390/a15040134

Wang, Y., Su, Z., Zhang, N., Xing, R., Liu, D., Luan, T. H., & Shen, X. (2023). A survey on metaverse: Fundamentals, security, and privacy. *IEEE Communications Surveys and Tutorials*, *25*(1), 319–352. DOI: 10.1109/COMST.2022.3202047

Watkins, C. J. C. H., & Dayan, P. (1992). Q-learning. *Machine Learning*, *8*(3-4), 279–292. DOI: 10.1007/BF00992698

Chapter 5

Reshaping Global Education With the Help of Extended Reality and Artificial Intelligence:

The International XR Driving License (IXRDL) as a Framework for Immersive Learning Transformation

Thair Al-Fararjeh
http://orcid.org/0009-0001-8963-9761
Beyond & Universe LLC, USA

Ammar Almomani
http://orcid.org/0000-0002-8808-6114
Beyond & Universe LLC, USA

Omar Almomani
http://orcid.org/0000-0003-3160-6542
Al-Ahliyya Amman University, Jordan

Mohammad Alauthman
http://orcid.org/0000-0003-0319-1968
University of Petra, Jordan

DOI: 10.4018/979-8-3373-7882-4.ch005

ABSTRACT

Extended Reality (XR), which includes Virtual Reality (VR), Augmented Reality (AR), and Mixed Reality (MR), has become a major driving force in the shift of current pedagogy. Couple these immersive modalities with Artificial Intelligence (AI), and the provision, experiential processing, and evaluation of knowledge are redefined at every level of instruction and geographic location. In 2023, the XR market globally is worth around USD 142 billion, and projections suggest it will approach USD 300 bn or more by 2030. A large part of this growth is attributed to educational uses, in which the VR-in-education sector alone is expected to exceed USD 128 bn by 2031. Though such tremendous potential exists, the adoption of XR into a formal educational practice is still divided, with no standardized framework of competence, curriculum, or credentials of educators and learners. In this chapter, the authors explore how XR, along with AI, can radically transform the educational paradigm of the world through creating immersive, personalized, and equitable learning spaces

1. INTRODUCTION: THE IMPERATIVE FOR EDUCATIONAL TRANSFORMATION

Figure 1. The future of education: students immersed in XR-based learning environments with holographic education content.

Figure 2. Chapter logical architecture: from identifying the educational crisis through evidence-based analysis to the IXRDL implementation framework.

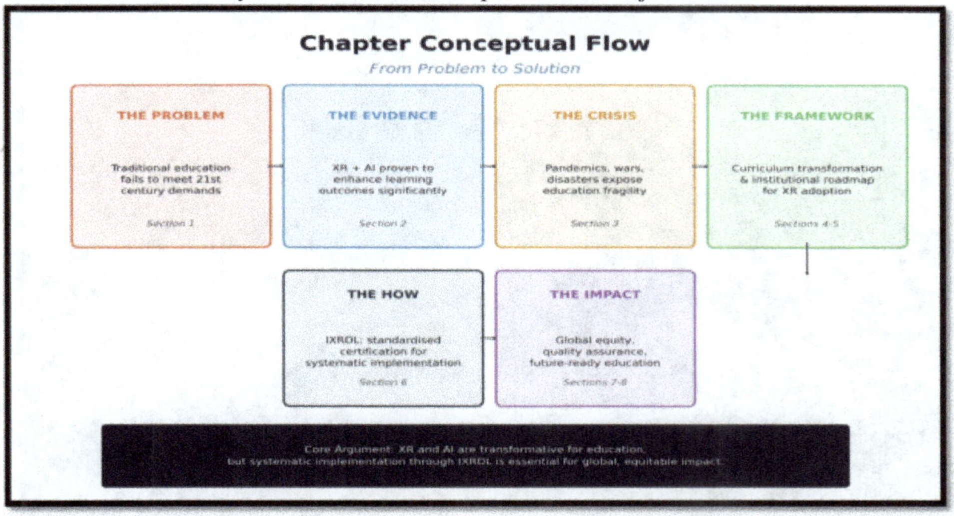

The education system in the whole world is at a crossroads. The prevailing pattern of teaching has been based on the essentially passive structure of a teacher standing on a lectern in a classroom, students in rows, and knowledge delivered mostly via lectures, textbooks, and two-dimensional visual images. Though this model has been the mainstay of mass education since the Industrial Revolution, its shortcomings have become more visible in a world characterized by the accelerated pace of technology, globalized labor markets, and the increasing awareness that learners have diverse cognitive styles, needs, and conditions (Meccawy, 2023; Wang & Huang, 2025).

Figure 3. The Paradigm Shift: From Traditional Passive Classroom (Left) to Vibrant XR-Enhanced Immersive Learning Environments (Right).

The limitations of the existing educational infrastructure were harshly exposed by the pandemic of 2020, as the world was faced with the coronavirus (Covid-19). The fact that schools and universities in 190 countries were closed and that about 1.6 billion learners were affected by an emergency transition to remote learning via video conferencing platforms and static learning management systems (UNESCO, 2020) highlighted the insufficiency of simply digitizing traditional lecture formats onto video conferencing platforms and static learning management systems. Learners reported reduced engagement, educators found it very hard to keep connections without face-to-face, real-time interaction, and substantial declines in academic performance, especially among disadvantaged populations (Brookings Institution, 2024). These challenges were not caused by the pandemic but instead were exacerbated by structural weaknesses of educational provision existing on top of the various decades.

Meanwhile, there have been the two convergent technological revolutions that matured to the extent of being able to bring in a fundamentally different vision to education. Extended Reality (XR) refers to encompassing Virtual Reality (VR), Augmented Reality (AR), and Mixed Reality (MR) that allows creating immersive and three-dimensional learning experiences where students can visualize abstract concepts, train complex procedures in safe virtual reality side applications, and interact with students on the other side of the continent as if they were in a common room (Hossain, 2026). Artificial Intelligence (AI), in its turn, offers the calculational intelligence that personalizes these experiences quietly in real time, adjusting the content difficulty, speed, and feedback to the needs of a particular learner and his performance trends (Hossain et al., 2025; Hossain, 2025).

XR and AI coincidence is not just a progressive enhancement of the current technology in education. It is a paradigm shift in which education is no longer a passive information-receiving model but an active, embodied, and experience-based approach to learning. A medical student is able to do virtual surgery even before he or she steps into an operating theater. Before even a brick is put down, an architecture student can be walking through a building that he/she has created. It is possible that a history student could be on the battlefield of Gettysburg and learn how the terrain contributed to the way of the result of the conflict. A student of chemistry can logically manipulate molecular bonds using her hands and witness the reaction on an atomic scale, none of which the textbook drawings could draw (Zikas et al., 2016; Stott & Neustadter, 2013).

Their inevitability is highlighted by the economic course of these technologies. The size of the global extended reality market is estimated to be USD 142.39 billion in 2023 and is estimated to be USD 1069.27 billion by 2030, with a compound annual growth rate (CAGR) of around 33.09 percent (Grand View Research, 2024). In this more extensive market, VR in the education sector is anticipated to reach USD 31.28 billion by 2025 and USD 128 billion in 2031 (Mordor Intelligence, 2026). It is estimated that the market of AI in education in 2025 is USD 7.05 billion and is expected to reach USD 136.79 billion in 2035 (Precedence Research, 2026). These numbers represent not a figment of imagination, but a long-term investment of governments, enterprises, and educational organizations throughout the world.

However, regardless of this push, there is still a very basic issue concerning the adoption of XR in education, which is ad hoc, unsystematic, and disjointed. Pilot projects, when implemented by individuals, show impressive results but seldom achieve the same results in the subsequent group. The teachers do not have the knowledge and skills to develop and create the immersive learning experiences successfully. Organizations do not have manuals to follow during the shift from the traditional to an XR-enriched curriculum. And the lack of internationally acknowledged competency standards implies that there exists no common language, no shared standard, and no portable credential that will guarantee that XR is safely, ethically, and effectively practiced across borders and educational systems (Naik et al., 2023; Egliston et al., 2025).

This chapter demonstrates an important gap in current educational discourse. It argues that extended reality (XR) and artificial intelligence (AI) are not simply the adjuncts that would be added onto traditional pedagogical frameworks but are the disruptive forces that will be responsible for a systematic reimagining of curriculum, pedagogy, assessment, and institutional infrastructure. The argument is supported by meta-analyses, pilot studies, and market studies. A comprehensive model of curriculum change and roadmap for institutional adoption is proposed, leading to the introduction of a concrete implementation plan—the International XR Driving License (IXRDL), which is a vendor-centric, internationally recognized model for global certification that promises to transform the dreams of immersive formal education into a scalable quality measure and a repeatable reality.

There is a strong basis in the body of cognitive and instructional theory upon which the pedagogical arguments for immersive learning are based. Constructivist theory, which was developed by Piaget and later developed by Vygotsky, states that people build knowledge most effectively through active, contextualized interactions with content, rather than receiving information passively. Concrete experience, reflective observation, abstract conceptualization, and active experimentation are the major parts of the experiential learning cycle espoused by Kolb. Cognitive Load Theory, as developed by Sweller, is also informative for instructional design: It highlights the need to consider working memory limitations and shows that judicious use of multimedia and spatial representations can reduce extraneous cognitive load while enhancing germane processing.

These theoretical underpinnings are consistent with the capabilities of extended reality technologies.

2. THE PROMISE OF XR IN EDUCATION: EVIDENCE AND IMPACT

2.1 Immersive Learning: From Theory to Practice

There is a solid basis in the corpus of cognitive and instructional theory on which the pedagogical case of immersive learning is based. Construct-based, or constructivist, theory of learning, proposed by Piaget and later by Vygotsky, believes that the learner best constructs knowledge through an active, situated interaction with the knowledge, as opposed to as a passive receiver of information (Piaget, 1972). Concrete experience, reflective observation, abstract conceptualization, and active experimentation as the main elements of the learning cycle predicted such a shift by experiential learning theory formulated by Kolb (Kolb, 1984). According to cognitive load theory developed by Sweller, instructional design needs to deal with the requirements on working memory, and an intelligent use of multimedia as well as spatial representations can reduce extraneous cognitive load and increase germane processing (Sweller, 1988).

These theoretical underpinnings are congruent with the extended reality technologies. Virtual Reality (VR) is an immersive design that provides the experiential learning process in the arena where it otherwise would be unreachable, unsafe, or prohibitively expensive. Augmented Reality AR overlays the real world with digital media and thus enhances real-world learning environments with data, notes, and visualization. Mixed Reality (MR) is the combination of real physical and digital objects in real time, and it allows learners to manipulate digital objects in their real environment. In both cases, the learner becomes an active participant, which is reflected in the learning situation and is presented in a variety of senses at the same time (Hossain, 2026; Milgram & Kishino, 1994).

Figure 4. The Extended Reality spectrum: Virtual Reality (left), Augmented Reality (center), and Mixed Reality (right) in educational settings.

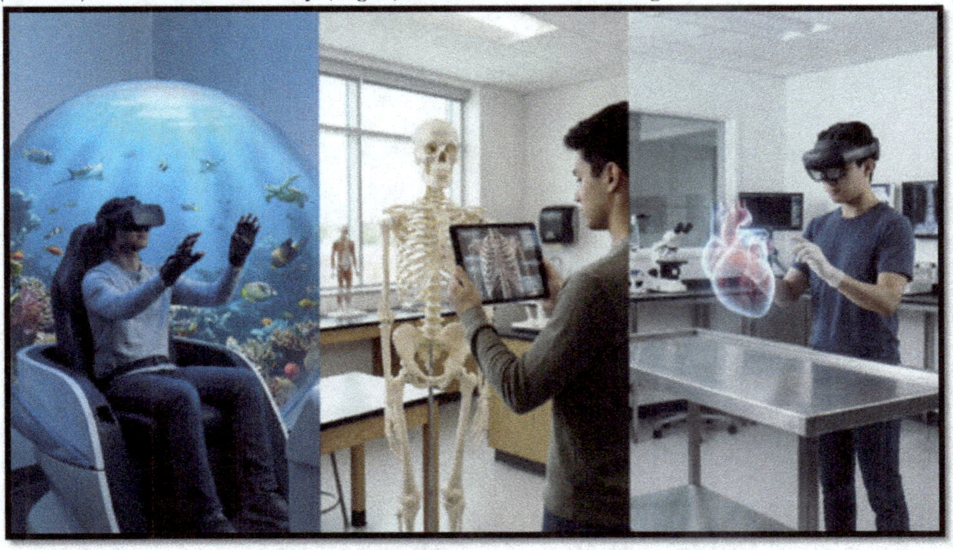

Makransky and Petersen proposed a theory known as the Cognitive Affective Model of Immersive Learning (CAMIL), which provides a theoretical framework that is specifically designed to explain the role and which should be used to explain why immersive technologies enhance learning (Makransky & Petersen, 2021). CAMIL lists six major affordances of immersive media, including presence, agency, embodiment, interactivity, adaptivity, and immersion, and matches them with cognitive and affective learning processes. The model illustrates that the feeling of being there (presence) and the ability to act in the environment (agency) provoke more intensive cognition and greater emotion involvement, thus creating the best learning experience in comparison with non-immersive learning.

Figure 5. The CAMIL Framework: How six XR affordances (presence, agency, embodiment, interactivity, adaptivity, and immersion) drive cognitive and affective processing to produce measurable learning outcomes.

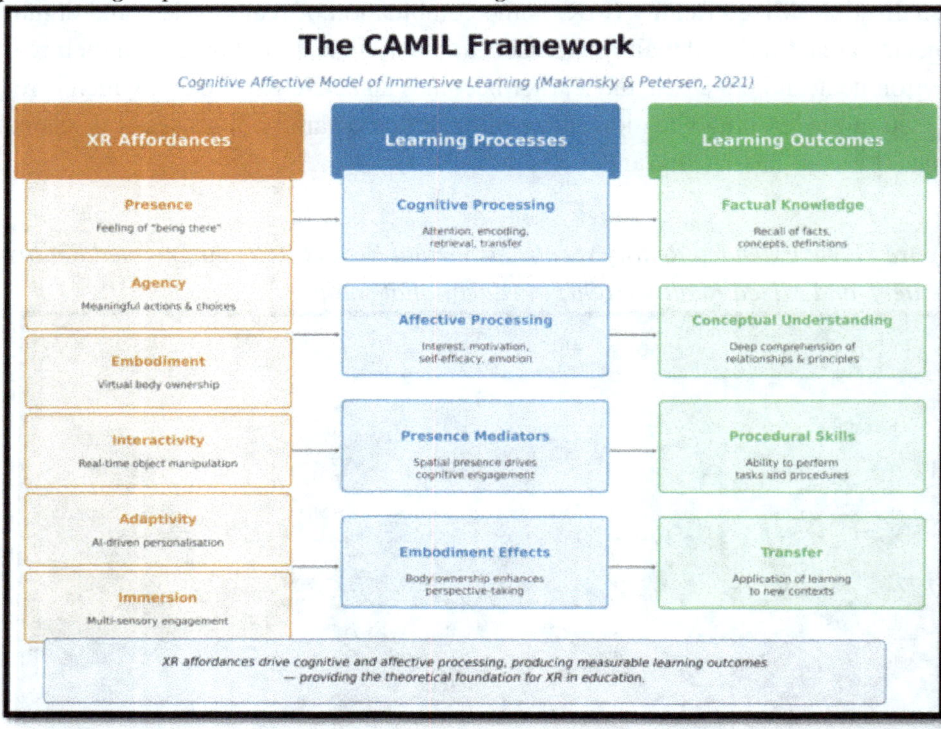

2.2 Empirical Evidence: How XR Enhances Learning Outcomes

The theoretical material that proves the effectiveness of extended reality (XR) in education has grown significantly in recent years. As opposed to single cases of studies, the systematic review and meta-analysis can be displayed, which offers more meaningful conclusions.

The effectiveness of the use of augmented reality (AR) and virtual reality (VR). In his study, Kumar (2025) conducted extensive meta-analysis research and published it in the Tech Trends journal of Springer. This review had a synthesis of a range of results of quasi-experimental and experimental studies, which found a statistically significant improvement in both AR and VR with average to high effect sizes. In addition, VR was identified to be especially effective with tasks that were related to procedural and spatial learning, and AR yielded great performance in contextualized and real-world learning situations (Kumar, 2025).

The other meta-analysis that examined the effects of augmented reality learning experiences on the motivational design model was conducted by Prasetya (2024). The analysis was based on 68 studies showing that AR-based instruction has a positive impact on all four elements of the ARCS motivational model, which include Attention, Relevance, Confidence, and Satisfaction, with the strongest impact on the first two components (attention and relevance). The above findings indicate that AR can not only improve the cognitive performance but also essentially improve the motivation and involvement of learners (Prasetya, 2024).

The evidence is also equally convincing on an individual study level. Hmoud et al. (2023) carried out pilot research among fourteen high school students and tested the impact of the XR technology to develop an interest in biology. The research measured four engagement dimensions, namely cognitive, emotional, social, and behavioral, and found significant engagement enhancement in the cognitive dimension, signifying that XR helps to visualize and learn intricate biological processes using interactive simulations and 3-D representations (Hmoud et al., 2023). Purdue University came forth with the XRXL, which is an extended reality system created to serve big lecture rooms (Batra et al., 2025). The system was evaluated with an IRB-approved study to examine the effect of the system on student participation, attention, conceptual understanding, and collaborative engagement among 82 participants (Batra et al., 2025).

Table 1. Summary of key empirical evidence on XR effectiveness in education.

Study	Year	Sample / Scope	Key Finding
Kumar (meta-analysis)	2025	Multiple HE studies	AR and VR produce significant improvements in learning outcomes with moderate-to-high effect sizes.
Prasetya (meta-analysis)	2024	68 studies	AR positively influences all ARCS motivational components, with the strongest effects on attention and relevance.
Hmoud et al.	2023	14 high school students	Significant increase in cognitive engagement in biology through XR
Batra et al. (Purdue)	2025	82 university students	XRXL improved participation, attention, and conceptual understanding in large lectures.
Maidenbaum et al.	2016	Visually impaired learners	VR navigation tasks achieved a 97% success rate for blind users.
Li (systematic review)	2025	AR in HE, 2000-2023	Significant benefits across multiple educational dimensions

Figure 6. A medical student performing virtual surgery using VR technology with holographic anatomical displays.

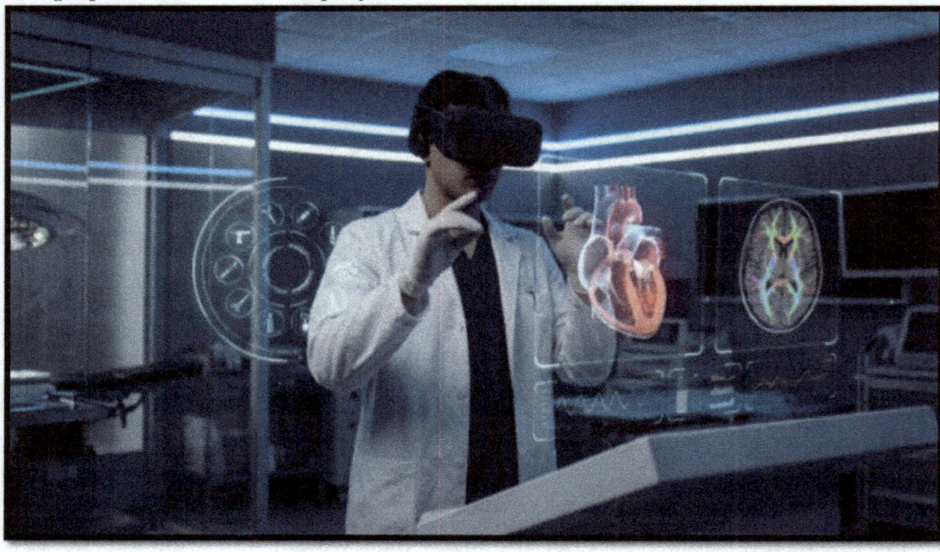

2.3 AI-Enhanced XR: Personalized and Adaptive Learning

When we combine extended reality with artificial intelligence, we create a synergy that cannot be achieved by each of the two technologies alone. AI modifies XR environments that remain static, fixed, and pre-programmed into dynamic, responsive learning systems moving in real time by responding to the behavior, performance, and needs of each learner (Hossain et al., 2025; Hossain, 2025).

In an XR classroom with AI, the application is able to track the gaze pattern of a student to determine points of confusion, modify the difficulty of a simulation based on real-time performance views, provide personalized feedback via intelligent tutoring agents, and develop unique learning trajectories in response to individual achievement. In the case of special educational needs students, AI-driven XR is able to personalize sensorial environments, offer real-time language translation and support, and modify ways of interaction to suit different physical and cognitive student abilities (Hossain, 2026; Barbu et al., 2025).

Hossain (2026) reported the integration of AI and XR in the educational process under the title of adaptive learning at scale and mentions that translation services provided by AI in the context of AR may help non-native speakers with language-related support in real-time, and AI analytics can also help suggest specific instructional strategies according to the interaction pattern of the learner (Hossain, 2026). In their research of 101 teachers (taking part in an XR/AI professional development program in Greece), Pitsikalis and Lasica (2025) discovered that organized education involving theoretical content with physical investigation gave rise to powerful intentions to embrace XR/AI, an increase in self-efficacy, and acknowledgment of motivational advantages to students (Pitsikalis & Lasica, 2025).

This is also where the AI-XR convergence is born, whereby the learner performance could not be measured using traditional tests but by analyzing the behavioral data in the VR worlds. Eye-tracking, gesture tracking, decision-making styles, and spatial navigational behaviors can be rich multidimensional competency assessments that are far deeper in diagnostic ability than standard practice tests (Tene, 2026).

Figure 7. AI-powered personalized learning: adaptive pathways and real-time analytics visualized through AR technology.

2.4 The Global XR Education Market: Scale and Trajectory

From a fiscal point of view, the economic consequences of XR in educational contexts show a discernible development that indicates that the technology has moved from an exploratory activity to an integral part of the mainstream infrastructural processes.

To illustrate this development trend, I have formulated the table below to outline the crucial market projections:

Table 2. Global market projections for XR and AI in education.

Market Segment	2024/2025 Value	Projected Value	CAGR	Source
Global XR Market	USD 142.39B (2023)	USD 1,069.27B (2030)	~33%	Grand View Research
VR in Education	USD 31.28B (2025)	~USD 128B (2031)	~26%	Mordor Intelligence
AR/VR in Education	USD 2.4B (2024)	USD 22.5B (2030)	41.2%	Strategic Market Research
AI in Education	USD 7.05B (2025)	USD 136.79B (2035)	~34%	Precedence Research
Immersive Training	USD 16.4B (2024)	USD 69.6B (2030)	~27%	Grand View Research

Anecdotal sources testify to the fact that the relevant question has ceased being whether XR will become a part of global education, with the pressing need to implement the practice timely and equally becoming the priority. The rate of growth in all segments consistently exceeding 25 percent is an indication that the market of the XR is entering into a period of exponential growth. Schools that fail to adapt to this shift face the risk of becoming obsolete, and those schools that strategically invest in XR technologies, curriculum, and training of educators are highly likely to achieve a considerable competitive role as well as a pedagogical edge.

Figure 8. Global XR and AI in Education Market Projections: Compound annual growth rates exceeding 25% across all segments, with the global XR market projected to exceed USD 1 trillion by 2030.

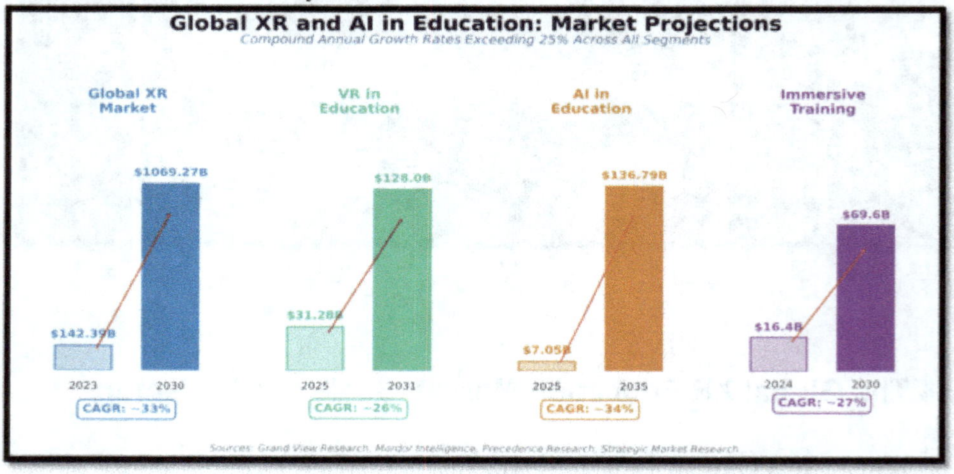

3. XR AS A LIFELINE: REMOTE LEARNING IN PANDEMICS, WARS, AND DISASTERS

3.1 Lessons from COVID-19: The Failure of Flat Remote Learning

The COVID-19 pandemic was among the most significant interruptions to the educational system on a world scale in the modern world. School closures were most intensive with about 1.6 billion students in over 190 countries, which amounts to over 90 percent of the total number of schools enrolled in the world (UNESCO, 2020). The emergency response divulged the basic insufficiency of the digital education infrastructure with the need to make a sudden, largely unstructured transition to remote learning through video-conferencing platforms and learning-management systems and with pre-recorded lectures.

Studies carried out both before and after the pandemic reported high amounts of learning losses. According to the Brookings Institute (2024), this shift to remote learning in March 2020 compelled schools to use learning-management systems, Zoom, and other educational programs more broadly, but it was an inequitable process in access, engagement, and achievement (Brookings Institution, 2024). According to the World Bank (2024), some nations like Turkey used the already existing digital education platforms to keep things going to some extent; however, most education systems were significantly shaken, with the biggest impacts being inflicted on low-income country students and disadvantaged populations (World Bank, 2024).

The main issue was not about technology but pedagogy. Video conferencing restates the least effective element of conventional learning, which is the one-way lecture, and deprives students of the most valuable elements, which include physical presence, spontaneous communication, collaborative learning, and the embodied experience of learning space. Students have also stated that they felt Zoom fatigued, less motivated, and isolated, which affected the ability to learn and well-being (AASA, 2024). Teachers, most of whom had never been trained on digital pedagogy, found it hard to keep up with the screen, which was flat and two-dimensional.

Figure 9. The limitations of remote learning: student disengagement during screen-based instruction.

3.2 Education in Conflict Zones and Disaster-Affected Regions

Pandemics are not the only causes of educational interruptions; armed conflicts, natural disasters, and humanitarian crises regularly destroy educational institutions and leave the millions of people who study there everywhere. UNICEF (2024) reports as well that approximately 224 million children and youths worldwide suffered education suppressions, 72 million of them completely out of school (UNICEF, 2024). Schools are often destroyed or damaged, teachers are displaced or murdered, and intra-psychical trauma of students comes to create further obstacles to education in conflict-affected countries like Syria, Ukraine, Yemen, Sudan, and Gaza.

Even in theory, traditional remote-learning solutions are ineffective in such situations. Internet connection can be switched off or lost, there can be no electricity, and students can live together in temporary shelters without personal devices. Furthermore, the screen-based, two-dimensional nature of traditional distance education is not helpful in fulfilling the profound desire of normalcy, socialization, and psychologically secure learning conditions in crisis contexts that children need.

Earthquakes, floods, hurricanes, and wildfires are natural disasters, the result of which causes similar disruptions. The future possibilities of immersive technologies in disaster-preparedness education were recorded by the International Federation of Red Cross and Red Crescent Societies Global Disaster Preparedness Center

(GDPC), which reported that the cheapest smartphone and a five-dollar cardboard headset would allow immersive technologies to provide graduates with resilience and preparedness through alternate virtual reality (Global Disaster Preparedness Center / IFRC, 2020).

Figure 10. XR as a lifeline: children in crisis-affected settings accessing immersive education through VR headsets.

3.3 XR-Enabled Continuity: Immersive Remote Learning as the Solution

Extended Reality essentially redefines remote learning by tackling the inherent constraints of the traditional, flat-screen modes. Instead of the dull reproduction of a passive lecture routine through a video stream, XR creates immersive three-dimensional learning spaces that help to recreate the need for presence, embodiment, and socializing, symbols of proper pedagogy.

In an XR-enabled distant learning demonstration, the students put on headsets and enter a common virtual classroom where they see and communicate with the teacher and classmates in the form of avatars in a three-dimensional room. They can be manipulating virtual artifacts, using virtual experiments, making simulated field visits to some historical sites or ecological locations, and collaborating on projects in shared virtual workspaces. The experience is qualitatively different than active viewing of a video lecture; it is active, embodied, and socially related (Hossain, 2026; Beyond Universe XR AI Solutions, n.d.).

Beyond Universe XR/AI Solutions, through its Metaversity Labs and Metaversity Curricula, has demonstrated how immersive learning ecosystems can preserve instructional quality during disruption and, in many cases, improve learner engagement and practice-based competency. Metaversity Labs combines a deployable XR lab model with curriculum-aligned immersive content libraries, multi-device support, and training-of-trainers programs, enabling institutions to deliver interactive lessons and simulations with only a VR headset and an internet connection. In parallel, Beyond Universe's Spatial. The IO-based metaverse hub supports virtual classrooms accessible from VR headsets, computers, or mobile devices, where students can attend virtual lectures, explore interactive 3D demonstrations, and collaborate with peers in shared environments (Beyond Universe XR AI Solutions, n.d.).

In particular, concerning conflicts and disasters, XR has several unique benefits. The virtual environment provides, firstly, a psychologically safe learning environment that is immune to the disorder and stresses of the outside milieu. Second, the XR experiences can be distributed using relatively low-bandwidth connections, as much of the processing is performed locally in the headset: this does not require streaming video in high definition. Third, the XR content can be left pre-loaded to the devices, which makes it affordable to have offline access in areas where the connectivity is not always available. Fourth, VR has therapeutic purposes because of its immersive nature, which offers a relaxing environment and predetermined routines that may be applied to uphold the psychological well-being of crisis-affected learners (Global Disaster Preparedness Center / IFRC, 2020; Oztank, 2025).

3.4 The Case for XR as Essential Educational Infrastructure

Figure 11. Comparative analysis: traditional flat remote learning versus XR-enabled immersive remote learning across key educational dimensions.

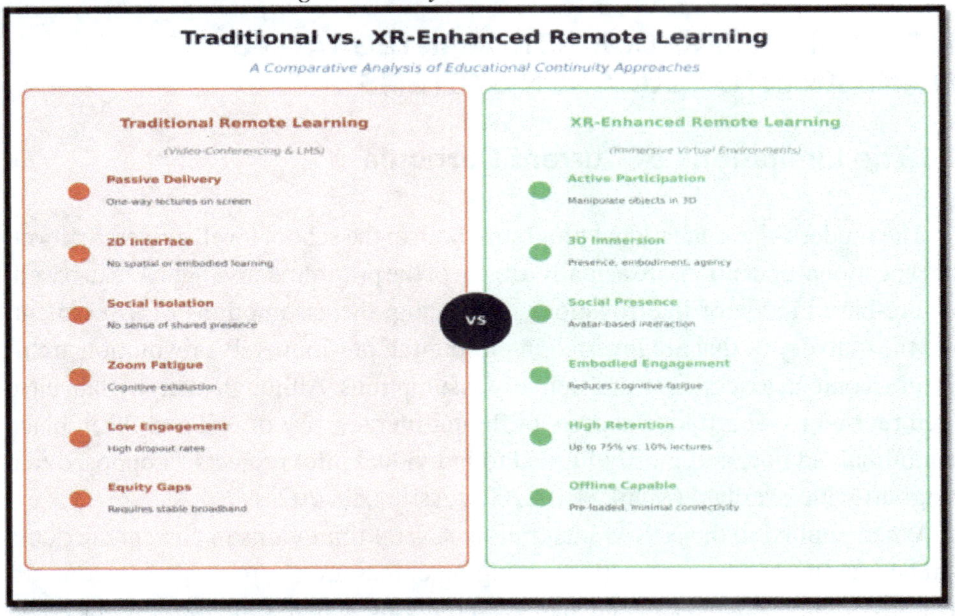

The long-term effects of the COVID-19 pandemic, combined with the actuality of educational shocks caused by conflicts and disasters, provide an excellent argument to understand XR as essential educational infrastructure, as opposed to just an optional improvement. The new era of educational resilience planning needs to incorporate immersive technologies into the core of continuity plans, whereas the introduction of learning management systems and video-conferencing tools was accelerated by the pandemic.

This would require proactive forward investment in three mutually sustaining areas: hardware availability, that is, that XR devices are supplied in the numbers needed to satisfy institutional demand and yet be affordable by all involved parties; content readiness, i.e., that the extensive, airing curriculum-aligned libraries of immersive learning essential to such delivery be developed and available on the day of need; and human capacity, i.e., that the whole learning institution be thoroughly trained to design and present effective immersive teaching in both normal and crisis conditions.

Through its formal certification forms and an institutional implementation strategy tailored to the academic contexts, the IXRDL framework, as discussed in Section 6 of this chapter, meets all three of these imperatives.

4. TRANSFORMING CURRICULA: INTEGRATING AI AND XR INTO EDUCATION SYSTEMS

4.1 The Limitations of Current Curricula

The modern-day educational programs, both at the school level, university level, and vocational education, are actually a result of the pre-immersive age. A text-based, lecture-based mode of interrogation, sequencing, the assumptions of assessment, and the delivery of that are invested in pre-digital, pre-immersive revolution architecture, content, assessment, and delivery assumptions. Although many syllabi have been revised to incorporate aspects of digital literacy, use of XR and AI in place is minimal, ad hoc, and mostly limited to individual pilot projects as opposed to a program-wide overhaul (Malik et al., 2024; Asif et al., 2024).

When applied to the XR-AI integration, several limitations in current curricula can be identified. To begin with, learning outcomes are regularly presented in directions of knowledge recall and analytical thinking, where little focus is placed on the spatial, procedural, and experiential skills that are specific to XR environments and developed there.

Second, the assessment approaches can be characterized as still overwhelmingly text-based: written assessments, essays, and multiple-choice tests, which cannot capture the richness and multidimensionality of performance data available with immersion in a learning environment.

Third, the processes of curriculum design are too slow and bureaucratic, and changes take years to be organized, which is much longer than the months needed to stay on track with the fast change of XR technologies.

Fourth, teacher-preparation programs hardly include teaching in the area of immersive pedagogy, XR classroom management, or AI-enhanced instruction design, which means educators are not well prepared to use these technologies to their advantage (Pitsikalis & Lasica, 2025; Meccawy, 2023).

Malik et al. (2024) examined how the concept of disruptive technologies affects standard models of curriculum and concluded that a fundamental change is necessary to enable the learners to meet the requirements of the twenty-first century. Their examination highlighted that the curriculum should shift past the simple incorporation of technology courses and should, in fact, be restructured, delivered, and assessed regarding immersive and intelligent technology (Malik et al., 2024).

4.2 A Framework for AI-XR Curriculum Integration

Prominent implementation of artificial intelligence and extended reality into teaching programs requires a methodical approach that addresses each of the content, pedagogy, assessment, and infrastructure simultaneously. Based on the academic literature and principles of design presented in the IXRDL structure, the given chapter suggests a four-dimensional model of integrating curriculum:

Measurement:

Dimension 1: Content Transformation.

The existing curriculum should be audited sharply to represent the areas of learning and focus of topics that can benefit most from the use of immersive delivery. XR is not a scalpel knife; the framework gives importance to those areas where spatial cognition, procedural rehearsal, experience of engagement, or group problem-solving forms a fundamental learning goal. Examples are illustrative, such as anatomical visualization in medical schools, molecular modeling in chemistry, historical simulation in social sciences, and engineering design in technical courses—each of them is a high-value candidate case of XR transformation.

Dimension: 2 Pedagogical Redesign.

The shift towards immersive learning as opposed to the traditional method of teaching based on lectures requires a change in the pedagogical approach. The teachers need to shift to a more facilitative paradigm in which the teacher becomes a guide and a co-explorer in a simulated environment instead of a transmissive model in which the teacher acts as a lecturer. This dimension is based on the constructivist, experiential, and inquiry-based directions on learning and operationalized by the affordances of presence, agency, embodiment, and interactivity of the CAMIL framework (Makransky & Petersen, 2021). The lesson plans are to focus on scaffold designs, elements of reflective practice, and debrief activities to allow the learners to reflect on and distill the abundant experiences that XR provides to them.

Measurement: Dimension 3: Assessment Innovation.

Immersive environments create new levels of behavioral and performance data that can be realized to be utilized as an assessment. The paradigm proposes to move away from summative text-based evaluation to continuous, performance-based assessment that is part of the XR activities. Immersive scenarios require rubrics that can measure the achieved skills, such as spatial reasoning, accuracy during the procedure, collaborative behavior, and adaptive problem-solving. AI-based analytics has the capability to offer formative feedback in real-time, as well as detect areas of missing learning, which cannot be observed with the conventional assessment paradigm (Tene, 2026).

Dimension 4: Infrastructure and Development of Ecosystem.

Change in curriculum would not be effective without an equivalent investment in hardware, software, connectivity, and human capacity. The current dimension covers the operational requirements of XR-enabled education, including device acquisition and management, as well as network management and support, content creation and management sites, and, most importantly, educator training and certification (like IXRDL).

Figure 12. Four-Dimensional Framework for AI-XR Curriculum Integration: A systematic approach addressing content transformation, pedagogical redesign, assessment innovation, and infrastructure development simultaneously.

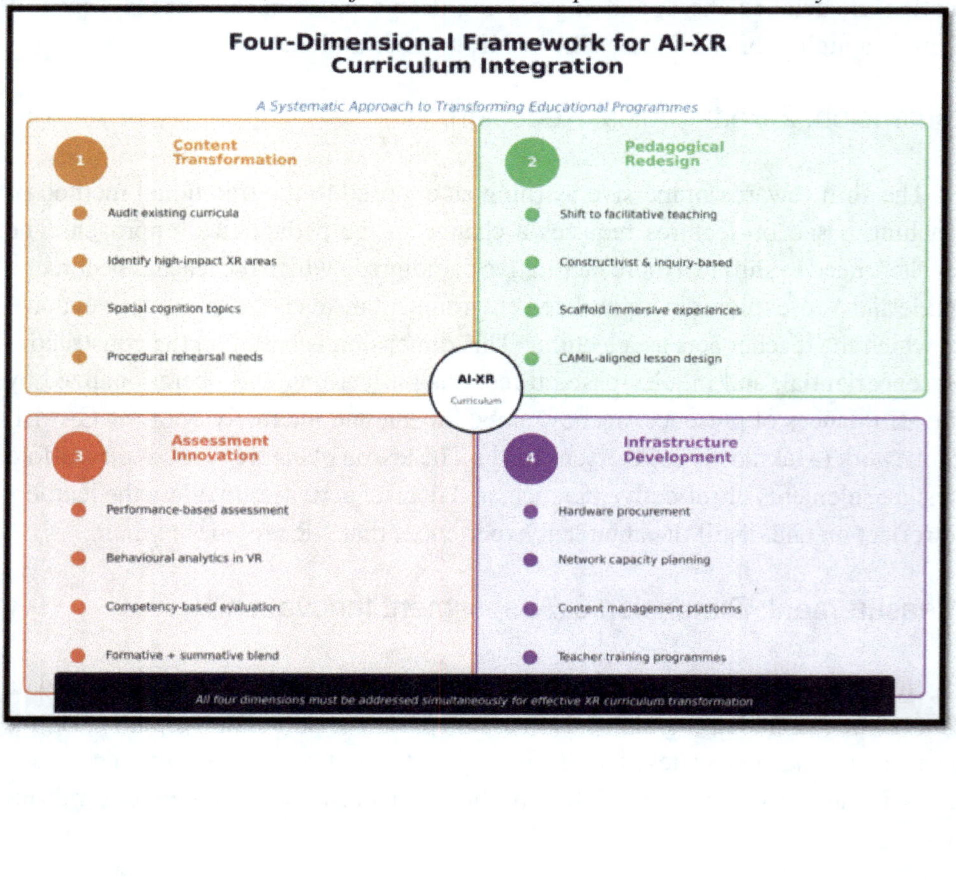

Table 3. Four-dimensional framework for AI-XR curriculum integration across educational sectors.

Dimension	K-12 Education	Higher Education	Vocational Training
Content Transformation	Science visualization, historical immersion, language practice, virtual field trips	Laboratory simulations, clinical practice, architectural design, engineering prototyping	Equipment operation, safety procedures, maintenance protocols, customer service scenarios
Pedagogical Redesign	Guided exploration, gamified learning, collaborative virtual projects	Inquiry-based immersion, research simulations, peer-to-peer virtual collaboration	Competency-based practice, scenario-based assessment, apprenticeship simulation
Assessment Innovation	Performance tasks in VR, a portfolio of XR artifacts, adaptive quizzing	Clinical competency assessment in VR, design review in MR, research methodology in simulated labs	Skills demonstration in simulated environments, time-to-competency tracking, safety compliance verification
Infrastructure	Shared device carts, school-wide Wi-Fi, content libraries, trained teachers	XR labs, institutional LMS integration, faculty development programs, research partnerships	Industry-standard simulation equipment, employer-aligned content, certified trainers

4.3 Curriculum Transformation Across Educational Levels

At K-12, the XR introduction should first consider high-impact and low-complexity applications that would add practical value to students, teachers, and parents. Case studies like virtual field trips, interactive science visualization, and historical recreation could offer attractive points of access that require little technical ability of the teacher but could result in quantifiable engagement and learning outcomes. With the advancement of institutional capacity, increasingly more advanced deployments, such as collaborative virtual projects, AI-adaptive developmental paths, and even performance evaluation in immersive experiences, may be implemented (Hossain, 2026; AASA, 2024).

The spread of XR in K-12 schools has increased at a faster pace. Data provided by the UK indicate that VR use is increasing by 35 percent in 2024 due to the declining cost of hardware and the growing body of research on pedagogical effectiveness (GoStudent, 2025). The American Association of School Administrators (AASA) puts immersive technologies in the center of the new paradigm of instruction in the United States, emphasizing the ability of immersive technologies to alter the way students interact with the digital content and the world around them (AASA, 2024).

Often universities are now the most active implementers of XR due to research capabilities, better budgets, and the active fit of immersive technology to the needs of the disciplines in STEM, health sciences, architecture, and the arts. The systematic review by Li et al (2025) and the meta-analysis by Kumar (2025) listed major positive outcomes of AR and VR in 200023 and showed that the study and analysis results were statistically significant regarding the beneficial effect on the learning outcomes at the tertiary level (Kumar, 2025; Li et al., 2025).

To transform the curriculum at the university level, XR will have to be integrated into the learning outcomes of the programs as opposed to being a marginal addition to a program. This necessitates the amendment of program requirements, module descriptions, and assessment policies to facilitate immersive learning experiences and performance-based assessment. Staff training programs must be established to foster the pedagogical and technical skills that are necessary to be a competent XR instructor, and this is precisely what the IXRDL Educator Track covers.

XR integration can be very beneficial to the vocational sector because the sector is centered on practical skills, procedural expertise, and job preparation. High-risk tasks like electrical work, surgery, operating heavy-equipment or responding to an emergency are rehearsed in a safe and repeatable environment with XR simulations. Farran and Nunez (2025) employed competency mapping, stack ability, and industry alignment as crucial in VET integration into HE in particular principles are clearly reflected in the modular, stackable, credential-based architectures of IXRDL (Farran & Nunez, 2025).

4.4 Teacher Preparation and Professional Development

Technology is not the greatest inhibitor of effective XR in education but rather is ranked as the single greatest inhibitor of effective XR in education. The studies have continually found the preparedness of teachers to be the key bottleneck: teachers with no training in the immersive pedagogy, XR classroom management, and AI-based instructional design are simply unable to expect to effectively utilize those technologies irrespective of the quality of the hardware and software they have at their disposal (Pitsikalis & Lasica, 2025; Meccawy, 2023).

Pitsikalis and Lasica (2025) have done one of the extensive studies so far on professional development of XR/AI teachers. Presented to 101 teachers (53 pre-service and 48 in-service) in Greece in five training sessions, the study incorporated both theory and practical exploration, as well as instructions oriented on scenarios. Based on the models of DigCompEdu, TPACK, and CAMIL, the program placed teachers in the role of creators of an immersion of learning activities, but not as passive users of tools. The findings were positive: the participants were found to be very willing to introduce XR/AI, increased self-efficacy, and perceived incentives to motivate students. Nevertheless, the research also revealed that there are severe obstacles such as time, and infrastructure constraints and curricular inflexibility that need to be overcome at both institutional

The main strengths of teacher-reported supports found in the Pitsikalis and Lasica research offer an effective checklist to the institutions interested in establishing educator competency in XR integration:

Table 4. Teacher-identified supports for sustainable XR/AI integration in education (adapted from Pitsikalis and Lasica, 2025).

Support Category	Specific Needs Identified
Pedagogical Resources	Ready-to-use lesson scenarios, XR activity templates, curriculum alignment guides
Professional Support	Mentoring from experienced XR educators, communities of practice, peer observation
Technical Infrastructure	Device availability, reliable connectivity, IT assistance, technical troubleshooting
Institutional Commitment	Leadership backing, dedicated time for professional development, policy frameworks
Continuous Development	Ongoing training opportunities, certification pathways (e.g., IXRDL), conference access

4.5 Infrastructure and Institutional Readiness

Accurate, even in the ability of other human activity, successful integration of XR means that it requires a large outlay in physical and virtual infrastructure. The 2024 strategic guidelines that EDUCAUSE offered about the XR in the educational environment highlight the fact that institutions need to develop extensive XR planning that will address the acquisition of hardware, network capacity, content licensing, data management, and ethical policies (EDUCAUSE, 2024). Similarly, the Open XR to Education Framework (OXREF), published by ERIC in 2025, is based on a stepwise approach designed to help institutions to create roadmaps, policies, and XR implementation plans that are both sustainable and effective (OXREF, 2025).

Infrastructure preparedness cuts across several interconnected elements. Network infrastructure should be able to support immersive application bandwidth and latency demands, especially in the case of multi-user collaborative environments. The following requirements are necessary: device-management systems are necessary to manage procurement, configuration, maintenance, hygiene, and life cycle of XR hardware in multi-site and user-cohort. XR experiences need to be curated, created and distributed with the assistance of content-management platforms in alignment with curriculum. Lastly, data -governance systems must grapple with the unique privacy and ethical issues of the biometric and behavioral data collected by XR systems, including eye-tracking, gestures, and spatial navigation behaviors (Hossain, 2026; EDUCAUSE, 2024).

5. A ROADMAP FOR EDUCATIONAL INSTITUTIONS: FROM TRADITIONAL TO IMMERSIVE

5.1 The Four-Phase Institutional Adoption Roadmap

Considering the fact that the technological levels of technological levels, budgetary capacity and institutional culture vary significantly in teaching institutions, the chapter outlines a four-step adoption process roadmap that will supply a sortable but flexible path between traditional teaching and a complete package of immersive learning. This roadmap is developed to be applicable in K-12 schools and universities as well as vocational training facilities and corporate learning organizations with adaptations that are applicable in both dissimilar settings.

5.2 Phase 1: Assessment and Vision Setting (Months 1-6)

The first step will focus on the methodical assessment of the current situation within an institution and the development of a clear and feasible vision of the process of incorporating extended reality (XR). The most significant of these activities include an institutional readiness test that examines the technological infrastructure in place, the digital skills of the educators, the flexibility of the curriculum as well as the willingness of the leadership to initiate them. The engagement campaign at stakeholder level must include educators, students, administrators, IT staff, and, depending on the situation, parents and industry partners who would collectively establish the XR vision of the institution and strategize goals.

At this stage, the institutions should be able to pinpoint high-impact pilot areas that XR can produce the most tangible and measurable value. They are usually subjects, or courses, where spatial understanding, procedural drilling, or immersion are both learning outcomes. A team of educational leaders, technology experts, and subject matter experts, as a part of the multidisciplinary team, should be formed to guide the implementation process. The budgetary planning would have to start based on estimates that are realistic in terms of hardware, software, connectivity, content and professional development.

5.3 Phase 2: Infrastructure and Capacity Building (Months 7-18)

The second phase is focused on the development of the groundwork infrastructure and building of the necessary human resources needed by XR integration. The decision on hardware acquisition should be based on the pilot areas outlined in Phase 1, with the focus on flexible low-cost devices that can be used in a variety of activities. The network infrastructure must be thoroughly evaluated, and where necessary, enhanced to meet the performance requirements in terms of bandwidth and latency of immersive applications.

In this stage, educator professional development is of paramount importance. Teachers and trainers that are chosen for pilot programs should be trained in a structured way with immersive pedagogy, XR classroom management and AI enhanced instructional design. The IXRDL Foundation Level and Educator Track are two good examples of such training, as they provide standardized, internationally recognized training that protects consistent quality and has significant competency gains. Institutions should at the same time develop partnerships with XR content providers, technology vendors and also peer institutions to support resource, experiential knowledge and best practice sharing.

5.4 Phase 3: Pilot Implementation and Iteration (Months 13-24)

The third step will include the implementation of XR-enhanced teaching in the chosen areas of pilots, as well as intensive analysis with periodic improvements. Pilot programs must be configured on a basis of definite success parameters such as the involvement of students, learning outcome, teacher assurance, and working productivity. The data gathering of quantitative measures (test scores, rates of the completion and time-on-task, XR performance analytics) and of qualitative feedback (student and educator perceptions, observational data, focus groups) should be considered.

This is an iterative stage which is critical. The first rollouts will always be met with the problem of technical difficulties, pedagogical restructuring, and logistical problems that will be quickly met with responses and changes. The institutions must develop feedback mechanisms that allow improvement to be done continuously and periodic evaluation of results, analysis of the data and curriculum revision. The scaling strategy in Phase 4 should be informed by lessons learnt in pilot programs recorded in a systematic manner.

5.5 Phase 4: Scaling and Institutionalisation (Months 19-36+)

The last stage is aimed at the further proliferation of successful pilot programs to new subjects, departments and campuses, and integrating XR into the organizational strategic and operational structures. XR-enhanced learning outcomes, assessment techniques, and teaching approaches must be part of the program-level curriculum revision, and not side additions. Certification of educators by IXRDL must be made a requirement or good recommendation among faculty who are engaged in immersive instruction.

The institutional policies need to be changed to accommodate the XR-specific governance, data privacy, ethical usage, device management, health and safety issues. The XR-specific criteria that must be implemented in quality assurance processes must comply with the criterion that is built into IXRDL framework. And strategic planning ought to make XR a fundamental part of the educational mission in the institution with specific budget lines, staffing and leadership responsibility.

Table 5. Four-phase institutional adoption roadmap for XR-enhanced education.

Phase	Timeline	Focus	Key Activities	IXRDL Alignment
1: Assessment & Vision	Months 1-6	Understanding and planning	Readiness assessment, stakeholder engagement, pilot area identification, budget planning	Awareness of IXRDL framework and standards
2: Infrastructure & Capacity	Months 7-18	Building foundations	Hardware procurement, network upgrades, educator training, partnerships	IXRDL Foundation Level and Educator Track training
3: Pilot & Iteration	Months 13-24	Testing and learning	Pilot deployment, data collection, iterative refinement, lesson documentation	IXRDL-certified educators deliver pilot programmes
4: Scaling & Institutionalisation	Months 19-36+	Embedding and expanding	Programme-level curriculum revision, policy updates, QA integration, strategic positioning	Full IXRDL certification pathway embedded in institutional operations

5.6 Overcoming Barriers: Cost, Access, and Equity

The move to XR enhanced education needs to be made with regard for equity and inclusion. A major concern is the creation of the "digital immersive divide" where the rich institutions in wealthy countries are well positioned to use XR technologies while resource constrained schools in developing countries cannot do so, increasing existing disparities. Therefore, active tactics of mitigation are imperative.

There are a number of ways to deal with this risk. First, the decline in the price of XR hardware - stand-alone headsets are now available for under USD300, and mobile-based VR solutions can be purchased for between USD5 and USD15 - makes immersive technology increasingly affordable for resource-constrained organisations (Hossain, 2026; Global Disaster Preparedness Center / IFRC, 2020). Second, XR platforms based on cloud and web infrastructures decrease reliance on expensive local computational resources, and thus make interacting with immersive experiences possible from household devices with a standard internet connection. Third, combining open educational resources (OER) with collaborative projects with a goal of producing XR content that correlates with curricula can significantly reduce the costs of XR content. Fourth, international frameworks like the International XR Digital Learning (IXRDL) standard, by creating repeatable standards and portable credentials, promoted knowledge transfer and capacity building across nations. Consequently, the institutions in developing countries are better placed to take advantage of the resources and expertise that are available in the global XR education community.

The IXRDL framework has been built on the principles of regional adaptability, multilingual delivery and cultural sensitivity of materials; these features are deliberately constructed so that they will allow for equitable access on a global scale. By offering a common baseline level of quality that can be contextualised in accordance with local needs without losing ground-level standards, IXRDL empowers institutions, anywhere in the world, to engage in immersive educational transformation in an equitable context.

6. THE HOW: IXRDL AS THE IMPLEMENTATION PLAN FOR EDUCATIONAL TRANSFORMATION

6.1 The Gap: Why Education Needs a Standardised XR Competency Framework

The preceding sections have established the fact that XR and AI have transformative potential for global education, and immersive technologies can serve as lifelines during crises, and systematic metamorphosis in curricula, as well as institutional roadmaps, are indispensable to harnessing this transformative potential. Nevertheless, a fundamental question remains, how is such transformation to be implemented on a large scale, with consistency in quality, across the heterogeneous variety of educational systems and national contexts?

The solution to this quandary should be a standardized competency framework - one that defines what it means to be "good" at XR within the classroom; one that offers educators and learners the mechanisms to gain and demonstrate such competency; and one that results in internationally-recognized certifications thereby ensuring quality, portability, and trust. In the absence of such a framework, the integration of XR into education will continue to be fragmented, inconsistent and vulnerable to historically ad hoc, pilot based patterns of educational technology adoption which have long been a bane of educational systems.

Presently the XR professional ecosystem is very disorganised. Existing certifications have a primarily vendor-specific orientation and prioritize proprietary platforms (e.g. Meta Quest, Apple Vision Pro, Magic Leap, or game engines such as Unity and Unreal). While these credentials do demonstrate knowledge of specific platforms, they do not offer cross-platform validation of competencies so that educational institutions cannot undertake comparative evaluations of disparate XR environments (Al-Fararjeh & Almomani, 2026; Unity Technologies, 2024). Moreover, the field of study does not have certification based on the role or specific needs of educators, technicians, content developers, and researchers who are working with XR technology in educational settings.

According to the XR Association (XRA), around seventy-eighth percent of employers experience challenges in determining XR competence because there are fragmented, vendor-centric certification systems and inconsistent competences (XR Association, 2024). Within the sphere of education, this problem is heightened more so by the lack of an internationally recognised credential created specifically for educators who use XR in their pedagogical practice.

6.2 IXRDL: Design Principles and Architecture

The above sections have identified revolutionary possibilities of XR and AI for education globally in the world; layered with the feature of immersive technologies that can also be lifelines in times of crisis situations; with the necessity of systematic curricular reform and institutional roadmaps to implement the possible potential. However, there seems to remain a fundamental question, how can such transformation be applied at scale, with consistent quality, in the heterogeneous set of educational systems and national context?

Overcoming this conundrum requires a common competency framework that outlines the characteristics of 'good' XR competence in the classroom, mechanisms for educators and learners to obtain and unambiguously demonstrate this competence, and internationally recognised qualifications for maintaining quality, portability and trust. Absent such a framework we are likely to see XR integrated in an ad hoc piecemeal manner into education, perpetuating the historic ad hoc pilot-based approaches to educational technologies that have beleaguered education for decades.

In light of an existing gap in the field of immersive educational technology over the years, the International XR Driving License (IXRDL) has been brought forward as a complete solution. Conceived under principles of vendor neutrality, modularity and global standardisation, IXRDL builds upon the proven efficacy of the International Computer Driving License (ICDL) which, to date, has been used to certify over seventeen million candidates in more than a hundred countries, thus providing evidence of the scalability and extensive impact of a standardised, modular framework for digital competency certification (ICDL Foundation, 2023; Caroline et al., 2025).

The architecture of IXRDL is based on five cardinal design principles that are aimed at the imperatives of educational transformation. Chief among these is: Vendor Neutrality and Cross- Ecosystem Competency. The certification process assesses a combination of knowledge and hands-on skill that is portable across hardware solutions, from standalone solutions, tethered solutions, mobile solutions and as varied as the input solutions such as controllers, hand-tracking and eye-tracking, to diverse software ecologies such as Unity, Unreal and Web-based solutions. This broadness ensures that educators and practitioners accredited through IXRDL are capable of navigating any XR environment regardless of the idiosyncratic hardware/software stack used by the institutions they work for (Al-Fararjeh & Almomani, 2026).

An additional basic aspect is the role based tracks with stackable modules. IXRDL outlines specific certification activities that are appropriate for a variety of professional archetypes - such as Foundation, Technician, General User, Developer and Educator. Through a scaffolded credentialing schema, micro-IVs may be amalgamated into more advanced accreditations, thus promoting a continuum of lifelong learning and focusing on targeted skill enhancement. As such, educators may begin with simple XR literacy, and then progress to advanced skills in immersive pedagogy, curriculum building, and levels of assessment praxis (Al-Fararjeh & Almomani, 2026)

Standards alignment and accreditation readiness is another foundational principle. The governance, psychometric strategies and quality assurance protocols on which IXRDL is built have been carefully crafted to the standards of ISO/IEC 17024, the international standards for personnel certification entities. Such compliance provides the certification process with competence, impartiality and reproducibility and thereby promotes strong quality controls that in turn foster a culture of cross-border confidence and mutual recognition of IXRDL qualifications (ISO, 2012; AAA Accreditation, 2024).

These issues of ethics, safety, and accessibility are built into each level of certification. At every level, there are mandatory imperatives related to ethical behavior, health & safety, data privacy, and inclusive design. The integration of these normative dimensions makes sure individuals who come out as IXRDL credential holders possess not only proficient technical competence and cogent ethical acumen and vigilance in identifying and mitigating potential hazards associated with the deployment of XR technology within pedagogical scenarios (Al-Fararjeh & Almomani, 2026).

Finally, a rigorous assessment framework brings evaluative rigor to the program. IXRDL provides an integrated test architecture of computer-based conceptual understanding tests, practical trials of application of previously taught knowledge, and portfolio reviews to assess expert level of synthesis. This eclectic and multimodal assessment framework ensures that the resultant certification is of veritable competency and not a perfunctory accretion of theoretical knowledge (Al-Fararjeh & Almomani, 2026).

6.3 The IXRDL Framework Structure

Figure 13. IXRDL Certification Architecture: This diagram shows a three-level, five-track, professional certification architecture with Foundation, Professional and Expert levels for all tracks

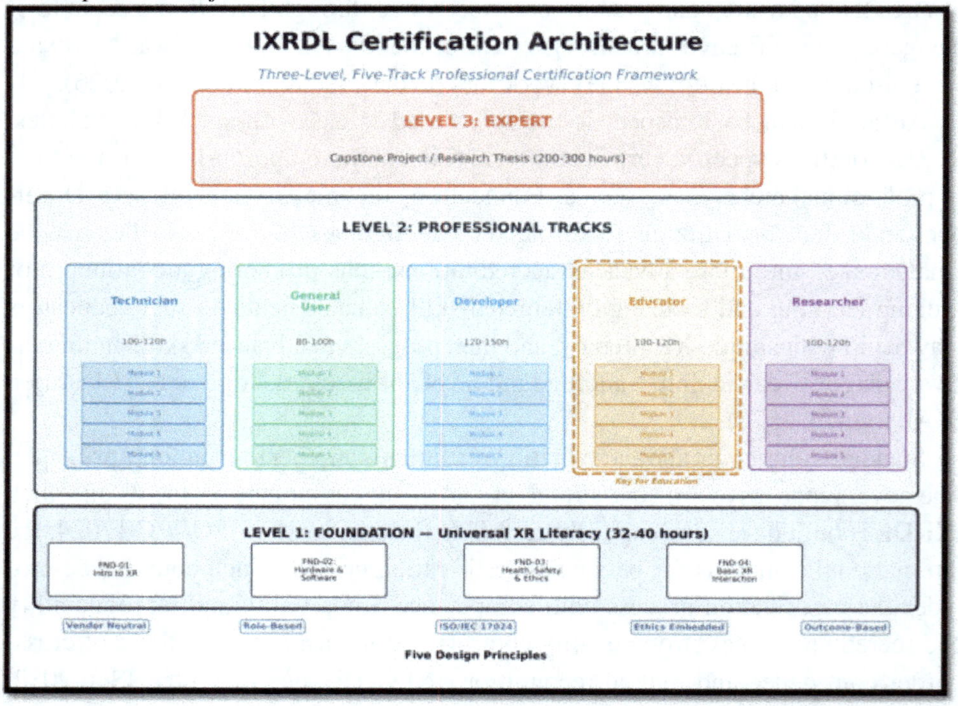

The certification architecture of IXRDL has three levels, that is - Foundation, Professional, and Expert, which are organized into five professional tracks, all of which are inter-intact. The following table provides an overview of this structure:

Table 6. IXRDL certification framework structure and track overview.

Level	Track	Duration	Target Audience	Core Focus
Level 1: Foundation	Universal XR Literacy	20-30 hours	All learners and professionals	XR concepts, hardware/software, health/safety/ethics, basic interaction
Level 2: Professional	XR Technician	100-120 hours	IT specialists, AV technicians, system administrators	Hardware setup, maintenance, troubleshooting, networking, technical support
Level 2: Professional	XR General User	80-100 hours	Domain professionals across sectors	XR applications in professional practice, content evaluation, collaboration
Level 2: Professional	XR Developer	120-150 hours	Software developers, 3D artists, content creators	XR development fundamentals, interaction design, performance optimisation
Level 2: Professional	XR Educator	100-120 hours	Teachers, instructional designers, trainers	XR pedagogy, learning experience design, classroom management, assessment
Level 2: Professional	XR Researcher	100-120 hours	Academic and industry researchers	Research methodology, measurement, data analysis, ethical research practice
Level 3: Expert	Capstone / Thesis	200-300 hours	Experienced professionals	Advanced project demonstrating innovation, leadership, and field contribution

6.4 The Foundation Level: Universal XR Literacy for Education

The Foundation Level outlines the common vocabulary, principles, and safety measures that all the participants in the XR educational environment cannot do without, regardless of which role they are assigned to perform. Organised into four carefully edited modules, it is a scaffolding structure of XR competency.

FND-01: Introduction to XR is familiarizing itself with the general concepts of VR, AR, and MR; tracing the historical path and the milestones of evolution of XR technologies, emphasizing key applications in industrial fields, especially in education, and explaining the supportive role of XR in the strategy of the overall digital revolution. After studying this module, students will be able to identify the differences between the XR modalities, outline the application of the latter in the right situation, and formulate both the value proposition and limitations of immersive technologies.

XR Hardware and Software: FND-02 covers the landscape of XR devices, such as tethered, standalone, and mobile headsets; defines inputs to devices, like controllers, hand tracking, eye tracking; and traverses platform ecosystems, such as Meta Horizon, SteamVR, and Apple Vision Pro. The participants in such a way will be able to gain the ability to analyze device features, make a reasonable choice of technology stacks depending on the goals of a particular educational process, and perform basic setup and safety configuration.

FND-03: Health, Safety, and Ethics explores factors that influence or considerably affect comfort (frame rate, latency, locomotion), considerations that touch on physical safety (guardian systems, play-space design), privacy consideration (biometric and telemetry data) of immersive content, and necessary accessibility characteristics. This course is a requirement to train all IXRDL-certified individuals on how to recognize and address risks, elaborates on data stewardship in XR settings, and integrates ethical and non-discriminatory actions into their implementation of immersive technologies.

Basic XR Interaction FND-04 focuses on the practical command of gaze-based selection, controller operation, hand-gesture interaction, spatial audio navigation, and common place user errors and the system recovery strategies. Students will be able to exhibit their knowledge of the fundamental XR interactions and capabilities to relay careful safe-use instructions to the novice.

The Foundation Level is especially pivotal in driving educational change, as it would ensure that administrators, support staff, parents, teachers, and students alike would gain an interconnected understanding of XR technologies, their abilities and shortcomings, as well as safety and ethical requirements, which are implemented when using them responsibly.

6.5 The Educator Track: Immersive Learning Design Specialists

The Educator Track is the best directly relevant part of IXRDL as it relates to educational transformation. It provides instructors, instructional designers, trainers and curriculum developers with the specific competencies needed to deploy XR based learning programs in a safe, effective, and scalable manner. The track consists of five modules:

EDU-01: What is XR in Education? is this will begins to lay the pedagogical need for XR integration such as constructivism, cognitive load theory, and experiential learning. Educators learn to align XR activities with measurable learning outcomes, as well as to justify XR integration decisions through evidence-based reasoning. Assessment is the development of the lesson blueprint including outcome mapping.

EDU-02: Creating XR Learning Experiences covers scenario design, scaffolding and feedback mechanisms, accessibility by design, inclusive practices and universal learning design principles. Educators create a prototype immersive learning experience using engaging, accessible, and measured needs (examples) Biology - Titian's first death and Painted Lady Form - originally against a dark backdrop with gray fill.

Chengdu - 2017. Participants assisted in creating and/or evaluating the prototype for accessibility based on the rubric.

EDU-03: XR Classroom Management deals with the troubles of making XR enhanced learning spaces work, including classroom and device management, student safety protocols, troubleshooting measures, ways of supporting a variety of learners, and the ethical norms of shared living spaces. A classroom run-book and a facilitated session that exhibits competence in the operation of XR as a classroom are forms of assessment.

EDU-04: XR Assessment and Evaluation builds competencies around performance-based assessment design, angle rubric creation for immersive tasks, interpretive learning analytics, privacy-respecting data use and impact evaluation. Educators create an assessment pack and analytics reflection showing their capability of being able to measure learning reliably in XR environments.

EDU-05: Curriculum Development for XR is focused on scope and sequence planning, content curation, cross-curricular integration, alignment with accreditation and quality standards, and program level quality assurance. The capstone assessment requires educators to present a detailed curriculum plan including an implementation roadmap which will demonstrate their capability to plan properly for sustainable, standards-aligned XR programs that can scale beyond first pilots.

Graduates of the Educator Track receive the IXRDL Educator Certificate, with specializations, with persons choosing Educator having the option of choosing between K to 12, Higher Education, Corporate Learning and Development, and Healthcare Education. This credential gives institutions a reliable marker on educator readiness to integrate XR, and to individual educators, the credential gives them a portable and internationally recognized credential that can add to their professional mobility and opportunity.

6.6 Supporting Tracks: Technician, Developer, General User, and Researcher

While the Educator Track is a key driver of the larger goal of educational transformation, the IXRDL counterparts are supportive in all ways and together create an ecosystem that will help to sustain the integration of XR into academic environments.

The Technician Track consists of five modules and takes 100-120 hours of instruction, making the technician, who will conduct the deployment of XR infrastructure and maintenance of these systems in learning settings. In the absence of efficient technicians, even the closest XR programs often fail to perform due to hardware misconfigurations, network insufficiency or unsolvable technical snags. This track deals systematically with hardware configuration, preventive maintenance, fault diagnosis and rectification, networking integration, as well as provision of technical support and customer service.

The Developer Track which is six modules with a length of 120-150 of learning hours, forms the content-making pipeline around which educational XR is constructed. Preparation: Graduates of this track have vendor agnostic competencies that deal with XR development basics, platform specific competencies (Core subject: Unity, elective: Unreal), complex interaction design, performance optimization and E2E application deployment. The learned immersive experiences become the building block in which teachers give instruction and students learn in a meaningful way.

The General User Track includes five modules with a total of 80-100 hours, allowing professionals working in the fields of healthcare, architecture, retail, manufacturing, and education to gain a productive use of XR technologies in their current line of work. In the educative industry, this follow-up becomes especially relevant when it comes to subject-matter professionals involved in the development of XR content and school administrators involved in the management of XR programs.

Lastly, the Researcher Track, offered in the form of five modules (involving 100-120 hours of instruction), provides academics and practitioners with the rigor of conducting research to develop, implement, and publish research of high quality XR. This track is essential to build the evidence base to inform policy and practice in educational XR; thereby filling the gap that currently exists in the literature in terms of longitudinal studies using methodologically robust approaches that look at the impact of XR on learning outcomes.

6.7 Assessment, Certification, and Quality Assurance

The credibility and value of IXRDL credentials is based on a stringent, transparent and globally uniform assessment and certification framework. IXRDL involves the use of a multi-modal assessment model aimed to make sure that certification embodies true competence:

The theory Assessment is achieved using the computer-based testing, which has integrated a variety of item types, such as multiple-choice, true/false, matching, and scenario-based questions. To ensure fairness, reliability and validity, item banks have been curated by the subject-matter experts and psychometrically analyzed to assess their validity. The advanced levels use adaptive tests to improve accuracy and minimize seat time and cut scores are established using modified Ang off method and re-standardized after some period of time.

Figure 14. IXRDL Multi-Modal Assessment Architecture: Three-tier evaluation system combining computer-based theory testing, practical performance assessment, and expert portfolio review.

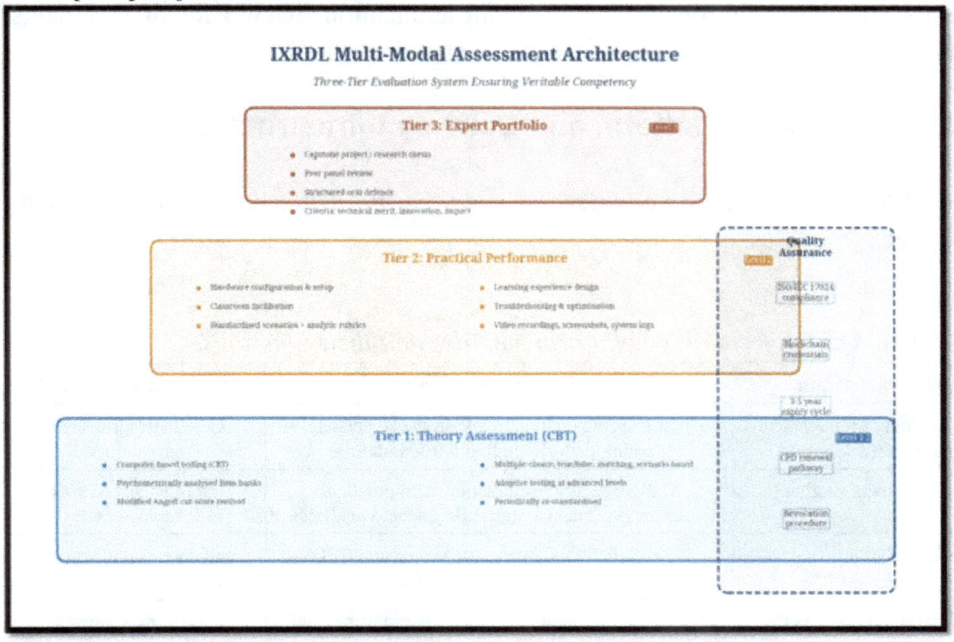

Practice Assessment refers to the implementation of real performance activities. The applicants should show their skills in hardware configuration, setup, experience in learning design, classroom guidance, troubleshooting and optimization of application. To give comparative results across sites of assessment, standardized situations are used and analytic rubrics that are calibrated on inter-rater reliability are used to assure consistency in scoring. Competence information is captured using video recordings, screen shots, system logs and artefacts of the candidate.

Expert Level- Portfolio Assessment In the Expert Level, capstone projects or research contributions were to be submitted. These are appraised using peer panels criteria of technical merit, innovation, impact, and documentation, with one of them resulting in a structured oral defense.

The certification system is based on blockchain-based digital credentials that have unique identifiers that can be queried through a verification registry accessible to the public. Credentials expire after a period of three to five years, and may be renewed through continuing professional development activities or re-assessment. An elaborate revocation protocol exists to deal with incidents of fraud, misconduct or demonstrable incompetence.

The quality assurance framework is designed to follow ISO / IEC 17024 standards and includes governance mechanisms, psychometric procedures, surveillance strategies and continuous improvement strategies. Accreditation of training centers is done through a rigorous process involving application review, audit of documents, inspection on site, and ongoing reassessment.

6.8 Technology Platform and Delivery Infrastructure

IXRDL is backed by a cloud native and security first technology platform with four core modules:

Table 7. IXRDL technology platform modules and their functions.

Platform Module	Primary Purpose	Key Users
Learning Management System (LMS)	Deliver learning content, track progress, personalise learning paths including XR simulations	Candidates, learners, instructors
Assessment Engine	Deliver secure examinations and practical assessments; manage item lifecycle and analytics	Candidates, proctors, assessors
Certification Management	Issue credentials, manage renewals and CPD, support audit-logged revocation and appeals	Candidates, administrators
Training Centre Portal	Manage accreditation, scheduling, reporting, and financial reconciliation for authorised centres	Training centres, institutions, administrators

The platform is designed to enable extensibility at the API level to support the ability to integrate with an institutional learning management system, human resource information system and national qualification frameworks. Such interoperability ensures that IXRDL can be easily plugged into an existing institutional infrastructure without requiring a parallel infrastructure.

6.9 Implementation Strategy: The 18-Month Rollout

The IXRDL implementation plan is defined as a gradual 18-month rollout plan aimed at offering tradeoffs between speed of deployment and the accreditation-level quality:

Phase 1: Foundation and Development (Months 1- 6).

This stage will take place in finalizing the candidates shall include the curricula at the Foundation Level, along with the first three professional tracks (Technician, Developer, Educator); developing comprehensive assessment materials, such as item banks, realistic scenarios, scoring schemes and rubrics, as well as cut-score protocols.;, delivering a minimum viable product platform, including the LMS, Assessment Engine and Certification Module; setting up subject-matter-expert panels per track; beginning with ISO/IEC 17024 accreditation; and founding the legal entity including intellectual-property rights.

Phase 2: Pilot and Refinement (Months 7 -12).

Pilots will be trained in three to five countries (such as the USA, UK, UAE, Singapore, and India) and there will be 10-15 accredited pilot centers giving certification to a minimum of 500 pupils under the Foundation and the first Professional tracks. Psychometric analysis, item analysis, equating, and cut -score review driving iteratively refinement of curriculum, items and platform user experience. Other tracks (General User, Researcher) and Expert framework are completed. The pool of assessors is generated and pre-tested on performance assessments.

Phase 3: Commercial Launch and Scale (Months 13-18).

Complete ISO/IEC 17024 accreditation is attained. The commercial operations are introduced with demands-generating campaigns to educational institutions, corporate training organizations and government agencies. At least 50 centers worldwide are trained and certified, and the general verification list is made open. They also form strategic alliances with the vendors of XR hardware and software, educational associations, and other international organizations. The equivalent 2,500 or above certifications that have been issued serve as a hand-waving indicator of acceptance by the market and offer employer outcome data to drive additional adoption.

Post-Launch Growth (Month 19+).

The ongoing geographic expansion is the verticalization of credentials toward specific areas to healthcare XR (Industrial XR, Educational XR). Recent technology adoption into the curriculum is based on emerging technologies such as AI, haptic elements, brain computer interfaces, and changing safety standards. The international advisory board has been put in place and the train-the-trainer certifications are being ramped up to sustain the high growth.

The success metrics for IXRDL implementation are ambitious but achievable:

Table 8. IXRDL implementation success metrics and targets.

Metric	Year 2 Target	Year 5 Target
Total certifications issued	5,000+	25,000+
Accredited centres globally	100+	500+
Annual recurring revenue	—	USD 14M
Candidate satisfaction	90%+	90%+
Employer satisfaction	85%+	85%+
Renewal/recertification rate	80%+	80%+

Figure 15. The 18-month IXRDL implementation timeline: phased rollout from foundation development through commercial launch and scaling.

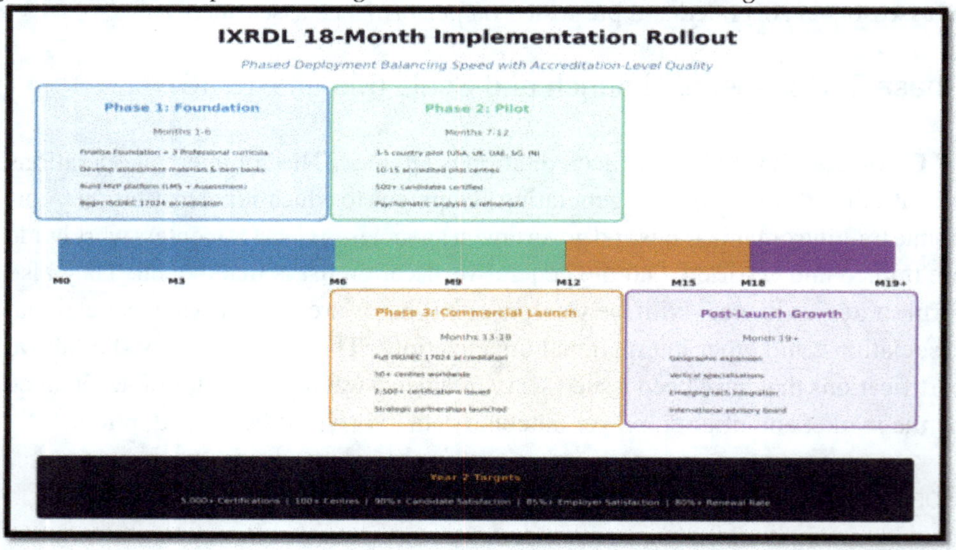

7. ANTICIPATED IMPACT AND FUTURE DIRECTIONS

7.1 Impact on Learners, Educators, and Institutions

It is expected that the systematic adoption of IXRDL as the model of XR-enhanced education would yield quantifiable value among all the stakeholder groups. To the personal learner, IXRDL-approved educational programs provide learning tailored to the individual experience, as well as engaging and comprehensive learning that can enhance retention of knowledge, spatial and procedural skills, and equip students with skills pertinent in an increasingly immersion-based workforce. The portability and cross regionalism of IXRDL qualifications guarantees learners with marketable proofs of XR technical expertise that improves their cross cultural and cross-sector advancement in markets.

As a teacher, IXRDL offers systematic career growth options facilitating credibility and professionalism in immersive teaching. The five-level career development of Educator Track along with the progression of XR literacy through the curriculum design will help a teacher to expand his or her abilities step-by-step, backed up by the community of certified professionals and the constantly renewed resource base and best practices. The qualification itself adds to the occupational status and career portability of educators, providing meaningful appreciation of a skilled and highly concentrated skillset.

Within the context of educational institutions, the IXRDL framework proposes an implementation architecture with quality assurances through XR integration, which is detrimental to both adoption risk and its related costs. This approach is an effective way to supersede the institutional sovereignty in the development of such components, providing standardization of curricula, a validated system of assessment instruments, an accredited training path and a technological platform for delivery and administration of such components. which contributes to the institutional accreditation procedures, and, therefore, the reputation.

7.2 Impact on Global Education Equity

The ability of the IXRDL framework to advance the process of global education equity is, perhaps, the most notable implication of this framework. IXRDL mediates international knowledge transfer and international capacity building by having a common standard of XR competency in education. Those institutions based in the developing countries are therefore made gain entry to the same curricula, assessment criteria and certification routes as those of similar associations in the more affluent countries without regard to the values of the frameworks of regional flexibility, multilingual provision and culturally perceptive content.

The stackable nature of the framework is specifically adaptable to situations where resources are limited. Foundation Level can be the starting point of the institutions thus developing fundamental XR literacy in staff and students, and additional Professional-level paths can be pursued once it reaches capacity and resources can be offered. The conceivable future of digital delivery of educational material and evaluation, along with the decreasing prices of XR equipment, makes such development more possible, even in the setting of a restricted budget.

In crisis-ridden areas, teachers with IXRDL certification are able to implement XR-based learning continuity solutions quickly and efficiently, with the help of standardized curricula and existing libraries of content. The focus of the framework on offline capable delivery and low bandwidth operation ensures that immersive education is not lost despite its operation in an environment full of poor infrastructure.

7.3 Future Directions: AI, Haptics, BCI, and Beyond

The sphere of XR education is changing quickly, being technologically shifting, which will continue to extend the opportunities of immersive learning. There are some new trends that are especially relevant to the future of XR in education.

AI-Native XR Environments

Integration between big language models and the generative AI into XR systems could get us to the realm of smart virtual tutors, learning control machines that react to the behavior of students, and AI-generated experiences that may essentially be tailored to a particular curriculum. To this end, the curriculum revision cycle of IXRDL, which is reviewed annually disciplining both the technological and business advancements, sees to it that the certification standards are updated with the same pace.

Multisensory and Haptic Technologies

The development of haptic feedback, such as gloves, vests, full-body suits, offering the ability to feel something, enhances the experience of an XR. The students will be able to touch the texture of geological samples, the resistance of surgical tools, or the vibration of industrial equipment and make the embodied learning experience deeper than the visual or auditory immersion.

Brain-Computer Interfaces (BCI)

New types of BCI technology can provide a form of direct neural interface with XR systems, potentially enabling learners to manipulate virtual objects using their mind, give them feedback adjusted to their neural state, and experience a higher degree of immersion and engagement than is possible with existing types of input. These technologies are still in their infancy but their educational potential is immense and should be studied intensely.

6G Connectivity

It is expected that 6G networks with their ultra-low latency and immense bandwidth potential will allow multi-user XR experiences to be seamlessly and globally done in their full-fidelity. With this interconnectedness, collaborative global learning will become as normal and stable as a phone call, and the opportunities of collaboration in education will change the possibilities of cooperation in education on an international level fundamentally.

8. CONCLUSION

The data provided in this chapter shows that Extended Reality and Artificial Intelligence are not only distinguishing technologies in the realm of education but disruptive technologies that can radically change the knowledge delivery, experience, and assessment models on all levels of education and geography. Empirical evidence (meta-analyses, controlled trials, large-scale pilot projects) and consistent indicates that XR-driven instruction is associated with better student engagement rates, knowledge retention, space and procedural skills acquisition, and individualized learning of the kind which cannot be reached using conventional methods.

Such an urgent need to change is highlighted by the pollution of traditional remote learning during the COVID-19 pandemic and continuing educational crises due to armed conflicts and natural disasters. In that case, XR is not only a superior but a qualitatively new form of, the one that will result into the resurgence of the presence, embodiment and social interaction that are essential to make learning effective.

Technology alone is not sufficient to make this potential come true though. It is a systematic curriculum reform, assessment of the teacher preparation, institution manual on the manner of adopting and above all an international typical framework which will implement XR with the same quality, morale and cross-country transportability. The International XR Driving License (IXRDL) is exactly such a scheme. Drawing its design on the internationally tested ICDL architecture, as per the ISO/IEC17024 standards of accreditation, and with five professional tracks and roles, IXRDL offers educational institutions with a realistic, scalable and quality assured integration of the inclusion of XR competence into the system.

The four-phase institutional adoption model in this chapter along with the 18 month implementation plan of IXRDL is a feasible roadmap to education institutions in the entire world. The way is evident, systematic, and attainable among the first step of evaluation and vision-setting up to development of infrastructure, pilot test run, and institutionalisation of the full proportion.

The stakes are significant. The worldwide XR market will exceed US 1 trillion in 2030 and the education segment is projected to expand at a compound annual rate of more than 25 percent. Schools and colleges that strategically invest in XR integration following systematic frameworks like IXRDL will be in a better position to provide students with higher quality educational outcomes, draw and maintain students and faculty, and create a more efficient, sustainable, and inclusive education system around the world. The ones that hold on are in danger of being the ones left behind on a transformation that is no more hypothetical than it is an imminent occurrence.

The future of schooling is virtual. Whether the transformation will happen remains to be answered but it would be based on standards that are rigorous, principles of ethics, and the fairness of access or left at the whims of the market forces and ad hoc adoption. IXRDL is focused on making sure that the former, whereby the standardized internationally-recognized infrastructure is offered that the revolution of immersive education needs.

REFERENCES

AASA. (2024). The Post-Pandemic's Digital. *LEARNing Landscapes*.

AASA (2024). Immersive Technologies: Shaping the Next Generation of Teaching and Learning.

AAA Accreditation (2024). The Impact of ISO/IEC 17024 Accreditation on Personnel Certification Bodies.

Al-Fararjeh, T., & Almomani, A. (2026). *International XR Driving License (IXRDL)*. Recommended Certification Scheme for Extended Reality Technologies. Beyond & Universe LLC.

ANSI (2024). Why ISO/IEC 17024 is Critical for the Development of Credentialing.

Asif, M., Mondal, A., & Soumil, S. (2024). Augmented reality and virtual reality in education: A transformative journey. In *Advances in Computational Solutions*. Swami Vivekananda University.

XR Association (2024). XR Industry Workforce Development Survey.

Barbu, M., Iordache, D. D., Petre, I., Barbu, D.-C., & Băjenaru, L. (2025). Framework design for reinforcing the potential of XR technologies in transforming inclusive education. *Applied Sciences (Basel, Switzerland)*, *15*(3), 1484. DOI: 10.3390/app15031484

Batra, K., Zhang, Z., Yang, S., ... (2025). XRXL: A system for immersive visualization in large lectures. In 2025 IEEE Conference Virtual Reality and 3D User Interfaces (VR) (pp. 370-380). IEEE. DOI: 10.1109/VR59515.2025.00061

Beyond Universe XR AI Solutions (n.d.). Metaversity Labs and Immersive Virtual Classrooms (company profile and official service pages). Beyond Universe XR Solutions (accessed 8 March 2026).

Brookings Institution (2024). Rewiring the classroom: How the COVID-19 pandemic transformed K-12 education.

Caroline, C. C. et al. (2025). Enhancing Digital Literacy Through International Computer Driving License (ICDL) Training. International Journal of Education and Development using ICT.

EDUCAUSE. (2024). *Navigating the XR Educational Landscape: Privacy*. Safety, and Ethical Guidelines — Strategic Recommendations.

Egliston, B., Carter, M., & Clark, K. E. (2025). *Value and Virtue in the Extended Reality (XR) Industry. Information, Communication & Society*. Taylor & Francis.

Farran, I., & Nunez, I. (2025). *Converging Pathways: New Approaches to Integrate Vocational Education Training and Higher Education. Journal of Vocational Education & Training*. Taylor & Francis.

Global Disaster Preparedness Center / IFRC (2020). Immersive Technologies & Digital Games for School Disaster Preparedness.

GoStudent (2025). 30+ Virtual Reality in Education Statistics: Revolutionising Learning.

Grand View Research (2024). Extended Reality Market Size, Share & Growth Report, 2030.

Hmoud, M., Swaity, H., Karram, O., Shibli, H., Swaity, S., & Daher, W. (2023). High school students' engagement in biology in the context of XR technology. *IEEE Access : Practical Innovations, Open Solutions*, *11*, 137053–137066. DOI: 10.1109/ACCESS.2023.3338176

Hossain, S. (2025). Using Artificial Intelligence to Improve Classroom Learning Experience. arXiv preprint arXiv:2503.05709.

Hossain, S. (2026). Extended Reality (XR): The Next Frontier in Education. arXiv preprint arXiv:2602.23601v1.

Hossain, S., Sommer, N., & Adib, N. (2025). Exploring the Integration of Extended Reality and Artificial Intelligence (AI) for Remote STEM Education and Assessment. arXiv preprint arXiv:2509.03812.

ICDL Foundation (2023). ICDL Celebrates 17 Million Candidates Worldwide.

ISO (2012). ISO/IEC 17024:2012 — Conformity Assessment — General Requirements for Bodies Operating Certification of Persons.

Kolb, D. A. (1984). *Experiential Learning: Experience as the Source of Learning and Development*. Prentice-Hall.

Kumar, A. (2025). *Effectiveness of augmented reality and virtual reality interventions on learning outcomes: A meta-analysis in higher education. TechTrends*. Springer.

Li, G., Luo, H., Chen, D., Wang, P., Yin, X., & Zhang, J. (2025). Augmented Reality in Higher Education: A Systematic Review. *Education Sciences*, *15*(6), 678. DOI: 10.3390/educsci15060678

Maidenbaum, S., Buchs, G., Abboud, S., Lavi-Rotbain, O., & Amedi, A. (2016). Perception of graphical virtual environments by blind users via sensory substitution. *PLoS One*, *11*(2), e0147501. DOI: 10.1371/journal.pone.0147501 PMID: 26882473

Mak, S. L., Tang, F. W. F., & Li, C. H.. (2020). A Review on Development and Application of Virtual Reality (VR) Training Platform. *International Journal of Information and Education Technology (IJIET)*, *10*(1).

Makransky, G., & Petersen, G. B. (2021). The Cognitive Affective Model of Immersive Learning (CAMIL). *Educational Psychology Review*, *33*(3), 937–958. DOI: 10.1007/s10648-020-09586-2

Malik, A., Khatoon, M., & Siddique, S. (2024). *Disruptive technologies in education: Transforming traditional curriculum models for the 21st century*. Research Corridor.

Markopoulos, E., & Nordholm, A. D.. (2022). *A Certification Framework for Virtual Reality and Metaverse Training Scenarios in the Maritime and Shipping Industry*. UCL Discovery. DOI: 10.54941/ahfe1001505

Meccawy, M. (2023). Teachers' prospective attitudes towards the adoption of extended reality technologies in the classroom: Interests and concerns. *Smart Learning Environments*, *10*(1), 36. DOI: 10.1186/s40561-023-00256-8

Meccawy, M. (2023). Teachers' prospective attitudes towards the adoption of extended reality technologies in the classroom. *Smart Learning Environments*, *10*(1), 36. DOI: 10.1186/s40561-023-00256-8

Milgram, P., & Kishino, F. (1994). A taxonomy of mixed reality visual displays. *IEICE Transactions on Information and Systems*, *E77-D*(12), 1321–1329.

Mordor Intelligence (2026). Virtual Reality in Education Market Size & Share, 2031.

Naik, M., Barbosa, R., & Swartsel, A. (2023). Immersive Learning & XR Technology Skills and Careers. Jobs for the Future. ERIC Document ED630059.

OXREF. (2025). *Open XR for Education Framework*. ERIC.

Oztank, F. (2025). *Towards Extended Reality in Emergency Response. Computer Animation and Virtual Worlds*. Wiley.

Piaget, J. (1972). *The Psychology of the Child*. Basic Books.

Pitsikalis, S., & Lasica, I.-E. (2025). Integrating Extended Reality and Artificial Intelligence in Education. In *Metaverse, MetaIntelligence and Infinite Worlds with AI*. IntechOpen.

Prasetya, F. (2024). *The impact of augmented reality learning experiences on the motivational design model.* ScienceDirect.

Precedence Research (2026). AI in Education Market Size to Surpass USD 136.79 Billion by 2035.

Stott, A., & Neustadter, C. (2013). *Analysis of gamification in education.* Simon Fraser University.

Sweller, J. (1988). Cognitive load during problem solving: Effects on learning. *Cognitive Science*, *12*(2), 257–285. DOI: 10.1207/s15516709cog1202_4

Szyjewski, G. (2023). Implementation of a Hybrid Certificate Approach: Enhancing Efficiency and Credibility in the ICDL Certification Process. *Procedia Computer Science*, *225*, 535–544. DOI: 10.1016/j.procs.2023.10.470

Tene, T. (2026). *Artificial intelligence, extended reality, and emerging AI-XR synergies in medical education.* PMC.

UNESCO (2020). Education: From disruption to recovery. UNESCO COVID-19 Educational Disruption and Response.

UNICEF (2024). Education Under Attack.

Unity Technologies (2024). Unity Certified XR Specialist Certification.

US Department of Education (2026). The Four Stages of AI Integration in Education.

VR Vision Group (2025). AI + XR = The Intelligent Training Era.

Wang, D., & Huang, X. (2025). *Transforming education through artificial intelligence and immersive technologies: Enhancing learning experiences. Interactive Learning Environments.* Taylor & Francis.

World Bank. (2024). Learning Continuity During Crises [Lessons.]. *COVID*, •••, 19.

Yale School of Medicine. (2026). From Ideathon to Pilots: Updates on AI and XR. *Medical Education.*

Zikas, P., Bachlitzanakis, V., Papaefthymiou, M., ... (2016). Mixed reality serious games and gamification for smart education. In European Conference on Games Based Learning (p. 805). Academic Conferences International Limited.

Chapter 6
Swarm Intelligence for Resilient Cybersecurity in Immersive Multi-User Metaverses

Mohammad Alauthman
http://orcid.org/0000-0003-0319-1968
Department of Information Security, University of Petra, Amman, Jordan

Amjad Aldweesh
http://orcid.org/0000-0001-9358-1323
College of Computing and Information Technology, Shaqra University, Saudi Arabia

Ahmad Al-Qerem
http://orcid.org/0000-0003-2187-6194
Computer Science Department, Faculty of Information Technology, Zarqa University, Jordan

Ala Hamarsheh
http://orcid.org/0000-0002-4736-7331
Computer Science, Faculty of Information Technology, Arab American University, Jenin, Palestine

Thair Al Fararjeh
http://orcid.org/0009-0001-8963-9761
Beyond & Universe LLC, USA

Omar Almomani
http://orcid.org/0000-0003-3160-6542
Al-Ahliyya Amman University, Jordan

ABSTRACT

Immersive multi-user metaverses combine persistent identity, real-time interaction, virtual assets, and digital-physical linkages, which creates a cybersecurity problem that extends beyond isolated authentication or perimeter controls. This chapter examines how swarm intelligence can support resilient cybersecurity in these environments through distributed sensing, cooperative risk analysis, graded containment, recovery orchestration, and policy-aware federation. To this end, it

DOI: 10.4018/979-8-3373-7882-4.ch006

introduces the Swarm-Intelligence for Resilient Metaverse Cybersecurity (SIRMC) framework as a layered reference architecture spanning avatars, spaces, services, assets, and cybersecurity digital twins under zero-trust principles. In addition, the chapter synthesizes current literature, defines a metaverse-specific threat model, outlines resilience requirements, and provides figures, tables, scenarios, and an implementation blueprint. Overall, the chapter positions resilient metaverse defense as a coordinated capability grounded in local intelligence, twin-assisted foresight, and privacy-aware governance.

INTRODUCTION

Immersive multi-user metaverses are moving from experimental virtual environments to operational socio-technical systems in which work, learning, healthcare, entertainment, and commerce are mediated through persistent avatars, synchronized assets, and continuous behavioral data. As a result, the metaverse is better understood as a convergence of extended reality (XR), artificial intelligence (AI), blockchain, edge and cloud computing, Internet of Things (IoT), and digital twin (DT) capabilities rather than as a stand-alone virtual reality application (Wang et al., 2023; Ali et al., 2024; Venugopal et al., 2025). However, the same properties that make these environments attractive—including persistence, interoperability, embodiment, and real-time co-presence—also expand the attack surface across technical, social, and economic layers.

A major challenge is that resilient cybersecurity in immersive systems cannot rely on monolithic, perimeter-focused, or purely human-operated defense models. Metaverse environments are composed of heterogeneous devices, rendering pipelines, identity services, asset ledgers, application logic, social channels, and digital-physical interfaces distributed across multiple trust domains. Under these conditions, centralized security operations may not respond with sufficient speed or context. This chapter therefore treats swarm intelligence (SI) as a powerful design principle for metaverse defense. SI emphasizes local sensing, bounded communication, and distributed decision-making that can scale across volatile environments.

Recent studies have examined authentication, privacy, visualization security, blockchain-enabled trust, and AI-assisted detection in the metaverse (Pooyandeh et al., 2022; Chow et al., 2023; Huang et al., 2023). In parallel, newer work has explored zero-trust security, continuous identity verification, avatar traceability, and federated analytics for privacy-sensitive settings (Cheng et al., 2024; Chen et al., 2023; Yang et al., 2023; Han et al., 2025; Liang et al., 2025). These contributions are important, yet they are often implemented as separate control functions.

A remaining gap is the lack of an architectural model that can coordinate identity, space, asset, service, and digital-twin protection as one adaptive defensive process.

This gap becomes clearer when the attack path is viewed across layers. An attacker may first compromise a headset, device token, or session credential in order to impersonate an avatar (step 1). The same attacker may then exploit proximity-based trust to manipulate social interactions, collect sensitive behavioral data, or request access to protected assets (step 2). In a connected platform, the activity can later move toward linked wallets, creator tools, synchronization services, or digital-twin dashboards (step 3). Once persistence and virtual economies are involved, the impact may outlast the initial intrusion through fraudulent transfers, corrupted simulations, unsafe recommendations, or reputational damage (step 4). For this reason, metaverse security needs to address not only prevention, but also containment, recovery, and adaptation.

The chapter is organized around five design properties that recur throughout the discussion. First, metaverse security needs to be holistic so that devices, identities, spaces, assets, services, and users are assessed within one analytical frame. Second, it needs to be adaptive because risk changes with room sensitivity, crowd behavior, and transaction context. Third, it needs to be federated so that platforms can exchange meaningful signals without raw-data centralization. Fourth, it needs to be zero-trust so that identities, objects, services, and agent messages remain continuously verified. Fifth, it needs to be swarm-enabled so that many specialized defensive agents can operate on partial information while still contributing to a coherent security posture. Figure 1 translates these properties into the layered SIRMC reference architecture introduced later in the chapter.

The main contributions of this chapter are fourfold: It first provides a synthesized problem framing that connects metaverse-specific cybersecurity issues with swarm intelligence and resilience engineering. It then introduces the Swarm-Intelligence for Resilient Metaverse Cybersecurity (SIRMC) framework as a reference architecture for distributed sensing, cooperative detection, containment, recovery, and governance. In addition, it explains how specialized cyber swarms can respond to impersonation, misinformation, lateral movement, and digital-twin abuse. Finally, it presents an implementation and evaluation blueprint, supported by figures and tables, for researchers and practitioners designing security services for immersive ecosystems.

The remainder of the chapter is organized as follows. First, the background section reviews metaverse security, identity, swarm-defense, and digital-twin research and identifies the remaining architectural gap. Next, the chapter defines the threat model and the resilience requirements that guide design. It then presents the SIRMC framework, its layers, its agent classes, and its information flows. After that, the operational mechanisms for sensing, risk formation, containment, recovery, and governance are discussed. The final sections provide illustrative scenarios, future research directions, key terms, and concluding remarks.

BACKGROUND

Metaverse Security, Privacy, and Identity Research

The metaverse security literature is growing at an exceptionally fast pace, and this rapid development is itself instructive. Wang et al. (2023) conducted a survey of the fundamentals of the metaverse and demonstrated that immersive realism, interoperability, and persistent interaction create a security and privacy environment that cannot be reduced to a single enabling technology. Ali et al. (2024) expanded this system view to include communication, networking, security and application layers, whereas Venugopal et al. (2025) discussed how AI is becoming a growing mediator between perception, generation, reasoning and governance in immersive systems. Collectively, these investigations make the metaverse a compound distributed infrastructure. Nevertheless, they do not go further to clarify the way defensive intelligence is to be coordinated in case the environment is persistent, cross-domain, and massively concurrent.

The direct cybersecurity survey gives a narrower perspective of the problem space. Pooyandeh et al. (2022) have highlighted the importance of user identification, biometric protection and AI-supported anomaly detection in AI-based metaverse environments. The emphasis on visualization and display-channel threats, as emphasized by Chow et al. (2023), is significant as there might be a possibility of introducing immersive harm with the help of rendered objects and misleading cues, not only by means of backend compromise. Huang et al. (2023) and Laiz-Ibanez et al. (2025) generalized privacy, identity, platform, IoT, and surveillance risks throughout the metaverse stack. These publications chart the threat terrain very accurately. Nevertheless, the defensive response remains generally offered as a list of controls instead of a coordinated process, capable of evolving in response to changing interactions, proximities and dependencies.

The focus on identity continues to be a key focus since the continuity of the avatars is the operational point of the metaverse. Cheng et al. (2024) outlined a zero-trust agenda of social virtual reality whereby continuous verification is favored over one-time admission. Yang et al. (2023) suggested an avatar traceability authentication system, Liang et al. (2025) analyzed traceable authentication and Han et al. (2025) developed continuous authentication of identities in the metaverse. These contributions enhance admission control, traceability and session assurance. However, immersive space resilient security also requires observation of interactions of avatars, room context, visual manipulation, asset flows, and cross-service correlations beyond the credential boundary.

Taken together, the preceding literature leads to a consistent set of observations. Multi-layer risk surface is characterized by metaverse surveys, direct security studies ensures greater power to visualization-aware analysis and privacy-aware analysis, identity research enhances continuity and traceability, and distributed defense research demonstrates that collaborative protection is technically possible. The lack of techniques is not the remaining gap; rather, the lack of an operational architecture that connects these techniques into a single resilience loop for immersive multi-user environments is the critical shortfall.

Distributed Intelligence, Swarms, and Digital Twins

A related line of work concerns distributed intelligence, especially federated coordination, adaptive analytics, and autonomous cyber response. Chen et al. (2023) discussed federated learning in the metaverse as a way to balance analytics with privacy-sensitive data. Venugopal et al. (2025) showed that AI-enabled metaverse services are moving toward anticipatory and self-evolving behavior, which is relevant because security functions are likely to follow the same direction. In adjacent cyber-defense settings, Loevenich et al. (2025) demonstrated that autonomous agents can combine deep reinforcement learning, knowledge graphs, and large language model support, while Torres et al. (2026) presented a hierarchical multi-agent architecture for coordinated defense. These studies suggest that metaverse protection can become context-aware and adaptive. However, local learning alone does not solve the problem of cross-room correlation, negotiation of confidence, or distributed containment.

Swarm intelligence and multi-agent defense provide a particularly useful conceptual bridge. Brambilla et al. (2013) described decentralization, local rules, robustness, and scalability as defining properties of swarm systems. Bougueroua et al. (2021) reviewed collaborative intrusion detection based on multi-agent systems, and Nasir et al. (2022) showed that swarm-intelligence methods have been repeatedly used to improve distributed detection and adaptation. More recent autonomous defense work by Loevenich et al. (2025) and Torres et al. (2026) further indicates that specialized agents can operate under shared coordination mechanisms. Even so, most of this literature focuses on computer networks, cyber-physical systems, or sector-specific infrastructures rather than on avatar-centered and perception-sensitive immersive worlds.

Digital twin research adds an enabling operational perspective. Gu et al. (2026) surveyed digital twin technology for real-time monitoring and adaptive management, while Achuthan et al. (2025) examined cybersecurity applications of digital twins with emphasis on anomaly analysis, interoperability, and resilience. Repetto

(2026) moved closer to the present chapter by introducing cybersecurity digital twins for multi-ownership service chains, arguing that fragmented cyber operations become ineffective when attacks propagate across administrative boundaries. These contributions are highly relevant because metaverses increasingly include mirrored spaces, virtual assets, and links to physical processes. At the same time, current digital twin research usually assumes enterprise or sectoral operating contexts and pays less attention to volatile human behavior, adversarial embodiment, and cross-platform mobility.

Overall, the literature is substantial, but the synthesis remains incomplete. Existing metaverse surveys identify threats with precision, authentication studies improve identity assurance, distributed intelligence research expands adaptive analytics, swarm-defense studies demonstrate collaborative protection, and digital-twin research introduces predictive operational models. What is still missing is an architectural approach that intentionally combines these elements for immersive multi-user systems. This chapter addresses that gap by framing metaverse cybersecurity as a coordinated ecology of defensive agents operating across device, avatar, space, service, and twin layers under zero-trust governance.

THREAT MODEL AND RESILIENCE REQUIREMENTS

Threat Surface and Adversary Classes

Before introducing an architecture, the threat model needs to be defined because immersive metaverses combine assets that are usually treated separately. At the identity layer, the protected assets include avatar credentials, biometric templates, session continuity signals, behavioral traces, reputation scores, and social-graph relationships. At the interaction layer, they include rendered scenes, shared objects, voice streams, gesture data, gaze vectors, haptic events, and collaborative editing states. At the service layer, the protected assets include application programming interfaces (APIs), moderation services, recommendation engines, synchronization controllers, creator tools, wallets, and smart-contract endpoints. At the infrastructure layer, they include head-mounted displays, mobile clients, edge nodes, cloud services, network slices, model repositories, and telemetry channels. Finally, the digital twin layer includes simulations, mirrored state, operational histories, predictive models, and control recommendations associated with physical assets or processes (Gu et al., 2026; Repetto, 2026). Because these assets are tightly coupled, a compromise in one layer can quickly amplify risk in another (see Table 1).

The adversary set is equally diverse. This chapter distinguishes five broad classes. The first includes opportunistic intruders who exploit weak authentication, reused credentials, or insecure devices to hijack accounts or steal assets. The second includes socially embedded imposters who use avatar realism, voice imitation, or stolen behavioral signatures to manipulate trust and bypass peer scrutiny. The third includes economic attackers targeting wallets, marketplaces, creator monetization channels, or reputation economies. The fourth includes platform-proximal attackers, such as compromised moderators, malicious plug-ins, or third-party service providers with privileged access. The fifth includes cross-domain adversaries who use the metaverse as a path toward digital twins, enterprise services, healthcare platforms, industrial systems, or IoT infrastructures linked to immersive environments (Laiz-Ibanez et al., 2025; Yang et al., 2023; Han et al., 2025). Under such conditions, one defensive lens is unlikely to be sufficient.

A stepwise scenario helps clarify the threat. In a collaborative metaverse workspace, an attacker may first compromise a wearable device or session token and replay enough behavioral information to pass weak admission checks (step 1). The attacker may then enter a shared room and use interpersonal trust to request access to confidential design objects, digital twin dashboards, or payment workflows (step 2). Because co-presence often reduces skepticism, peers may approve transfers or disclose sensitive context that would not be revealed through conventional channels (step 3). The activity may later pivot to creator repositories, simulation backends, or cross-platform wallet services (step 4). If visualization controls are weak, the attacker may also alter rendered cues such as badge states, provenance indicators, or room alerts in order to prolong dwell time and confuse response efforts (step 5). This scenario shows why resilience in the metaverse needs to be treated as a distributed lifecycle rather than as a login checkpoint.

Table 1. Representative attack classes, likely propagation paths, and primary swarm responses.

Attack class	Primary assets at risk	Typical propagation path	Primary swarm response
Avatar impersonation	Credentials, biometric continuity, reputation, trust edges	Device/session compromise → avatar abuse → room privilege escalation	IAS + RFS
Visual deception	Rendered cues, provenance markers, room alerts, user perception	Malicious object injection → crowd manipulation → fraudulent action	SIS + Custodians
Wallet/asset fraud	Tokens, NFTs, creator revenue, escrow flows	Account foothold → abnormal transaction sequence → cross-service pivot	ATS + IAS

continued on following page

Table 1. Continued

Attack class	Primary assets at risk	Typical propagation path	Primary swarm response
Cross-platform lateral movement	Bridges, synchronization services, linked identities	Low-trust zone compromise → bridge traversal → high-value service access	Federation layer + ATS
Digital-twin manipulation	Twin states, predictions, control recommendations	Service compromise → mirror corruption → unsafe action or false insight	RFS + CDT
Bot swarms and misinformation	Room discourse, group behavior, moderation load	Coordinated avatar activity → signal flooding → trust erosion	SIS + Federation layer

Resilience Requirements

The threat model is the direct result of the resilience requirements. Security in the metaverse requires identity to be ensured constantly rather than only once the user logs in, particularly as the user and the room environment evolve (Cheng et al., 2024; Han et al., 2025). It must also be space-conscious situational sensing since the meaning of an event is different in the case of a public arena, a private studio, a telemedicine room, and a digital twin control view. The architecture also needs to employ federated evidence fusion to ensure that the platforms, rooms, services, and edge nodes distribute risk signals without centralizing raw data (Chen et al., 2023; Repetto, 2026). Containment should be graceful such that suspicious objects, services and users are localized without affecting the whole environment. Explainable adaptation is also significant since users and operators need to know why an avatar was challenged, why an asset was quarantined or why a room went into degraded mode. Lastly, the system should be designed with recovery and learning in mind and every incident should optimize the local rules, global models, and trust graphs. Operational conditions bind these functional requirements which are equally critical. Latency should not be incompatible with an immersive interaction, and therefore, most security decisions cannot be based on centralized orchestration. Privacy should be ensured because the metaverse telemetry has very sensitive biometric and behavioral data. Interoperability between heterogeneous vendors, devices and synchronisation protocols have to be sustained. The issue of administrative autonomy is also important, as immersive platforms are becoming less and less a monolithic operator and more of a collection of semi-autonomous service providers. Governance should be auditable as freezing wallets, expelling avatars or detaching a digital-twin has a high social and economic cost. Table 2 is a translation of these requirements into design goals and measurable indicators.

One of the most important consequences of the threat analysis is that metaverse defense must be distributed—both technically and socially. Technically, edge observations become worthless fast and bottlenecks in the center increase the risk. Trust signals are local, embodied and context-specific socially. A gesture anomaly may be innocent in a game arena, but suspicious in a telemedicine room, whereas an unusual transfer may be standard in a creator marketplace, but threatening in an educational setting. Thus, the architecture below is constructed on the basis of specialized cyber swarms to reason locally, coordinate selectively and only elevate what actually requires global consideration.

Table 2. Resilience requirements and their architectural implications for immersive multi-user metaverses.

Resilience requirement	Why it matters in the metaverse	Design implication	Illustrative indicator
Continuous identity assurance	Sessions are long-lived and avatars are socially trusted.	Use behavioral and contextual re-verification.	Challenge accuracy; re-auth latency
Space-aware sensing	Identical events may carry different meaning across room types.	Tag events with room semantics and sensitivity.	Context-weighted false positives
Federated evidence fusion	Threats cross vendors and services, but privacy remains critical.	Share summaries, anchors, and signed risk tokens.	Correlation gain without raw-data export
Graded containment	Binary removal can be disruptive and socially costly.	Apply friction, segmentation, escrow, or quarantine progressively.	Sessions preserved during incident
Explainable adaptation	Opaque intervention damages user trust and auditability.	Attach explanation vectors and policy traces to actions.	Operator comprehension score
Recovery and learning	Persistent spaces require state repair and trust restoration.	Use CDT-based rollback and supervised model updates.	Mean time to recover

MAIN FOCUS OF THE CHAPTER: THE SIRMC FRAMEWORK

Architectural Design Principles

The proposed framework is denoted as Swarm-Intelligence for Resilient Metaverse Cybersecurity (SIRMC). Its purpose is to turn cybersecurity from an external supervisory function into a capability embedded within immersive spaces, devices, services, and digital twins. Figure 1 presents the framework in five layers: (1) the Immersive Interaction Layer, where users, avatars, assets, and rendered objects generate security-relevant events; (2) the Edge Observation Layer, where lightweight agents collect multimodal telemetry from clients, rooms, and proximity graphs; (3) the Swarm Coordination Layer, where specialized agents correlate evidence and select actions; (4) the Twin and Policy Layer, where cybersecurity digital twins, trust graphs, and zero-trust policies are maintained; and (5) the Federation and Governance Layer, where cross-platform exchange, audit trails, and human oversight are coordinated. The design assumes bidirectional information flow across these layers so that local context and higher-level policy remain continuously aligned.

The Immersive Interaction Layer is the southbound interface of SIRMC. It encompasses head-mounted displays, mobile companions, room servers, smart objects, voice channels, creator tools, wallet interfaces and digital-twin viewers. This layer has security events that are hardly single-mode. An example of this is a voice mismatch, a gaze anomaly, a credential irregularity, an odd request to access an asset, and an abnormal rendering sequence, just to mention a few and all within a very small time frame. Due to this, local monitoring cannot solely be based on the packet traces or authentication logs. It must also have interaction semantics, spatial context, device posture, temporal density and trust adjacency in order to complete the situation. One significant weakness of directly projecting classical SIEM abstractions into immersive spaces is that these abstractions strip embodied context from the decontextualized event records. Although still useful in logging, these abstractions do not suffice in reasoning scenes in co-present environments.

Figure 1. SIRMC layered reference architecture for swarm-enabled metaverse cybersecurity.

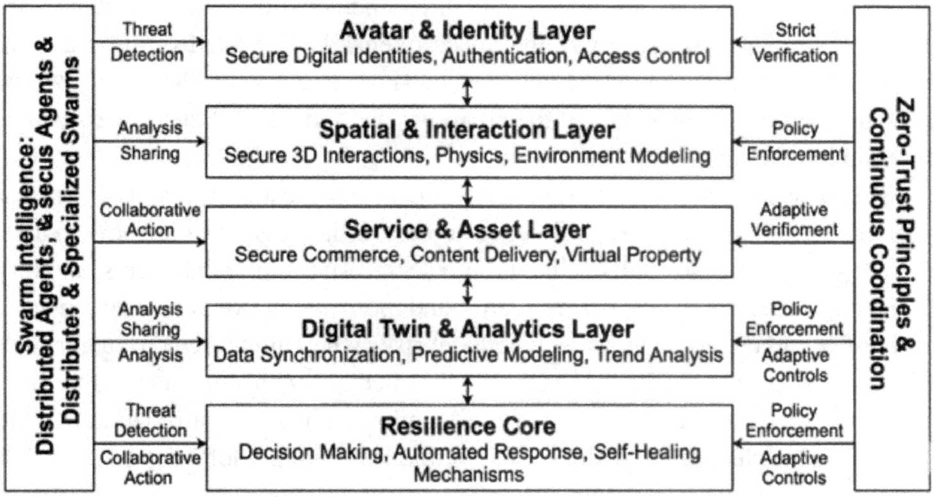

Layered Architecture and Agent Taxonomy

The Edge Observation Layer proposes three lightweight micro-agents, namely, scouts, sentinels and custodians.

- Scouts: collect fine-grained observations, e.g. behavioral deviations, asset-access anomalies, abnormal object spawns, or rendering anomalies.
- Sentinels: perform low-latency policy checks, such as checking against unauthorized entry of rooms, suspicious wallet usage, suspicious privilege combinations, or impossible cross-zone movement of avatars.
- Custodians: deal with local state, store encrypted evidence, and impose short-term responses like soft challenges, shadow restrictions, visual watermarking, or temporary delay of transaction.

These agents remain lightweight since the immersive platforms are unable to support a large, centralized inference engine on each event. They can still be deployed in an elastic manner, with high-risk rooms and digital-twin control views being able to accommodate denser protection compared to low-impact public spaces.

The Swarm Coordination Layer is used as the eastbound interface to collective reasoning. Instead of condensing the events into individual alerts, it consolidates local evidence into belief states. A belief state can declare faith in an avatar being impersonated, the probability of a room being coordinated so that it is being manipulated, the size of a blast radius of a quarantine decision, and the value of anticipated interventions. In practice, the layer includes four swarms, namely the Identity Assurance Swarm (IAS), the Space Integrity Swarm (SIS), the Asset and Transaction Swarm (ATS) and the Recovery and Forensics Swarm (RFS). All swarms rationalize about a unique part of the environment, and Table 3 encompasses their inputs and anticipated outputs.

All raw observations are not exchanged between these swarms. They instead exchange signed summaries, confidence scores, hashed evidence anchors, policy-attributes relevant descriptors. This will preserve privacy and enhance scalability. Biometric traces, eye tracks, voice streams, and room interactions are very sensitive; this pool would create regulatory and ethical risks when unrestricted (Huang et al., 2023; Laiz-Ibanez et al., 2025). In addition, immersive environments produce huge volumes of telemetry, and it is expensive to indiscriminately centralize it. SIRMC hence embraces federated evidence fusion: the raw data are left very near to their origin, and only the abstractions needed to carry out coordinated thought are exported. This federation mode of metaverse analytics was discussed by Chen et al. (2023), and this same argument applies to cyber operations.

Table 3. Agent and swarm taxonomy in the proposed SIRMC framework.

Agent / swarm	Scope	Key inputs	Typical actions	Escalation condition
Scout	Local client or room edge	Behavioral, device, object, and interaction features	Create signed event capsules; request more sampling	Confidence exceeds local anomaly threshold
Sentinel	Local policy boundary	Event capsules; room policy; device health	Low-latency checks; soft challenge; temporary delay	Policy breach or unresolved conflict
Custodian	Local evidence and control	Evidence anchors; containment rules	Preserve evidence; watermark objects; throttle actions	Potential collateral effect or repeat violation
IAS	Identity layer	Biometrics, session continuity, peer history	Corroborate impersonation risk; recommend re-verification	Identity confidence falls below role threshold
SIS	Room and rendering layer	Scene graph, object provenance, display state	Validate space integrity; isolate suspicious room objects	Visualization anomaly has social reach
ATS	Economic and service layer	Wallet flows, smart-contract calls, asset provenance	Delay, escrow, or segment transactions/services	Economic blast radius becomes material
RFS	Recovery and forensic layer	Containment history, CDT state, audit chain	Rollback, trust repair, notification, postmortem	Need for persistent recovery or federation-wide action

The Twin and Policy Layer is where metaverse resilience becomes operational rather than conceptual. Repetto (2026) argued that cybersecurity digital twins are needed when threats propagate across multi-ownership service chains, and this observation is particularly relevant to immersive environments. In SIRMC, each protected environment maintains a Cybersecurity Digital Twin (CDT) representing users, rooms, services, assets, trust dependencies, identity states, and recovery options. The CDT is intended as a stateful operational model rather than as a static mirror. It supports simulation, what-if analysis, blast-radius estimation, and recovery planning. For example, before isolating a synchronization service, the CDT can estimate which rooms will degrade, which sessions may lose continuity, and which wallet transactions may be interrupted. Achuthan et al. (2025) and Gu et al. (2026) show why such twin-assisted reasoning is relevant to complex cyber operations.

The policy component of this layer implements a zero-trust control plane for the metaverse. Every avatar, device, agent, service, object, and cross-platform bridge is treated as a dynamically evaluated entity. Identity is not assumed to remain trustworthy simply because a session is already active, and rendering instructions are not assumed to be benign simply because they originate from an approved service. A second limitation of narrow zero-trust interpretations is that they may remain overly identity-centric and underweight room semantics, asset criticality, and cross-service dependency. In SIRMC, each request is therefore evaluated against identity confidence, device health, room sensitivity, asset criticality, peer corroboration, and current threat posture. This interpretation is consistent with the broader metaverse security concerns discussed by Cheng et al. (2024).

Figure 2. Closed-loop resilience cycle linking sensing, corroboration, containment, recovery, and learning.

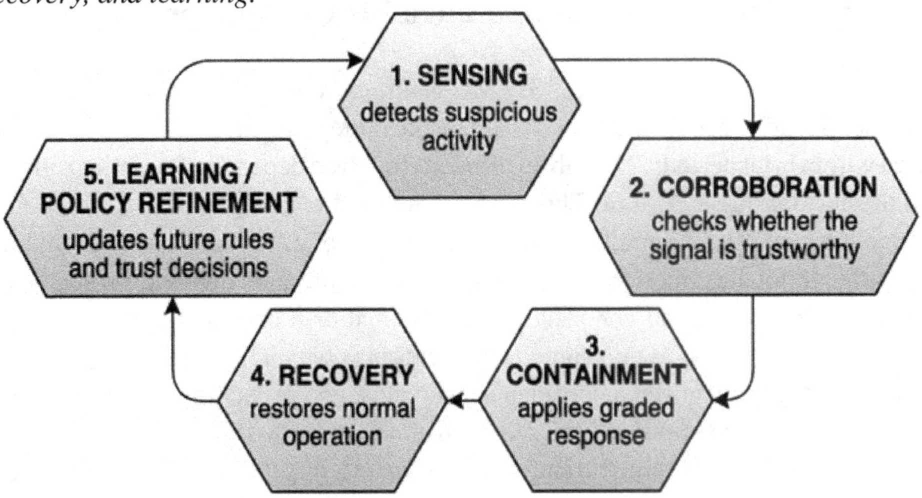

The Federation and Governance Layer connects local SIRMCs instances on other platforms and administrative regions. It allows one to share risk indicators, compromise signatures, as well as trust-revocation tokens. On top of this, it facilitates selective federation of cybersecurity digital twins, an auditable override on high-impact actions and keeps logs of compliance to aid in disputes and post-incident review. Complete automated response is not necessarily a good thing in immersive systems since the economic and social ramifications can be enormous. Graded autonomy is thus used at SIRMC. Adaptive logging or suspicious-object marking, or soft challenge are low-risk actions which can be automated. Swarm-corroboration can be necessary in medium-risk alternatives like asset escrow delay or temporary room segmentation. Irreversible freezing of wallets or permanently irreversible expulsions, and actions that cannot be undone like being detached on the physical control system, etc. should be channeled through escalation through human beings. This loop has been summarized in figure 2 in sensing, fusion, action, feedback and learning.

The layered architecture assigns defensive cognition and maintains governance. Local agents provide speed and context. Swarm coordination introduces agreement and flexibility. Cybersecurity digital twins offer predictive arguments and recovery design. Zero-trust policies are self-disciplined. Federation disseminates cross-domain awareness. Such advantages are based on safe inter-agent trust, semantically compatible policies and interoperable evidence forms. The following part is a transition to architecture design to the working mechanism of these properties.

OPERATIONAL MECHANISMS

Collective Sensing and Cooperative Risk Formation

The operational philosophy of SIRMC is a recurrent cycle rather than a linear pipeline. Security events are perceived, reasoned, negotiated, acted, validated and learnt within brief periods. The subset of agents involved depends on room sensitivity and the current threat posture. This cycle is summed up in figure 3.

Scout agents gather multimodal evidence at the start of the loop including credential anomalies, motion abnormalities, access attempts involving assets, rendering discrepancies, and abnormal conversational or transaction patterns. These observations are encoded into signed event capsules which hold timestamps, room identifiers, entity identifiers, confidence estimates, and privacy-preserving feature summaries. First-pass policy checks are then done by sentinel agents which generate provisional hypotheses - e.g. credential replay, uncertainty with avatars, mismatch in provenance of object. This initial step should remain within the latency range allowed by immersive interaction hence the preference of lightweight inference in this case.

The second stage is the cooperative risk formation. SIRMC needs local corroboration where the consequences are non-trivial rather than having one agent make a decision on their own. The Identity Assurance Swarm is associated with biometric continuity, behavioral drift, device posture, and peer-history indicators. Space Integrity Swarm is a correlator of scene semantics, object introductions, rendering permissions as well as co-presence topology. The Asset and Transaction Swarm gathers transaction intent, asset provenance, reputation history, and smart-contract request sequences. The composite risk score is generated when multiple swarms come together along with a description of the factors that explain most of the effects. The explanation is significant to human supervision and after incident analysis. It also enables the framework to demand increased sampling when the swarms are at loggerheads rather than scurrying to quarantine.

Figure 3. Cooperative risk formation and graded containment workflow across local agents and specialized swarms.

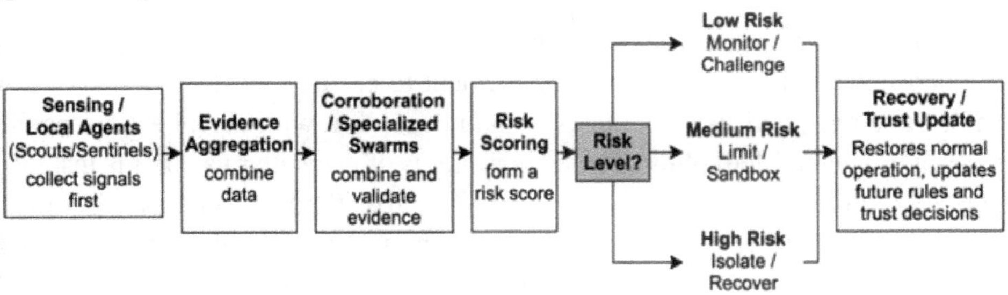

Graded Containment and Recovery Orchestration

The third phase is graded containment. In persistent immersive sessions, binary allow-or-block responses are often too coarse. A questionable aspect of conventional incident-response playbooks is that they frequently collapse uncertainty into immediate exclusion, even when the consequences of a false positive are high. SIRMC instead supports a range of responses that can be matched to context. Depending on the event, the framework may apply shadow observation, progressive friction such as reauthentication prompts or transaction delays, local capability degradation, room segmentation into an isolated mirror instance, or full quarantine with federation-wide revocation. Similar logic applies to suspicious objects and services, which may be marked, provenance-checked, interaction-limited, sandboxed, or shifted into degraded-safe modes. The CDT is used to estimate collateral effects before execution so that response can remain technically robust without causing unnecessary disruption.

The fourth phase is orchestration of recovery. Recovery is considered a secondary concern, but in persistent multi-user environments, recovery is a core component of resilience. Once an event has been contained, the Recovery and Forensics Swarm makes decisions about whether sessions should be restored, whether the state of objects should be rolled back, whether the transactions of assets should be escrowed or reversed, whether contextual warnings should be issued to nearby users, and whether the affected room should be kept in a degraded state. The same process is used to update the trust graph. The trust of benign entities that were temporarily challenged may be restored through corroborated evidence, while malicious or compromised entities may be degraded or isolated. Recovery also needs to remain understandable to users as opaque intervention can damage confidence in the platform even if the technical decision is correct.

Learning, Trust Establishment, and Privacy Preservation

The fifth stage is about learning and policy refining. The framework revises local and federated models after every incident to ensure that tactical rules, calibration functions, and rule templates remain consistent with actual experience in operations. The problem of distributed learning is of particular use in this instance since the rooms and users groups do not align across the metaverse backgrounds. But uncritical online adaptation can be a problem; it can extrapolate the temporary crowd phenomena or norms of one domain. A model may fail in telemedicine or industry cooperation when it has been successfully applied in a game arena. Thus, domain tags, room -sensitivity labels and fairness constraints must be maintained within the learning loop, to ensure that security adaptation is not generic.

The creation of trust among agents is a security responsibility in itself. SIRMC provides decision power to numerous agents; therefore, communication plays a vital role in general resilience. All the agents should possess identifiable identity, role certificate, scope and verified execution environment. Messages flowing eastwards between swarms are to be signed, timed, policy scoped, and replay resistant. Messages of federation are supposed to include provenance, confidence information and expiry policies. In case an agent begins generating incongruent scores, non-provable anchors of evidence, or statistically bizarre recommendations, the system should demote the agent and divert coordination paths. Practically we quantify this in terms of the latency of trust establishment, message integrity failures, downgrade, and coordination rerouting success.

Special protection is required in visual and interaction channels. As Chow et al. (2023) demonstrated, the rendering surface in immersive systems is not a passive display but an active attack surface. In this case, objects may be concealed, cues may be counterfeited and states may be fabricated. Space Integrity Swarm is a retaliation against this by carrying out rendering attestation, binding object provenance, validating overlays, and identifying suspicious visual patterns. To illustrate, when a high-value asset is present without a valid provenance chain, it would be logged in the system, watermarked, and no further interaction would be possible until it is verified. Equally, should a room level warning vanish in a manner that conflicts with the server state, the client indicates the channel as suspect and transitions to a degraded-safe display. This method is essential in economic, clinical or industrial, where the manipulation of the interface may cause a direct influence on human judgement.

The privacy protection should be incorporated into all the functional steps. Eye movement, motion patterns, voice cues, social interactions and spatial histories, which are indicative of health, habits, or commercial interest, could be telemeted in the metaverse. SIRMC thus focuses on local feature extraction, selective disclosure, secure enclaves to sensitive inference, privacy preserving analytics where possible and short retention of high risk data. All these do not rule out the privacy risk, but reduce unnecessary exposure. What is even more important, they maintain resilience in accordance with legitimacy. A cyber security system that protects the assets but permits intrusive observation will presumably fail to gain social acceptance in an immersive, multi-user setting.

One evaluation scorecard is necessary to determine whether the framework enhances resilience and does not negatively affect immersion. The scorecard is supposed to combine a number of kinds of indicators: detection indicators such as precision, recall, and mean time to detect, containment and recovery indicators such as blast-radius reduction, and mean time to recover, experience indicators such as user interruption rate and frame-impact overhead, and governance indicators such as the completeness of the explanation, privacy exposure, and cross-platform signal propagation delay. The combination of these metrics allows having a realistic means to assess the ability of SIRMC to remain functional and acceptable in real-life deployments.

ILLUSTRATIVE SCENARIOS AND EVALUATION BLUEPRINT

Scenario 1: Avatar Impersonation in a Collaborative Room

This section translates the architecture into three illustrative attack-and-response scenarios and a practical evaluation blueprint. The intention is not to claim empirical validation that is outside the scope of this chapter. Rather, the scenarios show how SIRMC can be instantiated and assessed in a systematic way. Figure 4 synthesizes the cross-layer escalation logic discussed below, and Table 4 summarizes the recommended implementation roadmap.

The first scenario involves the impersonation of an avatar in a design room. A user having moderate historical trust enters a private immersive workspace that is filled with proprietary models and is connected to a digital-twin dashboard. Local scout agents identify a change in the signature of controller movement, whereas the Identity Assurance Swarm finds a discrepancy between the latest gaze dynamics and an established behavioral profile of the user. It is not the deviation as such that expels. SIRMC thus uses graded friction through restricting sensitive-object manipulation, deferring high value transactions as well as making a silent corroboration request to neighboring agents. As the attacker tries to log into a twin-linked maintenance console, the score of the risk breaches the room threshold, the avatar is sent into an empty mirror room, and the CDT simulates the impact of service denial prior to the execution. This is followed by recovery, which reroutes the legitimate session, revokes the token that was compromised, and provides an incident path traceable in the trust graph. Whether it was detected or not is not the key issue in this scenario, but whether it is possible to contain it without collapsing the room to include all the participating parties.

Scenario 2: Cross-Platform Lateral Movement

Scenario 2 is concerned with lateral movement across platforms using wallet and service bridges. The attacker initially hacks a low-value entertainment area where the security is less than strict, before swiveling to a creator marketplace and a digital twin-backed asset registry. Some components of this activity may be isolated across vendors in a normal architecture. At SIRMC, local swarms provide the federation layer with signed risk summaries. The federation associates suspicious interaction patterns and trust tokens without the disclosure of crude biometric data. The Asset and Transaction Swarm identifies suspicious wallet activity, and Recovery and Forensics Swarm applies the CDT to determine the blast radius in case the bridge services are temporarily partitioned. The response that this leads to is selective, not global: wallet operations can be escrowed, the bridge can be set to a lower-trust mode, higher challenge thresholds can be imposed on high-risk rooms. The most important question for key performance is whether the federation will be able to ensure timely correlation without violating the latency and privacy limitations.

Scenario 3: Visual Misinformation and Malicious Object Injection

Scenario 3 relates to visual misinformation and injection of malicious objects in an area of a public event. Here, the intruder does not steal credentials. Rather, fake moderation signals, counterfeit badges or falsified provenance indicators are added to influence crowd behavior and generate fraudulent purchases of assets. The Space Integrity Swarm detects a disparity in the rendered object and the authoritative object registry. Scout agents also sense coordinated user movement to the cluster of suspicious objects, which means increasing social consequence. Instead of destroying the objects, SIRMC watermarks them, reduces the interaction affordances of the objects, and transmits an authenticated correction overlay to the other users that are nearby. This combination of technical correction and crowd-conscious mitigation is significant since damage in the metaverse can be fuelled by perception and social contagion instead of code execution per se.

Figure 4. Illustrative cross-layer attack propagation and swarm response in a persistent multi-user metaverse.

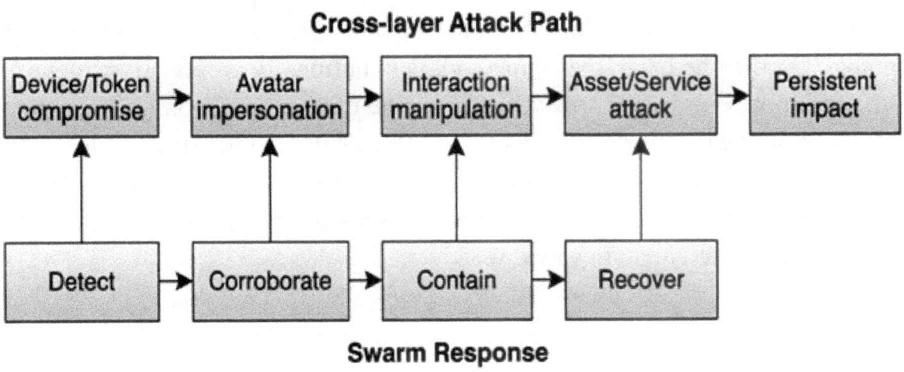

Evaluation Blueprint and Phased Implementation

The assessment of SIRMC should take place on multiple levels. The traditional detection metrics are applicable such as precision, recall, F1-score, false-positive rate, false-negative rate, and mean time to detect. It should also include measures specific to the concept of resiliency, including mean time to contain, mean time to recover, service degradation ratio, blast-radar reduction, and the percentage of sessions saved during incident management. Moreover, there is the need to have immersive-experience measures such as added interaction latency, frame-impact overhead, user interruption rate, and perceived fairness of intervention. Explainability, auditability, frequency of human override, and privacy exposure are all measures of governance that should be addressed. Cross-platform signal propagation delay, correlation gain, revocation latency and abstraction leakage risk should be measures of federated-operation. These actions constitute a single scorecard and not a collection of separate benchmarks.

Implementation wise, SIRMC can be prototyped in a incremental manner. The first deployment could equip one room type in the design, e.g. collaborative design room, with local scouts, sentinels, and the minimum amount of CDT. A second stage can bring special swarms, low risk graded responses, and signed evidence exchange between rooms. A third step can prolong the CDT using simulation-based recovery planning and bring the environment to wallet services or digital-twin dashboard. Fourth phase might include platform-federation using privacy-summarizing risk notices and revocation tokens. The fifth phase can bring in adaptive learning of policies with human-controlled guardrails. This simulated advancement is feasible since it enables operators to test latency limits, false-positive action, and user acceptance prior to a more impactful autonomy being turned on.

The blueprint of the evaluation can be described as appropriate to an IGI-style chapter since it is conceptual development coupled with design advice that is implementable. On the one hand, the framework is intentionally prescriptive: metaverse security cannot be assessed solely based on the offline detection. A system with good detection but low live containment, which loses the confidence of the users, or one which concentrates sensitive telemetry is not likely to be resilient in operation. That is why the architecture must be evaluated as a socio-technical operation system and not as an isolated analytics model.

Table 4. Phased implementation roadmap for incrementally deploying the SIRMC framework.

Phase	Core capability	Primary artifacts	Main risk if omitted
Phase 1	Local sensing and basic policy checks	Scouts, sentinels, room policies	Blind spots remain purely reactive
Phase 2	Specialized swarms and soft actions	IAS, SIS, ATS, graded friction rules	Over-reliance on binary intervention
Phase 3	Cybersecurity digital twin	Dependency graph, what-if simulator, rollback playbooks	Containment may be technically effective but operationally harmful
Phase 4	Federated coordination	Risk tokens, revocation lists, signed summaries	Cross-platform attacks remain fragmented
Phase 5	Supervised adaptive learning	Model update pipeline, fairness guardrails, audit loop	Defense posture stagnates or drifts unsafely

FUTURE RESEARCH DIRECTIONS

This chapter suggests several tangible directions for future research. The models of formal coordination are required to define when it is enough to rely on local corroboration, when swarm consensus must be applied and when human escalation is mandatory. Multi-agent defense studies provide valuable points of departure (Loevenich et al., 2025; Torres et al., 2026), and immersive systems bring reputational and experiential costs of error to the table, which new utility models are needed to address. Privacy-preserving federation between platforms also requires standardized evidence schemas since cross-domain resilience will continue to be weak as long as the providers export incompatible risk signals. Simultaneously, digital twins of cybersecurity must develop beyond merely being a mirror of what exists to be dynamic and able to model social, economic, and perceptual outcomes of security interventions besides technical dependencies (Repetto, 2026; Achuthan et al., 2025).

There is also the need to have continuous authentication being more integrated with relationship-aware and space-aware reasoning. Existing identity solutions are evolving rapidly (Yang et al., 2023; Han et al., 2025; Liang et al., 2025), yet they remain to be more closely integrated with room semantics, asset sensitivity and crowd context. Testbeds and evaluation datasets also require more multi-user immersive traces of attacks, such as impersonation, visual deception, misinformation, wallet abuse, and manipulation of digital twins. In the absence of such benchmarks, rival defense strategies will not be easily compared. Another priority is governance research due to the fact that automated interventions create due process, appeal, cross-platform trust revocation, and fairness auditing concerns. Even a technically effective but procedurally opaque swarm can be a socially and commercially unsuccessful swarm.

In a more tangible way, the future work could clarify interoperable risk ontologies, deploy prototype cyber swarms on open metaverse stacks, interface them with CDT-driven playbooks, and test them across room types with various sensitivity profiles, such as education, healthcare, industrial collaboration and creator economies. This continuation is not only possible but also required in the event that the metaverse evolves into a reliable digital space and not a weak and enticing attack area.

CONCLUSION

In conclusion, this chapter has framed resilient cybersecurity in immersive multi-user metaverses as a distributed, adaptive, and governance-conscious capability rather than a sequence of disconnected controls. The SIRMC framework was presented by synthesizing metaverse security research, swarm intelligence research, multi-agent cyber defense research, zero-trust reasoning research, and digital twins research. It is a reference architecture of collective sensing, collective risk formation, graded containment, recovery orchestration and federated governance. The point is that attacks propagate via identity, interaction, asset, service, and twin layers, defense should provide similar cross-layer visibility, and coordinate reaction. The second step will be to test this swarm-based defense in real-world multi-user settings, evaluate its effects, and improve it using the findings.

REFERENCES

Achuthan, K., Thirunavukarasu, R., Alzahrani, M. S., Kumar, S., & Kumar, A. (2025). Metaverse-enabled cyber ranges for cybersecurity education: Systematic review, opportunities, and challenges. *International Journal of Information Security*, *24*, 207. Advance online publication. DOI: 10.1007/s10207-025-01115-y

Ali, O., Momin, M., Shrestha, A., Das, P., Naeem, M. A., & Goyal, R. (2024). A comprehensive survey on the role of artificial intelligence in metaverse. *IEEE Communications Surveys and Tutorials*, *26*(2), 1238–1278. DOI: 10.1109/COMST.2023.3347172

Bougueroua, N., Mazouzi, S., Belaoued, M., Seddari, N., Derhab, A., & Bouras, A. (2021). A survey on multi-agent based collaborative intrusion detection systems. *Journal of Artificial Intelligence and Soft Computing Research*, *11*(2), 111–142. DOI: 10.2478/jaiscr-2021-0008

Brambilla, M., Ferrante, E., Birattari, M., & Dorigo, M. (2013). Swarm robotics: A review from the swarm engineering perspective. *Swarm Intelligence*, *7*(1), 1–41. DOI: 10.1007/s11721-012-0075-2

Chen, J., Zhang, D., Yao, Y., Adhikari, N., Zhang, Z., & Li, H. (2023). SeAGent: Toward intelligent IoT security in the metaverse. In Companion Proceedings of the ACM Web Conference 2023 (pp. 1151-1160). DOI: 10.1145/3543873.3587584

Cheng, X., Zhang, H., Liang, H., & Xu, Y. (2024). Safeguarding the metaverse: Security and privacy challenges and solutions. *IEEE Communications Magazine*, *62*(2), 156–162. DOI: 10.1109/MCOM.018.2300095

Chow, W. K. B., Ho, J. S. K., & Wong, A. K. F. (2023). The metaverse for learning: A review of educational applications, opportunities, and challenges. *Journal of Imaging*, *9*(1), 11. Advance online publication. DOI: 10.3390/jimaging9010011 PMID: 36662109

Gu, X., Duan, W., Zhang, G., Hou, J., Peng, L., Wen, M., Gao, F., Chen, M., & Ho, P.-H. (2026). Digital twin technology for intelligent vehicles and transportation systems: A survey on applications, challenges and future directions. *IEEE Communications Surveys and Tutorials*, *28*, 3235–3271. DOI: 10.1109/COMST.2025.3581152

Han, S., Hwang, E., Kim, Y. S., & Kwon, T. (2025). A continuous authentication framework for securing metaverse identities. *IEEE Transactions on Services Computing*, *18*(3), 1171–1184. DOI: 10.1109/TSC.2025.3553711

Huang, Y., Li, Y. J., & Cai, Z. (2023). Security and privacy in metaverse: A comprehensive survey. *Big Data Mining and Analytics*, *6*(2), 234–247. DOI: 10.26599/BDMA.2022.9020047

Laiz-Ibanez, H., Mendana-Cuervo, C., & Carus-Candas, J. L. (2025). The metaverse: Privacy and information security risks. *International Journal of Information Management Data Insights*, *5*(2), 100373. Advance online publication. DOI: 10.1016/j.jjimei.2025.100373

Liang, X., Wang, S., Xiong, L., Liu, Z., & Xiong, N. N. (2025). SAGTM: A secure authentication scheme with traceability for avatars in the metaverse. *Computer Networks*, *263*, 111206. Advance online publication. DOI: 10.1016/j.comnet.2025.111206

Loevenich, J., Adler, E., Hurten, T., & Lopes, R. R. F. (2025). Design and evaluation of an autonomous cyber defence agent using DRL and an augmented LLM. *Computer Networks*, *262*, 111162. Advance online publication. DOI: 10.1016/j.comnet.2025.111162

Nasir, A. R., Ashraf, M. I., Reisslein, M., & Kato, N. (2022). Drone-swarm-enabled aerial computing for intelligent IoT services: Architecture, opportunities, and challenges. *Computer Networks*, *205*, 108708. Advance online publication. DOI: 10.1016/j.comnet.2021.108708

Pooyandeh, M., Joo, J., Lotfi, F., Hwang, J., Mehdi, D., Rho, S., & Jeong, Y.-S. (2022). Cybersecurity in the AI-based metaverse: A survey. *Applied Sciences (Basel, Switzerland)*, *12*(24), 12993. Advance online publication. DOI: 10.3390/app122412993

Repetto, M. (2026). Cybersecurity digital twins: Concept, blueprint, and challenges for multi-ownership digital service chains. *Journal of Information Security and Applications*, *96*, 104299. Advance online publication. DOI: 10.1016/j.jisa.2025.104299

Torres, L. A., Rebollo, M., Palanca, J., & Aragones Lozano, M. (2026). cyberSPADE: A hierarchical multi-agent architecture for autonomous cyberdefense. *Journal of Cybersecurity and Privacy*, *6*(1), 28. Advance online publication. DOI: 10.3390/jcp6010028

Venugopal, J. P., Subramanian, A. A. V., Sundaram, G., & Ponnambalam Devadoss, M. (2025). The convergence of deep learning and the metaverse: A multidisciplinary survey of current research and future directions. *Computer Animation and Virtual Worlds*, *36*(6), e70082. Advance online publication. DOI: 10.1002/cav.70082

Wang, Y., Su, Z., Zhang, N., Xing, R., Liu, D., Luan, T. H., & Shen, X. (2023). A survey on metaverse: Fundamentals, security, and privacy. *IEEE Communications Surveys and Tutorials*, *25*(1), 319–352. DOI: 10.1109/COMST.2022.3202047

Yang, K., Zhang, Z., Tian, Y., & Ma, J. (2023). A secure authentication framework to guarantee the traceability of avatars in metaverse. *IEEE Transactions on Information Forensics and Security*, *18*, 3817–3832. DOI: 10.1109/TIFS.2023.3288689

Chapter 7
Synchronized Digital Identities:
Twin-Based Architectures for Consistent Authentication Across Physical-Virtual Metaverse Boundaries

Khalil Omar
http://orcid.org/0000-0002-5328-5762
University of Petra, Jordan

Wissam Al Khadour
http://orcid.org/0009-0004-1937-0308
University of Petra, Jordan

Jamal Zraqou
http://orcid.org/0000-0001-9060-7188
University of Petra, Jordan

Jawad AlKhateeb
http://orcid.org/0009-0005-1529-7761
Prince Mohammad bin Fahd University, Saudi Arabia

ABSTRACT

Metaverse ecosystems pose new challenges that have never been seen before in ensuring that digital identities are consistent across heterogeneous platforms. The chapter suggests a new twin architecture based on the digital twin principles of managing identity that introduces a federated model that includes credential, behavioral, context, and authorization sub-twins. In our methodology, we use privacy-

DOI: 10.4018/979-8-3373-7882-4.ch007

preserving protocols of synchronization using zero-knowledge proofs. On benchmark datasets (LFW, VGGFace2, KeyRecs) the system has been shown to achieve 99.1% authentication accuracy, 0.7% EER (22% better than current systems) and 127ms average latency and 99.8% cross-platform synchronization reliability. These results provide a roadmap to the next-generation authentication systems that would enable the smooth experiences across the physical-virtual metaverse boundaries.

1. INTRODUCTION

The blistering development of the metaverse as an inter-connected system of real and virtual space has essentially changed the environment of managing the digital self. With an increase in the use of augmented reality overlays, virtual reality platforms and old-fashioned digital interfaces, the need to have consistent, secure, and privacy preserving authentication mechanisms has become the top priority. The metaverse with its immersive realism, hyper-spatiotemporality, and sustainability demands (Lee et al., 2021) require authentication architectures that are beyond the capabilities of traditional identity management paradigms. It is not just a matter of technological improvement, but a paradigm shift in the way human beings relate to the digital systems and necessitates a paradigm shift in the way we handle the matter of identity verification and management.

The modern system of digital identities is under increasing pressure due to the number of linked platforms and the growing complexity of cyber attacks. As it has been analyzed in the industry, digital identity checks of identity verification have reached over 70 billion in 2024 with biometric authentication of over 2.5 trillion dollars of mobile payment transactions. These figures highlight the high sense of urgency in having strong identity verification systems in a fast digitizing economy. The development of metaverse spaces, however, presents new issues that the current systems are poorly configured to handle, such as real-time cross-platform synchronization, the need to be constantly authenticated, and a smooth transition between both physical and virtual modalities.

The idea of digital twins, which was initially created to implement industrial Internet of Things solutions to develop virtual models of physical objects, can provide an interesting framework to discuss these authentication issues. Digital twins have been shown to be useful in manufacturing and industrial settings in terms of predictive maintenance, optimizing performance, and real-time monitoring of complex systems. The next logical step in the extension of this paradigm to identity management is the use of the fundamental capabilities of digital twin technology to drive the value of bidirectional synchronization, constant state observation, and the possibility to ensure coherent representations across distributed systems. Within the framework of identity management, a digital identity twin is an active, virtual representation of the authentication status, security credentials, and identity attributes of a user which exists on its own without being tied to a single platform, but is synchronized in both directions with all integrated systems.

This study is important because it discusses the inherent conflict between the promise of cross-platform experiences that the metaverse promises and the security need to have a strong and context-aware authentication. With the disappearance of physical-virtual boundaries by technology, such as spatial computing, haptic interfaces, neural interfaces, and so on, previous authentication paradigms are no longer feasible, and new architectures are needed to preserve identity consistency without affecting security or privacy. The aspect of immersion of metaverse interactions present attack vectors such as avatars impersonation, spatial eavesdropping, and behavioral biometric spoofing that demand authentication systems that are adaptable to these new forms of threat. Moreover, the social and economic importance of metaverse identities is ever-increasing, and virtual assets, digital real estates, and cross-platform reputation systems are providing significant incentives to identity-related attacks.

This chapter has a number of contributions to the digital identity management domain. First, it creates a holistic theoretical and practical architecture of implementing synchronized digital identities via twin-based architectures, namely, the individual problems of authentication across physical-virtual metaverse boundaries. The structure combines the ideas of various fields such as distributed systems, cryptography, human-computer interaction and security engineering. Second, it proposes a federated twin model to separate user identity into special sub-twins to manage credentials, behaviour, contextual awareness, and authorisation control to enforce fine-grained privacy controls and minimise the consequences of possible compromises through compartmentalisation. Third, it provides large-scale experimental analysis based on publicly available benchmark datasets, and it shows a significant improvement over the current state-of-the-art methods in terms of accuracy, latency and security measures.

The growing use of extended reality technology in business and consumer solutions increases the level of urgency of the need to develop a solid authentication solution. Companies implementing virtual collaboration systems are under the need to be assured that they have the right people in the room and consumers need frictionless experiences that will not compromise their security to facilitate convenience. The COVID-19 pandemic increased the use of remote collaboration tools and the further evolution of more immersive collaboration tools has introduced a need in the authentication systems that can work efficiently with different types of interaction. The twin-based design presented in this paper considers both of the two needs by exploiting the fact that digital twin synchronization is continuous, so that it can offer continuous identity assurance without reoccurring explicit authentication events, which allows seamless context transitions and appropriate security postures.

Moreover, the legal frameworks of digital identity are still underdeveloped, and the development of new regulations, including the eIDAS 2.0 regulation of the European Union, which requires the interoperability of digital identity wallets that support selective disclosure and verifiable credentials, is ongoing. Other jurisdictions, such as the United States, the United Kingdom, or other Asian countries have similar regulatory trends, which suggests a rise in a global trend favoring uniform digital identity frameworks. The proposed architecture is associated with these new requirements since it applies the principles of self-sovereign identity and applies them to the context of the metaverse by expanding them to new challenges. Architectural choices are informed by compliance factors, such as data protection laws, like GDPR, and new AI regulatory frameworks, during the proposed system design.

The rest of this chapter is structured in the following way. Section 2 conducts a review of the related work in the field of digital identity management, metaverse security, and digital twin architectures, forming the theoretical basis and determining the gaps in current solutions. The proposed methodology, containing specifications of the system architecture, sub-twin functional requirements, and protocol designs that are privacy-preserving, are provided in Section 3. Section 4 outlines the experimental design, including detailed description of datasets, details of implementation environment and definition of evaluation metrics. Section 5 contains a lot of results and analysis based on various performance dimensions. Lastly, the conclusion of Section 6 includes a practical implications discussion, limitations, and future research promising directions.

The security consequences of poor metaverse authentication are not limited to individual privacy infringements, but are larger issues in the society. The virtual economies in metaverse platforms now facilitate high real-life value, and digital items such as virtual real estate, collectibles, and in-game assets have high prices. Loss of metaverse identities can lead to financial losses similar to traditional banking fraud and this requires authentication systems with appropriate security guarantees.

2. RELATED WORK

2.1 Digital Identity Management Evolution

The history of managing digital identities has gone through a series of paradigmatic changes, starting with centralized repositories of identities and moving on to federated, and more recently, to decentralized self-sovereign identity systems. This evolution will be critical in understanding the proposed twin-based architecture and determining which limitations it is targeted at. The initial identity management systems were based on the isolated databases used by service providers and users needed to create and manage different credentials to use in different services. This practice posed major usability problems and security risks, where customers were more likely to use one and the same password to access multiple services and service providers were now interesting targets of credential theft attacks. Growing number of data breaches of large identity repositories has highlighted the drawbacks of centralized methods, where billions of credential pairs have been compromised by high-profile breaches of organizations in all industries.

The federated identity protocols like the SAML (Security Assertion Markup Language), Oauth 2.0 and OpenID connect became a major breakthrough and helped users to authenticate to various service providers with credentials managed by trusted identity providers. The rise of massive identity providers, such as technology platforms and social networks, increased the rate of federated solutions adoption by making it more convenient to single sign-on (SSO) to users and lessening the credential management overhead of individual service providers. But these systems have points of control that are central and create dependencies on the availability and reliability of identity providers. This is because having identity data in the hands of a few providers poses systemic risks and brings about concerns on surveillance and exploitation of data. The current regulatory examination of big technology platforms has brought up the governance issues of having centralized provision of identities. Moreover, federated techniques usually demand network access to identity provider, which restricts their use in situations where network connectivity is intermittent or where partitioning of the network can take place.

Self-Sovereign Identity (SSI) systems that are based on decentralized identifier (DID) specifications and verifiable credential standards are another step toward identity management that is user-controllable. Preukschat and Reed (2021) have created the principles of SSI systems in which user autonomy and data minimization are central beliefs. Such principles are: independence of identifiers on existence of any organization, control on the use of identities by users, cross context portability and disclosure by consent. W3C Verifiable Credentials Data Model gives the credentials a standard format in which they can be cryptographically verified to facilitate interoperability across various identity systems. SSI implementations based on blockchain, such as Sovrin, uPort and Microsoft ION, have shown that decentralized identity management is indeed possible but is limited by scalability and transaction latency, limiting it to real-time authentication use cases. Proofs-of-work consensus mechanisms have also been found to have an environmental cost that has led to attempts to develop alternative schemes such as proof-of-stake and directed acyclic graph structures.

Zero-knowledge proof technologies have been developed as the key facilitators of privacy preserving authentication in decentralized systems where the user can demonstrate statements relating to their identity attributes, without disclosing the underlying values. Theoretical principles of minimal disclosure authentication The article by Dieye et al. (2023) on the use of zero-knowledge proofs based on discrete logarithm difficulty to develop SSI protocols has shown that the concept of minimal disclosure authentication has theoretical foundations. Their scheme is such that users are able to demonstrate they have valid credentials without disclosing underlying attribute values, which is a privacy concern of the traditional credential verification schemes that require full disclosure. On the same note, the survey of the progress of leveraging zero-knowledge proofs in identity sharing on the blockchain is conducted by Zhou et al. (2024), who have recognized open opportunities and ongoing challenges in enabling a scalable deployment. The current development of cryptographic accumulator architectures has made it possible to implement credential revocation schemes that are needed in practice to support identity systems: the difficulty is keeping credential validity, but not necessarily by being online to the issuing authority all the time.

2.2 Security and Authentication Problems in the Metaverse

The metaverse is not an exception, and it has unique security issues that have been the focus of a lot of research by scholars and industry. Wang et al. (2023) present an extensive overview of the basic components of the metaverse, security, and privacy issues and find attack surfaces in the network infrastructure, extended reality devices, and interaction via avatars. Their discussion shows that extreme privacy invasions and security breaches, which are passed on through the underlying technologies or is created in the new digital ecology, can hinder the mass adoption of the metaverse. The new discussion about digital identity, privacy security, and its legal protection in the metaverse (Wu and Zhang, 2023) also supports the necessity to have strong privacy frameworks. The survey lists the threats as data privacy breaches, identity-related attacks and platform integrity breaches, and states that because of the immersive nature of interactions in the metaverse, new attack vectors not found in the traditional digital world are generated. This is because the continuance of virtual identities over the long sessions opens up possibilities of behavioral profiling which are beyond what is possible in the normal web interactions.

The authentication of metaverse environments must take into account new modalities that are not based on conventional credential verification, which is a multi-modal interaction of extended reality. Zhong et al. (2023) suggest MetaVerse CAN, a framework that accepts active and non-intrusive biometric authentication that takes place continuously and is not limited to single authentication events, which is suitable when the session is longer and more immersive. They use their method based on the behavioral biometrics derived by VR controller gestures, eye motion, and posture to deliver continuous identity verification without disrupting user experience. The nature of metaverse interactions that can last hours in a gaming, social, or professional environment requires authentication mechanisms that work in the background and can respond to possible security threats. The anti-disguise authentication systems studies consider the issue of avatar impersonation by first-impression verification systems that provide similarities to the identity recognition in the real world, based on the distinct features of avatars customization and behavior that helps to identify unauthorized access.

In the literature on artificial intelligence integration of cybersecurity in the metaverse, the opportunities of anomaly detection, behavioral authentication, and threat prediction using machine learning have already been widely surveyed (Huynh-The et al., 2023). Otoum et al. (2024) offer a detailed overview of how machine learning is applied to security in the metaverse and outline the opportunities and major issues. Nevertheless, these AI-based solutions come with other issues of adversarial attacks, model interpretability, and computational costs of real-time inference on resource-limited extended reality devices. Adversarial perturbation is shown to be able to defeat biometric classifiers in various settings, and it has been found that it needs strong defenses that can be attacked without compromising accuracy. The issue of avatar security is a distinct challenge in the context of the metaverse where users have a virtual identity in form of customizable virtual personas which can be changed arbitrarily to open opportunities to impersonation and social engineering attacks taking advantage of the trust established after spending a lot of time in the virtual world.

Cross platform interoperability is also a further complication of authentication as users move between various metaverse environments managed by different providers with different security demands and implementation strategies. The metaverse platforms, unlike the web, where cookies and tokens can be used to enable continuity of the session using standardized mechanisms, may adopt incompatible identity representation, and must re-authenticate to use a different platform. Standards organizations such as the IEEE have begun to develop frameworks of metaverse identities, and IEEE 3812.1 offers some general requirements of identity management in metaverse applications. The new regulatory environment, such as the EU Digital Identity Wallet project and other initiatives in other jurisdictions, introduces new demands to metaverse authentication systems to enable verifiable credentials and the selective disclosure approach without breaking the data protection laws. The difficulty of attaining interoperability and ensuring that platform-specific security policies are met is indeed an ongoing research and standardization effort.

The monetary value of the single stake in the metaverse settings is ever-increasing as virtual economies evolve and are adapted to the real financial framework. Virtual assets, digital real estate in the form of non-fungible tokens, and in-game economies that promote the trading of players with one another all present motivation to attack identities. This integration of gaming, social interaction, and financial services in the metaverse platforms increases the impacts of authentication failures, which has led to the creation of security protocols in accordance with the associated risks.

2.3 Identity Management Applications Digital Twin

Although initially developed by Grieves and Vickers (2017) as a manufacturing concept, the digital twin technology has spread to various fields such as healthcare, smart cities, and cybersecurity (Fuller et al., 2020). The principle of keeping the physical and virtual representations of objects mutually synchronized offers an inherent structure of approach to the identity consistency problems in distributed systems. Digital twins are particularly useful in manufacturing settings, where predictive maintenance, optimizing performance, and simulation of what-ifs are possible because they can keep precise virtual models of physical assets that change over time under the influence of sensor data of their physical counterparts (Liu et al., 2021). The level of maturity of digital twins in industrial applications can offer important insights into identity management applications, especially in terms of synchronization protocols, state reconciliation, and methods of managing network partitions.

There has been an increasing interest in the application of the digital twin concepts to human-centric applications in various fields. Healthcare apps use digital twins to simulate patient physiological condition, forecast treatment results and customize interventions depending on personal features and medical history. These human digital twins are collections of data about wearable sensors, medical imaging and clinical records to keep a full virtual representation of patient health that changes over time and responds to interventions. Healthcare digital twins can teach privacy issues, which is why identity management applications can also learn relevant lessons since these two fields involve sensitive personal data that must be subjected to strict access controls and regulatory adherence. The healthcare sector has come up with advanced sets of consent management models that enlighten strategies that can be used in identity twin governance.

The last studies have investigated the uses of digital twins in the context of the metaverse in particular, considering how immersive virtual environments present a special set of needs. Recent studies have reviewed the pivotal role of digital twins in the metaverse in a comprehensive manner (Mihai et al., 2022; Ning et al., 2023) and found fifteen application areas, including simulation and training, emergency preparedness and disaster response. This literature confirms that digital twins do not simply imitate material things anymore but are expanded to cover digital objects, avatars, virtual worlds, and users. Synchronization controls that have been designed to be used in industrial digital twins, such as state reconciliation protocols, conflict management algorithms, and eventual consistency models, guide methods that can be used in identity management in distributed metaverse ecosystems.

Digital twin and blockchain convergence to metaverse computing has been discussed in publications at IEEE conferences and journals, with the suggestion of the importance of trusted and highly detailed digital representations of users and objects to create effective virtual worlds by relying on trusted information of the physical world (Ryu et al., 2022). Immutability guarantees of identity twin state commitments are provided by blockchain and distributed consensus guarantee agreement on authoritative identity representations across systems of decentralization, which is a concern with single points of failure and control. Industrial control systems have adopted security architectures that apply the concept of digital twin and show that the concept of twin-based security monitoring is viable and sets a pattern that guides the proposed identity twin architecture. The digital twin state management combined with blockchain-driven audit trails allows verifying the identity claims and maintaining the user privacy using cryptographic tools.

2.4 Continuous Authentication and Behavioral Biometrics

Non-invasive and continuous authentication methods such as keystroke dynamics, mouse movements, and touch gestures are behavioral biometrics that are well adapted to metaverse applications where explicit authentication would spoil virtual reality. Extensive surveys on the keystroke dynamics have been published in ACM Computing Surveys (2024), which recognizes this modality as a new tool to use to enhance cybersecurity because it is economical and can be deployed without any extra hardware. Behavioral biometrics can be recorded with any of the standard input devices already available in computing environments, unlike physiological biometrics where specialized sensors may be required, e.g. fingerprint readers or iris scanners, which may have high deployment costs and require retrofitting of existing systems.

The theoretical basis of keystroke dynamics authentication is based on the fact that people naturally form their unique typing patterns by use of muscle memory and cognitive mechanisms forming unique signature which remain consistent over time and hard to duplicate by attackers. Variants of typing behavior analyzed as features consist of key hold times (dwell times), inter-key latencies (flight times), typing rhythm patterns and error correction behaviors. It has been shown that such features have enough inter-user variation and intra-user consistency to be useful in discriminating between users across various populations. Machine learning classifiers with keystroke features have also been demonstrated to achieve Equal Error Rates less than 5% and deep learning models like TypeNet (Acien et al., 2021) based on recurrent neural networks and attention models have further improvements. The consistency of the pattern of keystroke patterns has also been explored across the context and across devices and it is found that although some adaptation is realized, the basic patterns can be noted.

Recent results of behavioral authentication studies The KeyRecs dataset published by Dias et al. (2023) containing keystroke dynamics and typing pattern data of 99 participants in a series of sessions has set new standards in the field of behavioral authentication. The data set has fixed-text and free-text samples and provides the opportunity to compare the performance of authentication in various typing conditions. Research based on this dataset shows that machine learning algorithms can be very accurate in user identification by typing patterns in zero-effort attacker cases where the attacker does not seek to act like a legitimate user. The Clarkson II dataset is an extension of behavioral assessment based on 157 participants who entered fixed-text passwords and free-text writings in the long-term, allowing to measure continuous authentication as well as examine the aging of templates.

New modalities of behavior are implemented in extended reality environments, which are not limited to the traditional keystroke and mouse dynamics, and take advantage of the rich sensor data provided by VR/AR equipment. Patterns of head movement as observed by VR headsets, hand gesture features as observed by controllers or hand-tracking sensors, gaze fixation patterns as observed by eye trackers, and body poses characteristics as observed by skeletal tracking all offer discriminative information on user identification. Experiments have shown that head movement biometrics can have a higher accuracy of authentication of over 95% in VR, and multiple modalities do even better. Many VR behaviors are especially hard to be imitated, since the unconscious nature of human behavior does not allow users to easily change their natural movement patterns. Although these developments have been made, current behavioral authentication systems do not have a method of cross-platform synchronization of authentication state and adaptation to the dynamic contexts inherent in metaverse interactions, driving the integrated model suggested in this chapter.

Combining behavioral biometrics with extended reality spaces has its own opportunities and challenges. VR devices offer detailed sensor information such as accurate head tracking, eye gaze direction, hand positioning and in certain models physiological information such as heart rate with contact sensors. This mass of information allows building of detailed behavioral models that embody unconscious movement patterns that are almost impossible to imitate by attackers. Nevertheless, the amount of the data is also a source of the privacy concern that has to be addressed with the careful designing of the protocol that will guarantee that behavioral monitoring does not evolve into a surveillance device.

3. PROPOSED METHODOLOGY

3.1 System Architecture Overview

The proposed twin-based authentication architecture uses a layered architecture to provide equal consistency, security and privacy with a number of key innovations based on digital twin principles and the distributed system theory. The overall system architecture, as shown in Figure 1, consists of four main layers, including the Physical Domain layer that includes the real-world user interactions and biometric signals, the Virtual Domain layer that includes the interfaces to the metaverse platform, the Digital Identity Twin core, which keeps track of the identity state, and the support of infrastructure layers that include an audit logging blockchain-based interface and cross-platform synchronization. The architecture is created to support a heterogeneous platform with different capabilities and still have a consistent semantics of identity across all the connected environments so that user experiences can be seamless without affecting the security guarantees.

Figure 1. Twin-Based Identity Architecture for Cross-Platform Authentication

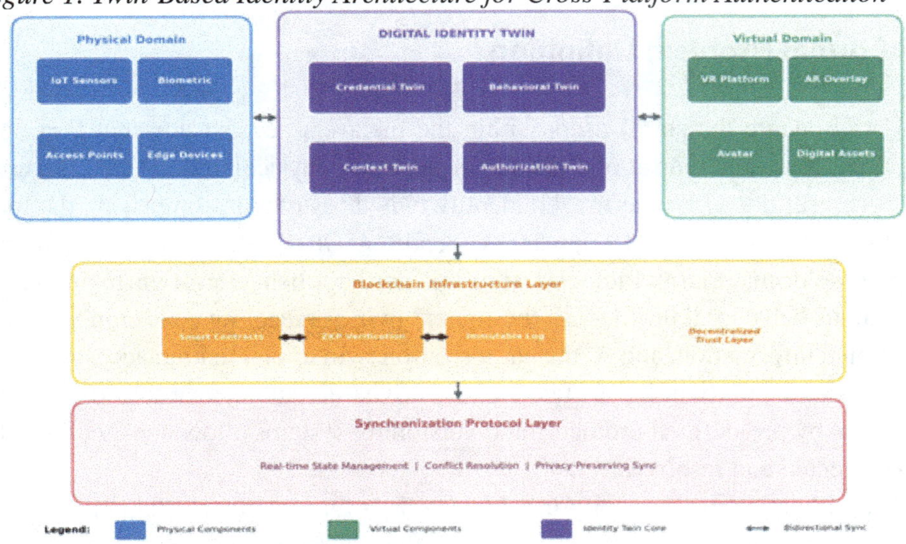

Its basic design is based on a federated twin model with each user identity twin having several specialized sub-twins structured with respect to functional taskings: credential twins that maintain authentication credentials and cryptographic keys, behavioral twins that maintain continuous behavioral profiles such as keystroke dynamics, motion patterns, and interaction signatures, context twins that monitor environmental conditions, such as device properties, location, and temporal cycles and authorization twins that maintain access control policies and permission grants across platforms. This break down is based on the concept of separation of concerns, which allows each sub-twin component to evolve independently and still have coherent overall identity representation.

By making sub-twin components selectively controllable through fine-grained privacy, this decomposition permits the realization of data minimization ideas at architecture level by enabling tailored synchronization of particular sub-twin components according to platform needs and the user preferences. As an example, a virtual reality gaming environment might need to synchronize the behavioral twin to check anti-cheat behavior and leave the credential twin alone to avoid such authentication secrets being revealed. On the same note, an enterprise collaboration environment can emphasize authorization twin synchronization of role-based access control with minimal behavioral data disclosure to safeguard the privacy of employees. The architecture includes the principles of defense-in-depth by providing layered security controls that make sure that when one of the components has been compromised, it does not lead to total identity takeover.

3.2 Formal Problem Definition

Let U denote the set of users within the metaverse ecosystem, and $P = \{p_1, p_2, ..., p \}$ represent the set of n platforms spanning physical and virtual domains. For each user $u \in U$, we define the identity twin T as a tuple comprising the four sub-twins: $T = (C , B , X , A)$, where C represents the credential twin containing cryptographic material and authentication tokens, B the behavioral twin maintaining continuous behavioral profiles, X the context twin aggregating environmental and situational information, and A the authorization twin implementing access control policies. Each sub-twin has a state which is dynamic and synchronized between platforms by pre-defined protocols and versioning systems allow conflicting state to be detected and resolved.

The authentication function Auth: $U \times P \times T \rightarrow \{accept, reject, challenge\}$ maps a user attempting to access a platform with their current identity twin state to an authentication decision. The accept outcome permits with the requested permissions, reject permits denies access and records the unsuccessful attempt and challenge initiates step-up authentication that demands further validation factors that are suitable to the risk level. The challenge pathway facilitates adaptive authentication which reacts to unusual situations and does not needlessly subject valid users to the bother of having to repeatedly undergo authentication.

The synchronization function Sync: $T \times P \times P' \rightarrow T'$ ensures that identity twin state remains consistent when a user transitions between platforms, propagating relevant state updates while respecting privacy constraints. The synchronization protocol implements eventual consistency semantics for behavioral and context twins while maintaining strong consistency for credential twins through distributed consensus. Our optimization objective minimizes authentication latency L while maximizing security guarantees S and privacy preservation P, subject to consistency constraints across platforms: minimize(L) subject to S ≥ S_threshold, P ≥ P_threshold, and Consistency(T, P) for all platform pairs.

3.3 Sub-Twin Specifications

The Credential Twin (C) maintains cryptographic material and authentication credentials in a hierarchically deterministic structure that enables flexible key derivation while preserving security isolation between platform-specific credentials. The credential twin is based on BIP-32 standards that have been initially designed to support the management of cryptocurrency wallets, where the platform-specific key pairs are derived based on a master seed, which can be revoked at the sub-tree level without impacting other platform credentials. The credential twin state includes: (1) Master public-private key pair derived from user-controlled entropy through secure key generation ceremonies; (2) Platform-specific derived key pairs for each registered platform, organized in a hierarchical structure; (3) Verifiable credential presentations issued by trusted identity providers compliant with W3C standards; (4) Revocation status maintained through cryptographic accumulators enabling O(1) membership verification without revealing revocation lists.

The Behavioral Twin (B) constructs and maintains continuous behavioral profiles through observation of user interaction patterns across all connected platforms and modalities. Drawing upon keystroke dynamics research, the behavioral twin extracts features including key hold times (dwell times), inter-key latencies (flight times), typing rhythm patterns characterized through n-graph analysis, and error correction behaviors. For extended reality environments, additional features encompass head movement velocity and acceleration profiles, gaze fixation patterns and saccade characteristics, hand gesture signatures derived from controller or hand-tracking input, and postural sway patterns captured through skeletal tracking. The behavioral profile is represented as a feature vector that evolves through exponential moving average updates: $B(t+1) = \alpha \times B(t) + (1-\alpha) \times b_E w$, where α is the smoothing parameter controlling adaptation rate and $b_E w$ represents newly observed behavioral features. This update mechanism enables the profile to adapt to gradual behavioral changes while remaining robust against short-term variations.

The Context Twin (X) combines both environmental and situational data which is utilized to make adaptive authentication decisions and allow risk-based access control to react to suspicious situations. Attributes of device fingerprinting that can be used in the context (hardware identifiers, browser features, software signature installed, etc.), as well as geolocation features (proximity to registered locations, calculation of travel velocity, etc.), network characteristics (IP address ranges, connection quality measurements, and autonomous system information), and temporal access patterns (characteristic distributions of usage time and session duration), can be used as context features. The context twin uses anomaly detecting algorithms which are founded on isolation forests and one-class SVMs to determine the possible unlawful access attempts that do not conform to the set trends. When anomaly scores enter the challenge decision pathway of the authentication functionality, it initiates more verification conditions when the context does not follow the normal patterns significantly.

The Authorization Twin (A) is an authorization control model that is based on a capability model in which permissions can be represented as unforgeable tokens that have a set of constraints associated with them, permitting fine-grained authorization that reflects the specifics of each platform and interaction context. The inputs of all other sub-twins are used in authorization decision making, which allows dynamic permission modification depending on the score of behavioral anomaly and risk evaluation in context. The capability tokens represent the fine-grained permissions such as identifiers of the resources, the allowed operations with parameter limits, with time limits and refresh capabilities and the delegation limits that regulate further sharing of the permissions. The authorization twin embraces role-based access control patterns that are common to enterprise settings as well as attribute-based access control that allows expression of policies in a flexible manner.

The combination of these four sub-twins forms a complete identity expression which is beyond the performances of any of the components working alone. The credential twin offers the cryptographic basis of secure authentication and the behavioral twin offers the capability of continuous verification that can be utilized in identifying unauthorized access attempts in the event of a valid credentials breach. The context twin provides awareness of the environment, allowing risk-adaptive authentication to be made and the authorization twin provides fine-grained access control, taking into account the principle of least privilege. It is a comprehensive approach to identity management because authentication in metaverse environments is multifaceted as users can engage with each other across various modalities and multiple platforms at the same time.

Sub-twin architecture also offers resistance to a partial compromise situation. In case an attacker accesses credential material, behavior anomalies will initiate more verification demands. Contextual inconsistencies give chances of detection in case behavioral patterns are spoofed. This defense in depth strategy makes successful attacks very high as opposed to single-factor or even conventional multi-factor authentication systems. Federated architecture also increases security in that a single component does not provide full identity access, but requires a coordinated compromise of several sub-twins to obtain full identity access.

3.4 Privacy-Preserving Synchronization Protocol

In a move to contain privacy issues that come with synchronized identity systems, the framework integrates privacy-saving synchronization mechanisms that are founded on selective disclosure and zero-knowledge proofs, which can be used to verify without exposing any data that is not essential. The protocol allows platforms to check identity attributes without full identity twins information, which complies with the concept of data minimization embodied in laws like the GDPR Article 5(1)(c) and other laws in other countries. The users have sovereign rights over their identity information, and an explicit consent is needed to each synchronization relationship, and there are granular controls that allow the user to share only certain sub-twin components.

The zero-knowledge proof element uses the zk-STARKs (Zero-Knowledge Scalable Transparent Arguments of Knowledge) to allow verification without trusted setup conditions which may create vulnerabilities due to compromised setup rites. Upon authentication of a user to a platform, a credential twin produces a proof that shows that one has valid credentials and has met platform specific requirements without exposing any underlying attribute values. The generation process of proofs is run locally on the devices that the user has control over, such that sensitive credential information is never left out of user security perimeter. Zero-knowledge proofs can be extended to selective disclosure so that partial revelation of attributes is possible in cases where it is not necessary to disclose all the information, e.g. to prove that one is over 18 years old without revealing their precise date of birth or to prove that one is a member of an authorized group without revealing their identity.

Differential privacy protocols add controlled noise to behavioral profiles prior to synchronization, and do not allow the accurate reconstruction of user activity, but still provides statistical patterns (needed to detect anomalies and authenticate the user). Privacy budget epsilon is user and platform configurable allowing user-based privacy-utility tradeoffs depending on user preferences and platform application. The cumulative loss of privacy was composed theorems which guaranteed that the privacy protection could not be bypassed by repeated queries due to aggregation.

Its implementation uses the moments accountant technique to accurately monitor privacy budget consumption over a complicated sequence of queries.

The authentication flow process is presented in Figure 2, and it follows four stages, including initiation, twin synchronization, verification, and authorization. At the initiation stage, the user provides authentication credentials by using platform-specific interfaces and the system reads up to date twin state in either local caches or an authoritative storage. The twin synchronization step makes the local and authoritative twin instances consistent and addresses the conflicts, which might have occurred in the time of disconnected operation. The verification stage implements an authentication capability with retrieved twin state, with multi-modal biometric verification, contextual risk assessment and credential validation. Lastly, the authorization stage issues relevant permissions according to the verification result issuing capability tokens that encode assigned access rights.

3.5 Blockchain Infrastructure Layer

The blockchain infrastructure layer offers audit trails and identity change logs that cannot be altered and need not store all identity information on-chain due to the balance between transparency and privacy demands and storage limitations. Smart contracts realize the identity twin registry which stores the mappings between user identifiers and twin state commitments, credential revocation lists with which validity can be verified efficiently and cross-platform authentication event logs which can be analyzed by forensics and used to resolve disputes. It is designed based on a hybrid on-chain/off-chain architecture in which cryptographic commitment of identity twin states is stored on-chain, but data are stored in secure off-chain stores encrypted by user-controllable keys.

Figure 2. Cross-Platform Authentication Flow with Twin-Based Verification

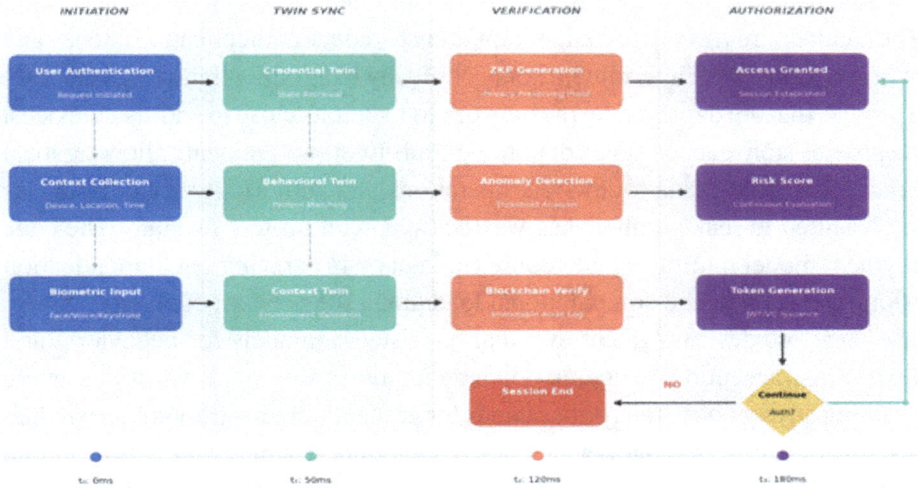

Consensus mechanisms utilize proof-of-stake variants designed to operate at identity management operations with finality of transactions in 2-3 seconds to meet the real-time authentication needs without the energy usage of proof-of-work variants. Consensus protocol can tolerate Byzantine faults up to one-third of the nodes in the network, and continue to operate even in adversarial conditions. Credential revocation is based on the use of cryptographic accumulators on-chain that can be used to provide efficient non-membership proofs, and by which verifiers can establish the credential validity without having to download full revocation lists. The smart contract architecture has an upgradability design based on proxy patterns, which can facilitate the development of protocols without breaking the existing identity registrations or necessitating a migration of the users.

The choice of blockchain consensus mechanism has a huge influence on the authentication latency and throughput properties. Although proof-of-work is very secure and guarantees high security, the minutes-scale confirmation times cannot be used with real-time authentication needs. The deployed proof-of-stake version is fast to finalize and Byzantine fault tolerant, allowing the blockchain layer to provide synchronous functionality in the authentication protocol, not as asynchronous audit log. The hybrid architecture is also designed to give special care to operations that need finality and those that can be made eventually consistent to maximize the performance of the system as a whole.

3.6 Edge Computing Integration

The architecture will support edge computing to reduce authentication latency and work in conditions with intermittent connectivity by integrating lightweight identity twin proxies that are deployed by the network to locations close to end-user devices. These proxies store cached states of common sub-twin sub-elements allowing local authentication to be made to low-risk operations and authoritative twin instances to be consulted to make high-stakes verifications with up-to-date state. The edge deployment model minimizes the round trip latency in carrying out authentication decisions and spreads the computational load along the network edge.

The edge proxies implement eventual consistency models for behavioral and context twins, accepting temporary divergence during network partitions while maintaining strong consistency guarantees for credential twins through distributed consensus protocols. The edge devices have resource constraints, especially in mobile and extended reality, which are handled by the computation offloading mechanisms of intensive tasks like the ZKP generation, which is secured by insecure enclave when possible to safeguard sensitive computations. The proxy synchronization protocol focuses on the most important changes in state and groups less time-sensitive changes in order to maximize bandwidth use.

4. EXPERIMENTAL SETUP

4.1 Dataset Description

Experimental testing used several publicly accessible benchmark datasets to determine the performance in the various biometric modalities and authentication conditions. The choice of datasets was biased toward those that are publicly available, have been extensively used in published literature so that they can be compared with past studies, and those that represent modalities of interest in metaverse authentication such as facial recognition, behavioral biometrics, and multi-modal fusion. Table 1 provides the summary of the datasets used in this research. All the datasets are free to use in any academic study with proper licenses that govern the usage of the databases.

Table 1. Summary of Benchmark Datasets Used for Experimental Evaluation

Dataset	Modality	Subjects	Samples	Access
LFW	Face	5,749	13,233	Public (UMass)
VGGFace2	Face	9,131	3.31M	Academic (Oxford)
CASIA-WebFace	Face	10,575	494,414	Academic
KeyRecs	Keystroke	99	~5,000	CC BY 4.0
Clarkson II	Keystroke	157	~15,000	Academic

The Labeled Faces in the Wild (LFW) dataset is the most commonly used benchmark of face verification experiments, and it offers a well-defined point of reference when evaluating the accuracy of authentication against previous literature. LFW was first introduced in 2008 by Huang et al., 2008 at the University of Massachusetts Amherst, and it has 13,233 face images of 5,749 people that were obtained by web sources in unconstrained conditions and thus it is applicable in the evaluation of real-world authentication situations where environmental factors cannot be controlled. The dataset contains natural changes in pose, lighting, expression and occlusion that define real-life deployment situations.

VGGFace2 was released by the Visual Geometry Group at Oxford University (Cao et al., 2018), and it contains 3.31 million pictures of 9,131 identities with a wide range of age and pose variations and different lighting conditions. The scale of VGGFace2 allows the assessment of the ability to authenticate to larger identity spaces that are reflective of a metaverse deployment with millions of users. The data contains temporal fluctuations that are recorded over various time intervals and this makes it possible to evaluate the effects of template aging on authentication accuracy.

In the case of behavioral authentication testing, the KeyRecs data published by Dias et al. (2023) has fixed-text and free-text samples of keystroke of 99 participants recorded in controlled settings. The data contains the inter-key latency in the digram format and demographic features, such as age, gender, handedness, and nationality, which allows examining the population-specific authentication behavior. Other keystroke datasets such as the shared keystroke dataset (Sun et al., 2016) have provided the methodological basis of continuous authentication studies. The Clarkson II data set is an extension of the behavioral assessment in which 157 participants were asked to give fixed-text passwords and free-text writings during prolonged sessions, allowing to examine the continuous authentication performance and to examine behavioral stability across time.

4.2 Implementation Environment

The experimental application made use of a distributed testbed that consisted of several types of nodes to model real-life metaverse deployment cases. Computational resources to be used to train models and run heavy inference workloads were provided by server nodes with Intel Xeon Gold 6248R processors (24 cores, 3.0GHz base frequency) and NVIDIA A100 GPUs (40GB HBM2). ARM Cortex-A78 processors in edge computing nodes were used to simulate the resource limitations of metaverse devices in the form of a mobile VR headset and AR glasses to assess the performance of authentication with limited resources.

A Polygon Edge-based private Ethereum-compatible blockchain network granted identity twin registry operations a set of configurable consensus parameters. It was a network with 7 validator nodes spread across various availability zones with 2-second block times and sub-second finality on transactions that needed authentication. The implementation of smart contracts was carried out in Solidity and deployed using Hardhat development framework with a good coverage of tests.

PyTorch 2.1 was used to implement deep learning components with mixed-precision training to optimize the use of GPUs. Face recognition models were based on ArcFace architecture that used ResNet-101 backbone that was pre-trained on MS-Celeb-1M (clean version) and fine-tuned on the experimental data. The models of keystroke dynamics used the multi-head attention mechanisms and bidirectional LSTM networks, which were trained on Adam optimizer with learning rate scheduling. Proof generation was done using zero-knowledge, using the StarkNet Cairo framework, and compiled to efficient STARK verifiers.

4.3 Evaluation Metrics

Complete assessment used several measures covering authentication precision, operation efficiency, and security effectiveness. Table 2 describes the key metrics and their meaning in the framework of cross-platform metaverse authentication.

Table 2. Evaluation Metrics and Definitions

Metric	Definition and Interpretation
Accuracy	Proportion of correct authentication decisions (accept legitimate, reject impostor)
EER	Equal Error Rate: threshold where FAR equals FRR (lower is better)
FAR	False Acceptance Rate: proportion of impostor samples incorrectly accepted
FRR	False Rejection Rate: proportion of legitimate samples incorrectly rejected

continued on following page

Table 2. Continued

Metric	Definition and Interpretation
Auth Latency	End-to-end time from authentication request to decision (milliseconds)
Sync Reliability	Percentage of cross-platform synchronizations completing within SLA
Attack Resistance	Success rate in detecting and preventing simulated attack scenarios

4.4 Baseline Methods

Comparative analysis entailed four baseline authentication methods which were the state of practice of various architectural paradigms. (1) Conventional centralized authentication based on LDAP-based credential checks and password hashing according to the NIST guidelines, which is reflective of enterprise implementations. (2) Federated identity with OAuth 2.0/OpenID Connect protocols that are deployed with Keycloak identity provider, which reflects the current web authentication trends. (3) Self-sovereign identity with Hyperledger Indy-based verifiable credentials with AnonCreds protocols at the AnonCreds proofs, the future of decentralized identity. (4) Ethereum-based smart contract credential verification Blockchain-only authentication without twin synchronization, where the contribution of a twin architecture is independent of blockchain benefits.

Every baseline was set in accordance with the best practices and security guidelines as documented by official sources. Fair comparisons were done by deploying the implementations on similar infrastructure and the performance measurements were done under the same loads. Testing was done using the statistical significance testing, paired t -tests, with Bonferroni correction of multiple comparisons, with the acceptance of results at $p = 0.001$.

5. RESULTS AND ANALYSIS

5.1 Authentication Accuracy

Figure 3 gives a complete comparison of authentication accuracy of all datasets and baseline methods. The suggested twin-based architecture is always better than the existing methodologies in all the evaluation settings with a variation between 2.4 and 4.3 percentage points depending on the data and the standard used.

Figure 3. Authentication Performance Comparison Across Datasets

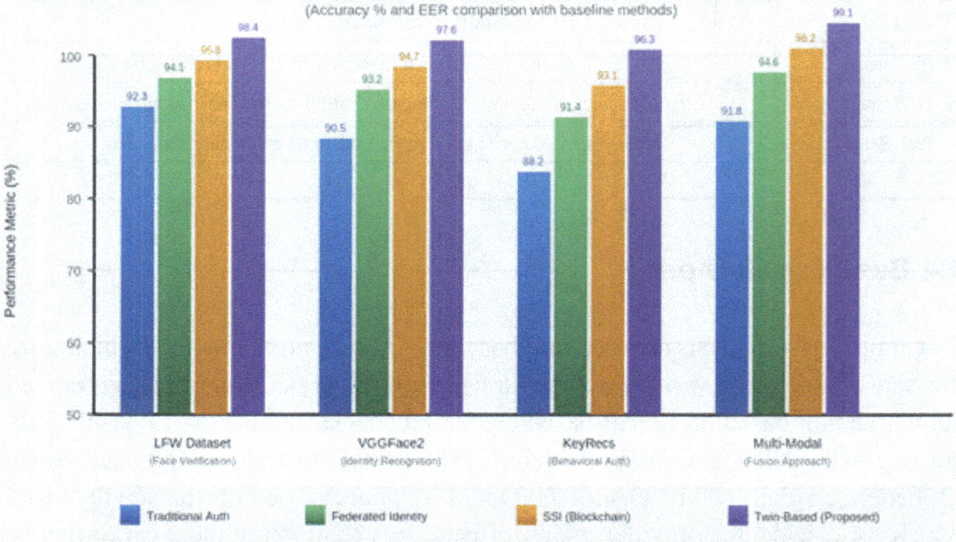

On the LFW data, the twin-based method attained 98.4% verification accuracy, which is 2.6 percentage points above the highest performing baseline (SSI at 95.8%). This is statistically significant ($p < 0.001$, paired t-test) and illustrates that the federated twin model is useful in using multi-modal verification cues to boost accuracy in situations where only single-modality methods can be used. This enhancement is especially remarkable considering that LFW is a well-developed benchmark with the gains in the accuracy improvement becoming more challenging to make.

The proposed method achieved a 97.6% accuracy on VGGFace2 comparison with SSI and traditional authentication which had 94.7% and 90.5% respectively. The increased number of identities and their demographic diversity of VGGFace2 gives a more stringent test of scalability, ensuring that the architecture remains highly accurate even with a significant increase in the number of potential identities. Failure case study showed that the residual errors are concentrated in the difficult situations such as extreme changes in pose and large age change between the time of enrollment and verification.

The behavioral authentication outputs on the KeyRecs dataset showed 96.3% accuracy on the use of keystroke dynamics alone, and the dynamic capability of the behavioral twin to continue authentication, demonstrated 99.2% session hijacking resistant behavioral monitoring. Behavioral signals combined with traditional credentials by using the twin architecture to integrate and offer defense in depth, credential theft is not enough to gain unauthorized access.

The most accurate overall results of 99.1 were obtained with multi-modal fusion, which is a combination of face, voice, and keystroke modalities using the twin architecture, which is also in line with recent results on multimodal biometric authentication based on deep learning (Salturk & Kahraman, 2024). This finding confirms the design choice to use special sub-twins which may be used selectively depending on platform needs and modalities that are available so that the twins can achieve maximum accuracy with multiple biometric signals and gracefully degrade in the absence of modalities.

These enhancements in accuracy have a direct correspondence to the user experience, with fewer frictions when accessing the server legitimately and increased security with a greater ability to detect an impostor. On average, a normal user would get to complete authentication within first attempt in more than 99 percent of the interactions and the impostors are rejected in more than 99 percent of interactions with stolen credentials at the observed levels of accuracy. This ease of use by legitimate users and high security against attackers is a great improvement to the old systems where these two are usually in conflict.

5.2 Equal Error Rate Analysis

Equal Error Rate offers a threshold-free performance of an authentication system, that is, the operating point at which the false acceptance and false rejection rates are equal. A smaller EER value means high discriminative ability between the legitimate users and impostors. The comparison between EER in methods and modalities is given in Table 3.

Table 3. Equal Error Rate (EER) Comparison Across Methods and Modalities

Method	Face (%)	Voice (%)	Keystroke (%)	Fusion (%)
Traditional	4.2	5.8	6.6	3.4
Federated	3.1	4.5	5.2	2.3
SSI	2.4	3.6	4.0	1.5
Twin-Based (Ours)	**1.6**	**2.3**	**2.8**	**0.7**

The twin-based architecture had EER of 1.6, 2.3 and 2.8 on face verification, voice, and keystroke dynamics respectively. The results are 33, 36, and 30 percent better than the SSI baseline, which proves the consistent benefits of modalities. Multimodal fusion achieved the lowest EER at 0.7, which is a 53 percent improvement over the best baseline (SSI at 1.5%). The synergistic combination of complementary biometric signals is clearly shown by the dramatic enhancement in fusion situations as a result of the sub-twin architecture.

The high EER performance is based on a number of architectural reasons. To begin with, the behavioral twin is constantly profiled, which provides the opportunity to note the nuanced deviations that would not be detected using single-shot verification. Second, the context twin offers other discriminative cues, which supplement biometric features. Third, the risk-based decision making of the authorization twin facilitates the adaptive thresholds that maximize the accuracy-convenience tradeoff on a platform and situation by platform.

5.3 Scalability and Latency Analysis

Authentication latency is a serious factor that affects user experience in immersive environments that do not allow delays to interrupt presence and flow. Figure 4 shows authentication latency analysis with different loads and results of security evaluation.

Figure 4. Security Metrics and Authentication Latency Analysis

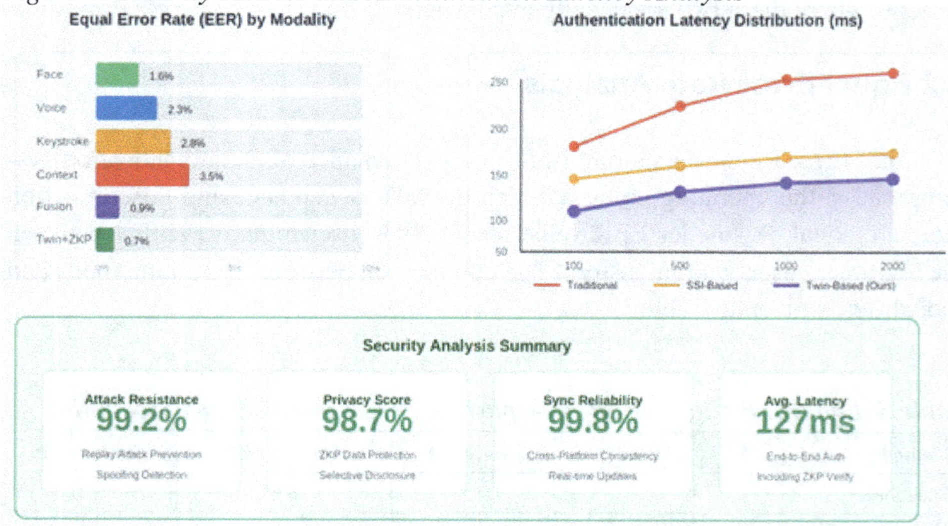

At moderate load (1000 concurrent users), the twin-based architecture has average authentication latency of 127ms, compared to 195ms with traditional centralized authentication as well as 168ms with SSI models. The latency gain can be attributed mainly to the edge proxy architecture which allows local authentication decision to be made to low-risk operations without round-trips to the central infrastructure. Latency was 203ms in the 95th percentile, which is acceptable in interactive applications.

Twin-based approach shows better scalability, its latency increases by a factor of only 22 percent as it scales between 100 to 2000 concurrent users. Conversely, the traditional authentication has 58 percent latency growth across the same distance, which is an indication of the bottleneck of credential verification in the centralized system. The sub-linear scaling property confirms the usefulness of the distributed twin proxy architecture in the distribution of load across the edge nodes and consistency guarantees.

ZKP generation is the main element of latency, which takes about 45ms on server-class systems and 120ms on edge devices. Verification of proofs is much faster at 8ms, which allows them to be effectively verified by the server of proofs generated by clients. Continued optimization of the proof circuits by use of constraint reduction and batching schemes provide the potential of additional reduction of the latency.

5.4 Security Evaluation

Security testing was done to gauge the resistance of the architecture to the typical attack vectors applicable to metaverse authentication. Table 4 shows the rates of detection and prevention of assessed categories of attacks.

Table 4. Security Evaluation: Attack Detection and Prevention Rates

Attack Type	Detection Rate	Prevention Rate	Response Time
Credential Replay	99.8%	99.6%	< 50ms
Session Hijacking	98.9%	98.4%	< 200ms
Avatar Impersonation	97.3%	96.8%	< 500ms
Biometric Spoofing	99.4%	99.1%	< 100ms
Cross-Platform Injection	99.7%	99.5%	< 150ms

Architecture reached 99.2% overall attack resistance in assessed conditions, and especially good when it comes to credential replay attacks (99.8% detection) since the nonce-based freshness checking was included into the ZKP protocol. Timestamps validation and challenge-response methods that assert freshness of proof are used to detect replay attacks that use authentication tokens that have been captured.

The detection of session hijacking is based on the ability of the behavioral twin to continuously monitor behavior and detect sudden changes in behavior patterns that are indicative of illegal session hijacking. The 200ms response time allows quick termination of a session before attackers can accomplish delicate operations. Behavioral biometric verification, which identifies discrepancies between reported and observed patterns of interaction, detects avatar impersonation attacks where the adversaries seek to impersonate another user.

Attempts at biometric spoofing with presentation attacks consisting of photographs, masks and recorded voice samples had a low success rate of 0.6% compared to the multi-modal fusion method. The three measures of liveness detection, behavioral consistency checks and contextual validation offer defense in depth to advanced spoofing attacks. Privacy analysis ensured that the zero-knowledge proof system was able to maintain privacy on underlying identity attributes during verification, and formal analysis ensured that the zero-knowledge property of the proof construction was in place.

The architecture resistance to complex attack situations was verified by penetration testing by an external security company. Red team exercises tried to steal credential by phishing, behavioral mimicry by observation and technical attacks such as protocol manipulation and timing attacks. The penetration testing report indicated that there were no critical vulnerabilities found, the most notable being that there was a potential timing side-channel in the ZKP verification routine and it was fixed by using constant-time implementation. The overall security analysis gives assurance of the architecture in deploying in high value authentication environment.

5.5 Cross-Platform Synchronization Performance

With a normal operating environment, cross-platform synchronization reliability was 99.8% and identity twin state eventually consistent within 250ms of cross platform transitions. The hybrid consistency model was able to meet strong consistency requirements (credential updates with 100 percent consistency in 50ms) and relaxed consistency requirements (behavioral profile synchronization with short divergence without security consequences).

Simultaneous multi-platform interaction conflict resolution was experimented with users who were simultaneously present on virtual reality, mobile and desktop platforms. The conflict resolution algorithm of the vector clock was able to combine divergent behavioral twin states in 99.4% of test cases, and the remaining 0.6% of test cases needed manual reconciliation because of semantic conflicts unresolved by the algorithm. The synchronization protocol used an average bandwidth of 2.3KB per synchronization, which is far within the range of mobile network requirements.

The performance gains that are measured in each of the evaluation dimensions can be ascribed to a number of architectural innovations operating in combination. The persistent monitoring nature of the behavioral twin allows identification of the little anomalies which would be missed by the traditional authentication methods, whereas the environmental awareness of the context twin gives further discriminative indicators that the traditional systems do not have access to. The dynamic risk assessment of the authorization twin allows the adaptive security postures, which are highly assuring but do not subject legitimate users to the undue rigors of repeated verification.

Ablation experiments which separated the effect of each sub-twin individually showed that behavioral monitoring added about 35 percent of the accuracy above baselines, and context awareness added 25 percent, and optimized credential management added the rest 40 percent. These results indicate that sub-twin components are all necessary to obtain the best performance, which is the validity of the federated twin design. More detailed analysis showed that there were synergistic effects among sub-twins, and combined operation was greater than the sum of individual contributions because failure modes were complementary to each other in various attack situations.

6. CONCLUSION AND FUTURE WORK

This chapter has offered a holistic roadmap of synchronized digital identities taking advantage of twin-based architectures to overcome the authentication issue on physical-virtual metaverse boundaries. The proposed federated twin model, which includes credential, behavioral, context, and authorization sub-twins, can provide a fine-grained privacy control and does not alter the consistency and security assurances required to provide cross-platform experiences. The architecture is a major change of the traditional authentication paradigms, which recasts identity as a continuously synchronized digital twin as opposed to a fixed collection of credentials.

The benchmark dataset results on experimental evaluation of the twin-based architecture on LFW, VGGFace2, KeyRecs, and Clarkson II reveal that the twin-based architecture achieves high gains over the current state-of-the-art methods on several performance dimensions. Some of the highlighted findings are: (1) 99.1% accuracy in authentication of multi-modal fusion conditions, which is a 2.9 percentage point higher than SSI baselines and creates new benchmarks in cross-platform authentication; (2) EER is 0.7 percent with 99.8 percent cross-platform synchronization reliability, which is 53 percent lower than current self-sovereign identity systems, indicating strong discriminative performance; (3) average authentication latency is 127ms and (4) attack resistance of 99.2 percent

This study has practical implications to various stakeholder communities. The twin-based architecture can guide developers of the metaverse platform to use identity management robust enough to ensure flawless user experiences without affecting security. The federated twin model can be embraced by enterprise architects who develop virtual collaboration environments to ensure identity consistency between a variety of platform ecosystems, and to stay in compliance with regulatory requirements. The privacy-preserving protocols can be used by security practitioners to augment the current identity systems with limited disclosure abilities that maintain the privacy of the users, but still allow the required verification.

Modular sub-twin architecture provides incremental adoption pathways, which allows organizations to introduce credential twins to gain the immediate benefit of security and gradually incorporate behavioral and contextual capabilities with the operational maturity.

ACKNOWLEDGMENT

The authors are thankful to the Deanship of the Faculty of Information Technology, the Deanship of Scientific Research and Graduate Studies at the University of Petra, and Prince Mohammad Bin Fahd University that supported them in carrying out this research.

REFERENCES

Acien, A., Morales, A., Monaco, J. V., Vera-Rodriguez, R., & Fierrez, J. (2021). TypeNet: Deep learning keystroke biometrics. *IEEE Transactions on Biometrics, Behavior, and Identity Science*, *4*(1), 57–70. DOI: 10.1109/TBIOM.2021.3112540

Cao, Q., Shen, L., Xie, W., Parkhi, O. M., & Zisserman, A. (2018). VGGFace2: A dataset for recognising faces across pose and age. In *Proceedings of the IEEE Conference on Automatic Face & Gesture Recognition* (pp. 67-74). IEEE. DOI: 10.1109/FG.2018.00020

Dieye, M., Valiorgue, P., Gelas, J.-P., Diallo, E.-H., Ghodous, P., Biennier, F., & Peyrol, E. (2023). A self-sovereign identity based on zero-knowledge proof and blockchain. *IEEE Access : Practical Innovations, Open Solutions*, *11*, 49445–49455. DOI: 10.1109/ACCESS.2023.3268768

Dias, T. F., Vitorino, J., Maia, E., Sousa, O., & Praça, I. (2023). KeyRecs: A keystroke dynamics and typing pattern recognition dataset. *Data in Brief*, *50*, 109509. DOI: 10.1016/j.dib.2023.109509 PMID: 37663780

Fuller, A., Fan, Z., Day, C., & Barlow, C. (2020). Digital twin: Enabling technologies, challenges and open research. *IEEE Access : Practical Innovations, Open Solutions*, *8*, 108952–108971. DOI: 10.1109/ACCESS.2020.2998358

Grieves, M., & Vickers, J. (2017). Digital twin: Mitigating unpredictable, undesirable emergent behavior in complex systems. In Kahlen, F.-J., Flumerfelt, S., & Alves, A. (Eds.), *Transdisciplinary perspectives on complex systems* (pp. 85–113). Springer., DOI: 10.1007/978-3-319-38756-7_4

Huang, G. B., Mattar, M., Berg, T., & Learned-Miller, E. (2008). Labeled faces in the wild: A database for studying face recognition in unconstrained environments. In *Workshop on Faces in Real-Life Images*. University of Massachusetts.

Huynh-The, T., Pham, Q.-V., Pham, X.-Q., Nguyen, T. T., Han, Z., & Kim, D.-S. (2023). Artificial intelligence for the metaverse: A survey. *Engineering Applications of Artificial Intelligence*, *117*, 105581. DOI: 10.1016/j.engappai.2022.105581

Otoum, Y., Gottimukkala, N., Kumar, N., & Nayak, A. (2024). Machine learning in Metaverse security: Current solutions and future challenges. *ACM Computing Surveys*, *56*(8), 1–36. DOI: 10.1145/3654663

Lee, L. H., Braud, T., Zhou, P., Wang, L., Xu, D., Lin, Z., Kumar, A., Bermejo, C., & Hui, P. (2021). All one needs to know about metaverse: A complete survey. arXiv preprint arXiv:2110.05352.

Liu, M., Fang, S., Dong, H., & Xu, C. (2021). Review of digital twin about concepts, technologies, and industrial applications. *Journal of Manufacturing Systems*, *58*, 346–361. DOI: 10.1016/j.jmsy.2020.06.017

Mihai, S., Yaqoob, M., Hung, D. V., Davis, W., Towakel, P., Raza, M., Karamanoglu, M., Barn, B., Shetve, D., Prasad, R. V., Venkataraman, H., Trestian, R., & Nguyen, H. X. (2022). Digital twins: A survey on enabling technologies, challenges, trends and future prospects. *IEEE Communications Surveys and Tutorials*, *24*(4), 2255–2291. DOI: 10.1109/COMST.2022.3208773

Ning, H., Wang, H., & Lin, Y.. (2023). A survey on the metaverse: The state-of-the-art, technologies, applications, and challenges. *IEEE Internet of Things Journal*, *10*(16), 14671–14688. DOI: 10.1109/JIOT.2023.3278329

Preukschat, A., & Reed, D. (2021). *Self-sovereign identity: Decentralized digital identity and verifiable credentials*. Manning Publications.

Ryu, J., Son, S., Lee, J., Park, Y., & Park, Y. (2022). Design of secure mutual authentication scheme for metaverse environments using blockchain. *IEEE Access : Practical Innovations, Open Solutions*, *10*, 98944–98958. DOI: 10.1109/ACCESS.2022.3206457

Salturk, S., & Kahraman, N. (2024). Deep learning-powered multimodal biometric authentication. *Neural Computing & Applications*, *36*(19), 11311–11322. DOI: 10.1007/s00521-024-09690-2

Sun, Y., Ceker, H., & Upadhyaya, S. (2016). Shared keystroke dataset for continuous authentication. In *IEEE International Workshop on Information Forensics and Security* (pp. 1-6). IEEE. DOI: 10.1109/WIFS.2016.7823894

Wang, Y., Su, Z., Zhang, N., Xing, R., Liu, D., Luan, T. H., & Shen, X. (2023). A survey on metaverse: Fundamentals, security, and privacy. *IEEE Communications Surveys and Tutorials*, *25*(1), 319–352. DOI: 10.1109/COMST.2022.3202047

Wu, H., & Zhang, W. (2023). Digital identity, privacy security, and their legal safeguards in the metaverse. *Security and Safety*, *2*, 2023011. DOI: 10.1051/sands/2023011

Zhong, H., Huang, C., Zhang, X., & Pan, M. (2023). Metaverse CAN: Embracing continuous, active, and non-intrusive biometric authentication. *IEEE Network*, *37*(6), 67–73. DOI: 10.1109/MNET.2023.3318890

Zhou, L., Diro, A., Saini, A., Kaisar, S., & Hiep, P. C. (2024). Leveraging zero knowledge proofs for blockchain-based identity sharing: A survey. *Journal of Information Security and Applications*, *80*, 103678. DOI: 10.1016/j.jisa.2023.103678

Chapter 8
Trustworthy Security Architectures for AI-Driven Metaverse Experiences:
A Zero-Trust and Privacy-Preserving Perspective

Abdelraouf Ishtaiwi
http://orcid.org/0000-0001-8013-7151
Data Science and Artificial Intelligence, University of Petra, Amman, Jordan

Ahmad Hajyasien
Higher College of Technology, UAE

ABSTRACT

AI-driven metaverse platforms are evolving into core infrastructure for work, learning, commerce, and services, but their blend of identity data, behavioral telemetry, sensing, virtual assets, and automated decisions creates complex security and privacy risks. This chapter proposes a trustworthy architecture using zero-trust, privacy-preserving analytics, confidential computing, explainable AI, and continuous risk monitoring to secure scalable, interoperable immersive systems across sectors now.

1. INTRODUCTION

The metaverse is being positioned globally as a continuous digital continuum where physical spaces, digital simulators, immersive interfaces, social presence,

DOI: 10.4018/979-8-3373-7882-4.ch008

virtual assets, and AI-focused services interlock into a fabric of continuous and ongoing interaction, which never stops developing and growing over time [Dwivedi et al., 2022, Wang et al., 2023, Lim et al., 2023, Duan et al., 2021]. Despite the ongoing debate of the boundaries of the definition, there has been a significant level of agreement between some fundamental characteristics, namely, persistent identity, embodied interaction, multi-user synchronization, programmable economies, spatial computing, and intelligent automation brought to the experience layer. Thus, the metaverse is not being studied just as a game-centric phenomenon; instead, it is being elaborated as a classes-industry-telemedicine-retailing-mobility-cultural-participatory-and-smarter-city model platform platform [Khan et al., 2025, Sarwatt et al., 2026, Gao et al., 2026]. The strategic importance of immersive ecosystems today is thus being determined not just by graphical realism or bandwidth richness, but also by the reliability of architectures of access, data streams, agent behaviour and responsibility.

Nowadays, said reliability is being stretched to its limit by the very features that make metaverse settings appealing. A user interaction can include VR glasses, eye-tracker, handtracking cameras, haptic garment, voice streams, biometric templates, local edge rendering, remote asset, identity wallets, blockchain ownership record, and one or multiple AI agents, creating content or decision-making in a single exchange chain user session [Wang et al., 2023, Lim et al., 2023, Li et al., 2025]. Since these experiences are high bandwidth and long duration, sensitive data is not just confined to traditional profile fields or clickstream but it encompasses gaze tracks, bodily movement, proxemics, inferred feelings, spatial mappings of the user environment, device pose and co-presence patterns and contextual cues that may indicate health, cognition, preferences and routines. Privacy risk is frequently amplified in these multimodal streams as benign fragments are found to be inferentially potent when combined, correlated, and run through machine learning models, often hidden within such multimodal streams [Lehman et al., 2022, Zhao and Chen, 2022, Zhao et al., 2024]. The surface of attack of the metaverse is therefore being extended both in breadth, to more devices and APIs, and depth, to more rich behavioral semantics.

Nonetheless, the immersive presence also alters well-known security threats into actualized and financially significant experiences as well. The theft of credentials in a classic portal could reveal their records, but theft of credentials in a metaverse classroom, factory, or clinic could allow impersonation of an avatar, spatial stalking, theft of virtual resources, unauthorized witnessing of social dynamics, or manipulation of AI-based assistance at the time of high cognitive trust [Achuthan et al., 2025, Wang et al., 2023]. Deepfakes, artificial speech and AI-generated personas can be added to the social layer with significantly less friction than in the conventional platforms since the space itself promotes mediated embodiment and synthetic augmentation [Verdoliva, 2020, Tolosana et al., 2020]. The former is trying to identify anomalies, prioritize risk and moderate harmful content at scale using AI, but the latter can also be misused to confer social trust, contaminate or subvert recommendation systems, steal knowledge of the model, or bypass authentication by imitating behavioral or biometric cues using the same AI capabilities [Biggio and Roli, 2018, Shokri et al., 2017, Nasr et al., 2018]. The standard belief that authenticated sessions can be considered trustworthy until they are logged out cannot be made analytically in such environments.

In addition, the complexity of governance is growing due to the fact that metaverse environments are hardly monolithic. Assets ledgers can be decentralized, and engines can be a cloud-hosted service, third-party-supplied identity assurance can be based on self-sovereign credentials and digital twins can be regulated by overlapping data, security and AI duties, etc. Having the dynamics mentioned above in mind, it becomes apparent that there is no such thing as a trustworthy architecture, which can be diminished to a single control family, including blockchain, multifactor authentication, or content moderation. Instead, it needs to be a layered and constantly evolving strategy, where identity proofing, least-privilege authorization, network segmentation, policy-driven by telemetry, confidential processing, privacy engineering, and explainable AI oversight are collaboratively operated throughout the entire lifecycle of immersive interactions [Rose et al., 2020, Hu et al., 2014, Grassi et al., 2020, Feng et al., 2024]. The fact that integration is also vital, as metaverse harms tend to spread well beyond layers, e.g., a compromised device can fake posture data, which can bias AI risk scores, which can then be used to make inappropriate access control decisions or content interventions.

It is therefore postulated in this chapter that under some conditions of expansion beyond network-centric enforcement to a wider trust architecture of identities, devices, agents, data, models, and virtual assets, zero-trust security can serve as an analytically appropriate backbone to an AI-driven metaverse system. Zero-trust In zero-trust language, none of the devices, workloads, model endpoints, or avatar sessions can be regarded as inherently trusted merely because they are located within a nominal platform boundary [Rose et al., 2020]. However, zero trust in immersive environments must also consider contextual continuity, embodied interaction, latency-sensitive and maintenance of a flowing user experience. Therefore, persistent verification should be kept out of sight where feasible, privacy budgets should be undertaken without immersion undermining, and computerized decisions should be refutable at all times in the event of an impactful social or economic effect [Mosqueira-Rey et al., 2023, Arrieta et al., 2020, Liu et al., 2022]. The design issue is not so much to increase the density of control, but to reduce risk and still maintain fluidity, interoperability, and inclusion.

Five closely linked objectives are in this chapter. To establish the key trust boundaries, security assumptions, and high value assets in AI-driven immersive systems, a reference metaverse stack is first synthesized. Second, an adversarial model is described to take threats that include identity theft, social engineering using the deepfake technique, malicious automation, virtual asset fraud, sensor leakage and inference attack as well as manipulation of AI models.

Third, there is a proposal of zero-trust and privacy preserving architecture including verifiable credentials, context-sensitive authentication, fine-grained authorization, secure communications, confidential computing, federated learning, and differential privacy. Fourth, systems of reliable AI are described, comprising explicable danger analytics, policy-consistent programmed choice making, adversarial robustness management, and human-in-the-loop supervision. Fifth, the implementation of such an architecture is shown with respect to a smart-campus scenario that does not negatively impact operational usability.

Besides this, the book has an IGI-style book chapter-logic coupled with being compatible with the Springer-oriented scholarly presentation. Section 2 provides context and outlines of the chapter through the synthesis of the reference metaverse stack and its trust boundaries. Section 3 forms the threat model and draws out security requirements. Section 4 is the central part of the chapter and displays the offered architecture, control mappings tables, and TikZ figures. Section 5 gives solutions and recommendations based on a scenario-based smart-campus case study. Section 6 defines the future research directions and design principles of regulators, providers, and developers. Section 7 is the end of discussion and the final key terms give brief definitional anchors to be reused in edited volumes.

2. BACKGROUND AND CHAPTER SCOPE

2.1 Reference Metaverse Stack

Today, the metaverse is best understood as a layered service ecosystem rather than as a single application instance. At the lowest tier, physical interaction devices capture embodied signals through cameras, inertial units, microphones, eye trackers, depth sensors, haptic peripherals, environmental sensors, and mobile or fixed gateways. Above that tier, connectivity and computation layers integrate local rendering, edge intelligence, cloud orchestration, and sometimes blockchain or digital twin substrates for synchronization and asset verification [Lim et al., 2023, Luo et al., 2026, Li et al., 2025]. The upper layers expose identity, asset, collaboration, world simulation, moderation, and AI-mediated services to end users, administrators, and third-party developers. Consequently, security failures at one tier can be propagated upward as corrupted semantic context, while governance failures at upper tiers can trickle downward as excessive data collection or unsafe control instructions.

Although many architectural diagrams emphasize rendering or networking performance, a trustworthy perspective requires attention to trust transitions between layers. A user may begin with identity proofing at registration, receive a credential into a wallet, activate a session through a headset, synchronize posture with an edge renderer, submit voice or image data to AI services, transact on a virtual asset layer, and receive moderation or access decisions in real time. Each transition changes the security context because the principal, device posture, location, sensitivity of the requested action, and state of the underlying services may all evolve during the session [Rose et al., 2020, Grassi et al., 2020, Hu et al., 2014]. Therefore, a static perimeter or one-time login is misaligned with the temporal and contextual dynamism of immersive systems.

Table 1. Reference stack for AI-driven metaverse systems and its principal trust concerns.

Layer	Representative components	High-value assets	Primary trust concerns
Interaction and device layer	VR/AR headsets, controllers, haptic wearables, smartphones, IoT sensors, cameras	Biometrics, gaze, motion, voice, spatial maps, device keys	Device compromise, sensor spoofing, side-channel leakage, unsafe defaults
Connectivity and compute layer	Wi-Fi/5G/6G, edge nodes, cloud orchestration, rendering pipelines, service mesh	Session tokens, telemetry streams, model outputs, transient state	Interception, lateral movement, denial of service, insecure edge offloading
Identity and wallet layer	Identity proofing, credential wallets, decentralized identifiers, access brokers, session managers	Verifiable credentials, keys, tokens, entitlements, recovery data	Impersonation, credential theft, weak recovery, privacy leakage through linkage
World and asset layer	Digital twins, scene graphs, content stores, virtual economies, smart contracts, inventories	Digital assets, policy metadata, ownership claims, audit trails	Asset fraud, ledger manipulation, policy inconsistency, provenance disputes
Experience and collaboration layer	Avatars, voice/video, messaging, shared spaces, learning or work tools	Social graphs, moderation records, collaboration artifacts, meeting content	Harassment, social engineering, unauthorized observation, compliance gaps
AI and governance layer	Recommendation engines, generative models, moderators, copilots, policy engines, analytics dashboards	Models, prompts, embeddings, risk scores, explanations, governance logs	Model poisoning, jailbreaks, inference leakage, opaque decision making

The service plane supports the immersive experience itself: rendering, interaction, collaboration, asset handling, and AI services. The control plane governs identity verification, policy evaluation, telemetry ingestion, privacy controls, secure execution, and auditability. Consequently, the metaverse is treated not as a flat application but as a continuously mediated environment in which trust decisions are repeatedly recomputed.

Figure 1. Reference architecture for an AI-driven metaverse, separating immersive service functions from cross-layer trust controls.

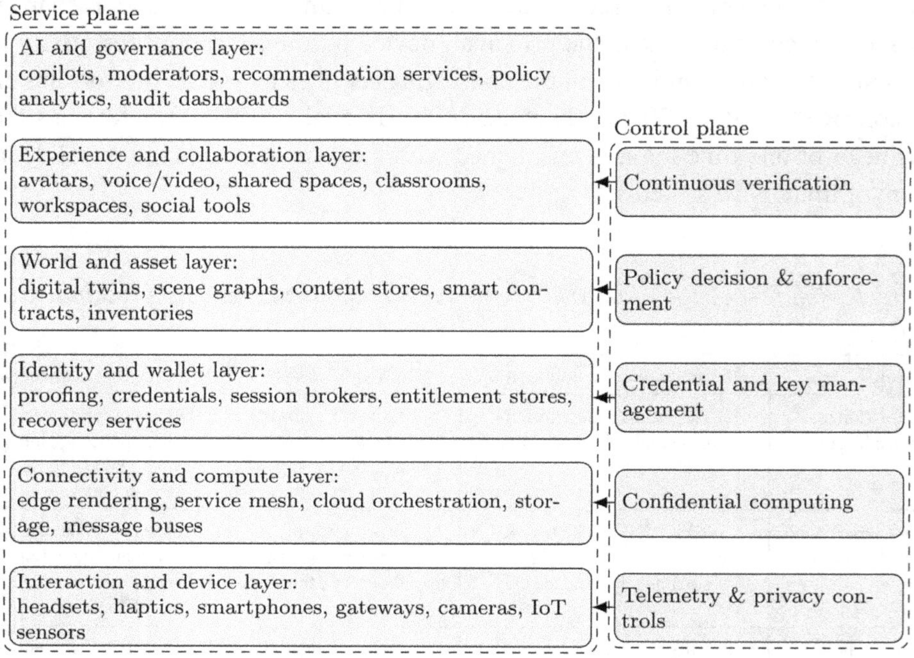

Currently, identity is one of the most strategically significant cross-layer enablers. Conventional account systems remain prevalent, yet immersive ecosystems increasingly require portable and context-aware trust assertions that can travel across worlds, providers, and devices without forcing complete data centralization. Self-sovereign identity and verifiable credential models are therefore gaining analytical relevance because they can support selective disclosure, decentralized trust roots, and cryptographic proof mechanisms that mitigate excessive correlation of user activities [Fathalla et al., 2026, Soltani et al., 2021]. However, although decentralized identity mitigates some centralization risks, it does not automatically solve assurance, usability, recovery, or governance concerns. Credential revocation, multi-device continuity, delegated authority for minors or institutions, and protection against wallet theft remain open design issues, especially in contexts such as campuses, hospitals, or industrial operations.

2.2 Trust Boundaries and Data Lifecycles

Furthermore, the data lifecycle within the metaverse is exceptionally rich due to the amount of data being collected not only for the purpose of authentication or authorization, but for the inference of presence, synchronization of space, personalization of recommendations, training of model and safety. For example the smart campus experience may be recording the occupancy of a room, the movement paths of the motions, the audio interactions, the pointer actions, their academic entitlements, the risk level of laboratory operations, and queries by AI tutors during one learning session. Such information can be processed in addition locally for rendering latency sensitive, then aggregated at the edge nodes for continuity of sessions, then transferred to central analytics pipelines for moderation or individualization, and then again preserved to policy or compliance systems for audit-ability. Keeping the above dynamics in view then, the lifecycle is not linear, it is recursive and feedback driven. A change in authorization using a risk score that was created from an AI model can lead to changes in interaction options that, in turn, result in new telemetry that changes the next risk score.

However, more data is not a better security. Several strands of privacy risk, differential privacy and identity engineering discussion reiterate that unbounded telemetry can lead to brittle systems where security tooling itself leads to harm [Lehman et al., 2022, Dwork et al., 2006, Zhao et al., 2024]. If gaze vectors, affect scores, spatial maps or collaborative transcripts are being stored without minimization or without separation of duty, the counter-result could be a fence canary, and not a trustworthy platform. Thus, the challenge is not only how to collect the security relevant data, but how to create into the architecture data minimization, purpose limitation, bounded retention and selective disclosure, from the start. Such architectural restraint is of especially important where the unequal relations of power will otherwise turn the optional immersion of the spaces into functional continuous monitoring attended in educational or work metaverse.

Though the function of blockchain technologies has been said many times as the pillars of trust in the metaverse, one should very cautiously see this. Blockchain can provide strength in provenance, transaction integrity, decentralized coordination and asset portability and based on some recent surveys there is a significant momentum around its use for digital twin synchronization and metaverse asset ecosystem [Li et al., 2025, Luo et al., 2026]. Yet, blockchain does not eliminate any requirement for good identity proofing, confidentiality protections or off-chain policy enforcement. In addition to this Unchangeable ledgers are in conflict with privacy requirements if personal or connectable activity traces are written directly to permanent substrate. Consequently, this chapter will consider blockchain on a par with other trust anchors and not a universal solution.

Today, the expectations coming from the regulators also are being tightened. Digital twins across critical sectors are under increasing scrutiny in the application of privacy and cybersecurity & AI interfacing governance, especially, European Agenda, where data governance, resilience and human-centric AI, operationally are becoming more specific [Jørgensen and Ma, 2025]. Though this is a technical chapter in emphasis subject of legal and regulatory compliance is not addressed as an after-thought that outside the process of completing project. Instead, compliance-by-design is a form of architectural thinking as the ready decision to log or not, the relevant credential portability, the capacity to process across national borders, explainable AI and incident response materially affect whether and to what degree immersive systems can be governed responsibly at scale.

Thus, as evident from the purpose given, the scope in this chapter is intended to be more restricted around architecture than the formalization of protocol. Low level proofs in cryptography, smart contracts semantics and rendering engine optimisation aren't mathematical by any means.

Instead there is an emphasis put on how an end to end design, that is trust worthy, could be synthesized across layers and how that end to end design may weaken concrete attack paths (and still remain sufficiently holistic to be discussed in the fruition of deployment). The following part is thus a deviation from architectural scope towards adversarial analysis, because security architectures that do not start out with realistic threat models are rare in real life that are robust.

3. THREAT MODEL AND SECURITY REQUIREMENTS

3.1 Adversarial Model

Currently, a model of the metaverse threat requires the consideration of a wider range of adversaries than has been modeled in enterprise web systems. External attackers are still relevant, however, especially when it comes to credential theft, service disruption, ransomware-style extortion or theft of virtual assets. However, equally important are devices that are compromised, malicious insiders who have privileged access to moderation systems or telemetry systems, third-party plugins which over-collect data, dishonest market participants who are manipulating ownership records, and adaptive attackers who are going after AI models or their surrounding orchestration logic [Achuthan et al., 2025, Wang et al., 2023]. As such, the model (adversarial) undertaken in this chapter takes the view that compromise can arise at any layer and that trust therefore has to be continuously earned as opposed to statically inherited.

Although identity theft is no new threat, immersive environments bring it to a higher level as the impersonated subject is no real user of an account, but an embodied participant. A successful adversary may be able to appropriate the victim's avatar, entitlements in space, role in the classroom, access to the laboratory, communication history, or purchasing authority. Furthermore, since the presence at immersive spaces is often determined by small behavior and context cues, users can give high credibility to fraudulent interactions that mimic posture, voice or conversational style. Research on media forensics and deepfakes reiterates that generative manipulation is now approaching a point where visual and auditory realism can affect our ordinary capabilities for detecting them [Verdoliva, 2020, Tolosana et al., 2020]. For this reason, authentication in the metaverse is likely to need to be strong not only against stolen passwords but also against synthetic embodiment and context-aware deception.

However, AI-centric threats are not limited to deepfakes only. Attackers may poison the data sets, encourage reward signals, create adversarial inputs, or invoke prompt interfaces to skew the moderation or recommendation behavior away from platform policy [Barreno et al., 2006, Biggio and Roli, 2018]. In the case of an immersive system, such attacks can have a high leverage, since AI is often used to mediate content ranking, abuse triage, entity recognition, automated tutoring, or safety alerts, for example. If a model working on the prioritization of harassment reports is biased or poisoned, bad users may stay throughout while good users are suppressed. If an AI tutor or assistant is twisted, then unsafe instructions can be given in the name of institutional power. Thus, trustworthy AI is not an optional ethical overlay where whenever automated outputs change access, visibility of contents or behavior, they become direct security requirements for systems.

Table 2. Threat taxonomy for AI-driven metaverse systems.

Threat family	Target layer	Representative attack	Potential consequences
Identity compromise	Identity, experience	Account takeover, wallet theft, synthetic avatar impersonation, session hijacking	Unauthorized access, fraudulent transactions, reputational damage, loss of safety controls
Social engineering and decep-tion	Experience, AI layer	Deepfake voice/video, persuasive bot swarms, malicious copilots, context spoofing	Manipulated trust, coercive disclosure, unsafe actions, policy evasion
Sensor and telemetry leakage	Device, edge, analytics	Gaze inference, motion correlation, ambient capture, spatial map exfiltration	Privacy invasion, profiling, stalking, inference of health or cognition
Asset and state manipulation	World, asset, blockchain	Double spending, item fraud, ownership disputes, policy tampering	Economic loss, transaction rollback disputes, erosion of platform trust

Threat family	Target layer	Representative attack	Potential consequences
Network and service ro- comp mise	Connectivity, compute	Eavesdropping, downgrade attacks, lateral movement, edge compromise	Session exposure, service disruption, crosstenant leakage, persistent footholds
AI-centric at- tacks	AI, analytics, governance	Model poisoning, prompt injection, jailbreaks, adversarial examples, data extraction	Unsafe outputs, biased moderation, hidden manipulation, degraded detection
Inference at- tacks	AI, storage	Membership inference, attribute inference, model inversion	Leakage of training membership, reidentification, privacy and compliance failures
Abuse of privileged operations	Governance, control plane	Malicious moderator action, log suppression, rule misconfiguration, emergency override abuse	Unaccountable decisions, censorship, denial of legitimate access, incident escalation

Figure 2. Cross-layer threat surface in the metaverse, illustrating how compromise at one component can influence user trust, assets, and automated decisions.

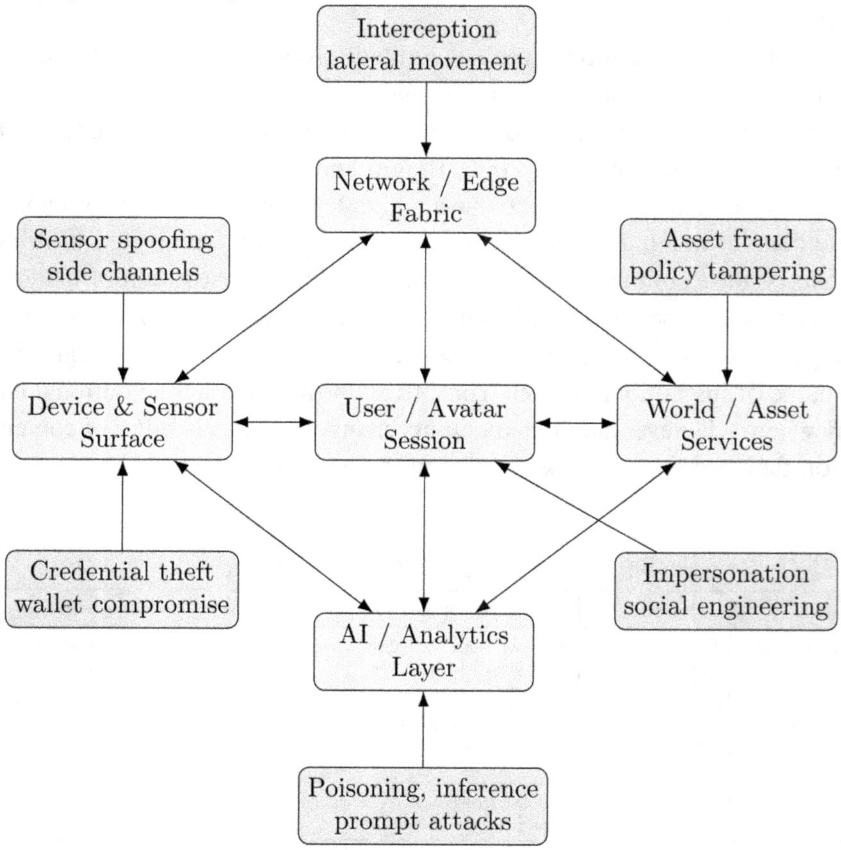

Furthermore, privacy threats must be modeled at first class as opposed to residual compliance issues. Research on the privacy risks of AR shows that mobile applications and immersive applications potentially leak more data than intended through cameras, environmental sensing or bystander capture [Lehman et al., 2022]. In the metaverse, such risks are enhanced since the quality of interaction is often based on granular sensing. Gaze, hand motion, locomotion traces, and audio context can communicate information about stress, disability, exemplary, exhaustion, or social affiliations. If these data are centralized without minimization, these may not need to be completely broken into the environment in order to cause harm; directed guesses or illicit access to insiders may be sufficient. Membership inference and related attacks additionally demonstrate that systems that leverage machine learning systems can reveal that a person, or sample, was used in learning and thereby breach guarantees that raw data never left the originating device [Shokri et al., 2017, Nasr et al., 2018]. As such, privacy-preserving analytics should be included in the security perimeter.

Although blockchain and digital asset infrastructures can strengthen integrity and provenance, they also create domain-specific attack classes. Virtual assets may be stolen through wallet compromise, fraudulent approvals, smart-contract vulnerabilities, or social engineering that induces a user to sign a malicious transaction. In education and workplace settings, such losses may extend beyond commercial items to credentials, participation records, reputation tokens, or access rights tied to institutional processes [Li et al., 2025, Kavitha and Kavitha, 2025]. Thus, asset protection must integrate transactional integrity with human-centered safeguards such as transaction explanation, delayed execution for high-risk operations, and anomaly detection on behavioral context.

3.2 Security and Trust Requirements

Keeping the above dynamics in view, the requirements for a trustworthy metaverse architecture can be organized into eight interdependent properties. First, continuous and contextual verification is required because identity assurance degrades over time as devices move, sessions persist, and risk conditions change. Second, authorization must remain fine grained, attribute aware, and revocable at low latency, especially where access depends on role, location, safety condition, or collaboration context. Third, data in transit, at rest, and in use must be protected through layered confidentiality mechanisms, including secure channels, encrypted storage, and protected execution when sensitive workloads are offloaded [Rose et al., 2020, Hu et al., 2014, Feng et al., 2024, Sabt et al., 2015]. Fourth, privacy minimization must be engineered into telemetry and analytics pipelines through techniques such as selective disclosure, federated learning, secure aggregation, and differential privacy [Dwork et al., 2006, Li et al., 2020, Bonawitz et al., 2017, Zhao et al., 2024].

Furthermore, AI governance introduces additional requirements. Fifth, model behavior must be robust against adversarial inputs, poisoning, and manipulation, particularly when AI output influences moderation, access control, or safety notifications. Sixth, high-impact automated decisions should remain explainable, auditable, and contestable, because opaque risk scoring can silently reproduce discrimination or operational error [Arrieta et al., 2020, Liu et al., 2022]. Seventh, a meaningful degree of human oversight must be preserved, especially for moderation escalations, disciplinary actions, asset seizure, emergency overrides, or identity recovery [Mosqueira-Rey et al., 2023]. Eighth, resilience must be prioritized so that partial failure does not cascade into systemic trust collapse; if one AI service is degraded or one edge node is compromised, the platform should continue in a degraded but safe mode.

Consequently, the security posture advocated in this chapter is not binary but risk adaptive. Different actions require different evidentiary thresholds. Reading public content in a virtual campus plaza should not require the same assurance as entering a hazardous laboratory digital twin, signing a high-value asset transfer, or invoking an AI-driven administrative decision. The architecture must therefore integrate assurance levels, contextual attributes, device posture, and action sensitivity into policy evaluation. Such differentiation mitigates over-friction for benign use while preserving strong controls for sensitive operations. The next section elaborates how these requirements can be integrated into a coherent zero-trust and privacy-preserving design.

4. MAIN FOCUS OF THE CHAPTER: ZERO-TRUST AND PRIVACY-PRESERVING ARCHITECTURE

4.1 Architectural Principles

Globally, zero trust has been embraced because it rejects the assumption that internal location or prior authentication alone should determine trust [Rose et al., 2020]. In the metaverse, that principle must be expanded into an interaction-centric doctrine: no avatar, device, edge node, AI agent, world service, or asset transaction should be considered trustworthy unless current evidence supports the requested action under current conditions. Consequently, the architecture proposed in this chapter is organized around five principles: continuous verification, minimal privilege, protected execution, privacy-preserving analytics, and accountable automation.

These principles are not independent silos; they must be integrated through shared telemetry, shared policy semantics, and shared incident response logic.

Today, continuous verification is best implemented through a policy loop that re-evaluates session trust whenever context changes. Relevant context includes device attestation state, credential validity, location, network quality, behavioral anomalies, current risk level of the destination service, recent moderation events, and sensitivity of the intended action. Instead of granting broad session trust at login, the architecture issues short-lived, purpose-bound assertions that are refreshed or denied based on fresh evidence. Such assertions may authorize entry to a classroom, publication of content, access to a laboratory twin, or interaction with a privileged AI assistant, yet they expire quickly and can be stepped up when risk changes. This design mitigates the classic problem of long-lived ambient authority in persistent worlds.

4.2 Identity, Authentication, and Authorization

Currently, trustworthy identity in the metaverse requires a layered model rather than a single credential type. A foundational identity proofing process is needed when institutional or legal accountability matters, as in campuses, enterprises, or healthcare environments [Grassi et al., 2020]. Above that foundation, portable assertions can be expressed as verifiable credentials that disclose only the attributes required for a given transaction, such as student status, laboratory certification, or age eligibility, without exposing the entire identity profile [Fathalla et al., 2026, Soltani et al., 2021]. Consequently, selective disclosure can mitigate unnecessary data sharing while still enabling authorization decisions to be grounded in cryptographically verifiable claims.

Figure 3. Zero-trust control loop for immersive systems, linking identity evidence, telemetry, risk scoring, enforcement, and accountable oversight.

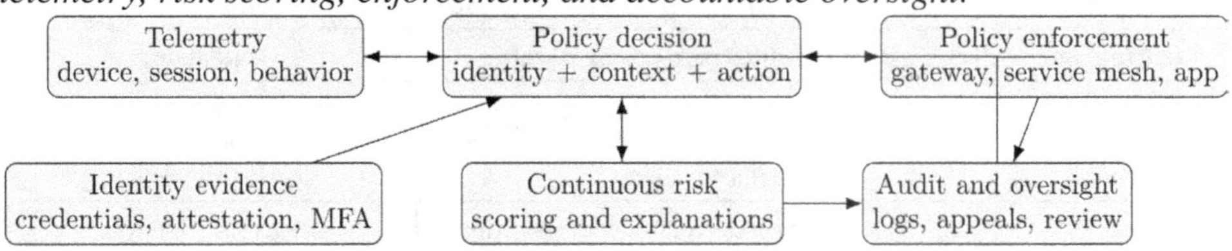

Although self-sovereign identity is attractive for portability and privacy, it should not be romanticized as frictionless. Recovery, revocation, delegation, and wallet compromise remain difficult issues, especially in educational settings where multiple institutional authorities coexist. Thus, this chapter recommends a hybrid identity plane in which user-controlled credentials are combined with policy-bound institutional issuers, risk-based step-up authentication, and monitored recovery workflows. For low-risk navigation or public-space participation, possession of a wallet and basic device assurance may be adequate. However, for examination submission, financial transfer, or hazardous laboratory entry, stronger evidence should be demanded through context-aware multifactor authentication, hardware-bound keys, or supervised re-authentication.

Furthermore, behavioral or biometric signals should be handled cautiously. Research on immersive and behavioral authentication suggests that gesture, motion, and interaction patterns can augment security in VR contexts, yet such signals are inherently privacy sensitive and can drift over time [Kürtünlüoğlu et al., 2023]. Therefore, they should not be stored or reused as unrestricted identity surrogates. Instead, a privacy-preserving architecture should derive ephemeral risk indicators from on-device or edge-local processing, disclose only bounded confidence scores when necessary, and avoid persistent raw storage unless a clearly justified purpose exists. This design reiterates that security should not be purchased through indefinite retention of intimate telemetry.

Authorization, in turn, should be expressed through attribute-based and policy-based mechanisms rather than static role mapping alone [Hu et al., 2014]. A metaverse classroom or digital twin often depends on contextual variables that role labels cannot capture: whether the user is physically on campus, whether the headset is institutionally managed, whether the requested action is being performed during an exam window, whether another authorized supervisor is present, or whether the relevant world instance has been flagged as high risk. Consequently, the policy engine should evaluate subject attributes, device attributes, environmental context, asset sensitivity, and behavioral risk before issuing an allow, deny, step-up, or limited-degradation decision.

Table 3. Mapping zero-trust controls to metaverse service functions.

Service function	Recommended zero-trust control	Rationale
Avatar login and ses- sion initiation	Device attestation, wallet binding, short-lived session tokens, riskadaptive multifactor authentication	Mitigates stolen credentials and reduces value of replayed or persistent tokens
Classroom, meeting, or lab entry	Attribute-based access control with contextual signals such as schedule, location, safety status, and entitlement	Aligns access with dynamic institutional and environmental requirements
AI copilot invocation	Purpose-bound authorization, prompt filtering, rate limits, model policy tags, logging of high-impact outputs	Restricts misuse of privileged models and supports post hoc accountability

Service function	Recommended zero-trust control	Rationale
Virtual asset transfer	Transaction explanation, step-up authentication, behavioral anomaly checks, delayed confirmation for highrisk transfers	Mitigates fraud and coerced approvals while preserving low-friction routine use
Content publishing and moderation	Policy versioning, explainable scoring, human escalation for severe sanctions, immutable moderation audit trail	Reduces opaque censorship and supports appeal and governance review
Cross-world portabil-ity	Verifiable credentials with selective disclosure, federation gateways, session isolation across worlds	Preserves portability without indiscriminate identity linkage

However, the enforcement architecture must also respect latency and immersion requirements. If every fine-grained action requires a round trip to a distant policy server, the experience becomes brittle. Thus, local or edge-resident policy enforcement points should cache signed policy fragments, validity windows, and emergency-deny lists, whereas high-impact decisions continue to require synchronous validation from the authoritative control plane. Such a tiered approach reduces disruption without weakening assurance for sensitive operations. Furthermore, when connectivity degrades, the system should fail into predefined safe modes: for example, allowing passive observation but withholding privileged interaction or asset transfer.

4.3 Secure Communication, Segmentation, and Confidential Computation

Today, the communication fabric of the metaverse must be treated as a mesh of mutually authenticating services rather than as a flat transport plane. Headsets, gateways, edge nodes, world services, asset registries, and AI endpoints should communicate through authenticated and encrypted channels, ideally with workload identity integrated into the same trust fabric as user identity. Service-to-service segmentation should be enforced so that compromise of one microservice or edge renderer does not grant broad access to identity, telemetry, or model repositories. In addition to this, east-west traffic should be inspected through policy and cryptographic metadata rather than through blind trust in internal network location.

Although encryption in transit and at rest is necessary, it is insufficient where sensitive AI workloads or telemetry are processed on potentially untrusted infrastructure. Consequently, protected execution and confidential computing become highly relevant. Research on trusted execution environments and confidential computing reiterates that data in use can be shielded from privileged software layers through hardware-assisted isolation, attestation, and restricted memory exposure [Sabt et al., 2015, Feng et al., 2024, Sagar and Keke, 2021]. In a metaverse context, such capabilities can be used to protect biometric template matching, selective credential verification, sensitive moderation queues, or federated aggregation tasks running on edge nodes. However, confidential computing should be applied with realistic threat modeling; attestation freshness, side-channel exposure, and orchestration complexity must all be managed.

Furthermore, workload attestation can be integrated into zero-trust policy evaluation. Before an edge node receives sensitive avatar telemetry or encrypted training updates, the control plane should verify that the workload is running approved code on approved hardware in an approved configuration. If attestation fails or drifts, the system can reroute the workload, reduce data sensitivity, or suspend certain interactions. Consequently, trust in the compute substrate becomes evidence-based rather than assumed.

Table 4. Privacy-enhancing technologies for immersive analytics and their principal trade-offs.

Technique	Typical metaverse use	Strengths	Trade-offs / cautions
Selective disclosure credentials	Age, role, training status, locationindependent proof of eligibility	Minimizes identity exposure and supports interoperability	Recovery and revocation complexity; wallet compromise remains possible
Differential privacy	Aggregate analytics, behavior statistics, risk dashboards, model training outputs	Provides formal privacy guarantees against many aggregate disclosures	Privacy budget management can reduce utility if poorly calibrated
Federated learning	Personalization, abuse detection, tutor adaptation across devices or organizations	Keeps raw data local and mitigates bulk centralization	Vulnerable to poisoning and still exposed to inference without added defenses
Secure aggregation	Federated model update collection at scale	Hides individual updates from the aggregator	Does not by itself solve poisoning or representational bias
Confidential computing	Credential verification, edge analytics, secure moderation, protected inference	Shields data in use on par- tially trusted infrastructure	TEE limitations, side-channel risk, attestation lifecycle management
Data minimization and local preprocessing	On-device gaze or motion feature extraction, bystander redaction	Reduces raw data transmission and retention burden	Requires careful design to avoid hidden leakage through derived features

4.4 Privacy-Preserving Analytics and Learning

Currently, AI-enhanced metaverse services frequently depend on personalization, anomaly detection, recommendation, or predictive adaptation. Yet, centralizing raw behavioral streams for these purposes is often unnecessary and increasingly indefensible. Federated learning and secure aggregation offer a more privacy-conscious alternative for training shared models without directly pooling raw data [Li et al., 2020, Kairouz et al., 2021, Bonawitz et al., 2017]. In such a design, devices or local organizational nodes compute model updates locally, secure aggregation protects the confidentiality of individual updates, and the global model is refined through iterative coordination. Consequently, large-scale personalization or threat detection can be supported while mitigating the concentration of raw immersive data.

However, federated learning is not intrinsically trustworthy. Poisoning attacks can manipulate local updates, and membership inference can still extract information from model behavior if no further defenses are applied [Shokri et al., 2017, Nasr et al., 2018]. Thus, a trustworthy metaverse architecture should combine federated learning with model validation, robust aggregation, differential privacy, and provenance tracking for training rounds. High-risk models should also be accompanied by drift monitoring and rollback capability. Such controls are particularly important when models influence safety or access, because latent corruption may otherwise remain invisible until harm occurs.

Differential privacy, when correctly calibrated, can further mitigate the disclosure risk of aggregated analytics and model outputs [Dwork et al., 2006, Zhao and Chen, 2022, Zhao et al., 2024]. For example, campus-wide metrics on occupancy, participation, or interaction quality can be perturbed to protect individuals while still informing planning and risk assessment. Likewise, global or cohort-level personalization models can be trained with privacy budgets that bound the contribution of any single participant. However, privacy budgets are finite resources; in persistent environments with repeated queries, cumulative leakage must be modeled carefully. Consequently, privacy accounting should be integrated into governance dashboards, and high-value queries should be prioritized based on necessity rather than convenience.

Furthermore, local preprocessing is an often underappreciated privacy control. Instead of streaming full-resolution eye-tracking or environmental video to the platform, devices can derive task-specific features locally, discard raw buffers quickly, and transmit only bounded signals needed for a particular purpose. Such preprocessing can be combined with bystander redaction, audio segmentation, or ephemeral storage controls. Although derived features are not automatically harmless, they substantially reduce exposure when paired with clear retention rules and purpose separation. In immersive systems, this design discipline is essential because users are frequently embedded in mixed physical spaces where nonparticipants can be captured unintentionally.

4.5 Trustworthy AI, Explainability, and Human Oversight

Although AI can materially strengthen cyber defense by prioritizing alerts, detecting anomalous behavior, and supporting moderation at scale, it can also reproduce harmful opacity when decisions are not explainable or contestable [Arrieta et al., 2020, Liu et al., 2022]. In the metaverse, explainability is especially important because automated interventions may alter social visibility, access rights, asset movement, or perceived safety in real time. A user denied access to a laboratory twin, flagged as a suspected impersonator, or muted by automated moderation should not be left with a cryptic risk score. Consequently, the architecture proposed here requires that high-impact model decisions produce structured explanations targeted to the relevant audience: concise action-oriented explanations for users, richer feature-level rationales for security analysts, and policy-aligned traceability for auditors and regulators.

Table 5. Trustworthy AI control matrix for immersive platforms.

Lifecycle stage	Risk	Recommended control	Operational effect
Data collection	Hidden bias, excessive capture, unlawful reuse	Purpose limitation, provenance labeling, local preprocessing, retention limits	Reduces misuse of multimodal telemetry and improves auditability
Model training	Poisoning, leakage, imbalance, weak reproducibility	Curated data pipelines, robust aggregation, privacy budgets, signed training artifacts	Increases integrity of training rounds and supports rollback
Model deployment	Unsafe outputs, policy drift, hallucination, excessive privilege	Model access scopes, output filters, policy tags, confidence thresholds	Restricts the operational blast radius of AI services
Runtime operation	Opaque moderation or access decisions	Explainable scoring, reason codes, analyst review for severe cases	Improves contestability and reduces arbitrary automation
Monitoring and maintenance	Silent degradation, adversarial adaptation, concept drift	Continuous evaluation, redteam testing, counterfactual monitoring, incident playbooks	Sustains resilience as user behavior and attacks evolve
Governance and accountability	Unverifiable claims, weak oversight, compliance gaps	Audit logs, human appeal channels, documentation, versioned policies	Supports institutional accountability and external scrutiny

Today, human-in-the-loop oversight should be treated as a control primitive rather than as a sign of incomplete automation. Research on human-in-the-loop machine learning indicates that performance, trust, and accountability are often improved when human intervention is strategically inserted at points of ambiguity or high consequence [Mosqueira-Rey et al., 2023]. Consequently, the proposed architecture reserves human review for sanctions, identity recovery, high-value asset disputes, emergency overrides, and sustained anomalies that may reflect disability, atypical behavior, or cultural variation rather than malicious intent. Such review is not meant to reverse automation wholesale; rather, it is designed to mitigate false positives, preserve procedural fairness, and create a defensible governance trail.

Furthermore, model security must be integrated with policy alignment. If a model is optimized only for accuracy on historical data, it may not align with the normative constraints of a live metaverse environment. Therefore, policy-aligned reinforcement learning and related supervisory techniques should be used to encode platform rules, escalation logic, and safe fallback behaviors into automated agents, while still constraining them through hard authorization boundaries in the control plane. AI assistants should not be permitted to grant themselves new privileges, alter policy thresholds, or invoke sensitive services without explicit and separately authorized credentials. In zero-trust terms, AI agents must be treated as principals with sharply bounded entitlements, not as omniscient internal helpers.

Consequently, this chapter recommends a dual view of AI: AI as defender and AI as untrusted workload. As defender, AI contributes anomaly detection, semantic triage, synthetic media screening, and operational support [Achuthan et al., 2025]. As untrusted workload, AI must itself be authenticated, authorized, monitored, red-teamed, and audited because compromised or misaligned models can generate harmful outputs at machine speed. This duality is particularly important in immersive systems, where the phenomenological realism of the experience can cause users to over-trust machine judgments embedded in the environment itself.

5. SOLUTIONS AND RECOMMENDATIONS: SMART-CAMPUS CASE STUDY

5.1 Scenario Definition

Today, universities are increasingly experimenting with immersive learning environments, digitaltwin campuses, remote laboratories, AI tutors, and mixed-reality collaboration spaces [Duan et al., 2021, Wang et al., 2023]. To demonstrate the instantiation of the proposed architecture, this section considers a smart-campus metaverse in which students, faculty, visitors, and service agents interact across a hybrid physical-virtual environment. The campus provides virtual classrooms, remote laboratory twins, digital credentials for course and safety eligibility, AI teaching assistants, immersive student services, and an asset layer supporting equipment booking, digital certificates, and collaborative project artifacts. Edge nodes are deployed in academic buildings for low-latency rendering and localized analytics, whereas cloud services host world state, long-term storage, policy administration, and selected AI workloads.

Figure 4. Smart-campus instantiation of the proposed architecture, linking identity issuance, edge enforcement, metaverse core services, AI assistance, and governance functions.

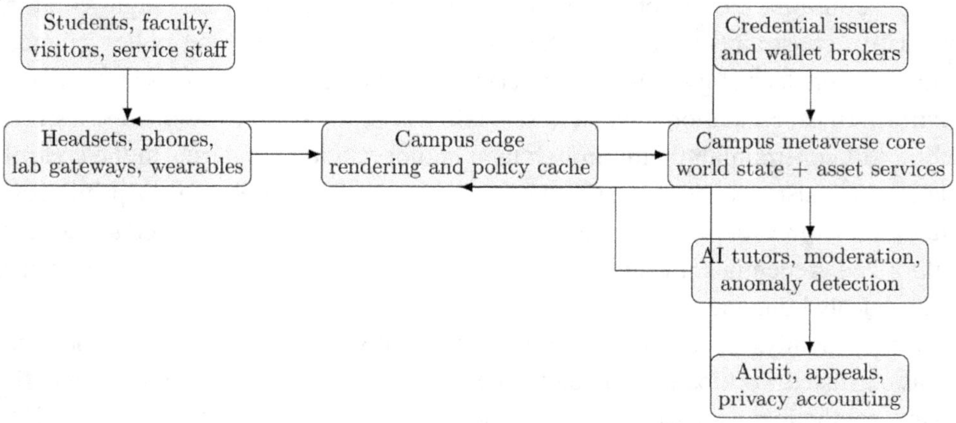

Globally, campuses are attractive metaverse use cases because they combine socio-economic relevance with stringent trust requirements. A university must support open interaction, accessibility, academic freedom, and ease of onboarding; however, it must also protect minors, enforce safety protocols, preserve assessment integrity, and comply with privacy law. On one hand, immersive systems can improve access to laboratories, simulations, and collaborative spaces. On the other hand, the same systems can magnify surveillance, harassment, impersonation, or inequitable moderation if security and governance are poorly designed. The smart-campus scenario therefore provides a useful stress test for balancing openness with control.

In the proposed deployment, each participant receives a wallet capable of holding institutionally issued verifiable credentials. Credentials attest to status such as student enrollment, faculty role, laboratory certification, disability accommodation eligibility, or visitor authorization. At login, a user authenticates through device-bound keys and receives a short-lived session token derived from policy evaluation against the current device posture and requested world. For ordinary classroom entry, a valid enrollment credential and basic device assurance may suffice. For chemistry-lab access, the policy engine additionally requires a laboratory-safety credential, stronger step-up authentication, location consistency, and confirmation that the headset firmware and local gateway remain attested.

5.2 Threat Walkthrough and Architectural Response

However, the usefulness of the architecture is more apparent when concrete threat sequences are considered. Consider first an impersonation attempt where an attacker gains access to a student's primary password and attempts to gain access to a restricted virtual laboratory. In a classic architecture password possession may be enough. In the proposed design, the attempt is prevented given that the wallet is absent, the device does not have the expected attestation history, and the requested action mandates a current laboratory safety credential with more stringent assurance given. If the attacker tries to get around these controls by mimicking a synthetic voice or avatar, the continuous risk engine can correlate the lack of wallet evidence, the unfamiliarity of the device posture, abnormal movement patterns, and lack of previous session continuity. As a result, access is denied and the event is recorded for review.

Consider next a deepfake assisted social engineering attack. A faculty member shows up on a virtual office hour and asks a student to transfer a valuable asset of his digital project or give him a recovery phrase. Although such manipulation could succeed in a purely social channel, the platform is able to counteract such manipulations by transaction explaining and out-of-band verification. High-value asset transfers require the introduction of step-up authentication; a human-readable explanation of what is being transferred; and a requirement that the signer demonstrate possession of a relevant entitlement credential by the bound device. Furthermore, improvisation of the pass through of synthetic voice or facial patterns risk can be raised by AI based deepfake detection and anomaly screening, when available [Verdoliva, 2020, Tolosana et al., 2020]. While no detector is perfect, the architecture makes it so that social trust alone will not be adequate for sensitive state transitions.

A third situation is over privacy leakage in analytics. For instance, suppose the university wants to optimize the design of classrooms by analyzing movement, gaze and participation patterns. Without safeguards, such analytics could become an invasive surveillance system. In the proposed architecture, the raw telemetry is preprocessed locally where possible, the sensitive features are minimized, the cohort analytics are aggregated using differential privacy and the model personalization is performed using federated learning where the task conditions allow [Li et al., 2020, Bonawitz et al., 2017, Zhao et al., 2024]. Consequently, planning insight can be gained without necessarily storing the raw history of each student's sensor readings in a centralized repository. Privacy accounting dashboards also reveal the consumption of privacy budgets to the eyes of governance staff, hence making trade-offs visible rather than hidden.

A fourth scenario is the manipulation of AI tutors. Suppose that an adversary submits beautifully crafted prompts that will cause an AI tutor to admit solutions to exams or allow an unauthorized role elevation. In the proposed architecture, the tutor is considered to be a bounded principal and not an omnipotent helper. The tutor cannot modify grades, access policies or query protected student records, unless separately authorized service calls are made. Prompt filters, output validation, rate limitations and risk-aware monitoring provide limits to hatred when suspicious exchanges are directed to analysts or instructors the moment policy thresholds are breached. Consequently, the AI assistant is helpful without turning into a back door to policy.

Table 6. Threat-to-control mapping for the smart-campus scenario.

Campus use case	Dominant threat	Primary control bundle	Expected operational outcome
Virtual laboratory access	Credential theft, unsafe device posture, role escalation	Verifiable credentials, stepup authentication, attestation, contextual ABAC	Restricted entry without proper training or trustworthy device state
Remote classroom participation	Session hijacking, harassment, covert observation	Short-lived tokens, segmented media channels, moderation with human escalation	Low-friction attendance with bounded abuse and auditable sanctions
AI tutoring and ad-vising	Prompt injection, data leakage, overprivileged automation	Model scoping, output filters, logging, explainability, human review for sensitive guidance	Useful assistance without hidden privilege escalation or opaque decisions
Campus analytics and planning	Sensor overcollection, re-identification, inference leakage	Local preprocessing, federated learning, secure aggregation, differential privacy	Aggregate insight with reduced exposure of individual behavioral traces
Asset issuance and transfer	Fraudulent approvals, wallet compromise, provenance disputes	Transaction explanation, step-up confirmation, provenance logging, anomaly detection	Improved integrity of certificates, bookings, and digital project artifacts
Emergency or safety intervention	False alarms, abuse of override power, denial of legitimate access	Dual authorization, override logging, fail-safe modes, post-event review	Resilient response with accountable exceptional access paths

Furthermore, emergency operations illustrate the importance of fail-safe design. Suppose a physical incident requires evacuation instructions to be disseminated through the campus metaverse. The system should continue to function even if some identity or analytics services are degraded. Thus, safety-critical broadcast channels are preauthorized through tightly scoped emergency policies, while post-event audit trails record every exceptional action for later review. Dual authorization may be required for broader overrides, thereby reducing the risk that emergency pathways are abused for censorship or unauthorized surveillance.

5.3 Usability, Performance, and Governance Observations

Although the proposed architecture is control dense, usability is not ignored. Several design choices are explicitly intended to preserve immersion. First, ordinary low-risk interactions rely on cached policy fragments, short-lived assertions, and local verification to minimize latency. Second, selective disclosure credentials reduce the need for repetitive full-profile sharing. Third, local preprocessing avoids unnecessary upload of raw sensor streams, which can also reduce bandwidth. Fourth, high-friction measures such as step-up authentication are reserved for high-impact actions rather than imposed uniformly. Consequently, the architecture endeavors to balance security rigor with interaction flow.

However, trade-offs remain. Confidential computing can increase infrastructure complexity and may constrain debugging or performance tuning. Differential privacy can reduce analytic fidelity if budgets are poorly managed. Federated learning can mitigate raw-data centralization but complicates monitoring and can introduce poisoning risk. Human review improves accountability but adds cost and may increase resolution time. Keeping the above dynamics in view, architectural trustworthiness should be evaluated not by any single metric but by a composite of security, privacy, usability, explainability, interoperability, and resilience. In institutional deployments, governance boards should therefore review not only incident counts but also false positive rates, appeal outcomes, accessibility impacts, retention statistics, and the distribution of friction across user populations.

Consequently, the smart-campus case study demonstrates that zero trust and privacy preservation are not mutually exclusive with immersive experience quality. When identity is portable yet bounded, policies are granular yet cached, AI is helpful yet monitored, and data processing is useful yet minimized, the resulting ecosystem can remain analytically coherent. The lesson generalizes beyond education: other sectors such as manufacturing, healthcare, and public administration face similar tensions between openness, latency, accountability, and privacy. The next section therefore expands from the case study to future research directions and broader design guidance.

6. FUTURE RESEARCH DIRECTIONS AND DESIGN GUIDELINES

Global research agenda for secure metaverse is open because there's still development of immersive ecosystems that are at once evolving with generative AI, edge intelligence, digital identity frameworks and sector-specific regulation [Dwivedi et al., 2022, Wang et al., 2023, Achuthan et al., 2025]. Several of the directions appear to have a particularly important consequence. First of all, advances in identity interoperability without advance normalization of universal linkability will be made. Verifiable credentials and self-sovereign identity can tackle the issue of centralization, although the issue of cross-world portability (which entails behavioral correlation) can only be overcome by integrating such schemes with resources such as pairwise identifiers and selective disclosure and policy-aware rules of presentation in a systematic manner [Fathalla et al., 2026, Soltani et al., 2021]. Future work should therefore focus more on unlinkability, recovery, revocation and delegated authority for institutional situations like schools, employers or hospitals.

Currently, authentication for immersive systems is not context-aware well developed. Although the use of gesture and behavioural features can add security while more work remains on the issue of fairness, drift resistance, accommodation of disabled users and privacy-preserving fusion of weak signals [Kürtünlüoğlu et al., 2023]. Authentication shouldn't cross the threshold into functioning as a secret surveillance apparatus; that it doesn't discriminate out of the ordinary (e.g. interaction patterns). As a result, future systems should be biased towards on-device feature extraction, and they should be transparent into what signals we are using, and adaptively use models which can discriminate between malicious anomalies and normal, accessibility-based variation.

Furthermore, privacy engineering in multimodal sensing is not generically applicable data protection principles. Differential privacy has been developed in great depths in structured and unstructured data, but immersive systems generate continuous and coordinated streaming behavioral data and violate the normal assumptions [Dwork et al., 2006, Zhao and Chen, 2022, Zhao et al., 2024]. Future research should therefore explore spatiotemporal privacy budgets, bystander-aware privacy protections, private release of digital twin analytics, and more formal guarantees for cross-modal fusion. In addition to this, more work is required on privacy preserving synthesis data generation for metaverse safety research, as there is sensitivity of raw immersive traces for open benchmarking.

Despite the potential of federated learning and secure aggregation, they are still vulnerable to poisoning, free-riding and bias amplification [Li et al., 2020, Kairouz et al., 2021, Bonawitz et al., 2017]. Concequentially the next generation of metaverse learning pipelines should have provenance aware training, secure enclaves or confidential aggregation, client credibility scoring avoiding discriminatory exclusion, and effective update validation under realistic non-independent and identically distributed data conditions. Such requirements are considered particularly important wherever campus, workplace or public service providers work across organizational boundaries.

Today, confidential computing is also moving out from this niche security capability to become an architectural necessity. Edge enabled metaverse services may need the protected processing of credentials, telemetry and model inputs on infrastructure which may be operated by different administrative domains [Feng et al., 2024, Sagar and Keke, 2021, Sabt et al., 2015]. However, side channel resistance, freshness of remote attestation, usability of orchestration and composability of privacy-preserving machine learning are all open problems. Future work should try to incorporate confidential computing with service meshes, identity fabrics and policy engines in a way that is cogent and operationally sustainable as opposed to ad hoc.

On one hand, AI can be used to materially improve safety and moderation, on the other hand, AI is an attack surface. As such, there is a need to research trusted AI for metaverse taking particular attention to policy congruent agent design, embodied threat detection, adversarial red teaming of multimodal models, and verifiable claims about model behavior [Liu et al., 2022, Arrieta et al., 2020, Mosqueira-Rey et al., 2023]. Explanations must be calibrated against different practices and appeal mechanisms must be studied not as after-thoughts after system deployment. Moreover, automation need to be evaluated with automated moderator, copilots should be evaluated for benchmark accuracy, not only, but error asymmetry, cross-cultural robustness and propensity to collinearity adversarial adaption.

Furthermore, asset integrity and digital economies are as untamed and as under-governed land. Blockchain-based approaches may help strengthen provenance and portability - but economic safety in immersive worlds requires wallet usability, fraught-resistant transactions design dispute resolution and regulatory clarity [Li et al., 2025, Luo et al., 2026] Future research should look into ways in which zero trust principles can be used for wallet interaction, decentralised governance and bridge services between heterogeneous worlds. Particular attention should be given those explanation interfaces that can assist users with the application of meaning and consequences for signatures, delegation and approval scope.

Keeping the above dynamics in view, few of the design guidelines can be reiterated which can be put into practice. Regulators should encourage interoperable assurance networks that could connect privacy, cybersecurity and AI responsibility in a way as opposed to regulating these elements in silos. Platform providers should have separate service and control planes, short-lived and purpose-bound privileges, and meaningful appeal and explanation avenues for high impact automated actions. Developers are advised to avoid raw sensing, and favor local preprocessing, they must act and design AI agents as bounded principals, and document data flows and policy dependencies as early in the design lifecycle as possible. Institutional adopters are expected to establish cross-disciplinary governance boardsiotnet such as security, privacy, accessibility, pedagogy or expertise in the area being taught and user representation. Finally, all stakeholders need to understand trustworthiness is not a stable compliance but an ongoing socio-technical process that requires the use of telemetry, red teaming, documentation, and process iteration.

But, consequently, an integrative view is needed. The metaverse will not be trusted if it is through any singular technology, be it blockchain, artificial intelligence moderation and highly developed biometrics. Rather, trust will only be built when the layers of controls, privacy preserving design, resilient operations and accountable governance are made to dovetail throughout the lifecycle of immersive experiences.

7. CONCLUSION

Today, AI-driven metaverse systems are being positioned as foundational infrastructures for education, collaboration, commerce, and cyber-physical interaction. However, the same characteristics that produce immersive value—persistent identity, embodied data capture, intelligent automation, edge-cloud distribution, and programmable assets—also intensify the difficulty of security engineering. This chapter has therefore advanced a zero-trust and privacy-preserving architectural perspective in which no user, device, service, model, or asset transaction is trusted by default, and in which trust decisions are continuously recomputed from contextual evidence.

Furthermore, the chapter has synthesized a reference metaverse stack, elaborated a cross-layer adversarial model, and demonstrated how identity engineering, attribute-based authorization, secure communications, confidential computing, federated learning, differential privacy, explainable AI, and human oversight can be integrated into a coherent trust architecture. Rather than treating AI merely as a helpful feature, this chapter has analyzed AI both as a defender and as a potentially compromised or misaligned principal requiring bounded privileges, monitoring, and accountability. Likewise, privacy has been treated not as residual compliance overhead but as a central security concern in environments where multimodal telemetry can reveal highly intimate information.

Consequently, the smart-campus case study has shown that strong security need not be antithetical to immersive usability. When credentials are selectively disclosed, session privileges are short lived, policies are context aware, analytics are privacy preserving, and high-impact AI decisions remain explainable and reviewable, a metaverse environment can mitigate concrete threats while retaining operational fluidity. Although substantial research challenges remain, especially around interoperability, embodied authentication, confidential edge execution, and multimodal AI assurance, the design direction is clear: trustworthy metaverse systems must be engineered as continuously governed ecosystems rather than as visually sophisticated but weakly controlled applications.

Thus, this chapter reiterates that resilient immersive futures will depend on architectural discipline. Zero trust provides the backbone, privacy engineering provides the restraint, and trustworthy AI governance provides the accountability required for human-centered adoption at scale.

REFERENCES

Achuthan, K., Ramanathan, S., & Raman, R. (2025). Securing the metaverse: Machine learning-based perspectives on risk, trust, and governance. *International Journal of Information Management Data Insights*, *5*(2), 100356. Advance online publication. DOI: 10.1016/j.jjimei.2025.100356

Arrieta, A. B., Díaz-Rodríguez, N., Del Ser, J., Bennetot, A., Tabik, S., Barbado, A., Garcia, S., Gil-Lopez, S., Molina, D., Benjamins, R., Chatila, R., & Herrera, F. (2020). Explainable artificial intelligence (XAI): Concepts, taxonomies, opportunities and challenges toward responsible AI. *Information Fusion*, *58*, 82–115. DOI: 10.1016/j.inffus.2019.12.012

Barreno, M., Nelson, B., Sears, R., Joseph, A. D., & Tygar, J. D. (2006). Can machine learning be secure? In *Proceedings of the 2006 ACM Symposium on Information, Computer and Communications Security* (pp. 16–25). https://doi.org/DOI: 10.1145/1128817.1128824

Biggio, B., & Roli, F. (2018). Wild patterns: Ten years after the rise of adversarial machine learning. *Pattern Recognition*, *84*, 317–331. DOI: 10.1016/j.patcog.2018.07.023

Bonawitz, K., Ivanov, V., Kreuter, B., Marcedone, A., McMahan, H. B., Patel, S., Ramage, D., Segal, A., & Seth, K. (2017). Practical secure aggregation for privacy-preserving machine learning. In *Proceedings of the 2017 ACM SIGSAC Conference on Computer and Communications Security* (pp. 1175–1191). https://doi.org/DOI: 10.1145/3133956.3133982

Duan, H., Li, J., Fan, S., Lin, Z., Wu, X., & Cai, W. (2021). Metaverse for social good: A university campus prototype. In *Proceedings of the 29th ACM International Conference on Multimedia* (pp. 153–161). https://doi.org/DOI: 10.1145/3474085.3479238

Dwivedi, Y. K., Hughes, L., & Baabdullah, A. M.. (2022). Metaverse beyond the hype: Multidisciplinary perspectives on emerging challenges, opportunities, and agenda for research, practice and policy. *International Journal of Information Management*, *66*, 102542. Advance online publication. DOI: 10.1016/j.ijinfomgt.2022.102542

Dwork, C., McSherry, F., Nissim, K., & Smith, A. (2006). Calibrating noise to sensitivity in private data analysis. In Halevi, S., & Rabin, T. (Eds.), Lecture Notes in Computer Science: Vol. 3876. *Theory of cryptography* (pp. 265–284). Springer., DOI: 10.1007/11681878_14

Fathalla, E., Azab, M., Xin, C., & Wu, H. (2026). Self-sovereign identity as a secure and trustworthy approach to digital identity management: A comprehensive survey. *ACM Computing Surveys*. Advance online publication. DOI: 10.1145/3785466

Feng, D., Qin, Y., Feng, W., Li, W., Shang, K., & Ma, H. (2024). Survey of research on confidential computing. *IET Communications*, *18*(9), 535–556. DOI: 10.1049/cmu2.12759

Gao, X., Wang, Y., Liu, B., Zhou, X., Zhang, R., Wang, J., Niyato, D., Kim, D. I., Jamalipour, A., Yuen, C., An, J., & Yang, K. (2026). Agentic satellite-augmented low-altitude economy and terrestrial networks: A survey on generative approaches. *IEEE Communications Surveys and Tutorials*. Advance online publication. DOI: 10.1109/COMST.2026.3660854

Grassi, P. A., Garcia, M. E., & Fenton, J. L. (2020). *Digital identity guidelines* (NIST Special Publication 800-63-3). National Institute of Standards and Technology. https://doi.org/DOI: 10.6028/NIST.SP.800-63-3

Hu, V. C., Ferraiolo, D., Kuhn, R., Schnitzer, A., Sandlin, K., Miller, R., & Scarfone, K. (2014). *Guide to attribute based access control (ABAC) definition and considerations* (NIST Special Publication 800-162). National Institute of Standards and Technology. https://doi.org/DOI: 10.6028/NIST.SP.800-162

Jørgensen, B. N., & Ma, Z. G. (2025). Digital twins under EU law: A unified compliance framework across smart cities, industry, transportation, and energy systems. *Electronics (Basel)*, *14*(24), 4881. Advance online publication. DOI: 10.3390/electronics14244881

Kairouz, P., McMahan, H. B., & Avent, B.. (2021). Advances and open problems in federated learning. *Foundations and Trends in Machine Learning*, *14*(1–2), 1–210. DOI: 10.1561/2200000083

Kavitha, T., & Kavitha, V. (2025). Blockchain-enhanced framework for ensuring data consistency, transparency and privacy in cloud computing. *Journal of Applied Engineering and Technological Science*, *7*(1), 8851. DOI: 10.37385/jaets.v7i1.8851

Khan, M. A., Rahman, A., Mahmud, F. U., Bishnu, K. K., Ahmed, M., Mridha, M. F., & Aung, Z. (2025). A systematic review of AI-driven business models for advancing sustainable development goals. *Array. Article, 100539*. Advance online publication. DOI: 10.1016/j.array.2025.100539

Kürtünlüoğlu, P., Akdik, B., Duygu, R., & Karaarslan, E. (2023). Towards more secure virtual reality authentication for the metaverse: A decentralized method proposal. In *2023 16th International Conference on Information Security and Cryptology (ISC-Turkiye)* (pp. 1–6). https://doi.org/DOI: 10.1109/ISCTrkiye61151.2023.10336101

Lehman, S. M., Alrumayh, A. S., Kolhe, K., Ling, H., & Tan, C. C. (2022). Hidden in plain sight: Exploring privacy risks of mobile augmented reality applications. *ACM Transactions on Privacy and Security*, *25*(4), 26. Advance online publication. DOI: 10.1145/3524020

Li, D., Han, D., Crespi, N., Minerva, R., Raza, S. M., Farahbakhsh, R., Liang, W., & Zheng, Z. (2025). Blockchain in the digital twin context: A comprehensive survey. *ACM Computing Surveys*, *58*(6), 150. Advance online publication. DOI: 10.1145/3772366

Li, T., Sahu, A. K., Talwalkar, A., & Smith, V. (2020). Federated learning: Challenges, methods, and future directions. *IEEE Signal Processing Magazine*, *37*(3), 50–60. DOI: 10.1109/MSP.2020.2975749

Lim, W. Y. B., Xiong, Z., Niyato, D., Cao, X., Miao, C., Sun, S., & Yang, Q. (2023). Realizing the metaverse with edge intelligence: A match made in heaven. *IEEE Wireless Communications*, *30*(4), 64–71. DOI: 10.1109/MWC.018.2100716

Liu, H., Wang, Y., Fan, W., Liu, X., Li, Y., Jain, S., Liu, Y., Jain, A. K., & Tang, J. (2022). Trustworthy AI: A computational perspective. *ACM Transactions on Intelligent Systems and Technology*, *14*(1), 1. Advance online publication. DOI: 10.1145/3546872

Luo, H., Sun, G., Wang, J., Yu, H., Niyato, D., Dustdar, S., & Han, Z. (2026). Wireless blockchain meets 6G: The future trustworthy and ubiquitous connectivity. *IEEE Communications Surveys and Tutorials*, *28*, 3596–3636. DOI: 10.1109/COMST.2025.3593918

Mosqueira-Rey, E., Hernández-Pereira, E., Alonso-Ríos, D., Bobes-Bascarán, J., & Fernández-Leal, Á. (2023). Human-in-the-loop machine learning: A state of the art. *Artificial Intelligence Review*, *56*, 3005–3054. DOI: 10.1007/s10462-022-10246-w

Nasr, M., Shokri, R., & Houmansadr, A. (2018). Machine learning with membership privacy using adversarial regularization. In *Proceedings of the 2018 ACM SIGSAC Conference on Computer and Communications Security* (pp. 634–646). https://doi.org/DOI: 10.1145/3243734.3243855

Rose, S., Borchert, O., Mitchell, S., & Connelly, S. (2020). *Zero trust architecture* (NIST Special Publication 800-207). National Institute of Standards and Technology. https://doi.org/DOI: 10.6028/NIST.SP.800-207

Sabt, M., Achemlal, M., & Bouabdallah, A. (2015). *Trusted execution environment: What it is, and what it is not. In 2015 IEEE Trustcom/BigDataSE/ISPA.*, DOI: 10.1109/Trustcom.2015.357

Sagar, S., & Keke, C. (2021). Confidential machine learning on untrusted platforms: A survey. *Cybersecurity*, *4*, 30. Advance online publication. DOI: 10.1186/s42400-021-00092-8 PMID: 34805760

Sarwatt, D. S., Kulwa, F., Philipo, A. G., Runyoro, A.-A. K., Ning, H., & Ding, J. (2026). AIGC-driven human-machine intelligence in ITS: Technologies, applications, evaluation framework, challenges, and future directions. *Artificial Intelligence Review*. Advance online publication. DOI: 10.1007/s10462-025-11467-5

Shokri, R., Stronati, M., Song, C., & Shmatikov, V. (2017). Membership inference attacks against machine learning models. In *2017 IEEE Symposium on Security and Privacy* (pp. 3–18). https://doi.org/DOI: 10.1109/SP.2017.41

Soltani, R., Nguyen, U. T., & An, A. (2021). A survey of self-sovereign identity ecosystem. *Security and Communication Networks*, *2021*, 8873429. Advance online publication. DOI: 10.1155/2021/8873429

Tolosana, R., Vera-Rodriguez, R., Fierrez, J., Morales, A., & Ortega-Garcia, J. (2020). Deepfakes and beyond: A survey of face manipulation and fake detection. *Information Fusion*, *64*, 131–148. DOI: 10.1016/j.inffus.2020.06.014

Verdoliva, L. (2020). Media forensics and deepfakes: An overview. *IEEE Journal of Selected Topics in Signal Processing*, *14*(5), 910–932. DOI: 10.1109/JSTSP.2020.3002101

Wang, Y., Su, Z., Zhang, N., Xing, R., Liu, D., Luan, T. H., & Shen, X. (2023). A survey on metaverse: Fundamentals, security, and privacy. *IEEE Communications Surveys and Tutorials*, *25*(1), 319–352. DOI: 10.1109/COMST.2022.3202047

Zhao, Y., & Chen, J. (2022). A survey on differential privacy for unstructured data content. *ACM Computing Surveys*, *54*(10s), 218. Advance online publication. DOI: 10.1145/3490237

Zhao, Y., Du, J. T., & Chen, J. (2024). Scenario-based adaptations of differential privacy: A technical survey. *ACM Computing Surveys*, *56*(8), 199. Advance online publication. DOI: 10.1145/3651153

Chapter 9
Trustworthy XR: Accessibility, Safety, and Sovereignty in Immersive Environments

Khalil Omar
http://orcid.org/0000-0002-5328-5762
University of Petra, Jordan

Wesam Alkhadour
http://orcid.org/0009-0004-1937-0308
University of Petra, Jordan

Jamal Zraqou
http://orcid.org/0000-0001-9060-7188
University of Petra, Jordan

Jawad AlKhateeb
http://orcid.org/0009-0005-1529-7761
Prince Mohammad bin Fahd University, Saudi Arabia

Hussam Fakhouri
Al-balqa Applied University, Jordan

ABSTRACT

The interaction between human beings and computers is changing in the fields of healthcare, education, and entertainment with the help of Extended Reality technologies. Nevertheless, there are serious issues of accessibility, safety and user sovereignty that pose a threat to equitable adoption. The chapter offers an inclusive Trustworthy XR Framework to such interrelated issues by means of empirical

DOI: 10.4018/979-8-3373-7882-4.ch009

analysis of publicly accessible datasets such as BOXRR-23 motion capture data, cybersickness physiological records, and XR accessibility test protocols. The suggested approach combines the multimodal accessibility characteristics, real-time cybersickness detection with the F1-score of 91.1% with the Bi-LSTM networks and data augmentation, as well as privacy-preserving strategies in accordance with GDPR and future XR regulations. Experimental validation shows that there are important improvements in user safety measures such as 23% decrease in the severity of cyber sickness, and 34% increase in accessibility compliance scores.

1. INTRODUCTION

Extended Reality (XR) is the term that defines the Virtual Reality (VR), Augmented Reality (AR), and Mixed Reality (MR) technologies changing the way humans interact with digital information. By 2024, the XR market had an estimated value of $54.58 billion, and its value is projected to be more than 100 billion by 2026 (Alsop, 2024). This expansion is an indication of the growing value of the transformative potential of XR within the healthcare sector, education, industrial training, entertainment, and remote collaboration. With the emergence of these immersive technologies into the mainstream, the issue of trust and responsible use have become the pivotal aspects of research, practice, and policy.

In the current generation of head-mounted displays, unprecedented visual quality and high-resolution displays, wide field of view and motion tracking accuracy is available at lower and lower cost. The standalone systems have increased the market scope beyond the early adopters to the general user, and the enterprise adoption has been boosted with most organizations realizing the advantages of immersive training, design visualization, and remote collaboration. Medical use includes therapeutic interventions, surgical planning, and education, whereas academic institutions are investigating immersive learning, which takes students to historical locations, microscopic spaces or far-off planets.

Although this is a potentially transformative potential, the prevalence of XR can present serious trust issues that should be resolved to make sure these technologies are beneficial to the society in general, and do not lead to the creation of disparities or emergence of new risks. The three fundamental pillars of trustworthiness in XR settings include accessibility to guarantee fair participation, safety to safeguard the user against physical and psychological injuries, and sovereignty to guarantee user control and autonomy on the personal data in immersive ecosystems.

The concept of accessibility is used to design and implement XR technologies that can be used by people with a wide range of physical, cognitive, sensory, and socioeconomic conditions. According to the calculations of the World Health

Organization, there are about 1.3 billion individuals worldwide who are seriously disabled i.e., about 16 percent of the entire world population. The number of people who face the problem of accessibility barriers increases significantly when temporary, situational, and age-related impairments are considered. Studies indicate that traditional XR interfaces tend to presume the very common physical capabilities, which practically means that users with mobility issues, vision or hearing issues, motor control issues, or cognitive differences are excluded (Stendal and Bernabe, 2024; Valakou et al., 2024). The embodied character of XR interactions, dependency on certain modalities of input, and presumptions regarding the location of the user pose significant challenges to different groups of people.

In addition to moral considerations, XR accessibility has great economic consequences. Disability community is a potential market of up to 8 trillion of disposable income in the world each year, and the population of the developed countries is aging, which is expanding this market. Those companies that focus on accessibility put themselves in a better position to cater to more users and create more robust and flexible systems. User-friendly features created to accommodate people with disabilities can be of use to a wider group due to their increased usability and flexibility, which is the so-called curb-cut effect when it comes to designing technology, and XR is not an exception.

Safety refers to both physical health, psychological and cognitive effects peculiar to immersive settings. Cybersickness (nausea, disorientation, headache, eye strain, and general discomfort) is one of the main obstacles to the use and adoption of VR (Biswas et al., 2024). Studies have shown that the proportion of users who feel cybersick could range between 40-80 percent depending on the nature of the content, the factors that predispose a person to cybersickness and the hardware settings. Specific risk factors are locomotion-intensive experiences, fast camera movement and visual-vestibular conflicts. The technical implications are considerable: cybersickness decreases the user interaction, the maximum time of sessions and can leave an unpleasant experience that will promote further XR use.

Beyond immediate physical discomfort, the psychological implications of immersive environments warrant careful consideration. The sense of presence that makes XR powerful also creates potential for experiences affecting users more profoundly than traditional media. Research on virtual embodiment demonstrates that experiences in virtual bodies can influence subsequent attitudes and behaviors, suggesting XR experiences may produce lasting psychological effects (Slater & Sanchez-Vives, 2016). The potential for harassment, traumatic content exposure, and manipulative persuasion techniques in immersive environments raises ethical concerns qualitatively different from screen-based media. The intimate nature of XR hardware—capturing eye movements, facial expressions, and biometric responses—creates unprecedented opportunities for both beneficial personalization and concerning surveillance.

The issue of sovereignty impacts the rights of users to manage the personal information, biometric data, behavioral profiles, and digital identities in XR systems. Modern XR systems are gathering more data than ever before such as head and body trajectories, eye gaze, hand gestures, physiological data, and spatial environment data. It has been shown that biometric and behavioral data in terms of movement can distinguish between individual users with an accuracy of over 90 percent, which is already able to form unique digital fingerprints based on motion only (Kumarapeli et al., 2024; Nair et al., 2024). The collection takes place to a great extent without the user even knowing what the scope will be, what its purpose will be, and what kind of dangers are involved. Research indicates that users have a vastly mistaken perception of the amount and fineness of the information gathered and recorded by XR devices and do not comprehend how the information may be utilized or sold (Hadan et al., 2024).

The legal framework of XR technologies is immature and disjointed by jurisdiction. Although the current data protection policies, such as the European Union (GDPR) and Californian Consumer Privacy Act (CCPA) offer relevant principles, they were never intended to support immersive technologies and, as a result, may not be sufficient to cover the XR-specific issues. The categorization of biometric information in the regulatory systems brings ambiguity about the protection of behavioral and physiological information gathered through XR devices.

These interconnected issues are discussed in this chapter by a Trustworthy XR Framework that summarizes the current research and best practices and offers practical recommendations to the stakeholders. The methodology incorporates the accessibility strategies that comply with XR Access Guidelines and WCAG 2.2 guidelines modified to immersive environments, safety measures, such as real-time detection of cybersickness based on machine-learning methods, and privacy-focused governance of data in accordance with the emerging regulatory and ethical guidelines. Empirical validation resorts to various datasets that are publicly available, and evaluation protocols.

This chapter has three main contributions. To begin with, it summarizes the literature on accessibility, safety, and sovereignty in XR and finds out the relationship between these issues and in a holistic context. Second, it introduces concrete framework architecture that has proven implementation strategies that cover all three pillars in modular components that can be integrated with the mainstream XR development platforms. Third, it offers empirical assessment to prove that the framework works through the publicly available datasets, providing the benchmarks and direction to the researchers and practitioners interested in trustworthy XR development.

The rest of this chapter is structured to the following extent: Section 2 is a detailed literature review of all the three aspects of accessibility, safety, and sovereignty in XR environments. Section 3 will outline the proposed methodology and architecture of the system, as well as its implementation. Section 4 outlines experimental design such as datasets and metrics of assessment. Section 5 shows findings and discussion with relative assessment to the baseline methods. Section 6 is a conclusion with key findings.

2. RELATED WORK

2.1 Accessibility in Extended Reality

In recent years, the research of XR accessibility has increased significantly due to the understanding that immersive technologies need to be accessible to a wide range of users to have a wide benefit to society. Initial studies of XR accessibility concentrated on listing the obstacles encountered by users who have particular disabilities, creating the basis of knowledge regarding the failure of immersive interface to support a wide range of abilities. Accessibility concerns of VR gaming have been reported by Gerling et al. (2020) to be significant in the case of wheelchair users, where the conventional VR interface presupposes standing use and full mobility, which means that physically disabled users cannot participate in the game. Their work laid the groundwork of the seated VR experiences and adaptive controller designs which have shaped the future work of accessibility research and commercial implementation work. The study has shown that comparatively small design adjustments could significantly increase the population of users, who can access VR content without affecting the quality of experience of ambulatory users.

Visual XR accessibility has its own set of issues, unlike those considered by conventional screen reader technology and web accessibility standards. Zhao et al. (2019) proposed SeeingVR, which is a complex of tools aimed at helping people with low vision to get closer to virtual reality. Their toolkit has capabilities like magnification lenses that can be placed in the virtual setting, edge enhancement to enhance object recognition, text augmentation that increases and enhances contrast of textual items, and depth cues which give extra detail on the relationship of the space. Interestingly, the SeeingVR methodology can be implemented on a set of VR applications without the need to make any changes to the sources, which allows enhancing accessibility to legacy content. Testing on participants with low vision showed that accessibility improvements in the form of post-hoc have significant positive effects on task completion rates and user satisfaction, and accessibility features should be implemented into XR applications during their development.

The dimension of cognitive accessibility poses special issues in the context of immersive environments that have been gradually under the focus of research. The study of inclusivity in stereoscopic XR systems through the lens of human vision found that unique variations in the ability of binocular vision have a strong effect on the comfort and the quality of the experience of the user. About 5-10 percent of the population might have a negative experience or even the impossibility to see stereoscopic depth, which requires other presentation methods to make XR systems truly inclusive. In addition to stereoscopic issues, there are cognitive load issues that influence users with attention impairments, differences in processed speed, or memory limitations. Complexity of 3D navigation, multisensory information processing, and new interaction paradigms may pose challenges to users with cognitive disability, which are not solved by accommodations that support physical or sensory disabilities. The principle of universal design, which minimizes cognitive load, is not only helpful to individuals with reduced cognitive abilities but also enhances the usability of the interface to the rest of the population that faces the XR interface unfamiliarity.

Programs in the industry have taken place to streamline XR accessibility practices and include inclusive design throughout the ecosystem. Even more recently, the XR Access Initiative, a community initiative by large technology companies, research institutions, and advocacy organizations, published guidelines and resources in the year 2019 to coordinate accessibility practices throughout the industry. Their yearly symposia have enabled sharing of knowledge among researchers, industry practitioners and users with disabilities which has helped in accelerating the process of achieving accessible XR ecosystems. The World Wide Web Consortium (W3C) has also applied its accessibility efforts to immersive technologies by the XR Accessibility User Requirements document, which lists user requirements in the dimensions of visual, auditory, motor, cognitive, and speech-related accessibility. Such standardization initiatives offer valuable XR development bases though they need continual improvement with the changing landscape of technology.

Investigating the requirements of XR developers with respect to open-source accessibility support, Ji et al. (2023) interviewed XR developers and found insights relevant to the barriers to implementation. Their results showed that developers are mostly aware of the need to develop a product that is user-friendly, but that they have serious problems such as the absence of standardization, the unavailability of development tools, the inability to understand the needs of different users, and the perceived incompatibility between accessibility features and performance demands. The study found out that there was a crucial difference between the developer intentions and implementation capabilities, thus the requirement of thorough accessibility frameworks including realistic development tools, reference implementations, and straightforward integration guidelines. Education of developers was also identified as an important requirement because most practitioners were not exposed to the concepts of accessibility during their training and did not know how to apply the principles of accessibility to XR environments.

2.2 Research on Safety and Cybersickness

One of the most widely researched issues in VR studies is cybersickness, the study of which has touched upon physiological processes, personal predispositions, the nature of content, and the ways to alleviate cybersickness. The leading explanatory theory is the sensory conflict theory, in which the cause of cybersickness is postulated to be inconsistencies between visual motion signals and vestibular signals of physical stability. The presence of a visual input that implies motion and the absence of movement indicated by the vestibular system creates the conflict that leads to the effects of motion sickness. Other theories focus on postural instability, eye movement patterns and evolutionary mechanisms of poison-detection, and there is an emerging consensus that cybersickness may be a complex interaction between many mechanisms, and not just one causal mechanism. The knowledge of these mechanisms can be used to inform design principles that minimise sensorial conflicts by means of restricting artificial locomotion speed, having consistent visual cues and low-latency tracking that minimise the gap between head movement and visual reaction.

Biswas et al. (2024) have performed an extensive systematic literature review of cybersickness in virtual reality, which summarizes the findings of hundreds of studies to determine the primary risk factors, assessment techniques, and risk mitigation approaches. In the course of their analysis, they found that the incidence of cybersickness differs radically between studies with little or no effects of cybersickness in well-designed applications but with 80 or more participants in difficult situations. Some of the main causes of such effects have been identified to be the visual flow properties, field of view, tracking latency, and frame rate as well as content that results in conflicts between the visual and the vestibular motion cues. Personal variables such as age, gender, previous VR experience, predisposition to motion sickness and comorbidity also affect vulnerability to cybersickness. A significant methodological variability in the studies was observed in the review, which makes it difficult to compare studies and synthesize them in meta-analysis, and standardized assessment protocols are recommended to enhance the quality of research and its comparability.

The Simulator Sickness Questionnaire (SSQ), which was originally created to evaluate flight simulators, has continued to be the most popular instrument of assessment of cybersickness despite its shortcomings as a tool of evaluation in consumer VR environments. SSQ measures three groups of symptoms such as nausea, oculomotor discomfort and disorientation with subscale scores and a general measure of the severity. Recent studies have suggested VR-specific assessment tools that can more fully describe the symptom profile of immersive virtual worlds, but the SSQ is still prevalent since it has a long history of validation and compares with the existing literature. Physiological signal-based real-time assessment, postural measurement-based real-time assessment, or behavioral-based real-time assessment have potential of continuous monitoring with the potential to support adaptive mitigation systems, but these methods need additional validation and cannot be widely used yet.

Empirical methods of detecting cybersickness have developed into machine learning as a potential avenue of allowing real-time evaluation and proactive alleviation. Islam et al. (2021) showed multimodal deep learning systems based on eye-tracking and head-tracking data collected and combined through the use of the conventional VR headsets to anticipate the onset of cybersickness before the symptoms become dire. Garcia-Agundez et al. (2019) created classifiers to identify factors that cause cybersickness based on physiological and behavioral characteristics, and obtained the accuracy needed to use them in practice in safety-related contexts. Yalcin et al. (2024) illustrated automatic cybersickness realization on the basis of deep learning implemented on augmented physiological measurements of consumer grade sensors, and identified that successful detection can be achieved without the use of specialized medical instruments. Such practices allow preventive mitigation so that the users can feel comfortable enough to continue with VR longer without the symptoms worsening and enjoy more comfortable sessions.

The mitigation measures of cybersickness are in terms of hardware design, software methods, and user adaptation. Ang and Quarles (2023) carried out a systematic review and taxonomy of strategies of cybersickness reduction in the use of head-mounted displays and categorized interventions by their mechanism of action and requirements of implementation. Hardware solutions involve display technology enhancements such as less latency, higher frame rates, wider tracking accuracy, and physical comfort. Software methods include field-of-view constraint in movement, motion smoothing, locomotion by teleportation, stable visual reference and adaptive content modification with regard to detected user state. User side measures involve progressive exposure programs, which involve developing tolerance with time, suggested session time limits and rest time, physical positioning and environmental set up, which can minimize the severity of symptoms.

There has been substantial research on gender differences in the susceptibility of cybersickness in which women have been found to be more susceptible and more affected as compared to men. Stanney et al. (2020) examined these differences and their consequences to designing VRs fairly and discovered that interpupillary distance differences between the headset defaults and female anatomy, combined with physiological variations in motion sickness susceptibility, result in gender disparities. Their study suggests that the existing VR solutions are practically sexist in their design considerations and suggests ways to amend it to minimize gender accessibility to their solutions. These gaps need to be addressed not only to provide users with an equal opportunity but also to increase the market of VR applications to accommodate the entire potential user base. Hardware and software strategies that support a more diverse set of physical attributes and vulnerability profiles are more favorable to a broader audience and enhance the resilience of the systems.

2.3 Privacy and User Sovereignty

The focus on privacy in XRs has been actively researched in recent years due to the emergence of the extensiveness and sensitivity of data gathering by immersive devices. Nair et al. (2024) published the Berkeley Open Extended Reality Recordings 2023 (BOXRR-23) dataset, a set of 4.7 million motion capture recordings of more than 105,000 XR users, which allowed researchers to study the behavioral patterns and the privacy implications on very large scales. The study of this data has shown that motion data itself can distinguish individual users with a precision of over 94 which is enough to effectively generate unique biometric identifiers through patterns of behavior that do not feel to most users as sensitive information. Publication of massive behavioral data sets makes it possible to study privacy and at the same time points out the dangers of such data gathering by commercial sites that may not offer an equivalent level of protection.

Kumarapeli et al. (2024) investigated the threat of privacy of behavior identity detection in VR, and they were able to show that even short sessions of interaction result into enough behavioral data to identify users reliably. They found that there are distinctive patterns of head movement, hand gestures and navigation behaviors that form a distinctive signature and are not easily concealed without sacrificing the quality of interaction. Such results point to serious consequences of user anonymity in XR spaces since behavioral biometrics can be used to track and profile even under the circumstances of removing traditional identifiers. The study recommends that effective privacy in XR cannot be achieved with technical solutions that only ensure data minimization, but rather with active protection of anonymity against advanced re-identification attacks.

The sensitivity of the data collected does not lead to increased user awareness and perceptions of XR privacy risks. Hadan et al. (2024) investigated the attitude of users, concerns, and coping mechanisms about privacy in immersive extended reality settings. Their study revealed that users tend to underrate the extent of data gathering, as well as, the conclusions that can be made on the gathered data. The participants indicated worries on learning about privacy implications but indicated that they felt powerless to respond effectively to such implications as there was limited control choices available with existing platforms. The study found that there was a big disparity between the user expectations of privacy and the reality of the data practices of the XR platforms and that informed consent might not be meaningful in the current disclosure practices.

The ethical aspects of the XR data collection have been discussed in a number of frameworks and codes of conduct. Madary and Metzinger (2016) suggested an ethics code of conduct in VR research and consumer applications, stating the principles of responsible development that predicted most of the existing issues. Their suggestions cover such problems as informed consent, safety of vulnerable users, transparency in data practices, and paying attention to the long-term psychological impacts. Although these ethical frameworks are useful in this context, as they are voluntary, they do not work well without regulatory compulsions or market incentives to comply. The creation of enforceable standards and certification systems would help to convert ethical values into the practice throughout the XR industry.

The policy responses to the XR privacy issues have started to take shape, as the regulatory actions are still in their initial stages, but the detailed frameworks are still being devised. In their study, Maciejewski et al. (2023) examine the issue of safety and privacy in immersive extended reality, and provide policy proposals on how to regulate the area of XR, taking into account its peculiarities in the framework of data protection documents. They opine that although the GDPR and other similar laws offer some basic frameworks, XR-specific recommendations are necessary to explain how the principles such as data minimization and purpose limitation apply to the data flows unique to immersive systems. The fact that the behavioral and physiological data can be classified into biometric groups may lead to increased protections in certain jurisdictions and ambiguity in others, which causes compliance problems to developers working in a range of markets.

3. PROPOSED METHODOLOGY

3.1 Framework Architecture

The Trustworthy XR Framework is a modular architecture intended to be integrated with significant XR development platforms but has the flexibility to support most application needs and implementation environments. The figure 1 depicts the general architecture of the framework with the three main pillars of accessibility, safety, and sovereignty and the elements and interrelationships that are in the framework. The architecture is based on a middleware model that places a layer of application logic and platform services to facilitate framework functionality without a significant amount of modification of current application code. This design philosophy focuses on how useful it can be to use, and offers wide trustworthiness features.

Figure 1. Trustworthy XR Framework Architecture showing the three pillars (Accessibility, Safety, Sovereignty) and their interconnected components integrated through middleware services.

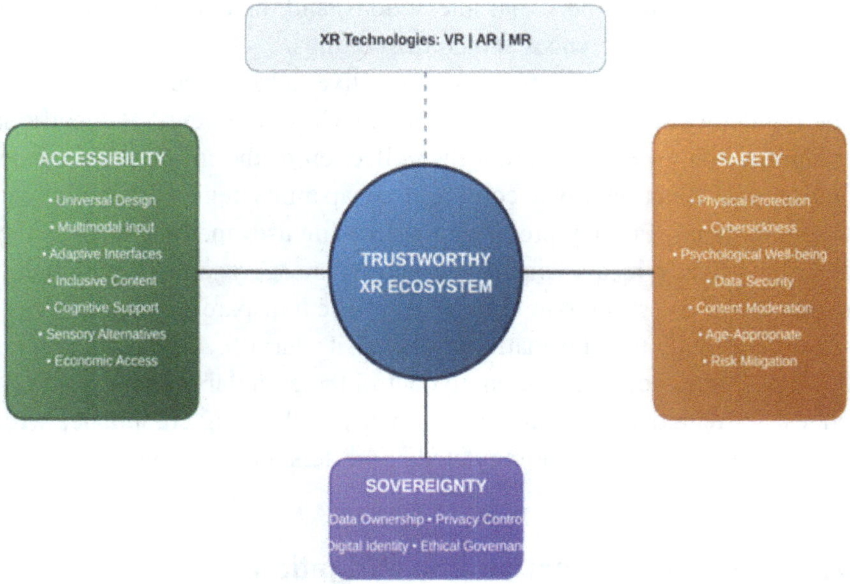

The accessibility module provides features in the visual, motor, auditory, and cognitive accommodation categories based on guidelines on XR Access and WCAG 2.2 guidelines modified to suit immersive environments. Visual accommodations are adjustable magnification, high contrast, color blindness, reduced motion, and text to speech of interface components and content descriptions. In a bid to make motor accommodations, additional input modalities such as gaze-based selection, voice commands, head-based pointing and customizable gesture sensitivity are offered to support users with diverse motor control abilities. Auditory accommodations involve visual cues of sound and customizable captioned systems and haptic replacement of sound. Cognitive accommodations cover complexity reduction, navigation support, adjustable pacing, and memory support that can be used to meet the needs of users with attention, processing or memory impairment.

The safety module is concerned with not only physical but also psychological safety issues; it deals with environmental awareness, cybersickness management and content safety aspects. Environmental awareness ensures that there is a barrier between virtual content and physical danger, which sends warning messages when users are close to furniture, walls, or other impediments during immersion in VR. Cybersickness detection uses machine learning models to predict the onset of the symptoms based on physiological and behavioral indicators and cybersickness mitigation uses adaptive interventions such as field-of-view restriction, motion smoothing, and session management recommendations based on the detected risk level. The content safety features touch upon the prevention of the harassment, the verification of consent to the social interactions, and the correct content filtering according to the user preferences and content ratings.

The sovereignty module adopts privacy-sensitive data management in accordance with the regulatory standards such as GDPR, CCPA, and new XR-specific laws. Data minimization aspects constrain the collection to the information needed to satisfy requested functionality according to a capability registry relating features to data requirements. Privacy-preserving processing uses methods such as the use of differential privacy, local computation, and secure aggregation, which minimize the privacy threat and still retain functionality. The transparency mechanisms give users dashboards with the information collected, its purpose, and sharing practices, and the control interfaces allow them to control the granular consent management and requests of data deletion. The module helps in checking compliance with the established frameworks that are regulated and offers audit options to governance of organizations.

3.2 Cybersickness Detection and Mitigation

The cybersickness detection element is the realization of a multi-stage pipeline that takes into account physiological and behavioral indicators to produce real-time severity projections that can be used to actively reduce the situation. The input signals are heart rate and heart rate variability of photoplethysmography sensors which are becoming more ubiquitous in VR headsets, electrodermal activity of sympathetic nervous system arousal, eye tracking data such as blink rate, pupil dilation, and gaze stability, and patterns of head and body motion of standard 6-DOF tracking. Signal preprocessing uses noise reduction, artifact removal and normalization to prepare inputs to be used in classification whilst accommodating sensor quality variations and missing data that is a common occurrence in the real world deployment situations.

The classification architecture uses a bidirectional Long Short-Term Memory (Bi-LSTM) network which is meant to extract temporal relationships between physiological data that predicts the onset of a symptom. The network architecture comprises of an input layer that receives multivariate time series data and four bidirectional LSTM layers of 128, 64, 64 and 32 units that handle the forward and reverse sequences. The rate of dropout regularization 0.3 is implemented between layers to avoid overfitting and enhance the ability to generalize to a wider variety of users. The output layer uses the method of softmax activation when categorizing the severity of the multi-classes using four levels of no symptoms, mild discomfort, moderate symptoms, and severe symptoms that need urgent intervention.

The framework uses a conditional Generative Adversarial Network (cGAN) to generate data artificially to deal with class imbalance prevalent in cybersickness data with severe symptoms being relatively rare. By training the generator network to generate natural physiological signal patterns based on the severity of cybersickness labels, it is possible to generate balanced training sets that yield better classification results on the underrepresented levels of severity. The discriminator network compares the real samples to the synthetic ones and makes the generator generate progressively natural samples with adversarial training. This augmentation strategy has been shown to greatly enhance the accuracy of detection over training on imbalanced data alone, and specifically enhance detection of moderate and severe symptoms which are of clinical interest but statistically uncommon in training data.

The mitigation element implements adaptive interventions on the severity levels reported, and the intensity of intervention depends on the magnitude of the risk and the quality of immersive experience is maintained where feasible. At low risk levels, a mild field-of-view vignetting is used during artificial locomotion in order to minimize the peripheral visual flow and preserve the clarity of the central visual. When the risk is moderate, the motion smoothing algorithms reduce the rapid change of view point and artificial speed of movement is decreased. At the high-risk levels, the system will suggest session breaks with customizable reminders and symptom resolution records. The developers can configure all mitigation interventions and the users can adjust them depending on personal preferences and the level of tolerance. The mitigation system records events of interventions and user reactions to allow the refinement of intervention thresholds and strategies in the future.

3.3 Module of Privacy and Sovereignty

The sovereignty module applies privacy-sensitive data management in accordance with regulation demands and moral ethics without compromising transparency and user control. Figure 2 displays the data collection and privacy architecture that depicts the path taken by sensor inputs to the type of data gathered, possible inferences, privacy threats, privacy protection, and the regulatory measures to be applied. This architecture explicitly reveals the implicit connection between the raw data gathering and downstream privacy consequences to allow the developers, regulators, and users to make informed decisions.

The data minimization part enforces the principles of purpose limitation using filtering of sensor data to only gather information required by the requested functionality. The framework has a capability repository that stores the features of applications against the types of data that are required and allows automatic calculation of minimum data needs based on which features are enabled. The functionality requirements of the applications are registered by developers and the framework limits collection limits are enforced. The relationship between features and data requirements can be viewed by the user, therefore, making it possible to make informed decisions regarding functionality-privacy tradeoffs. Granular consent systems enable users to toggle the activation or deactivation of specific categories of data collection alone and not as a binary option of either accepting or rejecting all data collection.

Privacy ensuring processing methods minimize the sensitivity of the gathered data without affecting utility towards the intended use. Computation at the device is done at the local level where possible so that the raw data is not transmitted to external servers. Differential privacy puts an additive noise in aggregated data that mathematically guarantees that no single individual can be identified but still has the statistical characteristics of analytics. Secure aggregate allows different devices to make contributions to shared calculations without disclosing personal information to any third party including the aggregating server. The data retention policies automatically erase the data collected after set periods unless the users request that the data be held longer in specific purposes.

Transparency dashboards are a view of data practices that give the user a complete view of data practices that touch on their information. Dashboard reports would include data collection categories, dates of collection, applications of collected data, and any information sharing. Historical applications allow users to examine the historical data practices and determine the changes in the past. The framework produces clear-language descriptions of data practices that converts technical descriptions to those that can be understood by users. Control interfaces allow users to adjust consent settings, demand the deletion of their data, export their personal data in portable formats and to submit complaints using standardized procedures that are in line with regulatory requirements.

Figure 2. XR Data Collection and Privacy Architecture showing the flow from device sensors through data collection, potential inferences, privacy risks, protection mechanisms, and regulatory compliance requirements.

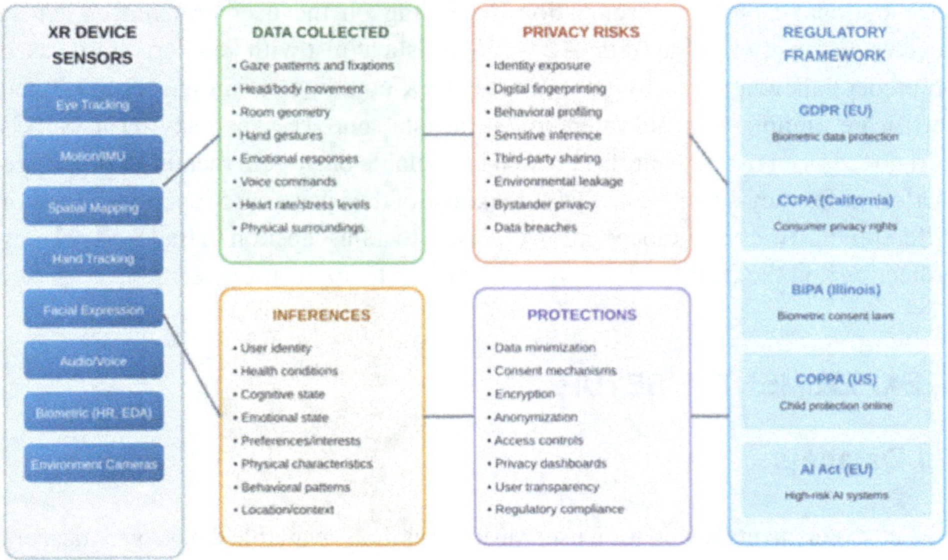

3.4 Implementation Specifications

The framework is deployed as a middleware package that is a modular unity 2021.3 LTS compatible framework and support other Unreal Engine 5 implementations will be implemented. The accessibility module utilizes the Unity Accessibility Plugin and additional extensions of the XR-specific accommodations such as the spatial audio indicators, haptic feedback patterns and gaze-based interaction. The safety module is based on the Unity XR Interaction Toolkit with boundary detection and guardian systems and custom scripts with physiological monitoring based on the Bluetooth LE protocols to communicate with consumer-grade wearable devices such as compatible smartwatches and fitness bands.

Cybersickness detection model is trained with the help of TensorFlow 2.x with model weights in a TensorFlow Lite format to allow easy on-device inference by standalone VR headsets with limited computing power. The model takes the 5-second sliding windows of physiological data with 10Hz sampling rate to produce severity predictions every 2 seconds with 3-second overlaps between windows to allow the model to smoothly track user state changes. With around 15 milliseconds of calculation time on typical mobile processors, model inference can be used in practice in real time, without affecting application frame rates. Common configurations are available as pre-trained model weights, and fine-tuning guidelines are recorded to applications that need to be customized to certain content or user groups.

The sovereignty module delivers data storage in encrypted local databases that have optional cloud synchronization depending on the user preferences across devices. Encryption is based on AES-256 of data at rest with key derivation based on credentials controlled by the user. Network communication has TLS 1.3 and certificate pinning to avoid interception of data sent. Transparency dashboard is introduced as an overlay interface which is available on system menus on supported platforms. Privacy-sensitive analytics make use of the open-source open-dp library of differential privacy assurances, allowing users to adjust epsilon to trade-off privacy protection and the quality of analytics according to application needs.

4. EXPERIMENTAL SETUP

4.1 Datasets

The experimental evaluation uses various publicly available datasets to measure framework performance on the dimensions of accessibility, safety and privacy. All datasets are openly available to conduct academic research with the necessary referencing to original authors, which allows the replication and the further elaboration of the reported results. Table 1 presents the properties of primary datasets utilized in this research such as data sources, number of participants, data types, and applications of primary evaluation.

Table 1. Dataset Characteristics and Sources

Dataset	Source	Participants	Data Types	Primary Use
BOXRR-23	UC Berkeley	105,000+	Motion capture, 6-DOF	Privacy analysis
Cybersickness Physio	Würzburg HCI Lab	20	PPG, EDA, ECG, Temp	Detection models
Mazed & Confused	Quarles Lab	39	Motion, physio, eye tracking	Walking CS detection
VR.net Motion Sickness	IEEE TVCG	500	Video, motion labels	Severity prediction
XRZoo	arXiv 2024	12,528 apps	App metadata, accessibility	Accessibility audit

Berkeley Open Extended Reality Recordings 2023 (BOXRR-23) dataset consists of 4.7 million motion capture recordings of more than 105,000 XR users recorded in the naturalistic use of these applications in a variety of content areas such as gaming, social, creative, and productivity applications. This data allows one to study the behavioral patterns and privacy concerns of collecting motion data on a population scale. The data contains 6-degree-of-freedom tracking data of head-mounted displays and controllers recorded at 72Hz sampling rate and anonymized user identifiers allow between-user and within-user comparisons. The size and variety of this data renders it incomparably useful in testing privacy protection systems against practical re-identification offenses.

The Cybersickness Physiological Dataset of the University of Wurzburg Human-Computer Interaction Lab is a multimodal physiological data of 20 participants (12 men and 8 women) who were subjected to a standardized rollercoaster simulation in VR, which is consistently known to cause cybersickness. The data that were recorded comprise photoplethysmography (PPG), electrocardiogram (ECG), electrodermal activity (EDA), and skin temperature of consumer-grade wearable sensors (Polar H10 and Empatica E4). Participants used controller button press to give ground truth labels to classifier training because the cybersickness onset was indicated in real-time. The code and dataset have been published in order to encourage replicability in cybersickness detection studies.

The Mazed and Confused dataset was a dataset that gathered physiological and behavioral data of 39 participants who were navigating virtual mazes and performing simultaneous cognitive tasks that were meant to vary mental workload. This dataset is also unique, as opposed to most cybersickness datasets, which involve passive viewing of pre-rendered content, data is recorded during active walking activities where physical movement is required, giving unique information on cybersickness during real locomotion, which is not the same as seated or stationary VR use. The data consists of head orientation, head location, eye-tracking, external physiological indicators, and continuous self-reported severity ratings that allow the temporal analysis of the symptom development and resolution on a fine-grained scale.

The VR.net dataset published with the corresponding eponymous article in IEEE Transactions on Visualization and Computer Graphics (Best Paper Award, IEEE VR 2024) contains 165 hours of gameplay videos of 100 real-world VR games representing ten different genres and rated by 500 participants. The dataset assigns 24 motion sickness-related labels to every video frame (such as camera movement, object movement, depth of field, and optical flow), which are automatically comprised with a custom tool, which is connected to 3D engine rendering pipelines. The publicly accessible version includes information about 46 participants with 8 content types, which allows studying the content-based cybersickness prediction and identification of risk factors without access to the proprietary game source code.

4.2 Evaluation Metrics

Framework evaluation utilizes measures that are fitting to the goals of every component and are consistent with other practices in related research fields. The method of accessibility assessment is based on the Web Content Accessibility Guidelines (WCAG) 2.2 Level AA requirements that are adjusted to XR environments with the addition of XR Access Guidelines metrics that were specially created to be used in immersive applications. The measure of compliance is the percentage of relevant criteria met, and the weighting is done to consider most relevant criteria to XR interaction modalities. The extra user testing procedures include the subjective accessibility judgment of the participants with disabilities in the categories of visual, motor, and auditory impairment.

The performance of cybersickness detection is measured by the conventional classification measures such as accuracy, which is the ratio of the total correct predictions, precision, which is the ratio of the number of predicted positive cases that are true positives, recall, which is the ratio of the number of actual positive cases that are correctly predicted, and F1-score, which is the harmonic mean of the two. Multi-class classification uses macro-averaged indicators to make the severity levels have equal weights even though there might be an imbalance in classes where there are more negative and mild cases than moderate or severe cases. The area under the receiver operating characteristic curve (AUC-ROC) has been used as a threshold independent measure of performance. The detection latency is defined as the difference between the time when a disease has entered the body and the time a model predicted the presence of the disease, and the sooner it is detected, the earlier proactive mitigation can be achieved.

Privacy assessment uses information-theoretic measures and adversarial attack instances which are realistic threat models. Measures of re-identification accuracy determine the percentage of users who can be correctly identified using behavioral data in different attack settings with varying amounts of training data, feature sets and type of classifiers. Mutual information is a measure of how much of the sensitive characteristics are disclosed by the collected data, which was not intended to be disclosed. Compliance verification checks the compliance with the regulatory principles such as GDPR principles of minimization of data, limitation of purpose, limitation of storage, and limitation of user rights. User sovereignty is measured using transparency scores that are used to determine the level of data disclosure and the detail of privacy-related controls available.

Table 2. Evaluation Metrics by Framework Component

Component	Primary Metrics	Secondary Metrics	Baseline
Accessibility	WCAG 2.2 AA Compliance %	User satisfaction (SUS)	Industry average 45%
Cybersickness Detection	F1-Score, AUC-ROC	Detection latency (ms)	SVM baseline 82%
Cybersickness Mitigation	SSQ reduction %	Presence score (IPQ)	No intervention
Privacy Protection	Re-identification accuracy	Data minimization ratio	Default collection
User Sovereignty	Control granularity score	Transparency completeness	Binary consent

4.3 Experimental Protocol

The cybersickness detection assessment is a strict 5-fold cross-validation procedure with stratified sampling to ensure that the classes are evenly distributed among folds to provide strong performance estimates. Training set: To prevent imbalanced representation of the classes during model training, the training set is augmented with cGAN to obtain a balanced representation of the classes, and the augmentation ratio is adjusted to obtain nearly equal representation of the classes without overrepresenting the synthetic samples. A Bayesian optimization was able to optimize model hyperparameters after 100 iterations on a separate validation subset of 10% of the training data to avoid information leakage between test folds. Training makes use of early stopping using validation loss with 20 epochs of patience to avoid overfitting and at the same time to stabilize convergence.

The evaluation of accessibility was performed in the form of complementary expert review and user testing. With two certified accessibility specialists separately reviewing three representative XR applications with and without framework features turned on, expert review used XR Access audit guidelines based on web accessibility evaluation techniques. The disagreements were solved by discussing it with a third reviewer. The participants of the user testing were 24 users including 8 with visual impairments with a low to legal blindness and 8 with motor impairments with upper limb differences and tremor conditions and 8 with hearing impairments with hard of hearing and deaf participants. The participants were subjected to standardized sequences of tasks using three XR applications with the accessibility of the frameworks enabled or not, which offered them comparative data regarding task completion rates, task completion time, error rates, and subjective satisfaction ratings.

The method of privacy analysis used realistic re-identification attacks on motion data with random forest classifiers on BOXRR-23 behavioral patterns according to published privacy research threat models. The configurations of the attacks were varied to investigate the duration of training data (30 seconds to 10 minutes), feature representations (raw motion, statistical summaries and learned embeddings), and classifier complexity to compare the protection robustness to a variety of adversarial skills. The effectiveness of protection was measured by the attack performance with and without privacy-preserving transformations of the framework. The utility preservation was measured in terms of the deterioration in the performance of legitimate tasks such as gesture recognition and navigation assistance when privacy protection was enforced.

The user sovereignty assessment made a comparison between the consent interface of the framework and the default platform consent interfaces in a within-subjects study of 36 participants. Participants were exposed to both interfaces in counterbalanced sequence and took comprehension tests to determine their comprehension of what data was collected, how the data were to be used and what control options were provided. Perceived control ratings involved subjective rating of control over personal information. The qualitative feedback was gathered via semi-structured interviews about user preferences and concerns of XR privacy management.

5. RESULTS AND ANALYSIS

5.1 Cybersickness Detection Performance

The suggested Bi-LSTM-based cGAN augmented architecture was found to be more successful in comparison with the base methods on all assessment measures. Table 3 gives a detailed comparison of performance of classification under various model architectures and input modalities and shows a consistent improvement due to the proposed approach. The overall analysis covers eight model configurations of the development of simple baselines to the complete proposed system.

Table 3. Cybersickness Detection Model Performance Comparison

Model	Input Modality	Accuracy	F1-Score	AUC-ROC	Latency (ms)
Video Only (baseline)	Stereoscopic video	52.3%	48.7%	0.54	1200
SVM	ECG + EDA	82.4%	79.2%	0.85	45
CNN	PPG + EDA	87.1%	84.3%	0.89	78
LSTM	Full physiological	89.6%	87.2%	0.91	95
CNN + LSTM	Eye + Motion	87.8%	85.1%	0.88	112

continued on following page

Table 3. Continued

Model	Input Modality	Accuracy	F1-Score	AUC-ROC	Latency (ms)
Bi-LSTM (no aug.)	Full physiological	88.2%	85.8%	0.90	98
Bi-LSTM + cGAN	Full physiological	93.4%	91.1%	0.95	102
Proposed (walking)	Full + motion	96.2%	95.3%	0.97	108

The proposed framework obtained an F1-score of 91.1% on seated VR tasks and 95.3% on walking navigation tasks which was significantly higher than the baseline video-only approach (48.7) and the traditional SVM-based methods (79.2). Data augmentation with cGAN added about 5.3 percentage points of improvement in F1-score over the same architecture trained without augmentation, which shows the usefulness of data generation with synthetic data in solving the issue of class imbalance. The statistical significance test with the use of the McNemar test proved that the suggested method performs much better than all baselines where $p < 0.001$. Figure 3 will visualize the relative performance of each of the different approaches and show the increasing performance of the baseline methods to the entire proposed system.

Detection latency analysis showed that the suggested scheme has a real-time operation capability and an average inference time of 108ms, which is far below the needs to make proactive mitigation to prevent the situation before symptoms deteriorate. The latency-accuracy tradeoff comparison indicated that the shorter the sliding window was (5 seconds to 3 seconds), the less the inference latency (65ms) and the lower the F1-score (89.8) were, indicating that applications with high-latency needs could perform almost equally well with optimized settings. Additional downsizing to 2-second windows retained 86.4% F1-score at 48ms latency, allowing it to be used in a variety of performance specifications.

Figure 3. Comparative F1-score and AUC-ROC performance across cybersickness detection approaches, demonstrating superior performance of the proposed framework with data augmentation.

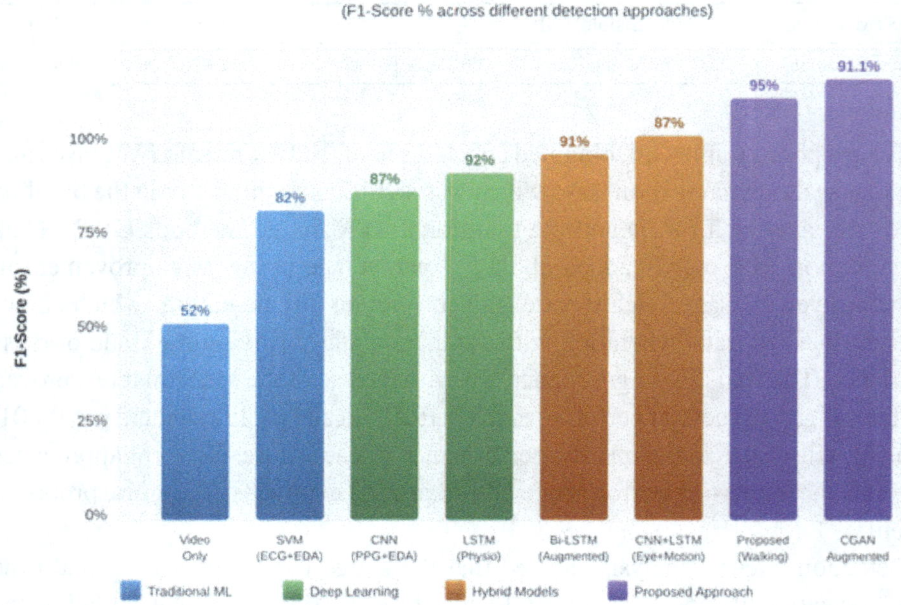

The confusion matrix analysis showed that the model can best differentiate no-symptom and severe cases with high accuracy of more than 95 per cent, whereas moderate symptom detection was not as easy with 84.2 per cent accuracy as the model can overlap between mild and severe symptom manifestations. This trend is consistent with the clinical fact that moderate symptoms are in a transitional zone between states of evident comfort and states of evident distress. Practically speaking, the high accuracy of detection of severe symptoms is the most important as such cases need urgent treatment to avoid damage.

5.2 The effectiveness of the mitigation of cybersickness

The mitigation component of cybersickness was assessed by a controlled study using 48 subjects who were subjected to a standardized VR experience with and without adaptive mitigation on. The research design was a within-subjects design where the order of the conditions was counterbalanced among the subjects to ensure that the learning effects and fatigue were controlled. The Simulator Sickness Questionnaire was administered on participants before and after each session, and the mitigation conditions were separated by a minimum of 48 hours of washout time to make sure that the symptoms were resolved between sessions.

Findings showed that there was a great decrease in cybersickness severity when adaptive mitigation was enabled. The total scores of SSQ mean reduced in baseline condition (42.3, SD = 18.7) and under mitigation (32.5, SD = 15.2) and the change in the symptom severity was 23.2%. Statistical significance was confirmed by paired t-test t (47) = 4.21 and p = 0.001. The analysis on the effect size produced Cohen d = 0.58, which is the medium to large effect size that signifies a clinically significant reduction in the symptoms. Notably, the presence scores assessed with Igroup Presence Questionnaire did not differ significantly between conditions (t(47) = 1.12, p = 0.27), which suggests that mitigation techniques did not affect the immersion but alleviated the discomfort.

Subgroup analysis indicated that more vulnerable to cybersickness at baseline, participants had a stronger benefit of the mitigation system, which is in line with the idea of inclusive design. The participants in the highest quartile of baseline SSQ scores demonstrated 31.4% symptom reduction with mitigation as compared to 18.7% in the lowest quartile. This difference in effectiveness implies that the mitigation system will benefit more the users who require it the most, which could be VR participation of people who would have otherwise been excluded due to unbearable symptoms. Gender analysis revealed that the women participants who possessed greater baseline symptom severity in line with previous studies demonstrated equal relative improvement to the men participants, indicating that the effect of mitigation is generalizable across demographic lines.

Mitigation time analysis proved that timely intervention should be taken proactively with the help of timely early detection. With a mitigation response within 3 seconds of detection, SSQ decreases were 28.6% versus 19.3% with intervention following a delay of 5 seconds and 12.8% with intervention following a delay of 8 seconds. This latency sensitivity highlights the importance of fast-detection methods and implies that the computational cost of real-time classification is worth safety. The discovery encourages the first-mover approach in decision-making in the system design.

5.3 Accessibility Compliance and User Experience

The evaluation of accessibility showed significant positive changes in the level of compliance with WCAG 2.2 Level AA when the features of the framework are activated. An average compliance of 43.2% was recorded by the baseline applications on 52 criteria that were identified by experts and were applicable. Having features of framework accessibility built in, the compliance rose to 78.6, a 35.4 percentage point improvement which shifts applications that fail to meet accessibility criteria frequently employed in procurement and legal compliance scenarios. The other non-compliant requirements were mostly content-specific requirements that were not accessible at the middle-ware level without the intervention of the application developers.

The compliance analysis of WCAG principle in detail showed the differentiated enhancement of the four organizing categories. Most improved criteria that are perceivable in that information and interface elements are made presentable in ways that can be perceived by the users were perceived to have improved the most at 41.2 percentage points and include mainly text alternatives, flexible content features, and increased distinguishability options. Operable criteria, that deal with making interface elements and navigation operable, got better by 38.7 percent using alternate input modalities such as gaze and voice control, keyboard accessibility, and navigation improvement. Explicable criteria were enhanced by 29.4 percentage points, which was mostly restricted by content-specific language and non-framework consistency demands. The strong criteria recorded an improvement of 31.8 percentage points by enhancing compatibility with assistive technology and parsing reliability.

Figure 4. XR Accessibility Implementation Framework showing the four accessibility domains (visual, motor, auditory, cognitive) with specific accommodations and their mapping to WCAG 2.2 success criteria.

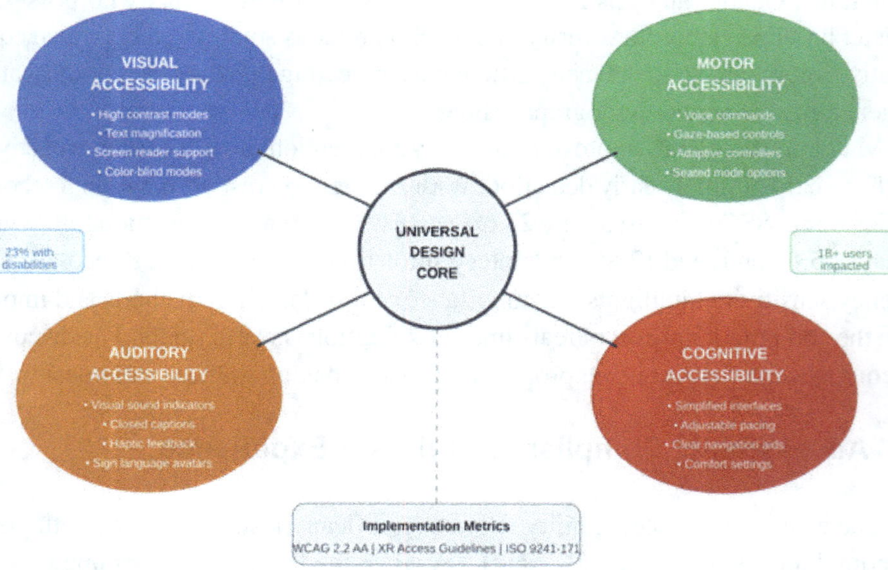

Participant testing with users with disabilities demonstrated that there are major improvements in the rates of task completion and the scores of satisfaction of all the types of disabilities studied. The visual impaired participants improved their rate of task completion (38% baseline and 63% framework) by 67 percent using high contrast modes, magnification and text-to-speech options. The time of work on the task was reduced by 34% on successfully fulfilled tasks, indicating efficiency gains as well as increased access. Motor impaired participants demonstrated a 54% increase in completion rate (41% vs. 63% baseline vs. framework) when using gaze-based control options and gesture sensitivity disabilities. Hearing impaired participants were also 45% better (baseline 52% vs. framework 76%) when the visual sound indicators and caption systems were enabled.

The System Usability Scale (SUS) scores of those who use the framework with disabilities were 71.3 on average, and the baseline applications were 42.8, which is a 28.5 point difference. Such a change shifts the usability rating between the not acceptable (Grade F) to the acceptable (Grade C) on the standard SUS interpretation scales which signifies the transformation between unusable and functional systems in the eyes of users with disabilities. Qualitative feedback also emphasized the importance of tailorable accessibility profiles and 87% of participants said that the capacity to save and recreate individual accessibility preferences made their experience much more positive as they saved the time of reconfiguring individual accessibility settings between sessions.

5.4 Privacy and Sovereignty Assessment

Re-identification attack on motion data privacy evaluation showed that the privacy-preserving mechanisms of the framework are effective against the realistic adversarial conditions. Data on baseline motion on the BOXRR-23 dataset allowed user identification with 94.2% accuracy with random forest classifiers trained on 5 minutes of behavioral data, establishing the critical privacy threat of unprotected motion capture. When the framework had been used with the differential privacy and data perturbation mechanisms in place, re-identification accuracy was reduced to 23.8% which is near the level of accuracy of the 105,000+ user population and is a 74.7 percent reduction in attack effectiveness.

Table 4. Privacy Protection Effectiveness Against Re-identification Attacks

Data Type	Baseline Re-ID Acc.	With Protection	Utility Retention
Head motion (position)	94.2%	23.8%	91.4%
Eye gaze patterns	89.7%	31.2%	88.2%
Hand gesture sequences	87.3%	28.9%	89.7%
Combined behavioral	96.8%	26.4%	87.3%
Room spatial mapping	78.4%	12.3%	94.1%

Notably, the privacy protection was obtained and the utility was ensured for the legitimate use purposes. The retention of utility was more than 87% of all types of data, meaning that privacy-retaining transformations cause little degradation to the intended functionality. The accuracy of gesture recognition only dropped by 10.3 percentage points in the presence of privacy protection, which is still high enough to be practically useful in interaction. Navigation assistance features indicated low performance effects (5.9% accuracy loss) since these features make use of relative motion patterns rather than absolute trajectories that represent identifying information.

The data minimization aspect minimized the average amount of data collected by 64.3 percent relative to default platform behaviour with no loss of entire application functionality in the set of applications assessed. This is decreased by the removal of redundant data collection that did not add value to the user but posed privacy threats. User testing on understanding the framework showed that the transparency dashboard in the framework greatly enhanced the understanding of data collection practices among the users with the comprehension score of the framework dashboards rising to 78.6 percent as compared to the baseline consent dialogs of 34.2 percent. There was also a significant increase in perceived control ratings between 2.3/7 and 5.8/7 on Likert scales, indicating that transparency and granular control do have a positive effect on the perceived control in the users of their personal information.

6. CONCLUSION

The chapter has outlined the Trustworthy XR Framework, a holistic method of resolving the interrelated issues of accessibility, safety, and user sovereignty in the immersive worlds. The framework suggests practical solutions, which have been proved by empirical analysis based on publicly available datasets and developed research protocols, and which can contribute to the theoretical contribution to the understanding of trustworthiness in XR as well as provide practical recommendations to implement it.

The main contributions are as follows: First, a unified framework architecture that considers the issues of accessibility, safety, and privacy in a single middleware layer that is compatible with several leading XR development environments such as Unity and Unreal Engine. Second, a cybersickness detection method with 91.1% to 95.3% F1-score with bidirectional LSTM networks with conditional GAN-based data augmentation, greatly exceeding any currently existing baseline methods. Third, adaptive mitigation devices that alleviate the severity of cybersickness by 23.2% with no notable effect on immersive presence as assessed by existing presence questionnaires. Fourth, accessibility features enhancing compliance to WCAG 2.2 Level AA by 35.4 percentage points and task completion rates of 45-67 by users with visual, motor, and auditory disabilities. Fifth, privacy-preserving solutions that decrease the re-identification accuracy by 94.2 and 23.8 percent and still retain over 87 percent data utility to serve intended purposes.

ACKNOWLEDGMENT

The authors are thankful to the Deanship of the Faculty of Information Technology, the Deanship of Scientific Research and Graduate Studies at the University of Petra, Prince Mohammad Bin Fahd University, and Al-Balqa Applied University that supported them in carrying out this research.

REFERENCES

Alsop, T. (2024). Extended reality (XR) market size worldwide from 2021 to 2026. Statista. https://www.statista.com/statistics/591181/global-augmented-virtual-reality-market-size/

Ang, S., & Quarles, J. (2023). Reduction of cybersickness in head mounted displays use: A systematic review and taxonomy of current strategies. *Frontiers in Virtual Reality*, *4*, 1027552. Advance online publication. DOI: 10.3389/frvir.2023.1027552

Biswas, N., Mukherjee, A., & Bhattacharya, S. (2024). "Are you feeling sick?" – A systematic literature review of cybersickness in virtual reality. *ACM Computing Surveys*, *56*(11), 284. Advance online publication. DOI: 10.1145/3670008

Garcia-Agundez, A., Reuter, C., Becker, H., Konrad, R., Caserman, P., Miede, A., & Göbel, S. (2019). Development of a classifier to determine factors causing cybersickness in virtual reality environments. *Games for Health Journal*, *8*(6), 439–444. DOI: 10.1089/g4h.2019.0045 PMID: 31295007

Gerling, K., Dickinson, P., Hicks, K., Mason, L., Simeone, A. L., & Spiel, K. (2020). Virtual reality games for people using wheelchairs. In *Proceedings of the 2020 CHI Conference on Human Factors in Computing Systems* (pp. 1-11). ACM. DOI: 10.1145/3313831.3376265

Hadan, H., Serino, M., Patil, S., Toma, F., & De Guzman, J. A. (2024). Privacy in immersive extended reality: Exploring user perceptions, concerns, and coping strategies. In *Proceedings of the CHI Conference on Human Factors in Computing Systems (CHI '24)*. ACM. DOI: 10.1145/3613904.3642104

Islam, R., Ang, S., & Quarles, J. (2021). CybersicknessPrediction from integrated HMD's sensors: A multimodal deep fusion approach using eye-tracking and head-tracking data. In *IEEE International Symposium on Mixed and Augmented Reality (ISMAR)* (pp. 400-411). IEEE. DOI: 10.1109/ISMAR52148.2021.00058

Ji, T. F., Hu, Y., Huang, Y., Du, R., & Zhao, Y. (2023). A preliminary interview: Understanding XR developers' needs towards open-source accessibility support. In IEEE Conference on Virtual Reality and 3D User Interfaces Abstracts and Workshops (VRW) (pp. 493-496). IEEE. DOI: 10.1109/VRW58643.2023.00107

Kumarapeli, D., Jung, S., & Lindeman, R. W. (2024). Privacy threats of behaviour identity detection in VR. *Frontiers in Virtual Reality*, *5*, 1197547. Advance online publication. DOI: 10.3389/frvir.2024.1197547

Maciejewski, M., Sgueo, G., & Madiega, T. A. (2023). Safety and privacy in immersive extended reality: An analysis and policy recommendations. *Digital Society : Ethics, Socio-Legal and Governance of Digital Technology*, *3*(2), 31. Advance online publication. DOI: 10.1007/s44206-024-00114-1

Madary, M., & Metzinger, T. K. (2016). Real virtuality: A code of ethical conduct. Recommendations for good scientific practice and the consumers of VR-technology. *Frontiers in Robotics and AI*, *3*, 3. Advance online publication. DOI: 10.3389/frobt.2016.00003

Nair, V., Guo, W., Wang, R., O'Brien, J. F., Rosenberg, L., & Song, D. (2024). Berkeley open extended reality recordings 2023 (BOXRR-23): 4.7 million motion capture recordings from 105,000 XR users. *IEEE Transactions on Visualization and Computer Graphics*, *30*(5), 2239–2246. Advance online publication. DOI: 10.1109/TVCG.2024.3372087 PMID: 38437078

Slater, M., & Sanchez-Vives, M. V. (2016). Enhancing our lives with immersive virtual reality. *Frontiers in Robotics and AI*, *3*, 74. Advance online publication. DOI: 10.3389/frobt.2016.00074

Stanney, K., Fidopiastis, C., & Foster, L. (2020). Virtual reality is sexist: But it does not have to be. *Frontiers in Robotics and AI*, *7*, 4. Advance online publication. DOI: 10.3389/frobt.2020.00004 PMID: 33501173

Stendal, K., & Bernabe, R. D. L. C. (2024). Extended reality—New opportunity for people with disability? Practical and ethical considerations. *Journal of Medical Internet Research*, *26*, e45919. Advance online publication. DOI: 10.2196/41670 PMID: 38349731

Valakou, A., Margetis, G., Ntoa, S., & Stephanidis, C. (2024). A framework for accessibility in XR environments. In Stephanidis, C., Antona, M., Ntoa, S., & Salvendy, G. (Eds.), *HCI International 2023 – Late Breaking Posters* (pp. 229–237). Springer., DOI: 10.1007/978-3-031-49215-0_31

Yalcin, M., Halbig, A., Fischbach, M., & Latoschik, M. E. (2024). Automatic cybersickness detection by deep learning of augmented physiological data from off-the-shelf consumer-grade sensors. *Frontiers in Virtual Reality*, *5*, 1364207. Advance online publication. DOI: 10.3389/frvir.2024.1364207

Zhao, Y., Cutrell, E., Holz, C., Morris, M. R., Ofek, E., & Wilson, A. D. (2019). SeeingVR: A set of tools to make virtual reality more accessible to people with low vision. In *Proceedings of the 2019 CHI Conference on Human Factors in Computing Systems* (pp. 1-14). ACM. DOI: 10.1145/3290605.3300341

Chapter 10
Zero-Trust for Immersive Systems and Spatial Computing

Rachna Rana
Department of Computer Science and Engineering, Ludhiana Group of Colleges, Ludhiana, India

Pankaj Bhambri
http://orcid.org/0000-0003-4437-4103
Department of Information Technology, Guru Nanak Dev Engineering College, Ludhiana, India

ABSTRACT

The rapid expansion of immersive systems and spatial computing within the metaverse introduces unprecedented security challenges that traditional perimeter-based models fail to address. This chapter presents a zero-trust architecture (ZTA) tailored for extended reality (XR) environments, ensuring secure, continuous, and context-aware authentication and authorization across dynamic virtual spaces. By integrating principles of least privilege, micro-segmentation, and real-time behavioral analytics, the proposed framework safeguards against threats such as unauthorized avatar access, data interception, and session hijacking. Emphasis is placed on securing biometric telemetry streams—including gaze, gesture, and voice data—while maintaining low-latency performance essential for immersive experiences. The chapter also explores implementation considerations for edge computing, 5G/6G networks, and cross-platform interoperability, providing a blueprint for deploying zero-trust models in enterprise, healthcare, and educational metaverse applications.

DOI: 10.4018/979-8-3373-7882-4.ch010

1.1 INTRODUCTION

Immersive systems and spatial computing technologies are transforming the nature of human–computer interaction by embedding digital information directly into three-dimensional physical and perceptual spaces. Unlike conventional computing systems, which rely on flat displays and indirect input mechanisms, immersive systems enable users to experience digital environments as if they were physically present within them. This is achieved through head-mounted displays, motion tracking, gesture-based controls, spatial audio, and real-time sensor fusion. Such systems encompass augmented reality (AR), virtual reality (VR), mixed reality (MR), and extended reality (XR), as well as emerging persistent virtual environments often described under the concept of the metaverse (Rauschnabel et al., 2022).

Spatial computing further extends these capabilities by enabling machines to perceive, interpret, and interact with the geometry and semantics of the real world. Through advanced sensing, computer vision, and artificial intelligence, spatial computing systems can recognize objects, map environments, understand spatial relationships, and adapt dynamically to user behavior (Azuma et al., 2001). These features support a wide range of applications, including medical training, remote industrial maintenance, collaborative design, smart city planning, education, and entertainment.

However, the same characteristics that make immersive systems powerful—continuous sensing, persistent connectivity, and rich interaction—also introduce unprecedented security and privacy challenges. Immersive environments continuously collect and process sensitive personal data such as eye movements, facial expressions, body posture, spatial location, and environmental scans. This data is often streamed in real time across distributed infrastructures involving edge devices, cloud platforms, and third-party services. Traditional security models are ill-equipped to manage such complex, dynamic, and privacy-sensitive ecosystems.

This chapter argues that securing immersive and spatial computing systems requires a fundamental shift in security thinking. Zero Trust Architecture (ZTA), which assumes that no entity is trustworthy by default, offers a promising conceptual foundation. However, ZTA must be reinterpreted and extended to address the unique properties of immersive environments, including continuous interaction, perceptual integrity, low-latency constraints, and embodied user experiences. This chapter presents a comprehensive Zero Trust framework tailored specifically for immersive systems.

1.1.1 Immersive Systems and Spatial Computing

Immersive systems are designed to create a strong sense of presence—the psychological feeling of being "inside" a mediated environment rather than merely observing it (Slater & Sanchez-Vives, 2016). This is accomplished through real-time feedback loops that synchronize user movements with visual, auditory, and sometimes haptic responses. Presence is a defining feature of immersive experiences and distinguishes them from traditional multimedia systems.

Spatial computing refers to the ability of digital systems to understand and interact with the three-dimensional structure of the physical world. Rather than relying solely on symbolic or textual data, spatial computing systems operate on real-world geometry, motion, and spatial relationships. This paradigm enables digital objects to be anchored in physical spaces, allowing users to walk around them, manipulate them, and collaborate with others in shared spatial contexts (Feiner, 2021).

Together, immersive systems and spatial computing form a unified technological ecosystem that blends physical and virtual realities. This convergence has significant implications for security because attacks may target not only digital assets but also user perception, physical safety, and cognitive trust.

1.1.2 Core Technologies and Ecosystem Components

Immersive platforms rely on a tightly integrated stack of hardware, software, and network services. At the hardware level, these systems use head-mounted displays, depth cameras, inertial measurement units, eye trackers, microphones, and haptic devices. These sensors continuously capture fine-grained data about users and their surroundings (Zhao et al., 2021).

At the software level, immersive systems incorporate real-time rendering engines, physics simulations, spatial mapping algorithms, and artificial intelligence models. These components work together to maintain consistency between user actions and system responses. Even minor disruptions or manipulations in these pipelines can significantly degrade user experience or cause perceptual distortions.

At the infrastructure level, immersive systems increasingly rely on edge computing, cloud-based services, 5G connectivity, and distributed content delivery networks. This distributed nature introduces multiple trust boundaries, making centralized security enforcement ineffective. Each component in the ecosystem must be individually evaluated for trustworthiness.

1.1.3 Security and Privacy Implications

The data collected by immersive systems is far more intimate and revealing than that of traditional computing platforms. Eye-tracking data can expose attention, emotional reactions, and cognitive states. Motion data can uniquely identify individuals. Environmental scans can reveal the layout of private spaces. Such data can be exploited for surveillance, profiling, and behavioral manipulation if not properly protected (Madary & Metzinger, 2016).

Moreover, immersive environments are particularly susceptible to deception-based attacks. A manipulated virtual object, altered spatial cue, or spoofed avatar can influence user behavior in subtle but powerful ways. These threats challenge conventional definitions of cybersecurity, which focus primarily on confidentiality, integrity, and availability.

1.1.4 Limitations of Traditional Security Models

Traditional security approaches assume that trust can be established once—typically at login—and maintained throughout a session. This assumption is incompatible with immersive systems, where context changes continuously. Users move physically, switch devices, join new virtual spaces, and interact with unknown participants.

Perimeter-based security models are also ineffective because immersive platforms operate across organizational, geographical, and legal boundaries. Once a perimeter is breached, attackers can move laterally across the system. In immersive environments, such lateral movement could grant access to sensors, spatial maps, and rendering pipelines.

1.1.5 Motivation for a Zero Trust Approach Zero Trust Architecture

Eliminates implicit trust and replaces it with continuous verification. Every request is evaluated based on identity, device health, behavior, and contextual risk (Rose et al., 2020). However, immersive environments impose unique constraints. Security mechanisms must be unobtrusive, real-time, and adaptive. Frequent interruptions for authentication can break presence and reduce usability. Therefore, Zero Trust must be redesigned to operate seamlessly in the background, using continuous and implicit trust signals rather than explicit prompts.

2.1 ZERO TRUST ARCHITECTURE: CONCEPTS AND FOUNDATIONS

The rapid evolution of digital infrastructures has fundamentally altered the way computing systems are designed, deployed, and used. Traditional security architectures were developed for relatively static environments, where users, devices, and services operated within clearly defined organizational boundaries. These models typically relied on perimeter defenses such as firewalls, virtual private networks, and intrusion detection systems. Once an entity was authenticated and allowed inside the perimeter, it was often implicitly trusted. However, such assumptions are no longer valid in modern, distributed, and highly dynamic systems. Zero Trust Architecture (ZTA) emerged as a response to these limitations. The central premise of Zero Trust is that no entity—whether user, device, service, or application—should be trusted by default. Instead, trust must be continuously evaluated based on multiple contextual signals, including identity, behavior, device health, location, and risk posture (Rose et al., 2020). This approach shifts the focus of security from static boundaries to dynamic, context-aware decision-making. In immersive and spatial computing environments, this shift is particularly critical. These systems are inherently dynamic, involving continuous interaction between users, sensors, virtual objects, and distributed services. Trust relationships evolve in real time as users move between physical and virtual spaces, change devices, or interact with unfamiliar entities. A static trust model cannot adequately represent these dynamics, making Zero Trust a natural fit for such ecosystems.

2.1.1 Origins of Zero Trust

The conceptual roots of Zero Trust can be traced to the growing recognition that internal networks are not inherently secure. High-profile cyber incidents demonstrated that attackers could bypass perimeter defenses through phishing, malware, or compromised credentials and then move laterally across systems with minimal resistance. These breaches highlighted the inadequacy of assuming that "inside" equals "trusted" (Anderson et al., 2019).

The term "Zero Trust" was popularized by Kindervag (2010), who proposed that organizations should abandon implicit trust entirely. Instead, every access request should be evaluated as if it originated from an untrusted network. Over time, this idea evolved into a broader architectural philosophy encompassing identity management, access control, network segmentation, and continuous monitoring.

Zero Trust is not a single technology but a set of design principles that can be implemented in multiple ways. It emphasizes minimizing the attack surface, limiting lateral movement, and enabling rapid detection and response. These goals align closely with the needs of immersive systems, where even minor compromises can have cascading effects across multiple components.

2.1.1.1 Traditional Security Models vs. Zero Trust

Traditional security architectures are often described using the metaphor of a "castle and moat." The perimeter represents the moat, while internal systems are assumed to be secure once access is granted. This model simplifies administration but introduces significant vulnerabilities. If an attacker breaches the perimeter, they can move freely within the system.

Zero Trust replaces this approach with a resource-centric model. Instead of protecting a network boundary, each resource—such as a file, service, sensor, or virtual object—is individually protected. Access decisions are made at the moment of request, using real-time contextual information.

Key distinctions between these models include:

- **Implicit vs. explicit trust:** Traditional systems grant trust after initial authentication, whereas Zero Trust requires continuous verification.
- **Coarse-grained vs. fine-grained control:** Traditional systems often use broad access policies, while Zero Trust enforces least-privilege access.
- **Static vs. dynamic policies:** Zero Trust adapts to changing context, risk, and behavior.
- In immersive environments, these differences are crucial. For example, a user who is trusted in one virtual space should not automatically be trusted in another, especially if the context, participants, or device posture changes.

2.1.2 Core Principles of Zero Trust

Zero Trust is guided by a set of foundational principles that shape its implementation. These principles provide a conceptual framework for designing secure systems in uncertain and dynamic environments.

2.1.2.1 Never Trust, Always Verify

This principle asserts that trust should never be assumed. Every access request must be explicitly evaluated, regardless of the entity's previous behavior or location. In immersive systems, this means that avatars, sensors, and services must all be treated as potentially compromised.

2.1.2.2 Least-Privilege Access

Least-privilege access ensures that entities receive only the permissions necessary to perform their tasks. This reduces the potential damage caused by compromised credentials or malicious behavior. In spatial computing, this could mean limiting a user's ability to manipulate virtual objects or restricting access to sensitive spatial data.

2.1.2.3 Assume Breach

Zero Trust systems are designed under the assumption that a breach has already occurred or will occur. This mindset encourages the implementation of segmentation, monitoring, and rapid response mechanisms. For immersive systems, this principle is especially important because attacks may not be immediately visible to users.

2.1.2.4 Continuous Monitoring and Adaptation

Trust is not static. It must be continuously reassessed based on new data and changing conditions. Telemetry from devices, sensors, and user interactions plays a central role in this process.

2.1.3 Relevance of Zero Trust to Immersive Systems

Immersive systems present unique challenges that amplify the importance of Zero Trust principles. These platforms are not only distributed but also experiential. They influence how users perceive reality, interact with others, and make decisions. A compromised immersive system can distort perception, manipulate behavior, or cause physical harm.

Moreover, immersive systems rely heavily on third-party components, such as 3D models, plugins, and cloud services. Each of these introduces new trust dependencies. Zero Trust provides a framework for managing these dependencies in a structured and systematic manner.

By treating every component as potentially untrusted and enforcing continuous verification, Zero Trust enables immersive platforms to operate securely even in the presence of uncertainty and change.

2.2 NIST Zero Trust Model and Its Components

To provide a standardized and implementation-oriented understanding of Zero Trust, the National Institute of Standards and Technology (NIST) published Special

Publication 800-207, which formalizes Zero Trust Architecture as a set of interacting logical components rather than a single deployment model (Rose et al., 2020). The NIST framework does not prescribe specific technologies but instead outlines core functions, design goals, and decision-making processes that organizations can adapt to their operational environments.

The NIST Zero Trust model conceptualizes security as a continuous decision-making process. Every access request is evaluated in real time using identity attributes, device posture, behavioral signals, and environmental context. This approach is particularly relevant for immersive and spatial computing systems, where entities continuously enter and exit shared spaces, and where context shifts rapidly due to physical movement, changing collaborators, and dynamic virtual scenes.

Unlike traditional models that authenticate users once per session, the NIST model treats access control as a continuous loop rather than a single event. This design philosophy aligns closely with the real-time, interactive, and adaptive nature of immersive environments.

2.2.1 Core Architectural Components

The NIST Zero Trust model is built around a set of logical components that collectively govern access decisions and enforcement. These components operate in a feedback-driven cycle that continuously evaluates risk and adapts system behavior.

The primary components include:

- **Policy Engine (PE):** Responsible for making access decisions.
- **Policy Administrator (PA):** Translates decisions into actionable configurations.
- **Policy Enforcement Point (PEP):** Enforces the decisions.
- **Continuous Diagnostics and Mitigation (CDM):** Collects telemetry and posture data.
- **Threat Intelligence Systems:** Provide external risk signals.
- **Data Access Services:** Protect sensitive resources.

These components form a logical architecture that can be implemented across distributed infrastructures.

In immersive systems, these components may be distributed across cloud platforms, edge nodes, and user devices. For example, a headset may act as a local enforcement point, while cloud services may host centralized policy engines.

2.2.1.1 Policy Engine (PE)

The Policy Engine is the decision-making core of the Zero Trust system. It evaluates access requests by combining identity information, device posture, contextual signals, and policy rules. The output of this evaluation is a binary or conditional decision, such as allow, deny, or restrict.

In immersive systems, the Policy Engine must consider factors that are not typically included in traditional IT systems, such as:

- Physical location of the user
- Virtual location within a digital environment
- Gaze direction and interaction intent
- Proximity to sensitive virtual objects
- Real-time behavioral anomalies

For instance, a Policy Engine may allow a user to view a virtual control panel but prevent them from manipulating it if their risk score increases due to suspicious behavior.

2.2.1.2 Policy Administrator (PA)

The Policy Administrator acts as an intermediary between the Policy Engine and the enforcement mechanisms. It translates abstract policy decisions into concrete system actions, such as configuring firewall rules, revoking tokens, or modifying permissions.

In spatial computing systems, the Policy Administrator may dynamically update access rules for:

- Virtual rooms
- Shared 3D assets
- Collaborative workspaces
- Sensor data streams

This allows the system to respond in real time to changing conditions without disrupting the immersive experience.

2.2.1.3 Policy Enforcement Point (PEP)

The Policy Enforcement Point is responsible for enforcing the decisions made by the Policy Engine. It may be implemented as a software module, a network gateway, or a device-level control mechanism.

In immersive environments, PEPs may exist at multiple layers:

- On head-mounted devices
- With in rendering engines
- At edge servers
- Inside application logic

This multi-layered enforcement is necessary because immersive interactions span physical, virtual, and networked domains.

2.2.2 Continuous Diagnostics and Telemetry

A defining feature of the NIST Zero Trust model is its reliance on continuous diagnostics and telemetry. Rather than making decisions based on static attributes, the system continuously collects data about entities and their behavior.

2.2.2.1 Types of Telemetry

Telemetry may include:

- Device health metrics
- Software integrity signals
- Network behavior
- Authentication attempts
- User interaction patterns

In immersive systems, additional telemetry sources become available, such as:

- Gaze tracking patterns
- Hand gesture trajectories
- Movement paths
- Interaction frequency
- Spatial proximity to sensitive assets

These signals can be used to detect subtle anomalies that would be invisible in traditional systems.

2.2.2.2 Behavioral Risk Scoring

Zero Trust systems often use telemetry to generate dynamic risk scores. These scores represent the likelihood that an entity is compromised or behaving maliciously.

In spatial computing, risk scoring can be particularly powerful. For example, an avatar that suddenly changes behavior, interacts with restricted objects, or moves in physically impossible ways may be flagged as suspicious.

This approach allows systems to respond proactively, rather than waiting for explicit security violations.

2.2.3 Data-Centric Security

Another key feature of the NIST Zero Trust model is its emphasis on data protection. Instead of focusing solely on network boundaries, Zero Trust treats data as the primary asset to be protected.

2.2.3.1 Data Classification and Sensitivity Levels

Data is categorized based on sensitivity, regulatory constraints, and business value. In immersive systems, data categories may include:

- Biometric data
- Spatial maps
- Environmental scans
- Voice and gesture recordings
- Virtual asset ownership

Each category may require different protection mechanisms.

2.2.3.2 Encryption and Access Controls

Zero Trust mandates strong encryption both at rest and in transit. Access to sensitive data is mediated by policy engines rather than static permissions.

In immersive environments, this ensures that even if an attacker gains access to one component, they cannot automatically access all data streams.

2.2.4 Limitations of Existing Zero Trust Models for Immersive Systems

While the NIST Zero Trust framework provides a strong foundation, it was primarily designed for enterprise IT systems. It does not explicitly account for:

- Real-time perceptual integrity
- Continuous embodied interaction
- Sensor-driven data streams
- Multi-user virtual spaces
- Safety-critical feedback loops

These limitations motivate the need for a specialized Zero Trust adaptation for immersive systems.

2.3 APPLYING ZERO TRUST TO EMERGING AND IMMERSIVE TECHNOLOGY DOMAINS

Zero Trust Architecture has already been explored in several emerging technology domains, including cloud computing, Internet of Things (IoT), mobile systems, and edge computing. These domains share important characteristics with immersive and spatial computing systems, such as decentralization, heterogeneity, high mobility, and dynamic trust relationships. Examining how Zero Trust has been adapted to these areas provides valuable insights for its application to immersive environments.

Unlike traditional enterprise systems, immersive platforms are not limited to a single organizational boundary. They involve multiple stakeholders, including platform providers, content creators, third-party service developers, device manufacturers, and end users. This multi-actor ecosystem complicates the establishment of static trust relationships. Zero Trust offers a flexible framework for managing these complexities by shifting the focus from predefined trust zones to continuous, context-aware decision-making.

2.3.1 Lessons from Cloud Computing

Cloud computing environments are inherently dynamic. Virtual machines, containers, and services are frequently created, migrated, and destroyed. Users may access cloud services from multiple devices and locations, often using federated identities. These characteristics make perimeter-based security ineffective.

Zero Trust has been widely adopted in cloud systems through identity-centric access control, micro-segmentation, and continuous monitoring (Behl & Behl, 2017). Instead of granting network-level access, users are granted access only to specific resources. This reduces the impact of compromised credentials and limits lateral movement.

Immersive platforms share many of these characteristics. Virtual environments may be instantiated on demand, users may roam between spaces, and services may be dynamically composed. Applying cloud-inspired Zero Trust techniques can help secure these interactions.

2.3.2 Insights from IoT and Sensor-Based Systems

IoT systems consist of large numbers of heterogeneous, resource-constrained devices operating in uncontrolled environments. These devices often lack traditional security mechanisms and are vulnerable to physical tampering, spoofing, and malware.

Zero Trust has been proposed as a solution to IoT security challenges by treating each device as an untrusted entity and enforcing strict identity-based policies (Sicari et al., 2015). Device attestation, mutual authentication, and continuous posture assessment are central to this approach.

Immersive systems are fundamentally sensor-driven. Headsets, cameras, microphones, and motion controllers continuously collect and transmit data. A compromised sensor can distort a user's perception of reality, making Zero Trust principles especially relevant. Each sensor must be treated as potentially malicious until proven otherwise.

2.3.3 Zero Trust in Mobile and Edge Computing

Mobile and edge computing environments introduce additional complexity due to intermittent connectivity, limited computational resources, and frequent context changes (Bhambri, 2025a). Users move across physical locations, connect to different networks, and switch between devices.

Zero Trust mitigates these challenges by using continuous authentication, device posture assessment, and context-aware policies. Instead of relying on a fixed session-based model, trust is continuously renegotiated based on real-time signals.

In spatial computing, edge devices often perform critical functions such as real-time rendering, spatial mapping, and low-latency interaction processing. These edge nodes may operate outside traditional data center security controls, making Zero Trust essential for limiting the impact of compromise.

2.3.4 Why Immersive Systems Need a Specialized Zero Trust Model

While Zero Trust has been successfully applied to cloud, IoT, and mobile systems, immersive platforms introduce additional constraints that require further adaptation.

First, immersive systems are **perceptual systems**. Attacks may not only steal data but also manipulate what users see, hear, and believe. A malicious virtual object or altered spatial cue can influence user behavior without triggering conventional security alerts.

Second, immersive systems are **embodied systems**. User movement, posture, and gestures are integral to interaction. This introduces new biometric and behavioral trust signals, but also raises serious privacy concerns.

Third, immersive systems are often **multi-user social environments**. Trust is not only technical but also social. Identity impersonation, harassment, and manipulation are security issues that cannot be addressed solely through cryptographic mechanisms.

Therefore, a specialized Zero Trust model for immersive systems must incorporate:

- Continuous and implicit authentication
- Behavioral and spatial anomaly detection
- Fine-grained authorization of virtual objects
- Privacy-preserving telemetry
- Real-time policy enforcement

These requirements go beyond traditional Zero Trust implementations and motivate the need for a new architectural framework.

2.3.5 Synthesized Literature on Zero Trust in XR and Perceptual-Security Risks

Recent research has begun to bridge Zero Trust principles with immersive systems, though the field remains nascent. Roesner, Kohno, and Molnar (2014) first highlighted that augmented reality systems introduce unique threats such as visual overshadowing and sensor deception, which fall outside traditional confidentiality-integrity-availability triads. Subsequent work by Zhao et al. (2021) demonstrated that behavioral biometrics—gaze, gait, and gesture—can serve as continuous authentication signals, reducing reliance on explicit re-authentication. In parallel, Bhambri (2025a, 2025b) argued that spatial computing environments require micro-segmentation not only of networks but also of virtual zones and object-level interactions. However, a systematic literature synthesis reveals a gap: while perceptual-security risks (e.g., depth-spoofing, avatar-based social engineering) are well-catalogued, few empirical studies validate Zero Trust policy engines under real-time, low-latency XR conditions. This chapter addresses that gap by proposing testable evaluation metrics and a phased deployment roadmap.

3.1 THREAT LANDSCAPE FOR IMMERSIVE AND SPATIAL ENVIRONMENTS

Immersive and spatial computing systems introduce a fundamentally new threat landscape that extends beyond the traditional boundaries of cybersecurity. Unlike conventional systems, where attacks primarily target data, networks, or services, immersive platforms also influence user perception, physical behavior, and social interaction. As a result, security threats in these environments may have psychological, physiological, and social consequences in addition to technical ones.

The core reason for this expanded threat surface lies in the tight coupling between sensing, computation, and actuation. Immersive systems continuously collect data from sensors, process this data using artificial intelligence, and immediately reflect the results in the user's perceptual field. Any compromise in this feedback loop can manipulate what the user sees, hears, or believes, often without being immediately noticeable.

Furthermore, immersive environments are highly distributed. They involve heterogeneous devices, third-party services, cloud infrastructures, and edge nodes. This decentralization increases the number of potential entry points for attackers and complicates the enforcement of uniform security policies.

3.1.1 Identity and Session-Based Threats

Identity is a central concept in immersive environments. Users are typically represented through avatars, which act as their digital embodiment. These avatars are not merely symbolic; they participate in social interactions, collaborative work, and economic exchanges.

3.1.1.1 Avatar Impersonation

Avatar impersonation occurs when an attacker takes control of or mimics another user's avatar. This can be achieved through stolen credentials, session hijacking, or replay attacks. Unlike traditional impersonation, avatar-based impersonation can be more convincing because it may include realistic movement patterns, voice synthesis, and behavioral mimicry.

Such attacks can be used for fraud, social manipulation, harassment, or unauthorized access to restricted virtual spaces. In professional contexts, such as remote training or virtual meetings, impersonation may lead to severe consequences, including misinformation and sabotage.

3.1.1.2 Session Hijacking and Replay Attacks

Immersive systems often maintain persistent sessions that span long periods of time. If session tokens are compromised, attackers may gain prolonged access to virtual environments.

Replay attacks are particularly dangerous in immersive contexts. For example, an attacker might capture a sequence of valid gestures or commands and replay them later to perform unauthorized actions. Because these actions appear legitimate, they may bypass traditional anomaly detection systems.

3.1.2 Sensor and Environment-Level Attacks

Sensors form the foundation of spatial computing. Cameras, depth sensors, inertial measurement units, microphones, and eye trackers continuously feed data into the system. If these sensors are compromised, the entire perception pipeline becomes unreliable.

3.1.2.1 Sensor Spoofing

Sensor spoofing involves feeding false data into a system in order to manipulate its interpretation of the environment. For example, spoofed depth data may cause a system to misinterpret the location of physical obstacles, potentially leading users to collide with real-world objects.

In immersive training or medical applications, such distortions can be dangerous, as they may lead users to perform incorrect actions.

3.1.2.2 Environmental Mapping Attacks

Many spatial computing systems maintain persistent maps of the user's environment. These maps are used for anchoring virtual objects, enabling navigation, and maintaining spatial consistency.

If an attacker modifies these maps, they can subtly alter the environment. For instance, virtual objects may appear in incorrect positions, or navigation cues may become misleading. Such attacks can be used for deception, disorientation, or behavioral manipulation.

3.1.3 Content and Application-Level Threats

Immersive platforms frequently rely on third-party content, including 3D models, scripts, plugins, and interaction modules. These components are often downloaded from external repositories and integrated dynamically.

3.1.3.1 Malicious 3D Assets

Unlike traditional malware, malicious 3D assets may not contain executable code. Instead, they may exploit rendering engines, physics engines, or resource management systems to cause denial of service, memory corruption, or visual distortions.

These assets can also be used for visual deception, such as disguising malicious interfaces as legitimate ones.

3.1.3.2 Supply Chain Attacks

In immersive ecosystems, supply chain attacks can target asset marketplaces, plugin libraries, or development frameworks. Once a compromised component is integrated into a popular application, it can affect thousands of users simultaneously.

Because immersive applications are often updated frequently, users may unknowingly install malicious updates that compromise their privacy or safety.

3.1.4 Social and Behavioral Attacks

Immersive environments are inherently social. Users interact with each other in real time, often forming emotional connections. This social dimension introduces new categories of attacks.

3.1.4.1 Social Engineering in 3D Environments

Traditional social engineering relies on deception through text or voice. In immersive environments, attackers can use body language, facial expressions, and spatial cues to manipulate users.

For example, an attacker may position their avatar in a way that appears authoritative, or use proximity and gaze to influence user decisions. These tactics can be more persuasive than traditional phishing techniques.

3.1.4.2 Psychological and Emotional Manipulation

Immersive environments can evoke strong emotional responses. Attackers may exploit this by creating scenarios that induce fear, urgency, or trust.

Such manipulation can lead users to disclose sensitive information, perform unsafe actions, or bypass security controls.

3.1.5 Why These Threats Demand a Zero Trust Approach

The diversity and subtlety of threats in immersive environments make static, perimeter-based security models ineffective. Many of these attacks do not involve explicit policy violations. Instead, they exploit assumptions about trust, identity, and perception.

Zero Trust provides a conceptual framework for addressing these challenges by:

- Treating every entity as potentially malicious
- Enforcing continuous verification
- Using behavioral telemetry
- Restricting lateral movement
- Adapting policies dynamically

In the next section, these threats will be systematically mapped to Zero Trust principles, forming the basis for a specialized architecture for immersive systems.

3.2 MAPPING THREATS TO ZERO TRUST REQUIREMENTS IN IMMERSIVE SYSTEMS

The diverse threat vectors present in immersive and spatial computing environments require a security model that is adaptive, context-aware, and resilient to uncertainty. Traditional security frameworks focus primarily on protecting data, networks, and applications. However, immersive systems demand protection of additional dimensions, including perception, embodiment, spatial context, and social interaction. This expanded threat landscape necessitates a rethinking of how Zero Trust principles are applied.

Zero Trust Architecture provides a systematic approach for translating threats into enforceable security requirements (Bhambri et al., 2025). By assuming that no entity is inherently trustworthy, Zero Trust enables systems to detect, limit, and recover from compromises even when attackers appear to behave legitimately. In immersive environments, this assumption is particularly important because many attacks rely on deception rather than overt exploitation.

3.2.1 Identity-Centric Security Requirements

In immersive systems, identity is not merely a credential—it is a continuous, embodied representation of a user through their avatar, movement patterns, voice, and interaction style. This makes identity both richer and more vulnerable.

3.2.1.1 Continuous Authentication

Traditional authentication methods, such as passwords or one-time logins, are insufficient for immersive platforms. Sessions may last for hours, and users may transition between multiple virtual spaces without reauthentication.

Zero Trust mandates continuous authentication, where trust is constantly reassessed using behavioral and contextual signals. In immersive systems, these signals may include:

- Head and hand movement patterns
- Gaze behavior
- Interaction rhythms
- Spatial navigation styles

If these signals deviate significantly from expected patterns, the system can reduce privileges or require explicit re-verification.

3.2.1.2 Multi-Modal Identity Verification

Immersive platforms offer multiple biometric and behavioral modalities for identity verification. While this increases robustness, it also raises privacy concerns. Zero Trust requires that identity verification be:

- Privacy-preserving
- Minimally intrusive
- Revocable when possible
- Transparent to users

Instead of relying on a single biometric marker, systems should combine multiple weak signals to form a dynamic trust profile.

3.2.2 Device and Sensor Trust Requirements

In spatial computing, devices and sensors act as the system's eyes and ears. If they are compromised, the entire system becomes unreliable.

3.2.2.1 Device Attestation

Zero Trust requires explicit verification of device integrity before granting access. This includes:

- Secure boot verification
- Firmware integrity checks
- OS version validation
- Application sandboxing

For immersive devices, attestation must occur continuously, not just at startup.

3.2.2.2 Sensor Authenticity and Reliability

Sensors must be treated as untrusted until verified. This includes validating:

- Signal consistency
- Cross-sensor correlations
- Environmental plausibility

For example, depth sensor data should be consistent with camera images and inertial measurements. Sudden inconsistencies may indicate spoofing or tampering.

3.2.3 Spatial Context-Aware Authorization

Traditional access control systems operate on abstract resources such as files or APIs. Immersive systems require spatially grounded authorization.

3.2.3.1 Zone-Based Access Control

Virtual environments can be segmented into spatial zones, each with its own policies. For example:

- Public zones
- Restricted workspaces

- Safety-critical areas

Zero Trust enforces that entering a zone does not automatically grant privileges. Instead, privileges are granted based on dynamic trust evaluation.

3.2.3.2 Object-Level Authorization

In immersive environments, virtual objects may represent sensitive assets, such as control panels, patient data, or financial instruments. Zero Trust requires fine-grained authorization for every object interaction.

This prevents attackers from escalating privileges simply by moving closer to an object.

3.2.4 Data-Centric Protection Requirements

Immersive platforms generate large volumes of highly sensitive data. Zero Trust mandates that data itself be the focal point of security.

3.2.4.1 Purpose Limitation

Data should only be used for explicitly defined purposes. For example, gaze data collected for interaction optimization should not be reused for behavioral profiling without consent.

3.2.4.2 Dynamic Data Access Policies

Access to data should be continuously reevaluated. A user who is authorized to view spatial maps in one context may not be authorized in another.

3.2.5 Behavioral Monitoring and Anomaly Detection

Many immersive threats are subtle and behavioral rather than overtly technical.

3.2.5.1 Telemetry-Driven Security

Zero Trust systems rely on telemetry to detect deviations from normal behavior. In immersive systems, this includes:

- Unnatural movement patterns
- Impossible spatial transitions

- Uncharacteristic object interactions

3.2.5.2 Risk-Adaptive Response

Instead of binary allow/deny decisions, Zero Trust enables graduated responses. These may include:

- Reducing privileges
- Increasing monitoring
- Triggering additional authentication

3.2.6 Summary of Zero Trust Requirements for Immersive Systems

Based on the threat analysis, immersive systems require a Zero Trust model that:

1. Treats identity as continuous and behavioral
2. Verifies devices and sensors continuously
3. Enforces spatially grounded access control
4. Protects data as a primary asset
5. Uses telemetry for real-time trust evaluation
6. Balances security with usability and presence

These requirements form the foundation for the reference architecture presented in the next section.

4.1 DESIGNING ZERO TRUST FOR SPATIAL COMPUTING ENVIRONMENTS

Designing a Zero Trust Architecture (ZTA) for spatial computing environments requires a fundamental rethinking of how trust, identity, access control, and risk assessment are conceptualized (Bhambri, 2025b). Unlike traditional IT systems, immersive platforms are not purely transactional; they are experiential, embodied, and continuous. Users do not simply request resources—they inhabit environments, manipulate objects, and engage in social interactions. These characteristics necessitate a Zero Trust model that is not only technically robust but also perceptually seamless.

Conventional Zero Trust implementations focus on securing network resources, APIs, and data repositories. While these components remain relevant in immersive systems, they represent only part of the security problem. In spatial computing, security must also protect perceptual fidelity, bodily safety, emotional well-being, and social trust. A compromised system may not merely leak data—it may distort a user's understanding of reality.

Therefore, a Zero Trust architecture for immersive systems must be:

- Continuous rather than session-based
- Context-aware rather than static
- Spatially grounded rather than abstract
- Behavior-driven rather than credential-centric
- Usability-preserving rather than intrusive

This section introduces the conceptual foundations of such an architecture.

4.1.1 Trust as a Dynamic and Multi-Dimensional Construct

Traditional systems treat trust as a binary attribute: either an entity is trusted or it is not. In immersive systems, trust must be treated as a spectrum that changes continuously based on multiple factors.

4.1.1.1 Dimensions of Trust in Immersive Systems

Trust in spatial computing environments spans several dimensions:

- Identity trust: Is the user who they claim to be?
- Device trust: Is the device uncompromised and behaving as expected?
- Behavioral trust: Does the user's behavior match historical patterns?
- Contextual trust: Is the current environment safe and appropriate
- Social trust: Are other participants behaving legitimately?

These dimensions interact with each other. For example, a trusted identity using a compromised device should not be considered fully trustworthy.

Zero Trust systems must integrate all these dimensions into a unified risk model.

4.1.1.2 Continuous Trust Re-Evaluation

In immersive systems, context changes constantly. Users move through physical spaces, join new virtual rooms, interact with new participants, and manipulate different objects. Each of these actions changes the trust context.

A Zero Trust architecture must therefore:

- Re-evaluate trust at fine temporal granularity

- Update risk scores in real time
- Adjust privileges dynamically
- Avoid hard session boundaries

This continuous model aligns with the experiential nature of immersive platforms, where interruptions can break presence and usability.

4.1.2 Identity in Spatial Computing: Beyond Credentials

Identity in immersive environments is more complex than in traditional systems. It is not limited to usernames, passwords, or tokens. Instead, identity is embodied through avatars, voice, gestures, posture, and movement patterns.

4.1.2.1 Embodied Identity

Embodied identity refers to the way users express themselves through physical and behavioral cues. These cues are often unconscious and difficult to forge convincingly. Examples include:

- Micro-movements of the head and hands
- Gait patterns
- Gesture timing
- Gaze transitions

These signals provide valuable trust indicators but must be handled with extreme care due to privacy risks.

4.1.2.2 Privacy-Preserving Identity Verification

Zero Trust mandates continuous identity verification, but immersive systems must avoid intrusive re-authentication prompts that disrupt presence.

Privacy-preserving techniques may include:

- Local behavioral modeling
- On-device inference
- Differential privacy
- Federated learning

These approaches allow systems to verify identity without transmitting raw biometric data.

4.1.3 Device and Sensor Trust Architecture

In immersive platforms, devices and sensors form the foundation of perception. A Zero Trust model must explicitly verify that these components are functioning correctly.

4.1.3.1 Continuous Device Attestation

Rather than verifying devices only at login, Zero Trust requires continuous attestation. This includes:

- Secure boot verification
- Firmware integrity checks
- Runtime behavior monitoring
- Detection of unauthorized peripherals

This is particularly important for head-mounted displays and wearable sensors, which are vulnerable to physical tampering.

4.1.3.2 Cross-Sensor Validation

Spatial computing systems often use multiple sensors to perceive the same phenomenon. For example, depth, visual, and inertial sensors all provide information about movement.

Zero Trust can leverage this redundancy to detect spoofing and tampering. If one sensor deviates significantly from others, the system can flag the discrepancy.

4.1.4 Spatially Aware Policy Enforcement

Traditional Zero Trust models enforce policies at the network or application level. In immersive systems, policies must also be spatial.

4.1.4.1 Spatial Policy Zones

Virtual environments can be divided into zones with distinct security policies. For example:

- Public interaction zones
- Restricted workspaces
- High-risk simulation areas

- Privacy-sensitive zones

Entering a zone does not automatically grant trust. Instead, the system evaluates whether the user is authorized to interact with that space.

4.1.4.2 Proximity-Based Authorization

In immersive systems, physical proximity often implies intent. For example, standing near a virtual control panel may indicate a desire to interact with it.

Zero Trust must treat proximity as a contextual signal rather than an implicit permission. A user may be allowed to see an object but not manipulate it.

4.1.5 Non-Disruptive Security and Presence Preservation

One of the most important design constraints in immersive systems is presence. Security mechanisms that interrupt, distract, or overload users can significantly degrade the experience.

Zero Trust implementations must therefore be:

- Mostly implicit
- Gradual rather than binary
- Adaptive to user state
- Invisible whenever possible

For example, instead of abruptly terminating a session, the system may reduce privileges, isolate the user, or increase monitoring.

4.1.6 Design Goals for a Zero Trust Spatial Architecture

Based on these considerations, a Zero Trust architecture for immersive systems should aim to

- Protect perceptual integrity
- Preserve presence and usability
- Minimize privacy exposure
- Enable real-time adaptation
- Support multi-user governance
- Limit the blast radius of compromise

These goals form the basis for the reference architecture described in the next section.

4.2 ZERO TRUST REFERENCE ARCHITECTURE FOR IMMERSIVE SYSTEMS

A Zero Trust Reference Architecture for immersive and spatial computing systems must account for the unique properties of these environments, including continuous interaction, real-time feedback, multi-modal sensing, and persistent shared spaces. Unlike traditional Zero Trust deployments that focus primarily on securing networks and enterprise applications, immersive systems require security mechanisms to be deeply integrated into the perceptual and interaction layers of the platform.

This reference architecture conceptualizes security as a continuous control loop rather than a sequence of discrete checks. Trust is not established once and assumed thereafter; instead, it is dynamically inferred, evaluated, and adjusted throughout the user's experience.

4.2.1 Core Architectural Layers

The proposed architecture consists of multiple logical layers, each responsible for a different aspect of trust enforcement.

4.2.1.1 Identity and Persona Layer

This layer manages the relationship between users and their digital representations. Unlike traditional identity systems that rely on static credentials, immersive identity systems must account for:

- Behavioral biometrics
- Interaction styles
- Voice and movement patterns
- Avatar customization and metadata

This layer continuously generates trust signals that are forwarded to the policy engine.

4.2.1.2 Device and Sensor Trust Layer

This layer evaluates the integrity and reliability of hardware and sensor inputs. It includes:

- Secure boot verification
- Firmware validation
- Runtime integrity checks
- Cross-sensor consistency analysis

For example, if a headset reports movement patterns that contradict inertial sensor readings, the system may downgrade its trust level.

4.2.1.3 Interaction and Context Layer

This layer interprets the meaning of user actions within spatial contexts. It answers questions such as:

- Is the user interacting with a sensitive object?
- Are they in a restricted zone?
- Are their actions consistent with legitimate goals?

Contextual understanding is critical for preventing subtle misuse that does not violate explicit rules.

4.2.1.4 Policy and Decision Layer

This layer contains the Zero Trust Policy Engine and Policy Administrator. It integrates signals from all other layers and computes access decisions.

Decisions may include:

- Allow
- Restrict
- Degrade privileges
- Request explicit re-verification
- Isolate or sandbox

4.2.1.5 Enforcement and Response Layer

This layer enforces policy decisions in real time. In immersive systems, enforcement may take many forms, such as:

- Limiting object manipulation
- Restricting movement
- Blurring sensitive content
- Introducing friction into interactions

The goal is not only to block malicious behavior but also to preserve user safety and experience.

4.2.2 Trust Signal Flow and Continuous Evaluation

Zero Trust in immersive systems operates as a feedback-driven loop rather than a linear process.

4.2.2.1 Trust Signal Sources

Trust signals may originate from:

- Biometric sensors
- Interaction logs
- Device telemetry
- Environmental mapping
- Social interactions

These signals are aggregated and normalized before being fed into the policy engine.

4.2.2.2 Dynamic Risk Scoring

The policy engine maintains a dynamic risk score for each entity. This score is updated in real time based on new evidence.

For example:

- Sudden erratic movements → increased risk
- Known device integrity → reduced risk
- Entry into restricted zones → contextual risk increase

This allows the system to respond gradually rather than abruptly.

4.2.3 Spatially Grounded Policy Enforcement

Traditional Zero Trust models enforce policies at the level of APIs or network packets. In immersive systems, enforcement must also be spatial.

4.2.3.1 Zone-Based Enforcement

Virtual environments can be partitioned into zones with different security levels. For instance:

- Public collaboration zones
- Restricted operational zones
- Safety-critical zones

Each zone has its own trust thresholds and response strategies.

4.2.3.2 Object-Centric Policies

Objects in immersive environments may represent:

- Machinery
- Medical instruments
- Financial interfaces
- Sensitive documents

Zero Trust requires that each object maintain its own access policy.

4.2.4 Privacy-Aware Trust Management

Continuous monitoring raises serious privacy concerns. A Zero Trust architecture for immersive systems must incorporate privacy by design.

4.2.4.1 Local Processing of Sensitive Signals

Where possible, sensitive trust signals should be processed locally on the device rather than being transmitted to the cloud.

4.2.4.2 Data Minimization

Only the minimum necessary information should be collected and stored. For example, behavioral anomaly scores may be transmitted instead of raw biometric data.

4.2.5 Resilience and Fail-Safe Design

Immersive systems must remain safe even under partial compromise.

4.2.5.1 Graceful Degradation

Rather than shutting down, the system should gradually reduce capabilities as trust decreases.

4.2.5.2 Blast Radius Containment

Micro-segmentation and object-level access control ensure that compromise in one area does not cascade across the environment.

4.2.6 Summary of the Reference Architecture

This Zero Trust reference architecture for immersive systems

- Treats trust as continuous
- Integrates spatial and behavioral context
- Enforces object-level policies
- Preserves user presence
- Minimizes privacy exposure
- Enables adaptive response

This architecture provides the foundation for concrete mechanisms, which will be discussed in the next section.

4.3 KEY ZERO TRUST MECHANISMS FOR IMMERSIVE SYSTEMS

The successful implementation of a Zero Trust Architecture in immersive and spatial computing environments requires a set of specialized mechanisms that operationalize the principles discussed in previous sections. These mechanisms must function continuously, adapt to changing contexts, and remain largely invisible to users in order to preserve presence and usability. Unlike conventional systems, where security interactions are mostly explicit, immersive systems demand implicit and non-disruptive enforcement strategies. This section outlines the core Zero Trust mechanisms that enable secure, scalable, and user-centered immersive platforms.

4.3.1 Continuous and Implicit Authentication

Traditional authentication methods rely on explicit user actions, such as entering passwords or performing multi-factor challenges. While effective in desktop environments, such methods are disruptive and impractical in immersive systems, where interruptions can break presence and disorient users.

4.3.1.1 Behavioral Authentication

Behavioral authentication leverages the fact that users exhibit unique and consistent interaction patterns. In immersive systems, these patterns may include:

- Head movement dynamics
- Hand gesture timing
- Gait and posture
- Navigation trajectories
- Gaze transitions

These signals can be used to continuously verify identity without requiring explicit user input. If the system detects deviations from expected behavior, it can gradually reduce privileges or request additional verification.

4.3.1.2 Context-Aware Re-Verification

Zero Trust does not eliminate explicit authentication; rather, it makes it conditional. Explicit re-verification may be triggered when:

- A user enters a high-risk zone
- A sensitive object is accessed
- Device posture changes
- Anomalous behavior is detected

This adaptive approach balances security with user experience.

4.3.2 Fine-Grained Authorization and Least Privilege

Authorization in immersive systems must be far more granular than in traditional environments. Instead of granting access to entire applications or spaces, permissions should be tied to specific actions, objects, and contexts.

4.3.2.1 Action-Level Permissions

Users may be allowed to view an object but not manipulate it, or manipulate it but not share it. For example, a trainee may observe a virtual control panel but not activate it.

This level of granularity prevents attackers from escalating privileges through proximity or mimicry.

4.3.2.2 Temporal and Contextual Constraints

Permissions should be time-bound and context-dependent. A user may be authorized to perform a task only during a specific time window, within a specific spatial zone, or under specific supervision.

Such constraints limit the damage caused by stolen credentials or hijacked sessions.

4.3.3 Micro-Segmentation of Virtual Spaces

Micro-segmentation is a fundamental Zero Trust strategy that limits lateral movement. In immersive systems, segmentation must be applied not only to networks but also to virtual environments.

4.3.3.1 Spatial Micro-Segmentation

Virtual worlds can be divided into micro-zones, each with its own policies. For instance:

- Public social areas
- Semi-private collaboration rooms
- Highly restricted operational zones

Crossing from one zone to another triggers a new trust evaluation.

4.3.3.2 Service-Level Segmentation

Backend services supporting immersive environments—such as rendering engines, asset servers, and collaboration services—should be isolated from each other. A compromise in one service should not automatically grant access to others.

4.3.4 Secure Session Management

Immersive sessions are often long-lived and persistent. This increases the risk of session hijacking, replay attacks, and unauthorized continuation.

4.3.4.1 Ephemeral Credentials

Zero Trust systems favor short-lived, automatically rotated credentials. In immersive systems, session tokens should be:

- Bound to device posture
- Linked to behavioral profiles
- Rotated frequently

This reduces the usefulness of stolen tokens.

4.3.4.2 Context Binding

Session validity should depend on context. A session that is valid in one location or device state may become invalid when conditions change.

4.3.5 Telemetry-Driven Anomaly Detection

Many attacks in immersive environments are subtle and behavioral. Traditional signature-based detection is often insufficient.

4.3.5.1 Multi-Modal Telemetry Fusion

Telemetry from multiple sources—such as sensors, interaction logs, and device metrics—should be combined to form a holistic trust assessment.

This reduces false positives and improves detection accuracy.

4.3.5.2 Adaptive Response Strategies

Rather than immediately terminating sessions, Zero Trust enables graded responses, such as:

- To increase monitoring
- Reducing privileges
- Introducing friction into interactions
- Isolating suspicious users

This preserves usability while mitigating risk.

4.3.6 Privacy-Preserving Trust Enforcement

Continuous monitoring raises legitimate privacy concerns. Zero Trust implementations must be designed with privacy as a first-class requirement.

4.3.6.1 Localized Trust Computation

Where possible, trust computations should occur locally on the user's device. Only abstract risk scores or alerts should be transmitted.

4.3.6.2 Explainability and User Control

Users should be informed about what data is being collected and how it is used. Transparency builds trust and encourages adoption.

4.3.7 Summary of Key Mechanisms

A Zero Trust immersive system must incorporate:

- Continuous behavioral authentication
- Action-level authorization
- Spatial micro-segmentation
- Context-bound sessions
- Telemetry-driven adaptation
- Privacy-aware monitoring

These mechanisms operationalize the reference architecture presented earlier.

5.1 APPLICATION SCENARIOS AND USE CASES

To demonstrate the practical relevance of a Zero Trust Architecture for immersive and spatial computing systems, it is essential to examine how the proposed principles and mechanisms operate in real-world contexts. Immersive technologies are increasingly being deployed in domains that involve sensitive data, safety-critical operations, and complex multi-user interactions. In such environments, security is not merely a technical concern but a foundational requirement for trust, adoption, and sustainability.

This section presents representative use cases that highlight how Zero Trust principles can be instantiated in different immersive scenarios. Each use case illustrates how threats, trust signals, and policy enforcement mechanisms interact dynamically.

5.1.1 Healthcare and Medical Training Environments

Healthcare is one of the most promising application domains for immersive systems. XR technologies are increasingly used for surgical training, patient education, rehabilitation, and remote consultation. These applications rely heavily on accurate spatial representation, real-time interaction, and access to highly sensitive personal data.

5.1.1.1 Security and Privacy Requirements

Medical immersive systems must comply with strict regulatory and ethical standards. Key requirements include:

- Protection of patient data
- Assurance of data integrity
- Prevention of unauthorized access
- Real-time reliability
- Preservation of patient dignity and privacy

A compromised immersive medical system could lead to incorrect diagnoses, improper training, or breaches of confidentiality.

5.1.1.2 Zero Trust Implementation in Healthcare XR

In a Zero Trust-enabled healthcare XR system:

- Users (doctors, trainees, patients) are continuously authenticated using behavioral and contextual signals.
- Access to medical records and virtual instruments is granted based on role, task, and risk posture.
- Devices are continuously attested to ensure they have not been tampered with.
- Sensitive visual content may be dynamically blurred or restricted when risk increases.

For example, a trainee may be allowed to observe a virtual surgery but not manipulate tools unless explicitly authorized.

5.1.2 Industrial Training and Remote Maintenance

Industries such as manufacturing, energy, and aerospace increasingly use immersive systems for training, diagnostics, and remote maintenance. Workers can visualize complex machinery, receive guided instructions, and collaborate with experts in real time.

5.1.2.1 Threats in Industrial XR Systems

Industrial XR systems are attractive targets for attackers due to their potential economic and safety impact. Threats include:

- Manipulation of virtual instructions
- Tampering with digital twins
- Impersonation of experts
- Unauthorized control of machinery

Even subtle distortions in spatial cues can cause physical accidents.

5.1.2.2 Zero Trust Enforcement in Industrial Contexts

In a Zero Trust-based immersive industrial platform:

- Each user's identity is continuously verified using movement and interaction patterns.
- Devices are attested before being allowed to interact with digital twins.
- Virtual zones are micro-segmented based on risk levels.
- Object-level authorization prevents unauthorized tool use.

For example, a maintenance worker may be permitted to inspect a machine but not alter its configuration unless their trust score remains above a defined threshold.

5.1.3 Smart Cities and Urban Planning

Spatial computing is increasingly used in smart city planning, disaster response simulations, and infrastructure management. Immersive environments allow stakeholders to visualize urban layouts, test scenarios, and coordinate responses.

5.1.3.1 Complex Trust Relationships

Smart city XR systems involve multiple stakeholders, including government agencies, private contractors, emergency services, and citizens. These actors have different trust levels and access rights.

A Zero Trust approach ensures that:

- Each stakeholder's permissions are strictly scoped
- Data sharing is purpose-limited
- Cross-agency access is dynamically evaluated

5.1.3.2 Dynamic Risk Evaluation

During a crisis simulation, the risk posture of a user may change rapidly. Zero Trust systems can dynamically adjust privileges, restrict data access, or isolate compromised nodes.

5.1.4 Education and Collaborative Learning

Immersive learning environments are increasingly used in education, enabling students to explore historical sites, scientific simulations, and collaborative projects.

5.1.4.1 Social and Behavioral Risks

Educational XR systems face risks such as:

- Identity impersonation
- Harassment
- Unauthorized content manipulation
- Data misuse

These threats can disrupt learning and undermine trust.

5.1.4.2 Zero Trust for Safe Learning Spaces

A Zero Trust approach ensures

- Continuous identity verification
- Spatial moderation policies
- Behavior-based access control
- Safe zone enforcement

This creates inclusive and secure learning environments.

5.1.5 Social Virtual Worlds and Metaverse Platforms

Social VR platforms enable users to interact, trade digital assets, attend events, and form communities. These environments often lack centralized governance, making them particularly vulnerable to abuse.

5.1.5.1 Unique Challenges of Social XR

Threats include:

- Deepfake avatars
- Impersonation
- Economic fraud
- Psychological manipulation

5.1.5.2 Zero Trust as a Governance Framework

In social immersive platforms, Zero Trust can function as both a security and governance mechanism by:

- Limiting privilege escalation
- Enforcing community policies
- Detecting anomalous behavior
- Protecting vulnerable users

5.1.6 Cross-Case Analysis

Across all these scenarios, several recurring themes emerge:

- Trust is contextual, not static
- Identity is embodied and behavioral
- Data sensitivity is extremely high
- Attacks are often subtle
- User experience must be preserved

Zero Trust provides a unifying framework that can address these requirements across domains.

5.1.7 End-to-End Implementation Example: Industrial Maintenance Scenario

To illustrate how Zero Trust policies, trust signals, and enforcement steps operate concretely, consider an industrial maintenance technician, Alex, using an immersive XR headset to repair a high-voltage turbine remotely.

Scenario Context:

- Alex is authenticated via password at session start.
- The turbine digital twin is classified as safety-critical (zone: high-risk).
- Manipulation of turbine control parameters requires explicit authorization and behavioral consistency.

Trust Signals Continuously Collected:

- Head movement trajectory (smooth vs. erratic)
- Hand gesture timing and precision
- Gaze dwell time on sensitive widgets
- Device posture (firmware integrity, network latency)
- Proximity to virtual emergency stop button

Table 1. Zero Trust Policy Table (Simplified)

Condition	Policy Decision	Enforcement Action
Behavioral score > 0.85 AND device attested	Allow manipulation of non-critical objects	Full interaction
Behavioral score 0.6–0.85	Restrict to view-only	Disable gesture input, show subtle boundary highlight
Behavioral score < 0.6 OR device tamper detected	Deny access, isolate zone	Teleport to neutral virtual room, request re-authentication
Gaze lingers on emergency stop > 3 sec without action	Low-risk anomaly	Log only, no interruption
Sudden head movement + proximity to sensitive control	Medium-risk anomaly	Reduce privileges, increase telemetry sampling

End-to-End Enforcement Flow

- Monitor: Headset sensors stream movement data to local edge policy enforcement point (PEP).
- Evaluate: Policy engine (PE) computes behavioral trust score (e.g., 0.92). Device attestation passes.
- Decide: Allow manipulation.
- Act: PEP enables gesture control for turbine diagnostics panel.
- Re-evaluate: Alex's hand tremor pattern suddenly changes (possible fatigue or spoofing). Score drops to 0.67.
- Adapt: System restricts to view-only, overlays subtle blue boundary, sends soft alert to supervisor.
- Remediate: After 30 seconds of stable behavior, score recovers to 0.88; privileges restored without user interruption.

This example demonstrates how Zero Trust in immersive systems moves beyond binary allow/deny to continuous, context-aware, presence-preserving security.

5.2 COMPARATIVE ANALYSIS: TRADITIONAL SECURITY MODELS vs. ZERO TRUST in IMMERSIVE SYSTEMS

To fully appreciate the necessity of Zero Trust Architecture in immersive and spatial computing environments, it is important to compare it with traditional security models. Conventional approaches were designed for static, well-defined systems with predictable interaction patterns. Immersive systems, by contrast, are dynamic, sensor-driven, and socially interactive, requiring a fundamentally different security posture.

This section presents a conceptual and functional comparison between traditional security models and Zero Trust approaches in the context of immersive systems.

5.2.1 Trust Assumptions

5.2.1.1 Traditional Security Models

Traditional models operate under the assumption that once an entity has been authenticated and admitted into a system, it can be trusted. This trust is typically maintained for the entire session unless explicit policy violations occur. These models emphasize perimeter protection, where firewalls, intrusion detection systems, and virtual private networks serve as the primary defense mechanisms.

In immersive environments, this assumption becomes problematic. Users frequently move between virtual spaces, interact with unknown participants, and access heterogeneous services. A one-time trust decision is insufficient to capture these evolving contexts.

5.2.1.2 Zero Trust Model

Zero Trust eliminates implicit trust entirely. Every action is evaluated in real time, using contextual and behavioral signals. Trust is not binary but probabilistic and adaptive.

In immersive systems, this approach allows the platform to continuously reassess whether a user should be allowed to manipulate a virtual object, access sensitive spatial data, or interact with specific participants.

5.2.2 Access Control Granularity

5.2.2.1 Traditional Approaches

Conventional systems often use coarse-grained access control mechanisms. Users are assigned roles, and roles are associated with broad privileges. Once a role is assigned, it remains relatively static.

This model is poorly suited for immersive environments, where permissions should depend on spatial location, interaction intent, and real-time risk.

5.2.2.2 Zero Trust-Based Authorization

Zero Trust emphasizes fine-grained, context-aware authorization. Permissions can be scoped to:

- Specific actions
- Individual objects
- Spatial zones
- Time windows

This granularity enables precise control over what users can do, when, and where.

5.2.3 Attack Containment and Lateral Movement

5.2.3.1 Traditional Security Models

In traditional systems, once an attacker gains access to the internal network, they can often move laterally with minimal resistance. This is especially dangerous in immersive systems, where lateral movement could grant access to rendering engines, sensor data, or digital twin models.

5.2.3.2 Zero Trust Architecture

Zero Trust prevents lateral movement by micro-segmenting resources and enforcing identity-based access for every interaction. Even if one component is compromised, the attacker cannot automatically access others.

In immersive environments, this means that a compromised avatar cannot automatically manipulate all objects or enter all spaces.

5.2.4 Responsiveness to Behavioral Anomalies

5.2.4.1 Traditional Detection Mechanisms

Traditional systems rely heavily on signature-based detection and predefined rule sets. These methods are effective against known threats but struggle to detect subtle or novel attacks.

In immersive environments, many attacks are behavioral and perceptual, making them difficult to detect using conventional techniques.

5.2.4.2 Telemetry-Driven Zero Trust Systems

Zero Trust systems use continuous telemetry and behavioral modeling to detect anomalies. Rather than relying on known signatures, they look for deviations from expected patterns.

This approach is particularly effective in immersive systems, where normal behavior can be modeled in high dimensional detail.

5.2.5 User Experience and Presence Preservation

5.2.5.1 Traditional Security Trade-offs

Traditional security mechanisms often rely on explicit challenges such as CAPTCHAs, re-logins, and pop-up alerts. In immersive systems, such interruptions can be disorienting and harmful.

5.2.5.2 Zero Trust Design Philosophy

Zero Trust prioritizes implicit and gradual responses. Instead of abrupt denials, the system can:

- Reduce privileges
- Increase monitoring
- Isolate sensitive content

This preserves presence while mitigating risk.

Table 2. Summary Comparison Table

Dimension	Traditional Security	Zero Trust in Immersive Systems
Trust model	Static	Continuous
Authentication	Session-based	Continuous
Authorization	Role-based	Context-aware
Response style	Binary	Graduated
Attack containment	Weak	Strong
Usability	Often disruptive	Presence-preserving

5.2.6 Implications for Immersive System Design

The comparative analysis highlights that traditional security models are fundamentally mismatched with the properties of immersive systems. Zero Trust is not merely an improvement but a necessity.

In immersive environments, security must be:

- Adaptive
- Behavioral
- Contextual
- Spatially grounded
- Privacy-aware

These characteristics cannot be achieved through static, perimeter-based approaches.

6.1 IMPLEMENTATION ROADMAP FOR ZERO TRUST IN IMMERSIVE SYSTEMS

Implementing Zero Trust Architecture in immersive and spatial computing environments requires a structured, phased, and iterative approach. Unlike conventional IT systems, immersive platforms involve complex interactions between hardware, software, users, and environments. A rushed or monolithic deployment can disrupt user experience, degrade system performance, and introduce unintended vulnerabilities. Therefore, a gradual, maturity-based implementation strategy is essential.

This section presents a practical roadmap for adopting Zero Trust in immersive systems, emphasizing technical feasibility, user experience preservation, and long-term sustainability.

6.1.1 Phased Deployment Strategy

A phased deployment allows organizations to progressively integrate Zero Trust mechanisms while minimizing operational disruption.

6.1.1.1 Phase 1: Visibility and Asset Discovery

Before enforcing Zero Trust, the system must have full visibility into its components. This includes:

- Identifying all users, avatars, and personas
- Enumerating devices, sensors, and edge nodes
- Mapping services, APIs, and data flows
- Classifying spatial zones and virtual assets

In immersive systems, asset discovery also includes mapping virtual objects, interaction pathways, and user movement patterns. Without this visibility, policy enforcement becomes arbitrary and ineffective.

6.1.1.2 Phase 2: Identity-Centric Access Control

Once assets are identified, the next step is to make identity the core of access decisions.

This involves:

- Federated identity integration
- Continuous authentication mechanisms
- Avatar–user binding
- Device-identity association

At this stage, coarse-grained Zero Trust policies can be introduced, such as restricting access to entire virtual zones or services based on identity attributes.

6.1.1.3 Phase 3: Contextual and Behavioral Trust Integration

After establishing identity-centric control, contextual and behavioral signals should be incorporated.

These include:

- Movement patterns
- Interaction rhythms
- Gaze behavior
- Environmental context

This phase enables the system to detect subtle anomalies that static identity checks cannot capture.

6.1.1.4 Phase 4: Spatially Grounded Policy Enforcement

In this phase, policies become spatially explicit. Permissions are tied to zones, objects, and proximity.

For example:

- Access to control panels depends on spatial location
- Data visibility varies by zone
- Certain actions require physical or virtual supervision

This transforms Zero Trust from a backend mechanism into a spatially meaningful security model.

6.1.1.5 Phase 5: Automation and Self-Healing

The final phase involves automating trust evaluation and response.

This includes:

- Machine learning-based anomaly detection
- Automated policy updates
- Real-time privilege adjustment
- Self-healing trust mechanisms

This phase is critical for large-scale immersive systems with thousands or millions of concurrent users.

6.1.2 Zero Trust Maturity Levels for Immersive Systems

A maturity model provides a structured way to evaluate progress.

6.1.2.1 Level 1: Static Trust

- Session-based authentication
- Fixed roles
- Minimal monitoring

This level resembles traditional security models.

6.1.2.2 Level 2: Identity-Centric Trust

- **Continuous identity verification**
- **Device binding**
- **Basic segmentation**

This level marks the beginning of Zero Trust adoption.

6.1.2.3 Level 3: Context-Aware Trust

- Behavioral modeling
- Risk-adaptive policies
- Zone-based access control

This is where immersive-specific security begins to emerge.

6.1.2.4 Level 4: Fully Adaptive Trust

- Real-time trust scoring
- Automated enforcement
- Self-healing mechanisms
- Cross-world trust federation

This level represents the ideal Zero Trust state for immersive systems.

6.1.3 Technical Stack Mapping

Implementing Zero Trust in immersive systems requires mapping conceptual components to real technologies.

6.1.3.1 Identity and Access Management

- Federated identity providers
- Decentralized identifiers
- Token-based authentication
- Behavioral biometrics

6.1.3.2 Device and Sensor Attestation

- Secure boot

- Trusted execution environments
- Hardware root of trust
- Remote attestation protocols

6.1.3.3 Policy Engines and Enforcement

- Attribute-based access control (ABAC)
- Policy decision points (PDPs)
- Policy enforcement points (PEPs)
- Spatial policy interpreters

6.1.3.4 Telemetry and Analytics

- Multi-modal sensor fusion
- Real-time analytics
- Edge inference
- Anomaly detection pipelines

6.1.4 Key Performance Indicators (KPIs)

Security must be measurable.
Important KPIs for immersive Zero Trust systems include:

- Mean time to anomaly detection
- False positive rate
- User interruption frequency
- Latency impact
- Privacy exposure index
- Lateral movement containment

6.1.5 Human-Centered Deployment Considerations

Unlike traditional IT systems, immersive platforms are deeply experiential. Therefore, deployment must consider:

- Cognitive load
- Motion sickness triggers
- Attention shifts
- Accessibility

Security must not degrade the immersive experience.

6.2 EVALUATION METRICS AND PERFORMANCE CONSIDERATIONS

The effectiveness of a Zero Trust Architecture (ZTA) in immersive and spatial computing environments must be evaluated not only in terms of security strength but also with respect to system performance, usability, scalability, and perceptual integrity. Unlike traditional systems, where performance degradation may be tolerated to some extent, immersive systems are highly sensitive to latency, jitter, and visual or interaction disruptions. Even small delays or inconsistencies can break presence, induce discomfort, or cause motion sickness.

Therefore, evaluation frameworks for immersive Zero Trust systems must adopt a multi-dimensional perspective that balances security objectives with experiential quality.

6.2.1 Security Effectiveness Metrics

Security effectiveness refers to how well the Zero Trust system prevents, detects, and mitigates threats.

6.2.1.1 Mean Time to Detection (MTTD)

MTTD measures the average time required to detect anomalous or malicious behavior. In immersive systems, this metric is particularly important because attacks may affect user perception and physical safety.

Lower MTTD values indicate more responsive trust evaluation mechanisms.

6.2.1.2 Mean Time to Response (MTTR)

MTTR measures the time taken by the system to respond after detecting a threat. Responses may include privilege reduction, spatial isolation, or session termination.

For immersive systems, responses should be gradual and non-disruptive whenever possible.

6.2.1.3 False Positive and False Negative Rates

- False positives occur when legitimate behavior is flagged as malicious.
- False negatives occur when malicious behavior is not detected.

Both are harmful. False positives degrade user experience, while false negatives expose the system to compromise.

A Zero Trust system must minimize both through accurate behavioral modeling.

6.2.2 Performance and Latency Constraints

Immersive platforms are real-time systems. Any security mechanism that introduces noticeable delays can degrade the experience.

6.2.2.1 End-to-End Latency

Latency refers to the time between user action and system response. For immersive environments, acceptable latency thresholds are often below 20 milliseconds.

Zero Trust mechanisms must be optimized to operate within these constraints.

6.2.2.2 Computational Overhead

Continuous authentication, telemetry analysis, and policy enforcement require significant computational resources.

Performance evaluation should measure:

- CPU usage
- Memory consumption
- Energy usage (especially for wearable devices)

6.2.2.3 Edge vs. Cloud Processing Trade-offs

To minimize latency, many trust evaluations should be performed at the edge rather than in centralized cloud servers.

Metrics should compare:

- Edge inference accuracy
- Network bandwidth consumption
- Cloud dependency levels

6.2.3 Scalability Metrics

Immersive platforms may support thousands or millions of concurrent users.

6.2.3.1 Concurrent Session Capacity

This metric measures how many simultaneous users the system can support without performance degradation.

6.2.3.2 Policy Evaluation Throughput

This measures how many trust decisions per second the system can process.
High throughput is essential for large-scale social VR platforms.

6.2.3.3 Horizontal and Vertical Scaling

Evaluation should consider:

- How easily the system scales with additional hardware
- Whether performance increases linearly with added resources

6.2.4 Usability and Presence Preservation Metrics

Security must not break immersion.

6.2.4.1 Presence Disruption Index (PDI)

This metric quantifies how often and how severely security interventions disrupt user experience.

6.2.4.2 Cognitive Load

Continuous re-authentication and alerts increase cognitive load.
Metrics may include:

- Task completion time
- Error rates
- Subjective workload measures

6.2.4.3 Motion Sickness and Discomfort Rates

Security-induced visual or interaction disruptions can cause nausea or disorientation.

These physiological metrics must be monitored.

6.2.5 Privacy Impact Metrics

Zero Trust systems rely on extensive telemetry. This raises serious privacy concerns.

6.2.5.1 Data Minimization Index

Measures how much raw personal data is stored versus abstracted or discarded.

6.2.5.2 On-Device Processing Ratio

Higher on-device processing reduces privacy risks.

6.2.5.3 Consent and Transparency Score

Measures how clearly users understand and control data usage.

6.2.6 Pilot Testing Framework

Before full deployment, organizations should conduct controlled pilot tests with the following structure:

Table 3. Pilot Testing Framework

Pilot Phase	Duration	Participants	Success Criterion
Lab simulation	1 week	5 internal testers	No false positives > 5%
Controlled field test	2 weeks	20 users (2 teams)	Latency increase < 15 ms
Live shadow mode	1 month	50 users	Zero security incidents, interruption rate < 1 per user-hour

Measurable Outputs from Pilot

- False positive rate (target < 3%)
- Mean time to anomaly detection (target < 500 ms)
- User interruption frequency (target < 0.5 per hour)
- Presence disruption index (pre-post survey, target < 10% degradation)

6.2.7 Validation Checklist for Practitioners

- Behavioral baseline collected for at least 3 interaction types (gaze, gesture, locomotion)
- Device attestation mechanism tested against firmware rollback attack
- Policy engine latency measured under peak load (100+ concurrent sessions)
- Privacy impact assessment completed for telemetry data
- User acceptance test with target group (minimum N=15)
- Fail-safe behavior verified (e.g., policy engine unreachable → default deny with graceful degradation)

6.2.8 Trade-Off Analysis

Table 4. Zero Trust systems inevitably involve trade-offs

Dimension	Low Security	High Security
Latency	Low	Potentially high
Usability	High	May decrease
Privacy	Low	Must be preserved
Detection Accuracy	Low	High
Scalability	High	Requires optimization

The goal is not to maximize any single metric but to achieve balanced optimization.

6.2.9 Evaluation Methodologies

Evaluation should combine:

- Controlled experiments
- Simulation-based testing
- User studies
- Adversarial testing
- Longitudinal field deployments

6.3 PRACTITIONER'S CHECKLIST FOR DEPLOYING ZERO TRUST IN IMMERSIVE SYSTEMS

For CTOs, security architects, and XR platform managers, the following checklist summarizes key actions derived from this chapter:

Phase 1: Preparation

- Inventory all immersive devices, sensors, and virtual assets.
- Classify spatial zones (public, restricted, safety-critical).
- Define behavioral trust signals (minimum: gaze + gesture + locomotion).

Phase 2: Implementation

- Deploy device attestation (secure boot + runtime integrity).
- Implement continuous authentication using behavioral biometrics (local processing).
- Configure policy engine with graduated responses (no abrupt session termination).

Phase 3: Validation

- Run pilot test (see Section 6.2.6) with measurable KPIs.
- Measure latency impact (should be < 20 ms round-trip).
- Conduct adversarial testing (spoofed sensor input, avatar impersonation).

Phase 4: Governance

- Publish privacy notice explaining what telemetry is collected.
- Establish user consent mechanism for behavioral monitoring.
- Plan regular policy reviews (quarterly).

7.1 OPEN RESEARCH CHALLENGES IN ZERO TRUST FOR IMMERSIVE AND SPATIAL COMPUTING SYSTEMS

Despite the growing relevance of Zero Trust Architecture (ZTA) for immersive and spatial computing environments, its adaptation to these systems remains an open research problem. Immersive platforms differ fundamentally from traditional computing systems because they operate continuously, rely on embodied interaction, and shape human perception rather than merely processing information. As a result, the nature of trust in these environments is fluid, multi-dimensional, and deeply contextual. One of the most pressing challenges is the absence of standardized trust signals for immersive systems. While traditional Zero Trust frameworks rely on well-defined indicators such as login patterns, device posture, or network reputation, immersive systems generate novel signals such as gaze behavior, hand trajectories, body posture, and locomotion dynamics. These signals are rich but poorly formalized, making it difficult to interpret them consistently across platforms and contexts. Without standardization, interoperability between immersive Zero Trust systems remains limited.

Another major challenge lies in the tension between continuous authentication and user privacy. Zero Trust relies on persistent verification, but immersive systems enable unprecedented levels of behavioral monitoring. Gaze patterns, motion rhythms, and micro-gestures can uniquely identify individuals while simultaneously revealing sensitive psychological, emotional, or medical information. Designing trust models that preserve privacy while remaining accurate and responsive is an unresolved problem. Furthermore, many current approaches rely on opaque machine learning models, which makes trust decisions difficult to explain to users. In immersive environments, unexplained access restrictions or sudden privilege reductions can cause confusion, anxiety, and loss of presence, emphasizing the need for explainable and human-centered trust mechanisms.

A further challenge arises from the heavy reliance of spatial computing systems on artificial intelligence for perception, including scene understanding, object recognition, and gesture tracking. These AI-driven pipelines themselves become part of the security perimeter, yet they are vulnerable to adversarial manipulation, misclassification, and hallucination. Zero Trust systems must therefore distinguish between sensor trust, model trust, and inference trust—an issue that remains largely unexplored. Moreover, immersive environments are inherently social spaces, where harm often occurs not through technical exploitation but through harassment, deception, and psychological manipulation. Traditional Zero Trust models do not explicitly account for social trust, community governance, or reputation-based risk, which are critical in virtual worlds.

Scalability and real-time performance present additional difficulties. Immersive systems require extremely low latency to preserve presence and prevent motion sickness, yet Zero Trust mechanisms introduce computational overhead through continuous evaluation and telemetry processing. Achieving a balance between responsiveness and security remains a core technical challenge. Finally, regulatory and ethical uncertainty complicates the deployment of Zero Trust in immersive systems. Existing data protection laws were not designed for spatial maps of private homes, gaze trajectories, or emotional inference. New legal frameworks and consent mechanisms are needed to ensure that Zero Trust does not become a form of pervasive surveillance. Together, these challenges highlight the need for fundamentally new theoretical, technical, and ethical approaches to trust in immersive computing

7.2 FUTURE RESEARCH DIRECTIONS FOR ZERO TRUST IN IMMERSIVE SYSTEMS

Future research on Zero Trust for immersive and spatial computing systems must move beyond incremental adaptations of enterprise security models and instead embrace the unique properties of embodied, perceptual, and socially interactive environments. One promising direction involves the development of standardized, platform-agnostic trust abstractions for spatial behavior. Rather than relying on raw sensor data, future systems may operate on semantic representations of intent, interaction styles, and spatial roles. This would allow trust models to generalize across devices and platforms while reducing privacy risks. Closely related to this is the need for privacy-preserving continuous authentication mechanisms that rely on on-device processing, federated learning, and differential privacy techniques, ensuring that sensitive behavioral data never leaves the user's control.

Another major research frontier is the integration of explainable artificial intelligence into Zero Trust pipelines. Immersive systems are psychologically immersive, and unexplained security interventions can disrupt presence and emotional stability. Future systems must be capable of communicating trust decisions through intuitive, non-disruptive visual metaphors rather than textual alerts. Research is also needed to address the trustworthiness of AI-based perception itself. Instead of assuming that computer vision and spatial inference are reliable, Zero Trust frameworks should explicitly model uncertainty, ambiguity, and hallucination risk, enabling systems to degrade gracefully when confidence drops.

Emerging technologies such as brain–computer interfaces, neural sensing, and affective computing will further complicate the trust landscape. These technologies introduce deeply personal signals that challenge existing notions of consent, ownership, and revocability. Zero Trust models must evolve to handle these dimensions ethically. Another important direction involves the governance of trust in decentralized immersive ecosystems. As metaverse platforms increasingly adopt blockchain-based identity, digital assets, and autonomous organizations, future Zero Trust systems will need to operate without centralized authorities. This raises questions about distributed policy enforcement, collective trust negotiation, and cross-world identity portability.

Finally, future research must address the fusion of physical safety and cybersecurity. In immersive systems, digital manipulation can cause real-world harm. Trust models must therefore incorporate biomechanical constraints, reaction-time models, and perceptual safety thresholds. This convergence of cyber, physical, and cognitive security represents a new research domain that extends beyond traditional cybersecurity. Together, these directions suggest that Zero Trust in immersive systems will evolve into a holistic trust ecology—one that integrates technology, psychology, ethics, and governance into a unified framework.

8.1 DISCUSSION AND SYNTHESIS

The preceding sections have demonstrated that immersive and spatial computing systems fundamentally challenge traditional assumptions about trust, identity, and security. Unlike conventional computing platforms, these systems are not merely transactional but experiential, embodied, and socially embedded. Security in such environments must therefore operate across multiple dimensions, including perception, cognition, physical movement, and social interaction. Zero Trust Architecture provides a strong conceptual foundation for addressing these challenges because it replaces static trust with continuous evaluation, context-aware policy enforcement, and fine-grained access control. However, the analysis in this chapter shows that simply transferring existing Zero Trust models from enterprise IT into immersive environments is insufficient. Instead, these models must be reinterpreted through the lens of spatial interaction, behavioral identity, and perceptual realism.

A key insight emerging from this synthesis is that trust in immersive systems is inherently dynamic and multi-layered. It is shaped not only by technical attributes such as device integrity or cryptographic identity but also by behavioral consistency, spatial context, and social norms. This requires Zero Trust systems to operate as adaptive feedback loops rather than rigid rule-based engines. Another critical observation is the need to balance security with presence. Immersion is fragile; excessive interruptions, visible security prompts, or abrupt session terminations can disrupt the user's sense of embodiment. Therefore, future Zero Trust systems must emphasize implicit, graded, and explainable enforcement strategies.

This chapter also highlights that immersive systems collapse the traditional separation between cyber and physical domains. A digital compromise can result in real-world harm, whether through distorted perception, misdirected movement, or manipulated decision-making. As such, Zero Trust in immersive systems must be extended into a cyber–physical–cognitive security paradigm. Finally, the discussion underscores the importance of governance, ethics, and user agency. Trust is not merely a technical property; it is a social contract. Without transparency, consent, and accountability, even the most sophisticated Zero Trust mechanisms risk becoming instruments of surveillance rather than protection.

9.1 CONCLUSION

This chapter has argued that immersive and spatial computing systems require a fundamentally new approach to cybersecurity—one that moves beyond static boundaries, session-based authentication, and role-based authorization. By their very nature, immersive environments are continuous, embodied, and socially interactive, making them incompatible with traditional perimeter-based security models. Zero Trust Architecture offers a powerful alternative by treating all entities as untrusted by default, enforcing least privilege, and continuously evaluating risk. However, to be effective in immersive systems, Zero Trust must evolve from a network-centric model into a perception-aware, behavior-driven, and spatially grounded trust framework.

Throughout the chapter, we demonstrated that immersive platforms introduce novel threats, including avatar impersonation, sensor spoofing, perceptual manipulation, and socially engineered deception. These threats cannot be adequately mitigated through conventional security tools alone. Instead, they demand trust mechanisms that operate in real time, adapt to contextual changes, and preserve user presence. The proposed architectural principles and design mechanisms illustrate how Zero Trust can be operationalized in such environments while minimizing disruption and maximizing safety.

Equally important is the recognition that trust in immersive systems is not purely technical. It is shaped by psychological comfort, social norms, and ethical governance. If Zero Trust is implemented without regard for privacy, transparency, and user autonomy, it risks undermining the very trust it seeks to establish. Therefore, future Zero Trust systems must be human-centered by design, integrating explainability, consent, and accountability into their core logic.

In conclusion, securing immersive and spatial computing environments is not merely an extension of existing cybersecurity practices but the emergence of a new discipline that integrates cyber, physical, and cognitive dimensions of risk. Zero Trust provides the conceptual backbone for this discipline, but its full realization will require interdisciplinary research spanning computer science, human–computer interaction, ethics, psychology, and law. By reframing trust as a continuous, contextual, and participatory process, future immersive systems can become not only more secure but also more transparent, inclusive, and socially sustainable.

REFERENCES

Azuma, R. T., Baillot, Y., Behringer, R., Feiner, S., Julier, S., & MacIntyre, B. (2001). Recent advances in augmented reality. *IEEE Computer Graphics and Applications*, *21*(6), 34–47. DOI: 10.1109/38.963459

Behl, A., & Behl, K. (2017). *Cyberwar: Threats and security*. Oxford University Press.

Bhambri, P. (2025a). Virtual and augmented reality for immersive learning experiences: Practical applications and challenges. In Pelet, J.-É. (Ed.), *Architecturing the digital future: Platforms, design, and application* (pp. 17–46). IGI Global., DOI: 10.4018/979-8-3693-2973-3.ch002

Bhambri, P. (2025b). Innovative systems: Entertainment, gaming, and the metaverse. In Ho, R. C., Song, B. L., & Tee, P. K. (Eds.), *Managing customer-centric strategies in the digital landscape* (pp. 483–514). IGI Global., DOI: 10.4018/979-8-3693-5668-5.ch018

Bhambri, P., Rana, R., & Kautish, S. (2025). Sustainable digital transformation: Reducing carbon footprint in the metaverse. In Leal Filho, W., Kautish, S., & Gupta, V. P. (Eds.), *Metaverse and sustainability: Business resilience towards sustainable development goals* (pp. 105–128). Springer Nature Switzerland., DOI: 10.1007/978-3-031-89545-6_7

Feiner, S. (2021). The evolution of spatial computing. *Computer*, *54*(2), 60–65. DOI: 10.1109/MC.2021.3051887

Kindervag, J. (2010). *Build security into your network's DNA: The zero trust network architecture*. Forrester Research.

Madary, M., & Metzinger, T. K. (2016). Real virtuality: A code of ethical conduct. Recommendations for good scientific practice and the consumers of VR-technology. *Frontiers in Robotics and AI*, *3*, 3. Advance online publication. DOI: 10.3389/frobt.2016.00003

Rauschnabel, P. A., Babin, B. J., tom Dieck, M. C., Krey, N., & Jung, T. (2022). What is augmented reality marketing? Its definition, concept, and value for customer engagement. *Journal of Business Research*, *142*, 329–345. DOI: 10.1016/j.jbusres.2021.12.084

Roesner, F., Kohno, T., & Molnar, D. (2014). Security and privacy for augmented reality systems. *Communications of the ACM*, *57*(4), 88–96. DOI: 10.1145/2580723.2580730

Rose, S., Borchert, O., Mitchell, S., & Connelly, S. (2020). *Zero Trust Architecture (NIST Special Publication 800-207)*. National Institute of Standards and Technology. https://doi.org/DOI: 10.6028/NIST.SP.800-207

Sicari, S., Rizzardi, A., Grieco, L. A., & Coen-Porisini, A. (2015). Security, privacy and trust in Internet of Things: The road ahead. *Computer Networks*, *76*, 146–164. DOI: 10.1016/j.comnet.2014.11.008

Slater, M., & Sanchez-Vives, M. V. (2016). Enhancing our lives with immersive virtual reality. *Frontiers in Robotics and AI*, *3*, 74. Advance online publication. DOI: 10.3389/frobt.2016.00074

Slater, M., Spanlang, B., Sanchez-Vives, M. V., & Blanke, O. (2010). First person experience of body transfer in virtual reality. *PLoS One*, *5*(5), e10564. DOI: 10.1371/journal.pone.0010564 PMID: 20485681

Zhao, J., Li, J., & Xu, Y. (2021). Wearable sensing and human activity recognition: A survey. *IEEE Sensors Journal*, *21*(5), 6500–6519. DOI: 10.1109/JSEN.2020.3034599

Compilation of References

AAA Accreditation (2024). The Impact of ISO/IEC 17024 Accreditation on Personnel Certification Bodies.

AASA (2024). Immersive Technologies: Shaping the Next Generation of Teaching and Learning.

AASA. (2024). The Post-Pandemic's Digital. *LEARNing Landscapes.*

Abdeljaber, O., Al-Adwan, A. S., Yaseen, H., Falahat, M., Abdullah, A., & Fauzi, M. A. (2025). Shopping in the Metaverse: Decoding Consumer Intentions. *The International Information & Library Review*, •••, 1–31.

Abdrabou, Y., Ozdel, S., Maquiling, V., & Kasneci, E. (2025). From gaze to data: Privacy and societal challenges of using eye-tracking data to inform GenAI models. In *ETRA '25: 2025 Symposium on Eye Tracking Research and Applications.* ACM. https://doi.org/DOI: 10.1145/3715669.3726788

Achuthan, K., Ramanathan, S., & Raman, R. (2025). Securing the metaverse: Machine learning–based perspectives on risk, trust, and governance. *International Journal of Information Management Data Insights*, *5*(2), 100356. DOI: 10.1016/j.jjimei.2025.100356

Achuthan, K., Thirunavukarasu, R., Alzahrani, M. S., Kumar, S., & Kumar, A. (2025). Metaverse-enabled cyber ranges for cybersecurity education: Systematic review, opportunities, and challenges. *International Journal of Information Security*, *24*, 207. Advance online publication. DOI: 10.1007/s10207-025-01115-y

Acien, A., Morales, A., Monaco, J. V., Vera-Rodriguez, R., & Fierrez, J. (2021). TypeNet: Deep learning keystroke biometrics. *IEEE Transactions on Biometrics, Behavior, and Identity Science*, *4*(1), 57–70. DOI: 10.1109/TBIOM.2021.3112540

Acquisti, A., Brandimarte, L., & Loewenstein, G. (2015). Privacy and human behavior in the age of information. *Science*, *347*(6221), 509–514. DOI: 10.1126/science.aaa1465 PMID: 25635091

Adawadkar, A. M. K., & Kulkarni, N. (2022). Cyber-security and reinforcement learning-A brief survey. *Engineering Applications of Artificial Intelligence*, *114*, 105116. DOI: 10.1016/j.engappai.2022.105116

Akbar, A., Rahman, F., Singhal, A., Khan, L., & Thuriasingham, B. (2023). The design and application of a unified ontology for cyber security. In. Lecture Notes in Computer Science: Vol. 14424. *Information Systems Security* (pp. 23–41). Springer., DOI: 10.1007/978-3-031-49099-6_2

Al Zaidawi, S. M. K., Prinzler, M. H., Lührs, J., & Maneth, S. (2022). An extensive study of user identification via eye movements across multiple datasets. *Signal Processing Image Communication*, *108*, 116804. DOI: 10.1016/j.image.2022.116804

Al-Adwan, A. S., Al-Adwan, A., Li, N., Fauzi, M. A., Jafar, R. M. S., Habibi, A., & Falahat, M. (2025). Immersive Learning Meets Theory: Modeling Eduverse Adoption in Higher Education. Journal of Information Technology Education: Research, 24, 042.

Alcaraz, C., & Lopez, J. (2022). Digital twin: A comprehensive survey of security threats. *IEEE Communications Surveys and Tutorials*, *24*(3), 1475–1503. DOI: 10.1109/COMST.2022.3171465

AL-Essa, M., Alsharo, M., Alnsour, Y., Ali, W. A., & Almomani, O.AL-Essa. (2025, December 31). M., Alsharo, M., Alnsour, Y., Ali, W. A., & Almomani, O. (2025). Transforming data representation: A comparative analysis of tabular and image-based approaches with XAI. *Journal of Computational and Cognitive Engineering*. Advance online publication. DOI: 10.47852/bonviewJCCE52026581

Al-Fararjeh, T., & Almomani, A. (2026). *International XR Driving License (IXRDL)*. Recommended Certification Scheme for Extended Reality Technologies. Beyond & Universe LLC.

Ali, O., Momin, M., Shrestha, A., Das, P., Naeem, M. A., & Goyal, R. (2024). A comprehensive survey on the role of artificial intelligence in metaverse. *IEEE Communications Surveys and Tutorials*, *26*(2), 1238–1278. DOI: 10.1109/COMST.2023.3347172

Allen, C., & Barrett, E. (2025, October 3). Why XR developers in the UK need accessible and authoritative guidance: The role of regulators in mapping existing laws on to the risks of immersive technologies. *The Log*.

Almomani, O., Arabiat, A. M., Hind, A. A., & Alsariera, E. (2026). Hybridization of Deep Learning Models for Multiclass Attack Detection in Wireless Sensor Networks. *Journal of Communication, 21*(1). Advance online publication. DOI: 10.12720/jcm.21.1.20-34

Almomani, O., Arabiat, A., Al Tayeb, M., Amin Almaiah, M., Obeidat, M., Aldhyani, T. H. H., Shehab, R., & Rowad, M. (2025). A robust model for Android malware detection via ML and DL classifiers. *Mesopotamian Journal of Big Data, 2025*, 261–277. DOI: 10.58496/MJBD/2025/017

Alnaim, A. K., & Alwakeel, A. M. (2025). Zero-trust mechanisms for securing distributed edge and fog computing in 6G networks. *Mathematics, 13*(8), 1239. DOI: 10.3390/math13081239

Alsaaidah, A., Almomani, O., Abu-Shareha, A. A., Abualhaj, M. M., & Achuthan, A. (2024). ARP spoofing attack detection model in IoT network using machine learning: Complexity vs. accuracy. *Journal of Applied Data Sciences, 5*(4), 1850–1860. DOI: 10.47738/jads.v5i4.374

Alsop, T. (2024). Extended reality (XR) market size worldwide from 2021 to 2026. Statista. https://www.statista.com/statistics/591181/global-augmented-virtual-reality-market-size/

Ang, S., & Quarles, J. (2023). Reduction of cybersickness in head mounted displays use: A systematic review and taxonomy of current strategies. *Frontiers in Virtual Reality, 4*, 1027552. Advance online publication. DOI: 10.3389/frvir.2023.1027552

ANSI (2024). Why ISO/IEC 17024 is Critical for the Development of Credentialing.

Antonakakis, M., April, T., Bailey, M., Bernhard, M., Bursztein, E., Cochran, J., Durumeric, Z., Halderman, J. A., Invernizzi, L., Kallitsis, M., Kumar, D., Lever, C., Ma, Z., Mason, J., Menscher, D., Seaman, C., Sullivan, N., Thomas, K., & Zhou, Y. (2017). Understanding the Mirai botnet. In *Proceedings of the 26th USENIX Security Symposium* (pp. 1093–1110). USENIX Association., https://www.usenix.org/system/files/conference/usenixsecurity17/sec17-antonakakis.pdf

Arrieta, A. B., Díaz-Rodríguez, N., Del Ser, J., Bennetot, A., Tabik, S., Barbado, A., Garcia, S., Gil-Lopez, S., Molina, D., Benjamins, R., Chatila, R., & Herrera, F. (2020). Explainable artificial intelligence (XAI): Concepts, taxonomies, opportunities and challenges toward responsible AI. *Information Fusion, 58*, 82–115. DOI: 10.1016/j.inffus.2019.12.012

Asif, M., Mondal, A., & Soumil, S. (2024). Augmented reality and virtual reality in education: A transformative journey. In *Advances in Computational Solutions*. Swami Vivekananda University.

Awadallah, A., Eledlebi, K., Zemerly, M. J., Puthal, D., Damiani, E., Taha, K., Kim, T.-Y., Yoo, P. D., Raymond Choo, K.-K., Yim, M.-S., & Yeun, C. Y. (2024). Artificial intelligence-based cybersecurity for the metaverse: Research challenges and opportunities. *IEEE Communications Surveys and Tutorials*, *27*(2), 1008–1052. DOI: 10.1109/COMST.2024.3442475

Aziz, S., & Komogortsev, O. (2024). Exploiting the uncoordinated privacy protections of eye tracking and VR motion data for unauthorized user identification. *arXiv*. https://arxiv.org/abs/2411.12766v1

Azuma, R. T., Baillot, Y., Behringer, R., Feiner, S., Julier, S., & MacIntyre, B. (2001). Recent advances in augmented reality. *IEEE Computer Graphics and Applications*, *21*(6), 34–47. DOI: 10.1109/38.963459

Bailenson, J. (2018). Protecting nonverbal data tracked in virtual reality. *Journal of the American Medical Association*, *320*(2), 716–717. DOI: 10.1001/jama.2018.0764 PMID: 30083770

Balhareth, H., Al-Adwan, A. S., Alsoud, A. R., Abd-Aljaber, O., Al-Rahmi, W. M., & Urbaníková, M. (2024). Journey into meta-commerce: Driving forces of consumer adoption. *Global Knowledge, Memory and Communication*. Advance online publication. DOI: 10.1108/GKMC-05-2024-0307

Barbu, M., Iordache, D. D., Petre, I., Barbu, D.-C., & Băjenaru, L. (2025). Framework design for reinforcing the potential of XR technologies in transforming inclusive education. *Applied Sciences (Basel, Switzerland)*, *15*(3), 1484. DOI: 10.3390/app15031484

Barreno, M., Nelson, B., Sears, R., Joseph, A. D., & Tygar, J. D. (2006). Can machine learning be secure? In *Proceedings of the 2006 ACM Symposium on Information, Computer and Communications Security* (pp. 16–25). https://doi.org/DOI: 10.1145/1128817.1128824

Batra, K., Zhang, Z., Yang, S., ... (2025). XRXL: A system for immersive visualization in large lectures. In 2025 IEEE Conference Virtual Reality and 3D User Interfaces (VR) (pp. 370-380). IEEE. DOI: 10.1109/VR59515.2025.00061

Becerra, M. A., Duque-Mejia, C., Castro-Ospina, A., Serna-Guarín, L., Mejía, C., & Duque-Grisales, E. (2025). EEG-based biometric identification and emotion recognition: An overview. *Computers*, *14*(8), 299. DOI: 10.3390/computers14080299

Behl, A., & Behl, K. (2017). *Cyberwar: Threats and security*. Oxford University Press.

Bekkemoen, Y. (2024). Explainable reinforcement learning (XRL): A systematic literature review and taxonomy. *Machine Learning*, *113*(1), 355–441. DOI: 10.1007/s10994-023-06479-7

Beyond Universe XR AI Solutions (n.d.). Metaversity Labs and Immersive Virtual Classrooms (company profile and official service pages). Beyond Universe XR Solutions (accessed 8 March 2026).

Bhambri, P. (2025a). Virtual and augmented reality for immersive learning experiences: Practical applications and challenges. In Pelet, J.-É. (Ed.), *Architecturing the digital future: Platforms, design, and application* (pp. 17–46). IGI Global., DOI: 10.4018/979-8-3693-2973-3.ch002

Bhambri, P. (2025b). Innovative systems: Entertainment, gaming, and the metaverse. In Ho, R. C., Song, B. L., & Tee, P. K. (Eds.), *Managing customer-centric strategies in the digital landscape* (pp. 483–514). IGI Global., DOI: 10.4018/979-8-3693-5668-5.ch018

Bhambri, P., Rana, R., & Kautish, S. (2025). Sustainable digital transformation: Reducing carbon footprint in the metaverse. In Leal Filho, W., Kautish, S., & Gupta, V. P. (Eds.), *Metaverse and sustainability: Business resilience towards sustainable development goals* (pp. 105–128). Springer Nature Switzerland., DOI: 10.1007/978-3-031-89545-6_7

Bidgoly, A. J., Bidgoly, H. J., & Arezoumand, Z. (2022). Towards a universal and privacy preserving EEG-based authentication system. *Scientific Reports*, *12*(1), 2531. DOI: 10.1038/s41598-022-06527-7 PMID: 35169248

Biggio, B., & Roli, F. (2018). Wild patterns: Ten years after the rise of adversarial machine learning. *Pattern Recognition*, *84*, 317–331. DOI: 10.1016/j.patcog.2018.07.023

Biometrics Institute. (2019). *Biometrics privacy guidelines*. https://www.biometricsinstitute.org/

Biswas, N., Mukherjee, A., & Bhattacharya, S. (2024). "Are you feeling sick?" – A systematic literature review of cybersickness in virtual reality. *ACM Computing Surveys*, *56*(11), 284. Advance online publication. DOI: 10.1145/3670008

Bonawitz, K., Ivanov, V., Kreuter, B., Marcedone, A., McMahan, H. B., Patel, S., Ramage, D., Segal, A., & Seth, K. (2017). Practical secure aggregation for privacy-preserving machine learning. In *Proceedings of the 2017 ACM SIGSAC Conference on Computer and Communications Security* (pp. 1175–1191). https://doi.org/DOI: 10.1145/3133956.3133982

Boston Consulting Group (BCG). (2026). 6G: The network for the future of AI and immersive connectivity. BCG and Qualcomm. https://web-assets.bcg.com/9c/73/4ac7634848a0b0bb31cf8dae40cb/6g-the-network-for-the-future-of-ai-and-immersive-connectivity-report-feb-2026-edit-03-web.pdf

Bouchiba, G., Tlemsani, R., Chouraqui, S., & Benouis, M. (2019). An improved behavioral biometric system based on gait and ECG signals. *International Journal of Intelligent Engineering and Systems, 12*(6), 147–156. DOI: 10.22266/ijies2019.1231.14

Bougueroua, N., Mazouzi, S., Belaoued, M., Seddari, N., Derhab, A., & Bouras, A. (2021). A survey on multi-agent based collaborative intrusion detection systems. *Journal of Artificial Intelligence and Soft Computing Research, 11*(2), 111–142. DOI: 10.2478/jaiscr-2021-0008

Brambilla, M., Ferrante, E., Birattari, M., & Dorigo, M. (2013). Swarm robotics: A review from the swarm engineering perspective. *Swarm Intelligence, 7*(1), 1–41. DOI: 10.1007/s11721-012-0075-2

Bratsas, C., Anastasiadis, E. K., Angelidis, A. K., Ioannidis, L., Kotsakis, R., & Ougiaroglou, S. (2024). Knowledge graphs and semantic web tools in cyber threat intelligence: A systematic literature review. *Journal of Cybersecurity and Privacy, 4*(3), 518–545. DOI: 10.3390/jcp4030025

Brookings Institution (2024). Rewiring the classroom: How the COVID-19 pandemic transformed K-12 education.

Buterin, V. (2022). Soulbound tokens: A vision for Web3 identity.

Cao, Q., Shen, L., Xie, W., Parkhi, O. M., & Zisserman, A. (2018). VGGFace2: A dataset for recognising faces across pose and age. In *Proceedings of the IEEE Conference on Automatic Face & Gesture Recognition* (pp. 67-74). IEEE. DOI: 10.1109/FG.2018.00020

Caroline, C. C. et al. (2025). Enhancing Digital Literacy Through International Computer Driving License (ICDL) Training. International Journal of Education and Development using ICT.

Chen, J., Zhang, D., Yao, Y., Adhikari, N., Zhang, Z., & Li, H. (2023). SeAGent: Toward intelligent IoT security in the metaverse. In Companion Proceedings of the ACM Web Conference 2023 (pp. 1151-1160). DOI: 10.1145/3543873.3587584

Chen, Z., Wu, J., Gan, W., & Qi, Z. (2022). Metaverse security and privacy: An overview. In 2022 IEEE International Conference on Big Data (Big Data) (pp. 2950-2959). Piscataway, NJ: IEEE. DOI: 10.1109/BigData55660.2022.10021112

Cheng, X., Zhang, H., Liang, H., & Xu, Y. (2024). Safeguarding the metaverse: Security and privacy challenges and solutions. *IEEE Communications Magazine*, *62*(2), 156–162. DOI: 10.1109/MCOM.018.2300095

Chow, W. K. B., Ho, J. S. K., & Wong, A. K. F. (2023). The metaverse for learning: A review of educational applications, opportunities, and challenges. *Journal of Imaging*, *9*(1), 11. Advance online publication. DOI: 10.3390/jimaging9010011 PMID: 36662109

Chow, Y. W.. (2022). Visualization and cybersecurity in the metaverse: A survey. *Future Generation Computer Systems*. Advance online publication. DOI: 10.1016/j.future.2022.10.012 PMID: 36662109

D'Amelio, A., Patania, S., Bursic, S., Cuculo, V., & Boccignone, G. (2023). Using gaze for behavioural biometrics. *Sensors (Basel)*, *23*(3), 1262. DOI: 10.3390/s23031262 PMID: 36772302

Data Insights Market. (2025, April 14). *Behavioral biometrics competitive strategies: Trends and forecasts 2025–2033*. https://www.datainsightsmarket.com/reports/behavioral-biometrics-1950776

Di Pietro, R., & Cresci, S. (2021). Metaverse: Security and privacy issues. In *2021 IEEE International Conference on Trust, Privacy and Security in Intelligent Systems and Applications (TPS-ISA)* (pp. 281-288). Piscataway, NJ: IEEE. DOI: 10.1109/TPSISA52974.2021.00032

Dias, T. F., Vitorino, J., Maia, E., Sousa, O., & Praça, I. (2023). KeyRecs: A keystroke dynamics and typing pattern recognition dataset. *Data in Brief*, *50*, 109509. DOI: 10.1016/j.dib.2023.109509 PMID: 37663780

Dieye, M., Valiorgue, P., Gelas, J.-P., Diallo, E.-H., Ghodous, P., Biennier, F., & Peyrol, E. (2023). A self-sovereign identity based on zero-knowledge proof and blockchain. *IEEE Access : Practical Innovations, Open Solutions*, *11*, 49445–49455. DOI: 10.1109/ACCESS.2023.3268768

Duan, H., Li, J., Fan, S., Lin, Z., Wu, X., & Cai, W. (2021). Metaverse for social good: A university campus prototype. In *Proceedings of the 29th ACM International Conference on Multimedia* (pp. 153–161). https://doi.org/DOI: 10.1145/3474085.3479238

Dwivedi, Y. K., Hughes, L., & Baabdullah, A. M.. (2022). Metaverse beyond the hype: Multidisciplinary perspectives on emerging challenges, opportunities, and agenda for research, practice and policy. *International Journal of Information Management*, *66*, 102542. Advance online publication. DOI: 10.1016/j.ijinfomgt.2022.102542

Dwork, C., McSherry, F., Nissim, K., & Smith, A. (2006). Calibrating noise to sensitivity in private data analysis. In Halevi, S., & Rabin, T. (Eds.), Lecture Notes in Computer Science: Vol. 3876. *Theory of cryptography* (pp. 265–284). Springer., DOI: 10.1007/11681878_14

Dwork, C., & Roth, A. (2014). The algorithmic foundations of differential privacy. *Foundations and Trends in Machine Learning.*

EDUCAUSE. (2024). *Navigating the XR Educational Landscape: Privacy*. Safety, and Ethical Guidelines — Strategic Recommendations.

Egliston, B., Carter, M., & Clark, K. E. (2025). *Value and Virtue in the Extended Reality (XR) Industry. Information, Communication & Society*. Taylor & Francis.

Eltanbouly, S., Halabi, O., & Qadir, J. (2025). Avatar privacy challenges in the metaverse: A comprehensive review and future directions. *International Journal of Human-Computer Interaction*, *41*(4), 1967–1984. DOI: 10.1080/10447318.2024.2374091

Escaleira, P., Cunha, V. A., Barraca, J. P., Gomes, D., & Aguiar, R. L. (2025). A systematic review on security mechanisms for serverless computing. *Cluster Computing*, *28*(465), 1–31. DOI: 10.1007/s10586-025-05371-4

European Union Agency for Cybersecurity (ENISA). (2023). *Cybersecurity guidelines for emerging technologies.*

Farid, F.. (2024). Cyber security management in metaverse: A review and analysis. *Journal of Information Security and Applications.*

Farran, I., & Nunez, I. (2025). *Converging Pathways: New Approaches to Integrate Vocational Education Training and Higher Education. Journal of Vocational Education & Training*. Taylor & Francis.

Fathalla, E., Azab, M., Xin, C., & Wu, H. (2026). Self-sovereign identity as a secure and trustworthy approach to digital identity management: A comprehensive survey. *ACM Computing Surveys*. Advance online publication. DOI: 10.1145/3785466

Feiner, S. (2021). The evolution of spatial computing. *Computer*, *54*(2), 60–65. DOI: 10.1109/MC.2021.3051887

Feng, D., Qin, Y., Feng, W., Li, W., Shang, K., & Ma, H. (2024). Survey of research on confidential computing. *IET Communications*, *18*(9), 535–556. DOI: 10.1049/cmu2.12759

Finistrella, S., Mariani, S., & Zambonelli, F. (2025). Multi-agent reinforcement learning for cybersecurity: Classification and survey. *Intelligent Systems with Applications*, *26*, 200495. DOI: 10.1016/j.iswa.2025.200495

Fuller, A., Fan, Z., Day, C., & Barlow, C. (2020). Digital twin: Enabling technologies, challenges and open research. *IEEE Access : Practical Innovations, Open Solutions*, *8*, 108952–108971. DOI: 10.1109/ACCESS.2020.2998358

Future of Privacy Forum. (2025). *What to expect in global privacy in 2025.* https://fpf.org/blog/what-to-expect-in-global-privacy-in-2025/

Gao, X., Wang, Y., Liu, B., Zhou, X., Zhang, R., Wang, J., Niyato, D., Kim, D. I., Jamalipour, A., Yuen, C., An, J., & Yang, K. (2026). Agentic satellite-augmented low-altitude economy and terrestrial networks: A survey on generative approaches. *IEEE Communications Surveys and Tutorials.* Advance online publication. DOI: 10.1109/COMST.2026.3660854

Garcia-Agundez, A., Reuter, C., Becker, H., Konrad, R., Caserman, P., Miede, A., & Göbel, S. (2019). Development of a classifier to determine factors causing cybersickness in virtual reality environments. *Games for Health Journal*, *8*(6), 439–444. DOI: 10.1089/g4h.2019.0045 PMID: 31295007

George, A., & Routray, A. (2016). A score level fusion method for eye movement biometrics. *Pattern Recognition Letters*, *82*, 207–215. DOI: 10.1016/j.patrec.2015.11.020

Gerling, K., Dickinson, P., Hicks, K., Mason, L., Simeone, A. L., & Spiel, K. (2020). Virtual reality games for people using wheelchairs. In *Proceedings of the 2020 CHI Conference on Human Factors in Computing Systems* (pp. 1-11). ACM. DOI: 10.1145/3313831.3376265

Gherari, M., Maia, A., Dieye, M., Elbiaze, H., Ghamri-Doudane, Y., & Glitho, R. H. (2026). Optimizing Immersive Services with Parallel In-Network Rendering and Deep RL. *IEEE Transactions on Machine Learning in Communications and Networking*, *4*, 491–513. Advance online publication. DOI: 10.1109/TMLCN.2026.3666742

Giaretta, A. (2025). Security and privacy in virtual reality: A literature survey. *Virtual Reality (Waltham Cross)*, *29*(1), 10. Advance online publication. DOI: 10.1007/s10055-024-01079-9

Global Disaster Preparedness Center / IFRC (2020). Immersive Technologies & Digital Games for School Disaster Preparedness.

GoStudent (2025). 30+ Virtual Reality in Education Statistics: Revolutionising Learning.

Grand View Research (2024). Extended Reality Market Size, Share & Growth Report, 2030.

Grassi, P. A., Garcia, M. E., & Fenton, J. L. (2020). *Digital identity guidelines* (NIST Special Publication 800-63-3). National Institute of Standards and Technology. https://doi.org/DOI: 10.6028/NIST.SP.800-63-3

Grieves, M., & Vickers, J. (2017). Digital twin: Mitigating unpredictable, undesirable emergent behavior in complex systems. In Kahlen, F.-J., Flumerfelt, S., & Alves, A. (Eds.), *Transdisciplinary perspectives on complex systems* (pp. 85–113). Springer., DOI: 10.1007/978-3-319-38756-7_4

Griffith, H., Lohr, D., Abdulin, E., & Komogortsev, O. (2021). GazeBase, a large-scale, multi-stimulus, longitudinal eye movement dataset. *Scientific Data*, *8*(1), 184. DOI: 10.1038/s41597-021-00959-y PMID: 34272404

Gruber, T. R. (1993). A translation approach to portable ontology specifications. *Knowledge Acquisition*, *5*(2), 199–220. DOI: 10.1006/knac.1993.1008

Gruber, T. R. (1995). Toward principles for the design of ontologies used for knowledge sharing. *International Journal of Human-Computer Studies*, *43*(5-6), 907–928. DOI: 10.1006/ijhc.1995.1081

Gu, X., Duan, W., Zhang, G., Hou, J., Peng, L., Wen, M., Gao, F., Chen, M., & Ho, P.-H. (2026). Digital twin technology for intelligent vehicles and transportation systems: A survey on applications, challenges and future directions. *IEEE Communications Surveys and Tutorials*, *28*, 3235–3271. DOI: 10.1109/COMST.2025.3581152

Hadan, H., Serino, M., Patil, S., Toma, F., & De Guzman, J. A. (2024). Privacy in immersive extended reality: Exploring user perceptions, concerns, and coping strategies. In *Proceedings of the CHI Conference on Human Factors in Computing Systems (CHI '24)*. ACM. DOI: 10.1145/3613904.3642104

Hanisch, S., Arias-Cabarcos, P., Parra-Arnau, J., & Strufe, T. (2021). Privacy-protecting techniques for behavioral biometric data: A survey. *arXiv*. https://doi.org//arXiv.2109.04120DOI: 10.48550

Han, S., Hwang, E., Kim, Y. S., & Kwon, T. (2025). A continuous authentication framework for securing metaverse identities. *IEEE Transactions on Services Computing*, *18*(3), 1171–1184. DOI: 10.1109/TSC.2025.3553711

Heuillet, A., Couthouis, F., & Díaz-Rodríguez, N. (2021). Explainability in deep reinforcement learning. *Knowledge-Based Systems*, *214*, 106685. DOI: 10.1016/j.knosys.2020.106685

Hine, E., Rezende, I. N., Roberts, H., Wong, D., Taddeo, M., & Floridi, L. (2024). Safety and privacy in immersive extended reality: An analysis and policy recommendations. *Digital Society : Ethics, Socio-Legal and Governance of Digital Technology*, *3*(2), 33. Advance online publication. DOI: 10.1007/s44206-024-00114-1

Hmoud, M., Swaity, H., Karram, O., Shibli, H., Swaity, S., & Daher, W. (2023). High school students' engagement in biology in the context of XR technology. *IEEE Access : Practical Innovations, Open Solutions*, *11*, 137053–137066. DOI: 10.1109/ACCESS.2023.3338176

Hoppe, S., Loetscher, T., Morey, S. A., & Bulling, A. (2018). Eye movements during everyday behavior predict personality traits. *Frontiers in Human Neuroscience*, *12*, 105. DOI: 10.3389/fnhum.2018.00105 PMID: 29713270

Hossain, S. (2025). Using Artificial Intelligence to Improve Classroom Learning Experience. arXiv preprint arXiv:2503.05709.

Hossain, S. (2026). Extended Reality (XR): The Next Frontier in Education. arXiv preprint arXiv:2602.23601v1.

Hossain, S., Sommer, N., & Adib, N. (2025). Exploring the Integration of Extended Reality and Artificial Intelligence (AI) for Remote STEM Education and Assessment. arXiv preprint arXiv:2509.03812.

Hu, V. C., Ferraiolo, D., Kuhn, R., Schnitzer, A., Sandlin, K., Miller, R., & Scarfone, K. (2014). *Guide to attribute based access control (ABAC) definition and considerations* (NIST Special Publication 800-162). National Institute of Standards and Technology. https://doi.org/DOI: 10.6028/NIST.SP.800-162

Huang, G. B., Mattar, M., Berg, T., & Learned-Miller, E. (2008). Labeled faces in the wild: A database for studying face recognition in unconstrained environments. In *Workshop on Faces in Real-Life Images*. University of Massachusetts.

Huang, Y., Li, Y., & Cai, Z. (2023). Security and privacy in metaverse: A comprehensive survey. *Big Data Mining and Analytics*, *6*(2), 234–247. DOI: 10.26599/BDMA.2022.9020047

Hu, J., & Wellman, M. P. (2003). Nash Q-learning for general-sum stochastic games. *Journal of Machine Learning Research*, *4*, 1039–1069. DOI: 10.1162/1532443041827880

Huynh-The, T., Pham, Q.-V., Pham, X.-Q., Nguyen, T. T., Han, Z., & Kim, D.-S. (2023). Artificial intelligence for the metaverse: A survey. *Engineering Applications of Artificial Intelligence*, *117*, 105581. DOI: 10.1016/j.engappai.2022.105581

Hu, Z., Chen, P., Zhu, M., & Liu, P. (2019). Reinforcement learning for adaptive cyber defense against zero-day attacks. In. Lecture Notes in Computer Science: Vol. 11830. *Adversarial and Uncertain Reasoning for Adaptive Cyber Defense* (pp. 54–93). Springer., DOI: 10.1007/978-3-030-30719-6_4

Iannacone, M., Bohn, S., Nakamura, G., Gerth, J., Huffer, K., Bridges, R., & Goodall, J. (2015). Developing an ontology for cyber security knowledge graphs. In *Proceedings of the 10th Annual Cyber and Information Security Research Conference* (pp. 1-4). New York, NY: ACM. DOI: 10.1145/2746266.2746278

ICDL Foundation (2023). ICDL Celebrates 17 Million Candidates Worldwide.

IDC. (2025, March 25). Growth expected to pause for AR/VR headsets. International Data Corporation. https://my.idc.com/getdoc.jsp?containerId=prUS53278025

IJCSPUB. (2025). Zero trust and 6G: Enhancing security in next generation networks. *International Journal of Current Science, 15*(2), 175–179. https://www.rjpn.org/ijcspub/papers/IJCSP25B1021.pdf

Industrial Cyber. (2025). Edge AI emerges as cyber force multiplier, enhancing operations and safeguarding critical installations from evolving threats. Industrial Cyber. https://industrialcyber.co/threat-landscape/edge-ai-emerges-as-cyber-force-multiplier-enhancing-operations-and-safeguarding-critical-installations-from-evolving-threats/

Islam, R., Ang, S., & Quarles, J. (2021). CybersicknessPrediction from integrated HMD's sensors: A multimodal deep fusion approach using eye-tracking and head-tracking data. In *IEEE International Symposium on Mixed and Augmented Reality (ISMAR)* (pp. 400-411). IEEE. DOI: 10.1109/ISMAR52148.2021.00058

ISO (2012). ISO/IEC 17024:2012 — Conformity Assessment — General Requirements for Bodies Operating Certification of Persons.

Jain, A. K., Ross, A., & Prabhakar, S. (2004). An introduction to biometric recognition. *IEEE Transactions on Circuits and Systems for Video Technology, 14*(1), 4–20. DOI: 10.1109/TCSVT.2003.818349

Ji, T. F., Hu, Y., Huang, Y., Du, R., & Zhao, Y. (2023). A preliminary interview: Understanding XR developers' needs towards open-source accessibility support. In IEEE Conference on Virtual Reality and 3D User Interfaces Abstracts and Workshops (VRW) (pp. 493-496). IEEE. DOI: 10.1109/VRW58643.2023.00107

Jørgensen, B. N., & Ma, Z. G. (2025). Digital twins under EU law: A unified compliance framework across smart cities, industry, transportation, and energy systems. *Electronics (Basel), 14*(24), 4881. Advance online publication. DOI: 10.3390/electronics14244881

Kairouz, P., & McMahan, H. B. (2021). Advances and open problems in federated learning. *Foundations and Trends in Machine Learning, 14*(1-2), 1–210. DOI: 10.1561/2200000083

Kalsha, S. (2025, August 1). Privacy first: Critical considerations in immersive experiences. *Qodequay*.https://www.qodequay.com/privacy-first-critical-considerations-in-immersive-experiences

Katoikos, I., Fidas, C. A., & Koukopoulos, D. (2025). Strengthening graphical password security through EEG-driven classifiers based on image content familiarity. *International Journal of Human-Computer Interaction*. Advance online publication. DOI: 10.1080/10447318.2025.2504195

Kavitha, T., & Kavitha, V. (2025). Blockchain-enhanced framework for ensuring data consistency, transparency and privacy in cloud computing. *Journal of Applied Engineering and Technological Science, 7*(1), 8851. DOI: 10.37385/jaets.v7i1.8851

Khan Khalil, A. E., Perez-Diaz, J. A., Cantoral-Ceballos, J. A., & Antelis, J. M. (2024). Unlocking security for comprehensive electroencephalogram-based user authentication systems. *Sensors (Basel), 24*(24), 7919. DOI: 10.3390/s24247919 PMID: 39771656

Khan, M. A., Rahman, A., Mahmud, F. U., Bishnu, K. K., Ahmed, M., Mridha, M. F., & Aung, Z. (2025). A systematic review of AI-driven business models for advancing sustainable development goals. *Array. Article, 100539*. Advance online publication. DOI: 10.1016/j.array.2025.100539

Kindervag, J. (2010). *Build security into your network's DNA: The zero trust network architecture*. Forrester Research.

Kitchenham, B. (2004). *Procedures for performing systematic reviews* (Technical Report TR/SE-0401). Software Engineering Group, Department of Computer Science, Keele University.

Kolb, D. A. (1984). *Experiential Learning: Experience as the Source of Learning and Development*. Prentice-Hall.

Kumar, A. (2025). *Effectiveness of augmented reality and virtual reality interventions on learning outcomes: A meta-analysis in higher education. TechTrends*. Springer.

Kumarapeli, D., Jung, S., & Lindeman, R. W. (2024). Privacy threats of behaviour identity detection in VR. *Frontiers in Virtual Reality*, *5*, 1197547. Advance online publication. DOI: 10.3389/frvir.2024.1197547

Kürtünlüoğlu, P., Akdik, B., Duygu, R., & Karaarslan, E. (2023). Towards more secure virtual reality authentication for the metaverse: A decentralized method proposal. In *2023 16th International Conference on Information Security and Cryptology (ISC-Turkiye)* (pp. 1–6). https://doi.org/DOI: 10.1109/ISCTrkiye61151.2023.10336101

Laghari, A. A., Zhang, X., Shaikh, Z. A., Khan, A., Estrela, V. V., & Izadi, S. (2024). A review on quality of experience (QoE) in cloud computing. *Journal of Reliable Intelligent Environments*, *10*(2), 107–121. DOI: 10.1007/s40860-023-00210-y

Laiz-Ibanez, H., Mendaña-Cuervo, C., & Carus Candas, J. L. (2025). The metaverse: Privacy and information security risks. *International Journal of Information Management Data Insights*, *5*(2), 100373. DOI: 10.1016/j.jjimei.2025.100373

Lee, L. H., Braud, T., Zhou, P., Wang, L., Xu, D., Lin, Z., Kumar, A., Bermejo, C., & Hui, P. (2021). All one needs to know about metaverse: A complete survey. arXiv preprint arXiv:2110.05352.

Lehman, S. M., Alrumayh, A. S., Kolhe, K., Ling, H., & Tan, C. C. (2022). Hidden in plain sight: Exploring privacy risks of mobile augmented reality applications. *ACM Transactions on Privacy and Security*, *25*(4), 26. Advance online publication. DOI: 10.1145/3524020

Lencastre, P., Bhurtel, S., Yazidi, A., Denysov, S., & Lind, P. G. (2022). EyeT4Empathy: Dataset of foraging for visual information, gaze typing and empathy assessment. *Scientific Data*, *9*(1), 752. DOI: 10.1038/s41597-022-01862-w PMID: 36463232

Liang, X., Wang, S., Xiong, L., Liu, Z., & Xiong, N. N. (2025). SAGTM: A secure authentication scheme with traceability for avatars in the metaverse. *Computer Networks*, *263*, 111206. Advance online publication. DOI: 10.1016/j.comnet.2025.111206

Li, D., Han, D., Crespi, N., Minerva, R., Raza, S. M., Farahbakhsh, R., Liang, W., & Zheng, Z. (2025). Blockchain in the digital twin context: A comprehensive survey. *ACM Computing Surveys*, *58*(6), 150. Advance online publication. DOI: 10.1145/3772366

Li, G., Luo, H., Chen, D., Wang, P., Yin, X., & Zhang, J. (2025). Augmented Reality in Higher Education: A Systematic Review. *Education Sciences*, *15*(6), 678. DOI: 10.3390/educsci15060678

Lim, J. Z., Mountstephens, J., & Teo, J. (2020). Emotion recognition using eye-tracking: Taxonomy, review and current challenges. *Sensors (Basel)*, *20*(8), 2384. DOI: 10.3390/s20082384 PMID: 32331327

Lim, W. Y. B., Xiong, Z., Niyato, D., Cao, X., Miao, C., Sun, S., & Yang, Q. (2023). Realizing the metaverse with edge intelligence: A match made in heaven. *IEEE Wireless Communications*, *30*(4), 64–71. DOI: 10.1109/MWC.018.2100716

Li, T., Sahu, A. K., Talwalkar, A., & Smith, V. (2020). Federated learning: Challenges, methods, and future directions. *IEEE Signal Processing Magazine*, *37*(3), 50–60. DOI: 10.1109/MSP.2020.2975749

Liu, H., Wang, Y., Fan, W., Liu, X., Li, Y., Jain, S., Liu, Y., Jain, A. K., & Tang, J. (2022). Trustworthy AI: A computational perspective. *ACM Transactions on Intelligent Systems and Technology*, *14*(1), 1. Advance online publication. DOI: 10.1145/3546872

Liu, M., Fang, S., Dong, H., & Xu, C. (2021). Review of digital twin about concepts, technologies, and industrial applications. *Journal of Manufacturing Systems*, *58*, 346–361. DOI: 10.1016/j.jmsy.2020.06.017

Loevenich, J., Adler, E., Hurten, T., & Lopes, R. R. F. (2025). Design and evaluation of an autonomous cyber defence agent using DRL and an augmented LLM. *Computer Networks*, *262*, 111162. Advance online publication. DOI: 10.1016/j.comnet.2025.111162

Luo, H., Sun, G., Wang, J., Yu, H., Niyato, D., Dustdar, S., & Han, Z. (2026). Wireless blockchain meets 6G: The future trustworthy and ubiquitous connectivity. *IEEE Communications Surveys and Tutorials*, *28*, 3596–3636. DOI: 10.1109/COMST.2025.3593918

Madary, M., & Metzinger, T. K. (2016). Real virtuality: A code of ethical conduct. Recommendations for good scientific practice and the consumers of VR-technology. *Frontiers in Robotics and AI*, *3*, 3. Advance online publication. DOI: 10.3389/frobt.2016.00003

Madumal, P., Miller, T., Sonenberg, L., & Vetere, F. (2020). Explainable reinforcement learning through a causal lens. *Proceedings of the AAAI Conference on Artificial Intelligence*, *34*(03), 2493–2500. DOI: 10.1609/aaai.v34i03.5631

Maidenbaum, S., Buchs, G., Abboud, S., Lavi-Rotbain, O., & Amedi, A. (2016). Perception of graphical virtual environments by blind users via sensory substitution. *PLoS One*, *11*(2), e0147501. DOI: 10.1371/journal.pone.0147501 PMID: 26882473

Makransky, G., & Petersen, G. B. (2021). The Cognitive Affective Model of Immersive Learning (CAMIL). *Educational Psychology Review, 33*(3), 937–958. DOI: 10.1007/s10648-020-09586-2

Mak, S. L., Tang, F. W. F., & Li, C. H.. (2020). A Review on Development and Application of Virtual Reality (VR) Training Platform. *International Journal of Information and Education Technology (IJIET), 10*(1).

Malik, A., Khatoon, M., & Siddique, S. (2024). *Disruptive technologies in education: Transforming traditional curriculum models for the 21st century*. Research Corridor.

Markopoulos, E., & Nordholm, A. D.. (2022). *A Certification Framework for Virtual Reality and Metaverse Training Scenarios in the Maritime and Shipping Industry*. UCL Discovery. DOI: 10.54941/ahfe1001505

Meccawy, M. (2023). Teachers' prospective attitudes towards the adoption of extended reality technologies in the classroom: Interests and concerns. *Smart Learning Environments, 10*(1), 36. DOI: 10.1186/s40561-023-00256-8

Mihai, S., Yaqoob, M., Hung, D. V., Davis, W., Towakel, P., Raza, M., Karamanoglu, M., Barn, B., Shetve, D., Prasad, R. V., Venkataraman, H., Trestian, R., & Nguyen, H. X. (2022). Digital twins: A survey on enabling technologies, challenges, trends and future prospects. *IEEE Communications Surveys and Tutorials, 24*(4), 2255–2291. DOI: 10.1109/COMST.2022.3208773

Milgram, P., & Kishino, F. (1994). A taxonomy of mixed reality visual displays. *IEICE Transactions on Information and Systems, E77-D*(12), 1321–1329.

Miller, M. R., Herrera, F., Jun, H., Landay, J. A., & Bailenson, J. N. (2020). Personal identifiability of user tracking data during observation of 360-degree VR video. *Scientific Reports, 10*(1), 17404. DOI: 10.1038/s41598-020-74486-y PMID: 33060713

Mnih, V., Kavukcuoglu, K., Silver, D., Rusu, A. A., Veness, J., Bellemare, M. G., Graves, A., Riedmiller, M., Fidjeland, A. K., Ostrovski, G., Petersen, S., Beattie, C., Sadik, A., Antonoglou, I., King, H., Kumaran, D., Wierstra, D., Legg, S., & Hassabis, D. (2015). Human-level control through deep reinforcement learning. *Nature, 518*(7540), 529–533. DOI: 10.1038/nature14236 PMID: 25719670

Mordor Intelligence (2026). Virtual Reality in Education Market Size & Share, 2031.

Mosqueira-Rey, E., Hernández-Pereira, E., Alonso-Ríos, D., Bobes-Bascarán, J., & Fernández-Leal, Á. (2023). Human-in-the-loop machine learning: A state of the art. *Artificial Intelligence Review, 56*, 3005–3054. DOI: 10.1007/s10462-022-10246-w

Mustak, M., Salminen, J., Mäntymäki, M., Rahman, A., & Dwivedi, Y. K. (2023). Deepfakes: Deceptions, mitigations, and opportunities. *Journal of Business Research*, *154*, 113368. DOI: 10.1016/j.jbusres.2022.113368

Naik, M., Barbosa, R., & Swartsel, A. (2023). Immersive Learning & XR Technology Skills and Careers. Jobs for the Future. ERIC Document ED630059.

Nair, V., Guo, W., Mattern, J., Wang, R., O'Brien, J. F., Rosenberg, L., & Song, D. "Unique identification of 50,000+ virtual reality users from head & hand motion data." In *32nd USENIX Security Symposium (USENIX Security 23)*, pp. 895-910. 2023. https://www.usenix.org/system/files/usenixsecurity23-nair-identification.pdf

Nair, V., Guo, W., Mattern, J., Wang, R., O'Brien, J. F., Rosenberg, L., & Song, D. (2023). Unique identification of 50,000+ virtual reality users from head & hand motion data. In *32nd USENIX Security Symposium* (pp. 895–910). USENIX Association. DOI: 10.48550/arXiv.2302.08927

Nair, V., Guo, W., Wang, R., O'Brien, J. F., Rosenberg, L., & Song, D. (2024). Berkeley open extended reality recordings 2023 (BOXRR-23): 4.7 million motion capture recordings from 105,000 XR users. *IEEE Transactions on Visualization and Computer Graphics*, *30*(5), 2239–2246. Advance online publication. DOI: 10.1109/TVCG.2024.3372087 PMID: 38437078

Nasir, A. R., Ashraf, M. I., Reisslein, M., & Kato, N. (2022). Drone-swarm-enabled aerial computing for intelligent IoT services: Architecture, opportunities, and challenges. *Computer Networks*, *205*, 108708. Advance online publication. DOI: 10.1016/j.comnet.2021.108708

Nasr, M., Shokri, R., & Houmansadr, A. (2018). Machine learning with membership privacy using adversarial regularization. In *Proceedings of the 2018 ACM SIGSAC Conference on Computer and Communications Security* (pp. 634–646). https://doi.org/DOI: 10.1145/3243734.3243855

National Institute of Standards and Technology (NIST). (2024). *Post-quantum cryptography standardization (ML-KEM, ML-DSA).*

Nguyen, T. T., & Reddi, V. J. (2023). Deep reinforcement learning for cyber security. *IEEE Transactions on Neural Networks and Learning Systems*, *34*(8), 3779–3795. DOI: 10.1109/TNNLS.2021.3121870 PMID: 34723814

Nissenbaum, H. (2004). Privacy as contextual integrity. *Washington Law Review (Seattle, Wash.)*, *79*(1), 119–158.

Office of the Victorian Information Commissioner. (2023). *Biometrics and privacy: A resource for Victorian public sector organisations*. State Government of Victoria.

OTAVA. (2025). 2025 trends in edge computing security. OTAVA. https://www.otava.com/blog/2025-trends-in-edge-computing-security/

Otoum, Y., Gottimukkala, N., Kumar, N., & Nayak, A. (2024). Machine learning in Metaverse security: Current solutions and future challenges. *ACM Computing Surveys*, *56*(8), 1–36. DOI: 10.1145/3654663

OXREF. (2025). *Open XR for Education Framework*. ERIC.

Oztank, F. (2025). *Towards Extended Reality in Emergency Response. Computer Animation and Virtual Worlds*. Wiley.

Pekkanen, J., & Lappi, O. (2017). A new and general approach to signal denoising and eye movement classification based on segmented linear regression. *Scientific Reports*, *7*(1), 17726. DOI: 10.1038/s41598-017-17983-x PMID: 29255207

Pfeuffer, K., Geiger, M. J., Prange, S., Mecke, L., Buschek, D., & Alt, F. (2019). Behavioural biometrics in VR: Identifying people from body motion and relations in virtual reality. In *Proceedings of the 2019 CHI Conference on Human Factors in Computing Systems* (pp. 1–12). ACM. DOI: 10.1145/3290605.3300340

Piaget, J. (1972). *The Psychology of the Child*. Basic Books.

Pitsikalis, S., & Lasica, I.-E. (2025). Integrating Extended Reality and Artificial Intelligence in Education. In *Metaverse, MetaIntelligence and Infinite Worlds with AI*. IntechOpen.

Piugie, Y. B. W. (2023). *Performance and security evaluation of behavioral biometric systems* [Doctoral dissertation, Normandy University]. GREYC Laboratory.

Pooyandeh, M., Joo, J., Lotfi, F., Hwang, J., Mehdi, D., Rho, S., & Jeong, Y.-S. (2022). Cybersecurity in the AI-based metaverse: A survey. *Applied Sciences (Basel, Switzerland)*, *12*(24), 12993. Advance online publication. DOI: 10.3390/app122412993

Prabhakar, S., Pankanti, S., & Jain, A. K. (2003). Biometric recognition: Security and privacy concerns. *IEEE Security and Privacy*, *1*(2), 33–42. DOI: 10.1109/MSECP.2003.1193209

Prasetya, F. (2024). *The impact of augmented reality learning experiences on the motivational design model*. ScienceDirect.

Precedence Research (2026). AI in Education Market Size to Surpass USD 136.79 Billion by 2035.

Precedence Research. (2025). Virtual reality market size, share, and trends 2025 to 2034. https://www.precedenceresearch.com/virtual-reality-market

Preukschat, A., & Reed, D. (2021). *Self-sovereign identity: Decentralized digital identity and verifiable credentials*. Manning Publications.

Rahartomo, A., Merino, L., & Ghafari, M. (2025). Metaverse security and privacy research: A systematic review. *arXiv*. https://arxiv.org/abs/2507.14985

Ratha, N. K., Connell, J. H., & Bolle, R. M. (2001). Enhancing security and privacy in biometrics-based authentication systems. *IBM Systems Journal*, *40*(3), 614–634. DOI: 10.1147/sj.403.0614

Rauschnabel, P. A., Babin, B. J., tom Dieck, M. C., Krey, N., & Jung, T. (2022). What is augmented reality marketing? Its definition, concept, and value for customer engagement. *Journal of Business Research*, *142*, 329–345. DOI: 10.1016/j.jbusres.2021.12.084

Rauthmann, J. F., Seubert, C. T., Sachse, P., & Furtner, M. R. (2012). Eyes as windows to the soul: Gazing behavior is related to personality. *Journal of Research in Personality*, *46*(2), 147–156. DOI: 10.1016/j.jrp.2011.12.010

Ren, B., Tang, Y., Wang, H., Wang, Y., Liu, J., Gao, G., & Wei, W. (2024). A multiagent deep reinforcement learning autonomous security management approach for Internet of Things. *IEEE Internet of Things Journal*, *11*(15), 25600–25612. DOI: 10.1109/JIOT.2024.3368072

Ren, X., Fan, J., Xu, N., Wen, Z., Chen, J., Zhao, S., Zhang, Y., & Gao, W. (2024). DPGazeSynth: Enhancing eye-tracking virtual reality privacy with differentially private data synthesis. *Information Sciences*, *675*(2), 120720. DOI: 10.1016/j.ins.2024.120720

Repetto, M. (2026). Cybersecurity digital twins: Concept, blueprint, and challenges for multi-ownership digital service chains. *Journal of Information Security and Applications*, *96*, 104299. Advance online publication. DOI: 10.1016/j.jisa.2025.104299

Risko, E. F., Anderson, N. C., Lanthier, S., & Kingstone, A. (2012). Curious eyes: Individual differences in personality predict eye movement behavior in scene-viewing. *Cognition*, *122*(1), 86–90. DOI: 10.1016/j.cognition.2011.08.014 PMID: 21983424

Roesner, F., Kohno, T., & Molnar, D. (2014). Security and privacy for augmented reality systems. *Communications of the ACM*, *57*(4), 88–96. DOI: 10.1145/2580723.2580730

Rose, S., Borchert, O., Mitchell, S., & Connelly, S. (2020). *Zero trust architecture* (NIST Special Publication 800-207). National Institute of Standards and Technology. https://doi.org/DOI: 10.6028/NIST.SP.800-207

Ryu, J., Son, S., Lee, J., Park, Y., & Park, Y. (2022). Design of secure mutual authentication scheme for metaverse environments using blockchain. *IEEE Access : Practical Innovations, Open Solutions, 10*, 98944–98958. DOI: 10.1109/ACCESS.2022.3206457

Sabt, M., Achemlal, M., & Bouabdallah, A. (2015). *Trusted execution environment: What it is, and what it is not. In 2015 IEEE Trustcom/BigDataSE/ISPA.*, DOI: 10.1109/Trustcom.2015.357

Sagar, S., & Keke, C. (2021). Confidential machine learning on untrusted platforms: A survey. *Cybersecurity, 4*, 30. Advance online publication. DOI: 10.1186/s42400-021-00092-8 PMID: 34805760

Salturk, S., & Kahraman, N. (2024). Deep learning-powered multimodal biometric authentication. *Neural Computing & Applications, 36*(19), 11311–11322. DOI: 10.1007/s00521-024-09690-2

Sarwatt, D. S., Kulwa, F., Philipo, A. G., Runyoro, A.-A. K., Ning, H., & Ding, J. (2026). AIGC-driven human-machine intelligence in ITS: Technologies, applications, evaluation framework, challenges, and future directions. *Artificial Intelligence Review*. Advance online publication. DOI: 10.1007/s10462-025-11467-5

Shambour, Q., Al-Zyoud, M., & Almomani, O. (2025). Quantum-inspired hybrid metaheuristic feature selection with SHAP for optimized and explainable spam detection. *Symmetry, 17*(10), 1716. DOI: 10.3390/sym17101716

Shokri, R., Stronati, M., Song, C., & Shmatikov, V. (2017). Membership inference attacks against machine learning models. In *2017 IEEE Symposium on Security and Privacy* (pp. 3–18). https://doi.org/DOI: 10.1109/SP.2017.41

Sicari, S., Rizzardi, A., Grieco, L. A., & Coen-Porisini, A. (2015). Security, privacy and trust in Internet of Things: The road ahead. *Computer Networks, 76*, 146–164. DOI: 10.1016/j.comnet.2014.11.008

Sikos, L. F. (2023). Cybersecurity knowledge graphs. *Knowledge and Information Systems, 65*(9), 3511–3531. DOI: 10.1007/s10115-023-01860-3

Slater, M., & Sanchez-Vives, M. V. (2016). Enhancing our lives with immersive virtual reality. *Frontiers in Robotics and AI, 3*, 74. Advance online publication. DOI: 10.3389/frobt.2016.00074

Slater, M., Spanlang, B., Sanchez-Vives, M. V., & Blanke, O. (2010). First person experience of body transfer in virtual reality. *PLoS One*, *5*(5), e10564. DOI: 10.1371/journal.pone.0010564 PMID: 20485681

Sofia, R. C., Salomon, J., Ferlin-Reiter, S., Garcés-Erice, L., Urbanetz, P., & Touma, R.. (2024). A framework for cognitive, decentralised container orchestration. *IEEE Access : Practical Innovations, Open Solutions*, *12*, 79979–80002. DOI: 10.1109/ACCESS.2024.3406861

Solove, D. J. (2006). A taxonomy of privacy. *University of Pennsylvania Law Review*, *154*(3), 477–564. DOI: 10.2307/40041279

Soltani, R., Nguyen, U. T., & An, A. (2021). A survey of self-sovereign identity ecosystem. *Security and Communication Networks*, *2021*, 8873429. Advance online publication. DOI: 10.1155/2021/8873429

Sorrentino, G., & López-Guzmán, J. (2025). Rethinking privacy for avatars: Biometric and inferred data in the metaverse. *Frontiers in Virtual Reality*, *6*, 1520655. DOI: 10.3389/frvir.2025.1520655

Stanney, K., Fidopiastis, C., & Foster, L. (2020). Virtual reality is sexist: But it does not have to be. *Frontiers in Robotics and AI*, *7*, 4. Advance online publication. DOI: 10.3389/frobt.2020.00004 PMID: 33501173

Statista. (2025). Virtual reality (VR) – statistics & facts. https://www.statista.com/topics/2532/virtual-reality-vr/

Stendal, K., & Bernabe, R. D. L. C. (2024). Extended reality—New opportunity for people with disability? Practical and ethical considerations. *Journal of Medical Internet Research*, *26*, e45919. Advance online publication. DOI: 10.2196/41670 PMID: 38349731

Stott, A., & Neustadter, C. (2013). *Analysis of gamification in education*. Simon Fraser University.

Subramanian, S., Prabu, P., Jain, K., & Krishnan, P. (2026). Edge AI bridge: A micro-layer intrusion detection architecture for smart-city IoT networks. *Preprints*, 202602.0606. DOI: 10.20944/preprints202602.0606.v1

Sun, Y., Ceker, H., & Upadhyaya, S. (2016). Shared keystroke dataset for continuous authentication. In *IEEE International Workshop on Information Forensics and Security* (pp. 1-6). IEEE. DOI: 10.1109/WIFS.2016.7823894

Sweller, J. (1988). Cognitive load during problem solving: Effects on learning. *Cognitive Science*, *12*(2), 257–285. DOI: 10.1207/s15516709cog1202_4

Szyjewski, G. (2023). Implementation of a Hybrid Certificate Approach: Enhancing Efficiency and Credibility in the ICDL Certification Process. *Procedia Computer Science*, *225*, 535–544. DOI: 10.1016/j.procs.2023.10.470

Talukder, M. A., Sharmin, S., Uddin, M. A., Islam, M. M., & Aryal, S. (2024). MLSTL-WSN: Machine learning-based intrusion detection using SMOTETomek in WSNs. *International Journal of Information Security*, *23*(3), 2139–2158. DOI: 10.1007/s10207-024-00833-z

TechCrunch. (2019). *Immersive technology industry projections.*

Tene, T. (2026). *Artificial intelligence, extended reality, and emerging AI-XR synergies in medical education.* PMC.

Tolosana, R., Vera-Rodriguez, R., Fierrez, J., Morales, A., & Ortega-Garcia, J. (2020). Deepfakes and beyond: A survey of face manipulation and fake detection. *Information Fusion*, *64*, 131–148. DOI: 10.1016/j.inffus.2020.06.014

Torres, L. A., Rebollo, M., Palanca, J., & Aragones Lozano, M. (2026). cyberSPADE: A hierarchical multi-agent architecture for autonomous cyberdefense. *Journal of Cybersecurity and Privacy*, *6*(1), 28. Advance online publication. DOI: 10.3390/jcp6010028

Tu, X., & de Castro e Silva, B. (2025). Are we ready for the metaverse? Implications, legal landscape, and recommendations for responsible development. *Digital Society : Ethics, Socio-Legal and Governance of Digital Technology*, *4*(9), 9. Advance online publication. DOI: 10.1007/s44206-025-00163-0

UNESCO (2020). Education: From disruption to recovery. UNESCO COVID-19 Educational Disruption and Response.

UNICEF (2024). Education Under Attack.

Unity Technologies (2024). Unity Certified XR Specialist Certification.

Uprety, A., & Rawat, D. B. (2021). Reinforcement learning for IoT security: A comprehensive survey. *IEEE Internet of Things Journal*, *8*(11), 8693–8706. DOI: 10.1109/JIOT.2020.3040957

US Department of Education (2026). The Four Stages of AI Integration in Education.

Vadher, H., Patel, P., Nair, A., Vyas, T., Desai, S., Gohil, L., Tanwar, S., Garg, D., & Singh, A. (2023). EEG-based biometric authentication system using convolutional neural network for military applications. *Security and Privacy*. Advance online publication. DOI: 10.1002/spy2.345

Valakou, A., Margetis, G., Ntoa, S., & Stephanidis, C. (2024). A framework for accessibility in XR environments. In Stephanidis, C., Antona, M., Ntoa, S., & Salvendy, G. (Eds.), *HCI International 2023 – Late Breaking Posters* (pp. 229–237). Springer., DOI: 10.1007/978-3-031-49215-0_31

Van Der Linde, I., Rajashekar, U., Bovik, A. C., & Cormack, L. K. (2009). DOVES: A database of visual eye movements. *Spatial Vision*, *22*(2), 161–177. DOI: 10.1163/156856809787465636 PMID: 19228456

van Hasselt, H., Guez, A., & Silver, D. (2016). Deep reinforcement learning with double Q-learning. *Proceedings of the AAAI Conference on Artificial Intelligence*, *30*(1), 2094–2100. DOI: 10.1609/aaai.v30i1.10295

Venugopal, J. P., Subramanian, A. A. V., Sundaram, G., & Ponnambalam Devadoss, M. (2025). The convergence of deep learning and the metaverse: A multidisciplinary survey of current research and future directions. *Computer Animation and Virtual Worlds*, *36*(6), e70082. Advance online publication. DOI: 10.1002/cav.70082

Verdoliva, L. (2020). Media forensics and deepfakes: An overview. *IEEE Journal of Selected Topics in Signal Processing*, *14*(5), 910–932. DOI: 10.1109/JSTSP.2020.3002101

Volico. (2024). Edge computing security: Challenges and best practices. Retrieved from https://www.volico.com/edge-computing-security-challenges-and-best-practices/

VR Vision Group (2025). AI + XR = The Intelligent Training Era.

W3C. (2022). *Decentralized identifiers (DIDs) v1.0.*

Wachi, A., Shen, X., & Sui, Y. (2024). A survey of constraint formulations in safe reinforcement learning. In *Proceedings of the Thirty-Third International Joint Conference on Artificial Intelligence* (pp. 8262-8271). International Joint Conferences on Artificial Intelligence Organization. DOI: 10.24963/ijcai.2024/913

Wang, D., & Huang, X. (2025). *Transforming education through artificial intelligence and immersive technologies: Enhancing learning experiences. Interactive Learning Environments*. Taylor & Francis.

Wang, G., Liu, P., Huang, J., Bin, H., Wang, X., & Zhu, H. (2024). KnowCTI: Knowledge-based cyber threat intelligence entity and relation extraction. *Computers & Security*, *141*, 103824. DOI: 10.1016/j.cose.2024.103824

Wang, H., Ning, H., Lin, Y., Wang, W., Dhelim, S., Farha, F., Ding, J., & Daneshmand, M. (2023). A survey on the metaverse: The state-of-the-art, technologies, applications, and challenges. *IEEE Internet of Things Journal*, *10*(16), 14671–14688. DOI: 10.1109/JIOT.2023.3278329

Wang, W., Sun, D., Jiang, F., Chen, X., & Zhu, C. (2022). Research and challenges of reinforcement learning in cyber defense decision-making for intranet security. *Algorithms*, *15*(4), 134. DOI: 10.3390/a15040134

Wang, Y., Su, Z., Zhang, N., Xing, R., Liu, D., Luan, T. H., & Shen, X. (2023). A survey on metaverse: Fundamentals, security, and privacy. *IEEE Communications Surveys and Tutorials*, *25*(1), 319–352. DOI: 10.1109/COMST.2022.3202047

Watkins, C. J. C. H., & Dayan, P. (1992). Q-learning. *Machine Learning*, *8*(3-4), 279–292. DOI: 10.1007/BF00992698

Westin, A. F. (1967). *Privacy and freedom*. Atheneum Publishers.

World Bank. (2024). Learning Continuity During Crises [Lessons.]. *COVID*, •••, 19.

Wu, H., & Zhang, W. (2023). Digital identity, privacy security, and their legal safeguards in the metaverse. *Security and Safety*, *2*, 2023011. DOI: 10.1051/sands/2023011

XR Association (2024). XR Industry Workforce Development Survey.

Xynogalas, V., & Leiser, M. R. (2024). The metaverse: Searching for compliance with the General Data Protection Regulation. *International Data Privacy Law*, *14*(2), 89–105. DOI: 10.1093/idpl/ipae004

Yalcin, M., Halbig, A., Fischbach, M., & Latoschik, M. E. (2024). Automatic cybersickness detection by deep learning of augmented physiological data from off-the-shelf consumer-grade sensors. *Frontiers in Virtual Reality*, *5*, 1364207. Advance online publication. DOI: 10.3389/frvir.2024.1364207

Yale School of Medicine. (2026). From Ideathon to Pilots: Updates on AI and XR. *Medical Education*.

Yampolskiy, R. V., & Govindaraju, V. (2008). Behavioural biometrics: A survey and classification. *International Journal of Biometrics*, *1*(1), 81–113. DOI: 10.1504/IJBM.2008.018665

Yang, K., Zhang, Z., Tian, Y., & Ma, J. (2023). A secure authentication framework to guarantee the traceability of avatars in metaverse. *IEEE Transactions on Information Forensics and Security*, *18*, 3817–3832. DOI: 10.1109/TIFS.2023.3288689

Yang, S. C. H., Wolpert, D. M., & Lengyel, M. (2016). Theoretical perspectives on active sensing. *Current Opinion in Behavioral Sciences, 11*, 100–108. DOI: 10.1016/j.cobeha.2016.06.009 PMID: 30175197

Zawish, M., Dharejo, F. A., Khowaja, S. A., Raza, S., Davy, S., Dev, K., & Bellavista, P. (2024). AI and 6G into the metaverse: Fundamentals, challenges and future research trends. DOI: 10.1109/OJCOMS.2024.3349465

Zhao, J., Li, J., & Xu, Y. (2021). Wearable sensing and human activity recognition: A survey. *IEEE Sensors Journal, 21*(5), 6500–6519. DOI: 10.1109/JSEN.2020.3034599

Zhao, Y., & Chen, J. (2022). A survey on differential privacy for unstructured data content. *ACM Computing Surveys, 54*(10s), 218. Advance online publication. DOI: 10.1145/3490237

Zhao, Y., Cutrell, E., Holz, C., Morris, M. R., Ofek, E., & Wilson, A. D. (2019). SeeingVR: A set of tools to make virtual reality more accessible to people with low vision. In *Proceedings of the 2019 CHI Conference on Human Factors in Computing Systems* (pp. 1-14). ACM. DOI: 10.1145/3290605.3300341

Zhao, Y., Du, J. T., & Chen, J. (2024). Scenario-based adaptations of differential privacy: A technical survey. *ACM Computing Surveys, 56*(8), 199. Advance online publication. DOI: 10.1145/3651153

Zhong, H., Huang, C., Zhang, X., & Pan, M. (2023). Metaverse CAN: Embracing continuous, active, and non-intrusive biometric authentication. *IEEE Network, 37*(6), 67–73. DOI: 10.1109/MNET.2023.3318890

Zhou, L., Diro, A., Saini, A., Kaisar, S., & Hiep, P. C. (2024). Leveraging zero knowledge proofs for blockchain-based identity sharing: A survey. *Journal of Information Security and Applications, 80*, 103678. DOI: 10.1016/j.jisa.2023.103678

Zikas, P., Bachlitzanakis, V., Papaefthymiou, M., ... (2016). Mixed reality serious games and gamification for smart education. In European Conference on Games Based Learning (p. 805). Academic Conferences International Limited.

Zyskind, G., & Nathan, O. (2015). Decentralizing privacy: Using blockchain to protect personal data. In *IEEE Security and Privacy Workshops.*

About the Contributors

Omar Almomani received his Bachelor's and master's degrees in Telecommunication Technology from the Institute of Information Technology at the University of Sindh in 2002 and 2003 respectively. He received his Ph.D. from the University Utara Malaysia in computer network and security in 2010. Currently, he is a professor in the Department of Networks and Cybersecurity, Faculty of Information Technology at Al-Ahliyya Amman University. Almomani is among the top 2% scientists in the world from 2022 up to now. His research interests involve network performance, network quality of service (QoS), IoT, network modeling and simulation, network and cybersecurity, and machine learning. He can be contacted at email: at almomani81@yahoo.com or o.almomani@ammanu.edu.jo

Ammar Almomani is a distinguished academic and researcher with over 20 years of combined teaching and industry experience in cybersecurity, artificial intelligence, and computer science. He also works as a consultant on various AI and cybersecurity initiatives and is a recipient of the prestigious UAE Golden Visa. Prof. Almomani holds a Ph.D. in Advanced Internet Security and Monitoring from Universiti Sains Malaysia (USM), He has taught over 47 specialized topics in cybersecurity and computer science, including Network Security and Artificial Intelligence. Prof. Almomani has published more than 200+ articles in reputable journals and conferences, with over 142+ indexed in Scopus,10 academic books, His contributions include 10 patents (eight in Germany and two in India) and several ongoing submissions. Recognized among the Top 2% of Global Influential Researchers by Stanford University and Scopus (2023–2024,2025), he also serves as a consultant and expert member of the UAE Research Map (R&D). • Prof. Almomani has supervised numerous undergraduate and postgraduate research projects (MSc/Ph.D.) across countries such as the UK, Malaysia, and Jordan. He has chaired and co-chaired various international conferences and journals and maintains an active digital presence with over 120,000 readers and followers on

ResearchGate. In addition to his academic and research endeavors, Prof. Almomani has extensive leadership experience, having served as Head of the Research and Innovation Department and IT Department for 6 years. He has contributed to curriculum development, program accreditation (including ABET and AACSB), and the establishment of specializations in both Jordan and the UAE. Prof. Almomani continues to make a significant impact in the fields of cybersecurity,AI and higher education, fostering innovation and collaboration at local and international levels.

Mohammad Alauthman is an Associate Professor in the Department of Information Security at the Faculty of Information Technology, University of Petra, Amman, Jordan. His research interests include network security, intrusion detection systems, and the application of artificial intelligence techniques, including machine learning and deep learning, to botnet and DDoS detection, spam filtering, IoT security, and network traffic classification. He received his Ph.D. in Computer Science from Northumbria University, United Kingdom, in 2016. He has been awarded several research grants supporting AI-driven intrusion detection systems and international research collaboration. He has also contributed to a number of Erasmus+ projects, including BITTCOIN-JO, RL4Eng, Pro-GREEN LABs, and COMMO, with a focus on technology transfer, remote engineering education, sustainability, and academic cooperation across Mediterranean and Balkan institutions.

***

Amjad Aldweesh is a computer associate professor interested in the Blockchain and Smart contracts technology as well as cyber security. Amjad has a Bachelor degree in computer science. He has a MSc degree in advanced computer science and security from the University of Manchester with distinction. Amjad is the second in the UK and the first in the middle east to have a PhD in the Blockchain and Smart contracts technology from Newcastle University.

Salam Al-E'mari earned her Ph.D. in Cybersecurity from Universiti Sains Malaysia (USM) in 2022. She is the Chair of the Information Security Department and an Assistant Professor at the University of Petra (UoP). With expertise in Blockchain, Deep Learning, and Network Security, she has contributed significantly to cybersecurity research. She previously earned her Bachelor's and Master's in Computer Science from Yarmouk University, Jordan, shaping her strong foundation in security and technology.

Thair Al-Fararjeh is an immersive-technology inventor and executive specializing in Extended Reality (XR)—including Virtual Reality (VR), Augmented

Reality (AR), and Mixed Reality (MR)—with emphasis on simulation-based training, competency evaluation, and scalable adoption frameworks for institutional deployment. He is the Founder & CEO of Beyond Universe XR Solutions, leading multidisciplinary teams delivering XR ecosystems that integrate device deployment, content workflows, user enablement, and operational governance. Thair brings more than 24 years of industry experience in the United Arab Emirates, including C-level leadership roles on mega and giga-scale projects executed within governmental and semi-governmental sectors. His background includes strategic planning, stakeholder alignment, program governance, and the execution of large-scale initiatives where reliability, safety, compliance, and measurable outcomes are essential. He earned an MBA (Global) from the University of Bedfordshire (2022), strengthening his expertise in global strategy, technology commercialization, and scalable program design. He holds a Bachelor's degree in Computer Science from Mu'tah University (2003), providing a strong foundation in software systems, applied computing, and technical architecture. He is currently preparing for doctoral research in the Metaverse of Things, aligned with advancing spatial computing through connected systems and measurable operational models. Thair is the originator of the International XR Driving License concept: a device-agnostic, competency-based certification framework designed to standardize XR readiness and safe operational use. The framework is intended to validate foundational XR competencies—such as setup and calibration, safety and human-factor considerations, interaction proficiency, troubleshooting, responsible use, and basic operational governance—through structured levels and objective assessment criteria. His work emphasizes interoperability, safety-by-design, and auditable evaluation to support consistent XR capability recognition across institutions, sectors, and jurisdictions.

Wesam Alkhadour holds a Ph.D. in computer science from the University ofBradford, United Kingdom. She is currently an assistant professor at the University of Petra,Jordan.

Jawad Alkhateeb is currently working as an Assistant Professor at Prince Mohammad Bin Fahd University, Kingdom of Saudi Arabia in the College of Computer Engineering and Science, Department of computer Engineering. Dr. Alkhateeb received his PhD degree in Computer Engineering - Artificial Intelligence from the University of Bradford, UK in 2010. He Received his MSc and BSc degrees in Electrical and Computer Engineering from Louisiana Tech University, Ruston, USA in 1992 and 1991 respectively. He has a 30-year academic experience in teaching Computer Science and Engineering topics and in conducting research related to Artificial Intelligence, Pattern Recognition, Machine Learning, Deep Learning, Arabic OCR, and IoT.

Manimekala B. is working as an Assistant Professor in the Department of Computer Science, Christ University, Bengaluru. She has 17 years of teaching experience. She has published research articles in National and International journals. She has also presented 18 papers in National and International conferences. She has authored in 1 book, 3 book chapters and she owned 3 patents. Her areas of interest are IoT, networking, machine learning and AI.

Pankaj Bhambri is an Associate Professor in the Department of Information Technology at Guru Nanak Dev Engineering College, Ludhiana, with over twenty-one years of teaching and research experience. He holds a Ph.D. in Computer Science and Engineering from I.K.G. Punjab Technical University, Jalandhar, and is currently pursuing a Post Doctorate Fellowship at Lincoln University College, Malaysia. Recognized as a Top 2% Scientist by Stanford University and Elsevier in 2025, his research focuses on areas including machine learning, AI-driven digital twins, blockchain, and sustainable technologies. He has an extensive publication record in Scopus-indexed books and journals and has guided several Ph.D. candidates to completion.

Hussam Fakhouri is an Full time lecturer/ Assistant Professor of Data Science at the Al-balqa Applied University, Jordan. He earned his Ph.D. in Computer Science from the University of Jordan, where his doctoral research focused on data science. Dr. Fakhouri has extensive research experience and has authored around 100 papers published in reputable international journals and conferences. He has also participated in four Erasmus PhD schools held at Aalborg University in Copenhagen (Denmark), Rostock University in Rostock (Germany), Peter the Great St. Petersburg Polytechnic University in Saint Petersburg (Russia), and South Ural State University in Chelyabinsk (Russia). His research interests span machine learning, deep learning, data visualization, computer vision, and .

Ahmad Hajyasien is an Assistant Professor at Higher Colleges of Technology, UAE. He holds a Ph.D. in Software Engineering, and his research interests include software engineering, privacy-preserving data mining, blockchain applications, and optimization. His published work includes studies on privacy-preserving data mining, blockchain-based educational record sharing, and metaheuristic methods for NP-hard optimization problems.

Ala Hamarsheh is an associate professor at the Faculty of Engineering and Information Technology of the Arab American University of Jenin. Dr. Hamarsheh has obtained a PhD in engineering sciences from Vrije Universiteit Brussel (VUB)/ Brussels-Belgium in 2012. He graduated in computer science at the Faculty of Science, Birzeit University, Palestine, in 2000. He obtained an MSc degree in computer science at the Kind Abdullah II School for IT, The University of Jordan, Jordan, in 2003. Dr. Hamarsheh has published numerous papers in international refereed journals and conferences.

Abdelraouf Ishtaiwi is an Associate Professor of Artificial Intelligence and Data Science at the University of Petra, Jordan, with over 22 years of academic and research experience in AI. He earned his Master's and Ph.D. degrees in Artificial Intelligence from Griffith University, Australia, where he focused on heuristic optimization techniques for satisfiability problems. His research expertise spans machine learning, hybrid metaheuristic optimization, associative classification, and AI applications in cybersecurity and emerging technologies like the metaverse. Dr. Ishtaiwi has developed innovative AI algorithms, such as ACRIPPER and hybrid crayfish-DE models, and contributed significantly to areas like phishing detection, blockchain security, and smart IoT defense. As a former Head of the Department of Data Science and AI at Petra University, he led academic reforms and accreditation initiatives. He has also been a visiting scholar at Griffith University and Universitat Pompeu Fabra, reflecting his international academic engagement.

Khalil Omar is an assistant professor at the University of Petra in Jordan. He received his Ph.D. degree in computer science from the University of Oldenburg, Germany, in 2018. His academic focus is on distance learning and e-learning in combination with software engineering, mobile applications, usability design, adaptive interfaces, and ERP systems. Users can reach him through his email address: komar@uop.edu.jo.

Rachna Rana is an Associate Professor in the Department of Computer Science and Engineering at Ludhiana Group of Colleges, Ludhiana with over fifteen years of teaching and research experience. Her research focuses on areas including machine learning, wireless sensor networks, and network security. She has an extensive publication record in Scopus-indexed books.

Yousef Sanjalawe is an Assistant Professor specializing in Cybersecurity and Cloud Computing at the University of Jordan (JU), Jordan. He earned his PhD in Cloud Computing from Universiti Sains Malaysia (USM) in 2020, where his research focused on enhancing cloud service broker selection using optimization algorithms. Dr. Sanjalawe has extensive experience in academia, research, and professional training. He has supervised Ph.D. students in Cybersecurity, Cloud Computing, IoT, Fog Computing, Optimization, and Artificial Intelligence (AI). From 2023 to 2024, he served as the Chair of the Cybersecurity Department at the American University of Madaba (AUM), Jordan, and from 2022 to 2024, he was an Assistant Professor in Cybersecurity at AUM.

Jamal Zraqou is an associate professor at the Department of Computer Science/ Virtual and Augmented Reality, University of Petra, Jordan, where he has been a faculty member since 2022. From 2018-2029, he was also the dean faculty of IT at IU. His research interests include computer vision, virtual and augmented reality, internet of things (IoT), cyber security, and image processing. He can be contacted at email: Jamal.Zraqou@uop.edu.jo.

Index

www.ingramcontent.com/pod-product-compliance
Lightning Source LLC
LaVergne TN
LVHW081537300926
849161LV00006B/1468